# THE TRUTH ABOUT CAMP DAVID

# THE TRUTH ABOUT CAMP DAVID

•

## THE UNTOLD STORY ABOUT THE COLLAPSE OF THE MIDDLE EAST PEACE PROCESS

•

CLAYTON E. SWISHER

NATION BOOKS
NEW YORK

THE TRUTH ABOUT CAMP DAVID: THE UNTOLD STORY ABOUT THE COLLAPSE OF THE MIDDLE EAST PEACE PROCESS



Maps courtesy of Jan de Jong.
Photographs of Stockholm courtesy of Gidi Grinstein.
White House photographs from Camp David courtesy of Clinton Presidential Materials Project.
Remaining photographs courtesy of the author.

Published by Nation Books
An Imprint of Avalon Publishing Group
245 West 17th St., 11th Floor
New York, NY 10011

Nation Books is a co-publishing venture of the Nation Institute and Avalon Publishing Group Incorporated.



Library of Congress Cataloging-in-Publication Data is available.

ISBN 1-56025-623-0

9 8 7 6 5 4 3 2 1

*Book design by Pauline Neuwirth, Neuwirth & Associates, Inc.*

Printed in the United States of America
Distributed by Publishers Group West

*Dedicated to the valiant American troops, diplomats, and operators in the Middle East, who continue to pay the consequences for Washington's misguided policy in the region.*

# *Contents*


| | | |
|---|---|---|
| | Persons Interviewed or Consulted | ix |
| | Maps | xiii |
| | Introduction | xix |

**• PART ONE •**
*Barak Takes Charge*

| | | |
|---|---|---|
| ONE | An Israeli Deus Ex Machina | 3 |
| TWO | Misgivings About Barak | 14 |
| THREE | Leaning Toward Syria | 34 |
| FOUR | The Palestinians Accept a Bad-Faith Bargain | 47 |

**• PART TWO •**
*Barak Opts for Syria First*

| | | |
|---|---|---|
| FIVE | "Find Me a Way to Fudge It" | 61 |
| SIX | Showdown at Shepherdstown | 77 |
| SEVEN | Collapse of the Israeli-Syrian Track | 90 |
| EIGHT | The Truth About Geneva | 110 |

**• PART THREE •**
*The Camp David Disaster*

| | | |
|---|---|---|
| NINE | Gathering Storm Clouds | 133 |
| TEN | Roadblocks and Reversals | 164 |
| ELEVEN | A Dose of False Hope | 183 |

| | | |
|---|---|---|
| **TWELVE** | The Decision to Go for Broke | 213 |
| **THIRTEEN** | Camp David 2000 | 250 |
| **EPILOGUE** | The Politics of Blame | 335 |
| | Notes | 406 |
| | Acknowledgments | 437 |
| | Index | 441 |

# *Persons Interviewed or Consulted*

**THE UNITED STATES**

Madeleine K. Albright, former U.S. Secretary of State
John Podesta, former Chief of Staff to the President
Maria Echaveste, former Deputy Chief of Staff to the President
Joe Lockhart, former White House Press Secretary
Bruce Riedel, former Senior Director for the Near East, National Security Council
Robert Malley, former Adviser for Arab-Israeli Affairs, National Security Council
Dennis Ross, former Special Middle East Envoy, State Department
Martin Indyk, former U.S. Ambassador to Israel, State Department
Ned Walker, former U.S. Ambassador to Israel, State Department
Toni Verstandig, former Deputy Assistant Secretary, Near Eastern Affairs, State Department
Aaron Miller, former Deputy Special Middle East Envoy, State Department
Jonathan Schwartz, Deputy Legal Adviser, State Department
Gemal Helal, Senior Adviser and Translator for the President, State Department

Melissa Boyle Mahle, Senior Field Operative to Israel/Palestine, Central Intelligence Agency

Unnamed senior intelligence officers and unattributed officials

**ISRAEL**

Gilead Sher, former Chairman of the negotiating team (Palestinian Track)

Uri Sagi, retired General and former Chairman of the negotiating team (Syrian Track)

Amnon Lipkin-Shahak, retired IDF Chief of Staff and former Minister of Transportation

Dan Meridor, former Finance Minister and Ambassador-at-Large

Natan Sharansky, former Minister of Housing and Absorption

Ami Ayalon, former Director, Shin Bet

Gidi Grinstein, former advisor to PM Barak

Unattributed officials

**PALESTINE**

Nabil Shaath, PLO Foreign Minister

Nabil Abu Rudeineh, Chief of Staff to President Yasser Arafat

Saeb Erekat, former Chairman of the negotiating team

Mohammed Dahlan, former PLO National Security Advisor

Gamal Abouali, former legal advisor, negotiations support unit

Omar Dajani, former legal advisor, negotiations support unit

Ghaith al-Omari, NSU legal advisor

### SYRIA

Walid Moallem, Deputy Foreign Minister
Riad Daoudi, Legal Advisor to late Syrian President Hafez al-Asad
Bouthaina Shabban, Spokesperson, Ministry of Foreign Affairs and Translator to Hafez al-Asad
Imad Moustapha, Syrian Ambassador to the United States

### SAUDI ARABIA

Rihab Massoud, Minister, Embassy of the Kingdom of Saudi Arabia

### EGYPT

Nabil Fahmy, Egyptian Ambassador to the United States
Hishem Youssef, Spokesman for Amr Moussa, Secretary General of the Arab League

### SWEDEN

Pär Nuder, Minister for Policy Coordination to Prime Minister Goran Persson

### CARTER ADMINISTRATION OFFICIALS, BROKERS OF THE SUCCESSFUL 1978 CAMP DAVID SUMMIT

Jimmy Carter, former President of the United States and Nobel Laureate
Walter Mondale, former Vice President of the United States
Samuel Lewis, former U.S. Ambassador to Israel

## ACADEMIA AND OTHERS

William Quandt, Vice Provost, University of Virginia, former Adviser to President Carter on Arab-Israeli Affairs at the National Security Council

Ehud Sprinzak, former Dean of the Lauder School of Government, Diplomacy and Strategy at the Interdisciplinary Center in Herzliya, Israel

Haydar Abdel Shafi, Founder, Palestinian Red Crescent Society, former Palestinian Delegate to the 1991 Madrid Conference on the Middle East

# Golan Heights, 1923–2000

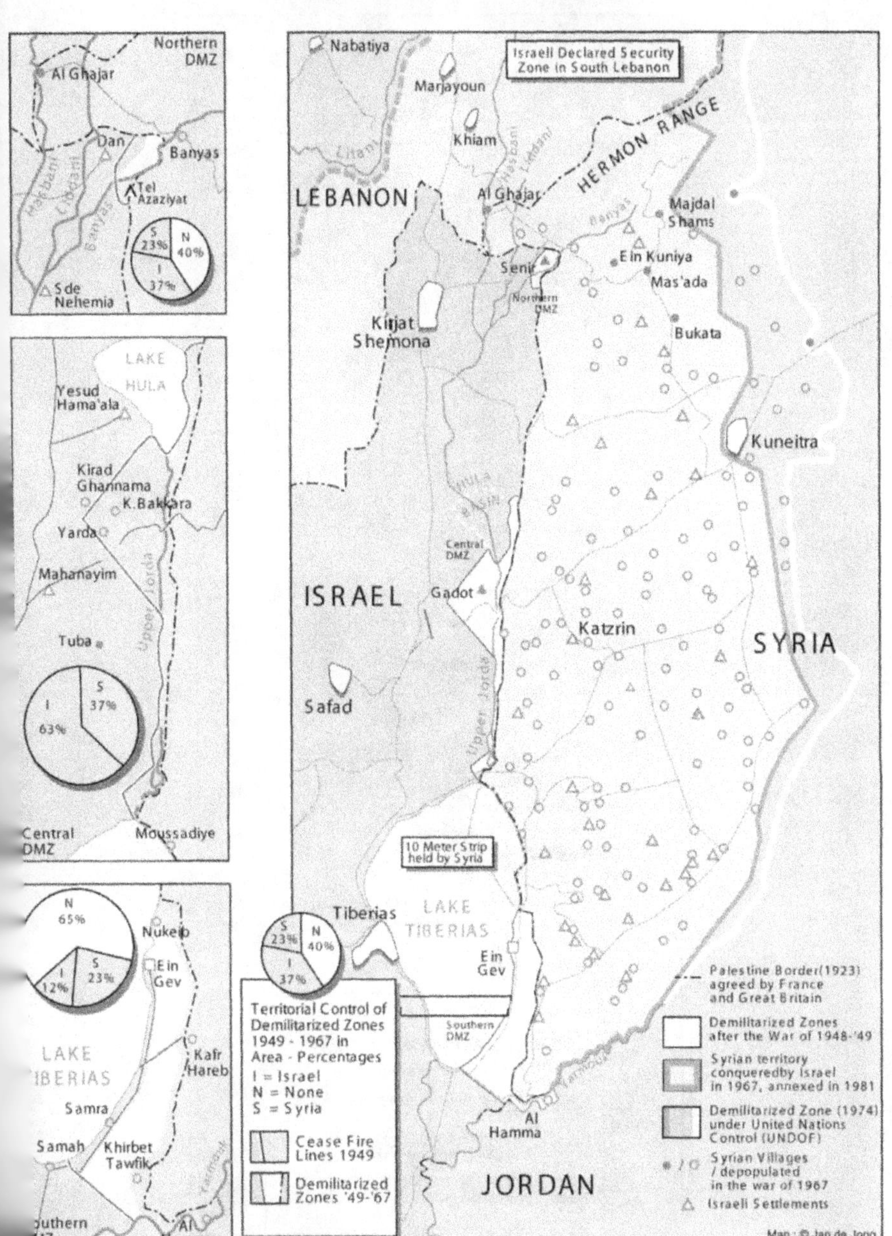

Northern DMZ
Al Ghajar
Dan
Banyas
Tel Azaziyat
Hasbani
Liddani
Banyas
S 23%
N 40%
I 37%
Sde Nehemia
LAKE HULA
Yesud Hama'ala
Kirad Ghannama
K.Bakkara
Yarda
Mahanayim
Upper Jordan
Tuba
S 37%
I 63%
Central DMZ
Moussadiye
N 65%
I 12%
S 23%
Nukeib
Ein Gev
LAKE TIBERIAS
Kafr Hareb
Samra
Samah
Khirbet Tawfik
Al Hamma
Nabatiya
Marjayoun
Khiam
Israeli Declared Security Zone in South Lebanon
HERMON RANGE
LEBANON
Al Ghajar
Majdal Shams
Ein Kuniya
Mas'ada
Senir
Northern DMZ
Bukata
Kirjat Shemona
Kuneitra
Central DMZ
ISRAEL
Gadot
Katzrin
SYRIA
Safad
10 Meter Strip held by Syria
Tiberias
LAKE TIBERIAS
Ein Gev
S 23%
N 40%
I 37%
Territorial Control of Demilitarized Zones 1949 - 1967 in Area - Percentages
I = Israel
N = None
S = Syria
Cease Fire Lines 1949
Demilitarized Zones '49-'67
Southern DMZ
Al Hamma
JORDAN
Palestine Border(1923) agreed by France and Great Britain
Demilitarized Zones after the War of 1948-'49
Syrian territory conqueredby Israel in 1967, annexed in 1981
Demilitarized Zone (1974) under United Nations Control (UNDOF)
Syrian Villages / depopulated in the war of 1967
Israeli Settlements
Map : © Jan de Jong

# Sharm-Esh-Sheikh, 1999

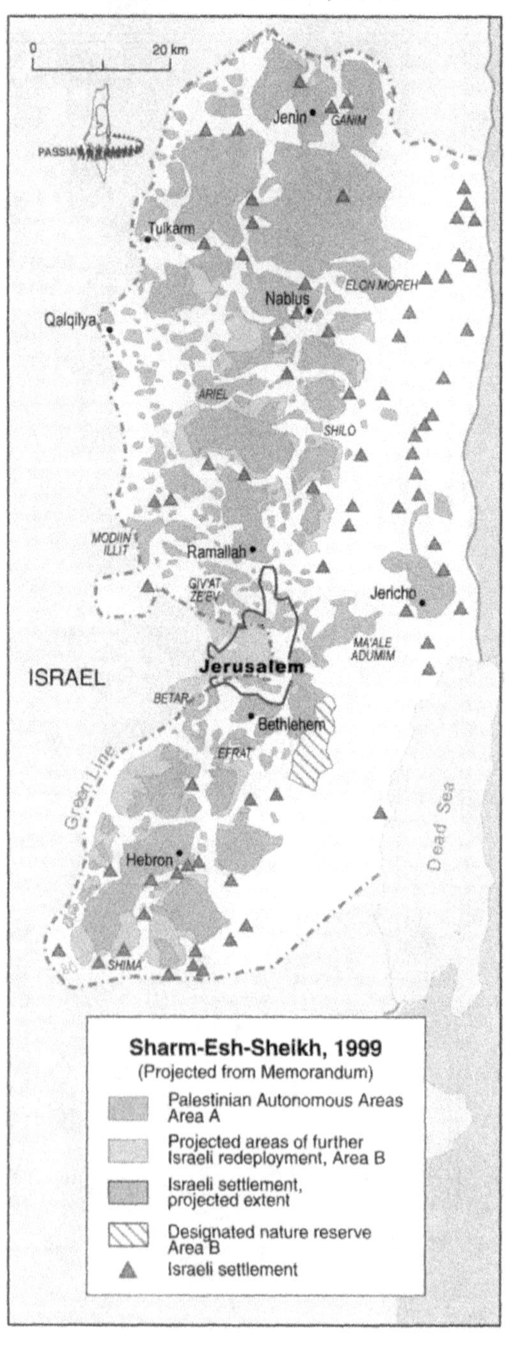
0
20 km
PASSIA
Jenin
GANIM
Tulkarm
ELON MOREH
Nablus
Qalqilya
ARIEL
SHILO
MODIIN ILLIT
Ramallah
GIV'AT ZE'EV
Jericho
MA'ALE ADUMIM
ISRAEL
Jerusalem
BETAR
Bethlehem
EFRAT
Green Line
Dead Sea
Hebron
SHIMA
Sharm-Esh-Sheikh, 1999
(Projected from Memorandum)
Palestinian Autonomous Areas Area A
Projected areas of further Israeli redeployment, Area B
Israeli settlement, projected extent
Designated nature reserve Area B
Israeli settlement

## West Bank and Gaza Strip, March 2000

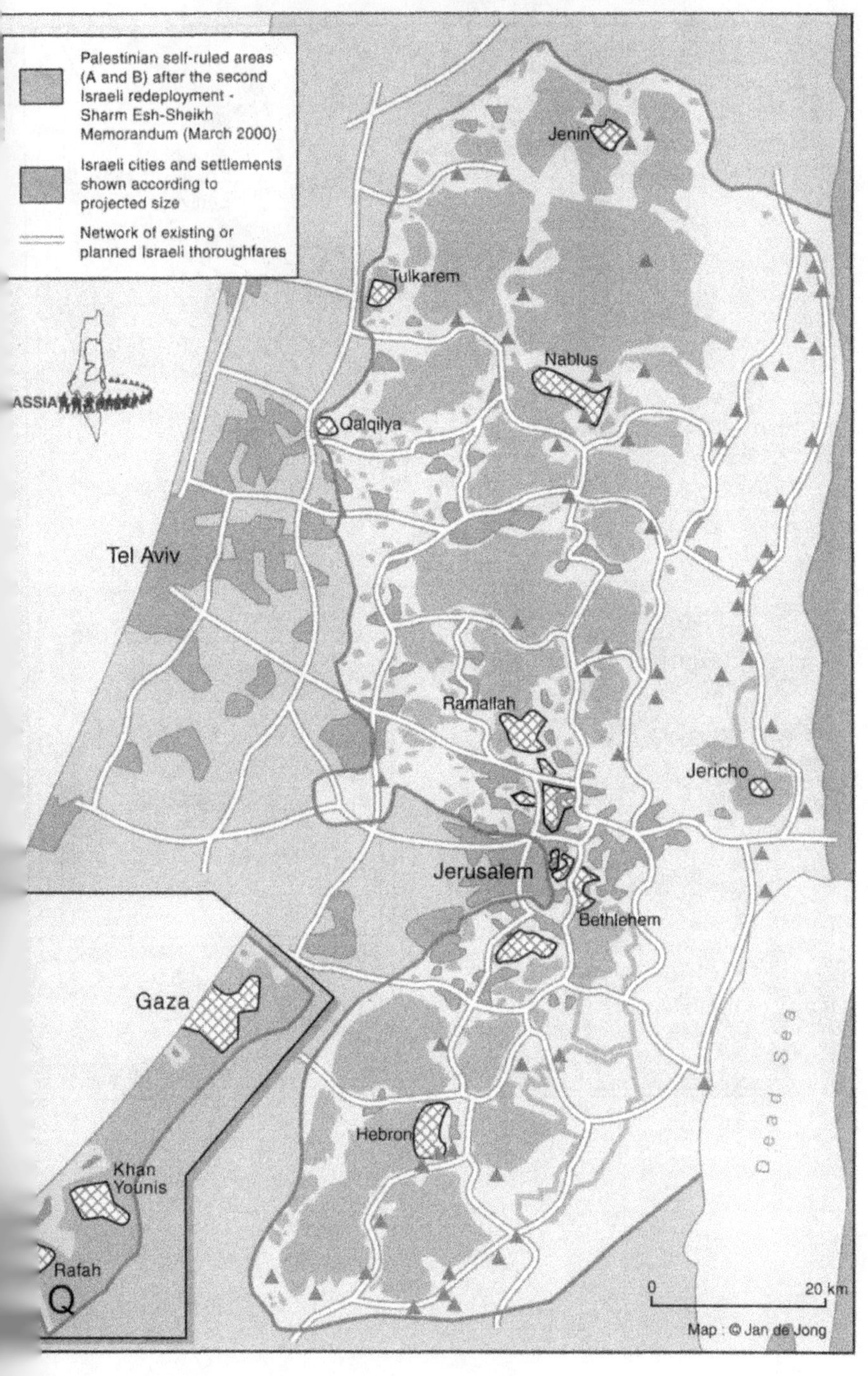

Palestinian self-ruled areas (A and B) after the second Israeli redeployment - Sharm Esh-Sheikh Memorandum (March 2000)
Israeli cities and settlements shown according to projected size
Network of existing or planned Israeli thoroughfares
Jenin
Tulkarem
Nablus
Qalqilya
Tel Aviv
Ramallah
Jericho
Jerusalem
Bethlehem
Gaza
Hebron
Dead Sea
Khan Younis
Rafah
0
20 km
Map : © Jan de Jong

# The Gaza Strip, 2000

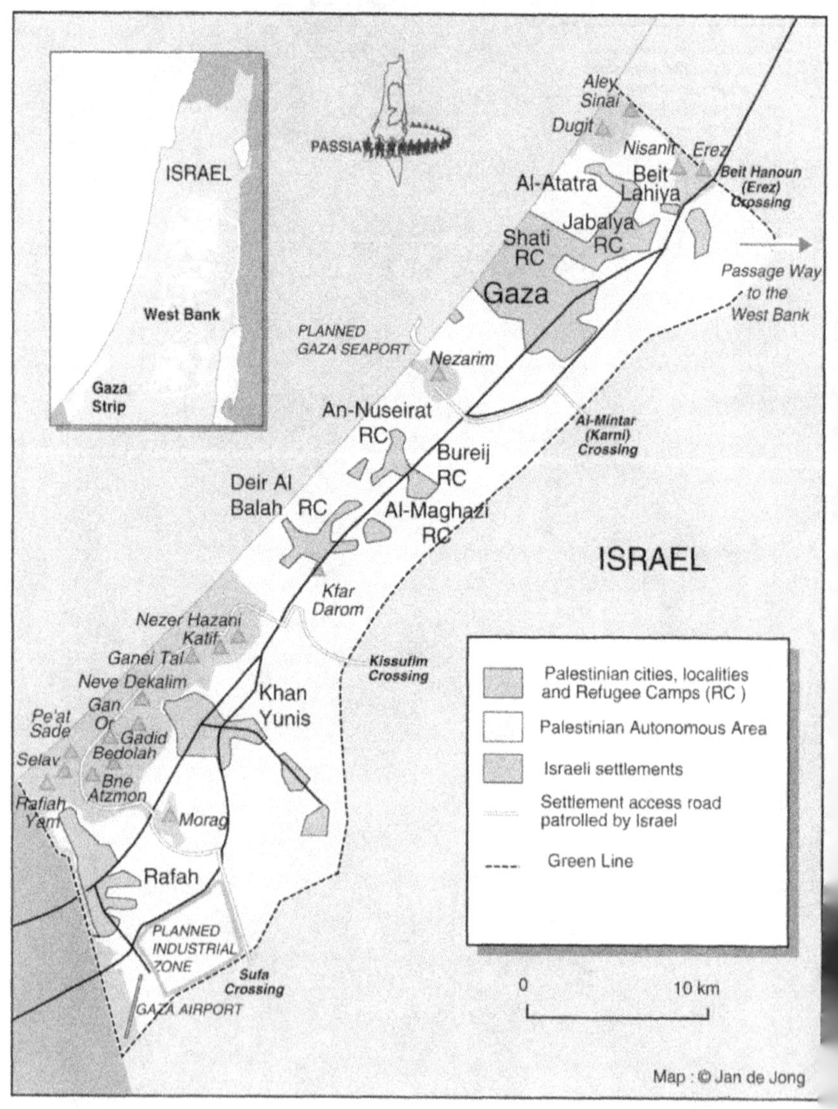

ISRAEL
West Bank
Gaza Strip
PASSIA
Aley Sinai
Dugit
Nisanit
Erez
Beit Hanoun (Erez) Crossing
Al-Atatra
Beit Lahiya
Jabalya RC
Shati RC
Gaza
Passage Way to the West Bank
PLANNED GAZA SEAPORT
Nezarim
An-Nuseirat RC
Al-Mintar (Karni) Crossing
Bureij RC
Deir Al Balah RC
Al-Maghazi RC
ISRAEL
Kfar Darom
Nezer Hazani
Katif
Ganei Tal
Neve Dekalim
Kissufim Crossing
Khan Yunis
Pe'at Sade
Gan Or
Gadid
Bedolah
Selav
Bne Atzmon
Rafiah Yam
Morag
Rafah
PLANNED INDUSTRIAL ZONE
Sufa Crossing
GAZA AIRPORT
Palestinian cities, localities and Refugee Camps (RC )
Palestinian Autonomous Area
Israeli settlements
Settlement access road patrolled by Israel
Green Line
0
10 km
Map : © Jan de Jong

# Israeli Proposed Final Status–2000 (Camp David Talks)

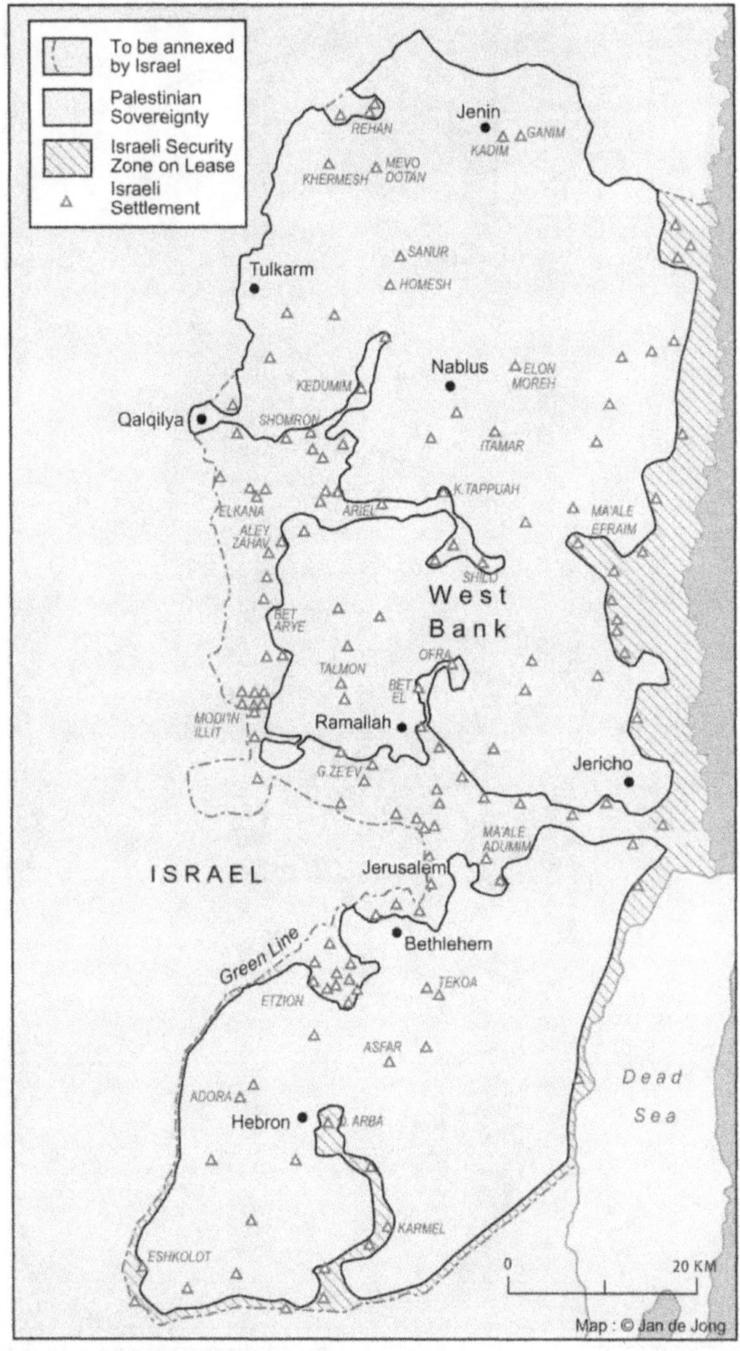

To be annexed by Israel
Palestinian Sovereignty
Israeli Security Zone on Lease
Israeli Settlement
Jenin
REHAN
GANIM
KADIM
KHERMESH
MEVO DOTAN
SANUR
Tulkarm
HOMESH
Nablus
ELON MOREH
KEDUMIM
Qalqilya
SHOMRON
ITAMAR
K.TAPPUAH
ELKANA
ARIEL
MA'ALE EFRAIM
ALEY ZAHAV
SHILO
West Bank
BET ARYE
OFRA
TALMON
BET EL
MODI'IN ILLIT
Ramallah
Jericho
G.ZE'EV
MA'ALE ADUMIM
ISRAEL
Jerusalem
Bethlehem
Green Line
TEKOA
ETZION
ASFAR
Dead Sea
ADORA
Hebron
Q. ARBA
KARMEL
ESHKOLOT
0
20 KM
Map : © Jan de Jong

## Israeli Proposed Final Status–2001 (Taba Summit)

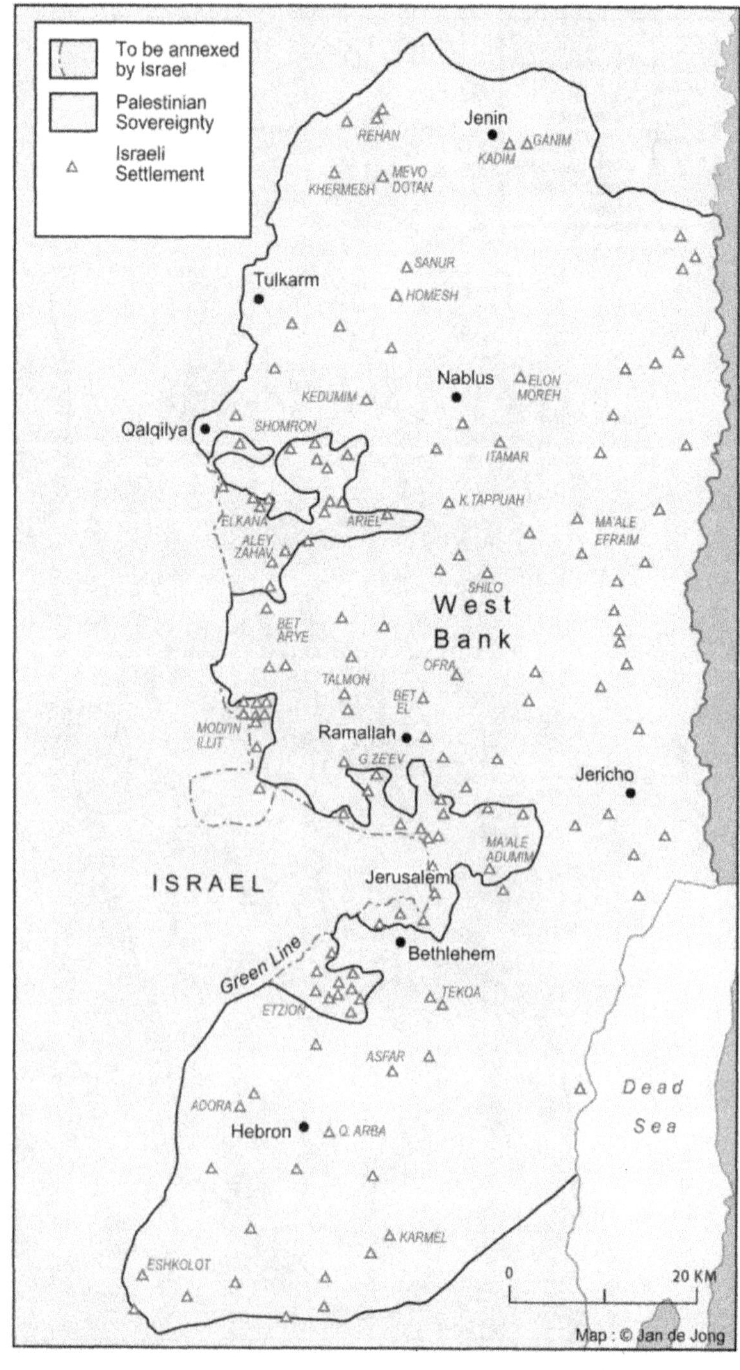

# *Introduction*

**THE CATASTROPHIC TERROR** attacks of September 11, 2001, set in motion a series of events that we are still feeling today. In response, the Bush administration declared war not only against al-Qaeda but against terrorism throughout the world. After invading Afghanistan and overthrowing the Taliban regime, the United States then unleashed its arsenal on Iraq. The administration claimed the main reason was to eliminate the threat of nuclear, biological, and chemical weapons, and that Saddam Hussein was in some way connected to al-Qaeda. This has been proven false by numerous independent investigative commissions and journalistic reports.

The administration has also invoked another claim: the selfless desire to bring democracy and freedom to the Iraqi people, and indeed the entire Middle East. But it is impossible for Arabs and Muslims to take these claims seriously, given the longstanding American support for Israel's thirty-seven-year occupation of the West Bank, Gaza Strip, and the oft-forgotten Golan Heights. The primary reason for Arab and Muslim anger against America has been and remains unbridled support for Israel's oppression of the Palestinians; it also stands as a betrayal of the American ethos of life, liberty, and property. Indeed, American support for Israel's occupation has recruited legions to the ideology of bin Ladenism and bolstered not only anti-American sentiment through the world but also resurrected the evil rumblings of anti-Semitism.

One of the chief reasons the Bush administration has done nothing constructive to resolve the Israeli-Palestinian conflict and enhance U.S. national security interests in the Middle East is its adoption of a set of myths regarding the failure of the Oslo peace process under the helm of President Bill Clinton. Most Americans bought into the government and media spin. The Palestinians, we were told, rejected a generous Camp David deal that would have brought peace to the region and allowed them to achieve self-determination, instead choosing the path of violence by launching an intifada whose eventual goal is the destruction of the state of Israel. Why should the United States help the Palestinians if they "are either unready or unwilling to help themselves," the category of the damned alluded to in the Bush administration's September 2002 National Security Strategy?

As much of my book is focused on criticizing this theory, I should be the first to acknowledge how persuasive it could be, and that I originally bought into it. In the summer of 2001, after taking a class on the Arab-Israeli conflict during the course of my graduate studies, my professor posed the following question: "What was the biggest missed opportunity for Middle East peace?" Here's my response at the time:

> The biggest missed opportunity was Camp David 2000. At Camp David, both parties were ripe for conflict resolution. Ehud Barak showed the ability to think in abstract terms—outside of conventional wisdom. Barak's bold move toward territorial compromise belongs in a category with [Egyptian president] Anwar Sadat's 1977 visit to Jerusalem. What was lacking at Camp David was a Palestinian leader with the ability to take risks and accept that he would not get 100 percent of concessions. Barak's honorable intentions of settling all claims came as a shock to Arafat.

I did not begin to revisit my assumptions until the September 11 attacks, when, after long days of work at Ground Zero, I found myself drowning in anguish and alcohol as I and my colleagues asked each other, "Why do they hate us?"

I began to reflect on little things I had witnessed in the course of my travels and experiences as a special agent with the State Department's Diplomatic Security Service. Part criminal investigator and part international bodyguard, I had both the honor and the pleasure of protecting the Secretary of State and visiting Arab and Israeli leaders in support of the Oslo process, including trips to Jerusalem, Ramallah, Washington, and Camp David.

This book grew out of a project for my graduate thesis, when I conducted a series of detailed interviews with senior diplomats—American, Israeli, Palestinian, and Syrian—who were directly involved in those negotiations. I eventually held more than forty such interviews, with 500 pages of transcipts from digitally recorded depositions and notes. Some of these officials have been very outspoken on the issue, but some have never made public comment until now. These accounts were supplemented by internal government documents supplied to me that are currently unavailable to the public, interviews with top academics, journalistic accounts, my own reading on the conflict, and my training and experience as a onetime U.S. government gumshoe. I have provided footnotes for claims or ideas that are not my own. Where confidentiality and privacy requests were made, I have scrupulously honored those requests (to the point of extreme frustration, I might add, in the case of certain individuals who continue to speak differently on the subject in public).

If we are ever to repair our relations with the Arab and Muslim world, we must have an honest and open examination regarding our role in the Arab-Israeli conflict. Too many American, Israeli, and Arab lives depend on it. Considering all the threats facing our country in the Middle East, the time for petty politics and mythification has passed.

There are many sides to this complex story, yet the one-sided mantra of Arab blame is still all-pervasive. What follows is a considerably more nuanced account, with enough blame to be shared by many actors in this drama. As I see it, this is the real Camp David.

• **PART ONE** •

# BARAK TAKES CHARGE

## • ONE •

# *An Israeli Deus Ex Machina*

THE WINTER OF 1999 was not a good time for U.S. President Bill Clinton. Just before Christmas of 1998, the House of Representatives had impeached him for "high crimes and misdemeanors," all stemming from an embarrassing independent counsel investigation into his adulterous relationship with White House intern Monica Lewinsky. Clinton was only the second president in U.S. history to suffer such an indignity, and during the previous year his personal life had been exposed by the media, the public, the FBI, federal grand juries, and, finally, Congress. The matter was not put to rest until February 1999, when the Senate voted for an acquittal. Clinton had less than two years left in his presidency to repair his damaged legacy. Nevertheless, it was the consensus of many observers that if any politician could pull off such a miracle, Bill Clinton, a political phoenix, could.

Middle East peacemaking was an area in which Clinton had exerted great personal efforts in the past. There would, no doubt, be significant risks if he redoubled these efforts, given the special U.S. relationship with Israel and the political land mines this could pose. But there could also be significant payoffs, as evidenced by the 1994 conferral of the Nobel Peace Prize upon former Israeli Prime Minister Yitzhak Rabin, his Foreign Minister Shimon Peres, and Chairman of the PLO Yasser Arafat for concluding the Oslo Accords in 1993.

Clinton's first term had given hope that the Arab-Israeli conflict might peacefully conclude on both the Palestinian-Israeli track (with the 1993 beginning of the Oslo peace process) and on the Syrian-Israeli track (with the 1994 pledge by Rabin to fully end Israel's occupation of the Syrian Golan Heights in exchange for full peace). But since Rabin's 1995 assassination by Yigal Amir, a far-right-wing opponent of the Oslo process, Clinton had been awaiting the arrival of an Israeli leader who was empowered and willing to fulfill Rabin's tantalizing vision of peace. Clinton's second term, which should have allowed for bolder presidential moves[1] since re-election was not an option, was initially bogged down on the Middle East peace front by the tenure of the obdurate and unwilling Israeli Prime Minister Benjamin Netanyahu.

Time was not in the Clinton administration's favor. Already in the winter of 1999, the State Department was deeply embroiled in faltering negotiations that later produced a U.S.-led NATO air campaign in Kosovo. With few rewards reaped, it was a puzzling intervention challenged by many critics. As a result of the State Department's miscalculation that the bombing of Serbia and Kosovo would take only three days before compelling Yugoslav President Slobodan Milosevic's surrender, the chief protagonist of this war, U.S. Secretary of State Madeleine K. Albright, became involved in a longer-than-expected imbroglio from the winter of 1999 to mid-summer, and thus was unable to fully devote her attention to the demanding duties of Middle East peacemaking. The Middle East portfolio slowly moved closer to President Clinton through his National Security

Adviser, Sandy Berger, and his small cadre of experts at the National Security Council (NSC). The State Department, though committed elsewhere and with slower-moving parts, was in the loop, but not through the usual Secretary of State channels. Clinton's Special Middle East Coordinator at the State Department, Dennis Ross, and his Assistant Secretary of State for Near East Affairs, Martin Indyk, kept a close eye on developments through their own direct channels to the NSC and White House. Ross began reporting more directly to Berger, who had instant access to the president,[2] as did Indyk, who was known to call on a daily basis.[3]

From war in Kosovo to peace in the Middle East was just one of the many startling turns during Clinton's waning tenure as president. Leaving behind the somber mood of his impeachment, the spring of 1999 brought hope to the administration that political changes in Israel might rekindle the peace process. Israel's most highly decorated general, Ehud Barak, had emerged as a candidate for prime minister and was pledging to fulfill Rabin's vision of peace. For Clinton, the announcement of Barak's candidacy was the deus ex machina that could revive the dying hopes of Oslo. It was no secret that the Clinton administration had not had productive relations with incumbent Netanyahu. But Clinton, now wiser after six years in office, had to make sure that history—at least when it came to the conditions surrounding Netanyahu's rise—did not repeat itself.

• • •

**From the outset** of his 1996 campaign for prime minister, Netanyahu had bluntly proclaimed his anti-peace agenda at rallies, stating that "we are here to prevent the establishment of a Palestinian state." Initially, Clinton had little to worry about, as Netanyahu's candidacy appeared to be a long shot. This changed drastically during the winter and spring of

1996, as an escalation of violence in the region increased the popularity in Israel of Netanyahu's "security-driven" rhetoric.

Labor incumbent Shimon Peres, who had succeeded the slain Rabin in November 1995, faced a difficult time building campaign support for negotiations with the Palestinians. There had been a long period without Palestinian terror attacks in Israel, but the dovish Peres felt the need to do something to project the image to hawks that he was aggressive on security. He made the fateful decision to approve the assassination of Hamas bomb-maker Yahya Ayash, but found unmanageable the horrific tempest of retaliatory violence that followed: four bombings in just nine days, killing fifty-eight Israelis.

Peres phoned Palestinian Authority leader Yasser Arafat, who promised to do his part and exert every effort to confront terror. Arafat viewed Peres as a partner for peace and, with overwhelming public support—at that time many Palestinians saw the terror attacks as undermining Oslo's hope for Palestinian freedom—he was able to order his security services to wage an internal war against Hamas. Looking back at that period, Peres recalled the result of Arafat's heavy-handed campaign, "He killed twenty of the Hamas leaders; he arrested thousands of them. He did something that nobody else did—he shaved their beards!"[4]

Even this harsh repression, however, was not enough for Israeli public opinion, which had to decide whether to stay the course of negotiations with Peres or retreat to the security platform being offered by Netanyahu.

Clinton also interceded, hoping that his popularity within Israel would tip the scales in Peres's favor. To boost the candidate he felt was most likely to conclude a future peace agreement, Clinton helped convene a summit of Arab leaders to promote Peres in the weeks preceding the election at the Egyptian resort of Sharm el-Sheikh. He next attended a well-publicized memorial ceremony with Peres at Rabin's gravesite in Jerusalem. As the May 1996 election neared,

Clinton sequestered Peres and Arafat together for a press event in Washington. He even made a pledge of $1 billion to aid Israel in its fight against terror.

International supporters of Netanyahu also got involved. Seeking the emoluments of having a right-wing leader in office, followers of the messianic Orthodox Jewish group Chabad began channeling massive foreign contributions into Netanyahu's campaign coffers. None of Netanyahu's notoriously secular practices really mattered to the Chabadniks: His opposition to territorial partition and a Palestinian state, which they viewed as a religious crime, overrode any other differences. Under the leadership of Australian tycoon Joseph Gutnick, and with contributions from tax deductible, nonprofit Chabad affiliates in the United States, international members of Chabad successfully rallied the 1996 campaign around the slogan of "Bibi's good for the Jews."

Peres didn't have as much campaign money, but that was the least of his problems. Fighting between Israeli occupation forces in Lebanon and the Shiite resistance group Hezbollah had flared up, and a spate of Israeli casualties along the Israel-Lebanon border buttressed Netanyahu's standing among the Israeli public. Peres lost support from the usually pro-Labor Arab Israeli voters—twenty percent of the country's population—following the Israeli military's shelling of the UN refugee camp of Qana in southern Lebanon. Outraged at the killing of over one hundred civilians, most Arab Israelis condemned Peres as a "war criminal" and boycotted the elections. Netanyahu managed a Likud victory by just one-half of one percent.

Netanyahu's 1996 campaign tactics—especially his reliance on foreign contributions—had narrowly outgunned the Clinton administration's attempt at electoral interplay in favor of Peres. Given the administration's open support for Peres, it's not surprising that relations with the new prime minister got off to a bad start. And they got worse as time progressed. Former White House press secretary Joe Lockhart, who was at that time tasked with providing a positive spin on the many meetings between Clinton and Netanyahu, reflected rather bluntly on Netanyahu's character:

> Netanyahu was one of the single most obnoxious individuals you're going to come into—just a liar and a cheat. He would open his mouth and you would have no confidence that anything that came out of it was the truth. With Barak and Arafat, you were in the margin of error. I mean these were two relatively honest guys who had the right motive.[5]

Any attempts to negotiate substantive agreements between Israelis and Palestinians under Netanyahu were mired in delay, provocative actions, and trickery. In September 1996, against the advice of security advisers, Netanyahu opened a passageway along Jerusalem's Western Wall without consulting the Waqf, the Muslim authority for the city's holy sites. This resulted in days of rioting and gun battles between the Israeli army and Palestinian security forces, in which fifteen Israeli soldiers and nearly eighty Palestinians were killed, with hundreds wounded. Netanyahu delayed the scheduled turnover of Hebron, insisting on further revision of earlier agreements, and he continued the unabated expropriation of Palestinian land and settlement construction; especially controversial was that of Jabal Abu Ghneim, near Jerusalem, which was renamed Har Homa. After a Security Council resolution condemning the construction was vetoed by the United States, violent Palestinian demonstrations erupted. In 1998, the erratic Israeli leader tried the last-minute ploy of conditioning the Israeli government's acceptance of the Wye River Agreement on Clinton's release of convicted U.S. spy Jonathan Pollard. Clinton nearly succumbed to Netanyahu's blackmail demands until George Tenet, the director of the CIA, threatened to resign. It was an embarrassing episode for Clinton. And getting Netanyahu's signature on the Wye Agreement proved to matter little. Even as the ink was drying on Wye, Netanyahu put egg on Clinton's face and on the entire U.S.-Israeli "special relationship" by continuing to renege on Israel's commitments to withdraw from occupied Palestinian land.

• • •

**Like many Israelis,** Clinton urgently felt the need for a Labor victory in 1999 to bring about serious negotiations. Mindful of the last Israeli election, Clinton realized that endorsing Ehud Barak's candidacy would require striking the right political balance. At first there were not-so-subtle gestures, such as Clinton's refusal to meet with Netanyahu.[6] What followed was a behind-the-scenes mission to help Barak's campaign, beginning with Barak's hiring of Clinton's own political triumvirate—Stanley Greenberg, James Carville, and Robert Shrum. Importing the same "soft-money" scheme employed during the 1996 Clinton re-election campaign, these heavyweight American consultants were able to guide Barak in raising vast sums of soft money—just as was done by the Netanyahu campaign in 1996—through both foreign and nonprofit donations. Many of the big guns who contributed to Clinton's campaign were called in.[7] Oblique fundraising schemes were employed. For example, a wealthy Jewish financier, Charles Bronfman, the CEO of Seagram's, was able to funnel over $500,000 to Barak's public-relations team, all through the Israeli nonprofit medium of "sending money to collect data on polls and social issues."[8]

The relationship of Barak's campaign with U.S. financers and advisers began to attract attention in the press. Reports surfaced that his team had illegally raised an estimated $10 million in the United States. The American consultancy even took a strange, Watergate-like twist, complete with a burglary at Stan Greenberg's Washington, DC, office. Local police never recovered Greenberg's stolen computer files, which contained Barak's campaign finance records.[9] But nearly a year later, evidence of malfeasance surfaced following a criminal investigation in Israel of Barak's close political advisers. The Israeli government comptroller responded by levying Barak with a $3.2 million fine.[10]

The 1999 campaign alliance would help cement Clinton's special political bond with Barak, though Clinton was clearly familiar with him from his earlier days as a rising political figure in Israel. As Israel Defense Forces (IDF) chief of staff under Rabin and later foreign minister under Peres, Barak had participated in the 1994 signing of the Israeli-Jordanian peace agreement and in secret channel negotiations in Washington over the issue of Israeli-Syrian peace.

The Clinton administration had pushed very hard for the successive Israeli governments to fulfill Rabin's pledge for a Syrian-Israeli peace agreement.[11] And to the great delight of Clinton, Barak began incorporating bold campaign pledges to make this his priority. "I promise you that if we create the next Government we will be out of Lebanon by June 2000, with security assurances, and deep into talks with Syria," said Barak.[12]

But Clinton would have to walk a tightrope. While Barak's campaign speech proposing Syrian-Israeli negotiations made Clinton happy, it raised concerns among the Palestinians, who, after years of patience with the slow-moving Oslo Accords, feared being left behind. Despite watching the Netanyahu government renege on Israel's Wye River obligations, the Palestinian Authority was still carrying out its unpopular and unrewarded pledge to cooperate with Israel in suppressing organizations like the anti-Oslo Islamist group Hamas. Though Netanyahu complained that more could be done, even senior members of the Israeli intelligence bureaucracy, like General Amos Gilad, heaped praise on Palestinian security cooperation, which he acknowledged was "intensive."[13]

Yet despite these efforts, the Palestinians still had not fulfilled their hopes of achieving statehood by the end of the five-year interim period mandated by the original Oslo Accords of 1993. To placate his own frustrated constituencies as elections in Israel neared—land seizures and settlement construction in the territories continued at a rapid pace, infuriating the Palestinian people and causing them to lose hope in the Oslo process—Arafat gathered international and domestic support for making a unilateral declaration of independence on May 4, 1999.[14]

Declaring Arafat's efforts a "security threat," and sensing an opportunity to garner last-minute support from extremist and right-wing constituencies, Netanyahu responded with his own threat to annex unilaterally the Israeli-controlled areas of the West Bank if such a declaration was made.[15] To ease these tensions, which could only help Netanyahu as the May 17 elections approached, Clinton made a personal appeal to Arafat.

In an April 26 letter, Clinton promised that he would use his remaining time in office to push for a Palestinian-Israeli final-status agreement within a "reasonable period of time," culminating in a Washington summit meeting. Clinton also laid out the U.S. bona fides as an honest broker committed to Palestinian freedom. Playing to Arafat's concerns, Clinton passionately remarked:

> Mr. Chairman, I know that you and your people have faced great difficulties in the past several years. Clearly the Oslo process has not made the kind of progress we would have hoped to see. Much time has been wasted and many opportunities have been lost. . . . The agreement we helped facilitate between you and Prime Minister Netanyahu at Wye carried with it a great deal of progress. The first phase was implemented. Unfortunately, the second and third phases have not been.

> The Palestinians have implemented many of their commitments for the second phase, and I appreciate your efforts, particularly in the security area where Palestinians are engaged in a serious effort to fight terror.
>
> . . . It is important that you continue these efforts and fulfill all of your commitments. We will continue to work actively for implementation by Israel. . . .
>
> As May 4 approaches, I also understand that you face enormous pressures and challenges in trying to realize Palestinian aspirations and keep hopes for peace alive. In your effort to deal with these challenges, I am asking that you continue to rely on the peace process as the way to realize the aspirations of your people. Indeed, negotiations are the only realistic way to fulfill those aspirations. In this context, and in the spirit of my remarks in Gaza, we support the aspirations of the Palestinian people to determine their own future on their own land. As I said in Gaza, I believe Palestinians should live free today, tomorrow and forever.[16]

Inveigled by Clinton's words, which an elated Arafat described as "more than positive," the Palestinian Authority backed away from the May 4 declaration.[17] After learning of the letter, which alluded to Palestinian freedom, the Barak campaign condemned Clinton for drafting what they believed was tantamount to a "Balfour Declaration for the Palestinians which harms the security of the state."[18]

All of this, Clinton understood, was for Barak's own showing in the polls. At all times he was apprised of Barak's political reality, due to the mutual employment of the pollster Greenberg.[19] Clinton had a longstanding relationship with Greenberg, dating back to his days as a paid consultant during Clinton's 1990 Arkansas gubernatorial re-election campaign.[20] The benefit of having Greenberg also working in Barak's camp was the back channel of information it produced. Greenberg would become business partners in Israel with Tal Zilberstein, Barak's campaign manager, and he later customized polling statistics for Clinton that specifically highlighted the political realities facing Barak and the policies that could or could not be expected to receive support.[21]

The polls were yet another factor that would uniquely align Clinton's presidency with Barak, highlighting the empathy of a U.S. president who, in addition to his reverence for political polls, was already well-known for his unbridled support for Israel. Clinton's Deputy Chief of Staff, Maria Echaveste, reflected on the use of Greenberg's polls:

> Polls in the way that President Clinton used them, was really to try to understand . . . what was the political reality that Barak was operating under? What was the atmosphere? What could be supported? What *would* be supported? I don't know if he [Clinton] could make the distinction. . . [22]

When the Israelis cast their votes on May 17, it was evident that Clinton had handled things well. He had prevented Arafat from declaring statehood and thereby prevented Netanyahu from making good on his threats to annul the Oslo Accords. He had also given just the right level of endorsement while keeping a more proper—at least in public—distance from the Barak campaign, so as not to repeat the mistakes made under Peres.

Election-night returns gave Barak a victory that was nothing short of a historic landslide.[23] For Clinton, it was a master stroke that put the stars in near-perfect alignment and on course for a deal, or so it seemed. Barak's election could now provide Clinton the opportunity to be remembered not for scandalous relations with an intern but for brokering the supreme cause of Middle East peace. It had been some of the most important work of his presidency, and it could be a crowning achievement that would overshadow all else in his legacy. Clinton now had the chance, as he termed it, "to atone for sins" by fostering Middle East peace.[24]

• TWO •

# *Misgivings About Barak*

**NATURALLY, NOT EVERYONE** in the Arab world reacted as positively to Barak's election as his chief U.S. endorsers. But even those optimists who were closely aligned with Barak would have to find immediate ways to rationalize the mixed messages he laced throughout his internationally televised election-night victory speeches on May 17, 1999. At the Dan Hotel in Tel Aviv, Barak began by extolling Leah Rabin, wife of the slain prime minister, and Shimon Peres, a principal architect of the Oslo peace process, which Barak had once openly opposed. Next, he effusively praised Rabin:

> I would like to mention in particular that one special person who had a unique role in our reaching this moment, somebody who was my commander and guide and the person who led me into politics, our teacher and guiding light: Yitzhak Rabin. I know that if Yitzhak is looking down at us from heaven, he is proud of us today, just as we are proud of him, and he knows that together we will fulfill his heritage.[1]

Barak's promise to "fulfill [Rabin's] heritage" was interpreted ambiguously by a watchful Arab world, particularly among the Palestinian citizens of Israel, who, as one-fifth of the electorate, felt invested in Barak after block-voting to help secure his win.[2] Speaking later before a crowd of jubilant Israelis attending a 2 A.M. celebration in Tel Aviv's Rabin Square, Barak delivered a speech that stunned his Arab supporters. Contrary to the inflated hopes of some Palestinians, they were given their first indication of what to expect:

> We will move quickly toward separation from the Palestinians within four security Red Lines: a united Jerusalem under our sovereignty as the capital of Israel for eternity, period; under no conditions will we return to the 1967 borders; no foreign army west of the Jordan River; and most of the settlers in Judea and Samaria will be in settlement blocs under our sovereignty. Any permanent arrangement will be put to a national referendum. In the long run, you, the people of Israel, will decide.[3]

Many were shocked by these statements. Barak had made a campaign promise to withdraw all Israeli troops from Lebanon within a year of his election, but the Lebanese would only make peace so long as the Syrian track had been satisfied and only if there was positive movement on the Palestinian track that promised an imminent solution to the fate of several hundred thousand Palestinians still living in Lebanese refugee camps. After Barak's victory speeches, Lebanese Prime Minister Salim al-Hoss said: "There is no difference between Barak and Netanyahu and the best proof of that is his speech after he was elected. He ruled out withdrawal to the June 4, 1967 lines."[4] The chief Palestinian negotiator, Saeb Erekat, echoed these reservations; saying, "Barak did not go into whether he would implement the Oslo Accords or the Wye River Agreement or stop settlement, which is necessary to give a serious push to the peace process."[5]

Retired General Amnon Lipkin-Shahak, who like Barak had served as the Israeli Army's chief of staff and whom Barak later named as his minister for transportation and tourism, ruefully observed:

> The errors that Barak made started after Barak was elected. The first speech that Barak gave was from the Palestinian point a "No! No! No!" speech. I will *not* give back Jerusalem. I will *not* accept any Palestinian refugees. I will *not* leave the Jordan Valley. They [the Palestinians] thought—especially after Netanyahu's period—that they played a major role in the Israeli elections. And they were waiting immediately after the elections . . . [to] get a reward for what they did during the elections.[6]

Palestinians saw Barak's declarations as violating the first article of the Oslo Accords; namely, that any permanent settlement would be based on implementation of UN Security Council Resolution 242, which calls for, among other things, an Israeli "withdrawal from territories occupied" in the June 1967 conflict and a just solution to Israel's displacement of Palestinian refugees. Even though Barak ruled both of these premises out, there had been no corresponding public criticism from U.S. negotiators or, surprisingly, from America's Arab allies like Egypt and Jordan, who had reached separate agreements with Israel based on Resolution 242.

Instead, Barak was welcomed with open arms. His hardline rhetoric was dismissed as a tactical maneuver by a man who, at worst, was trying to mollify the religious and settler constituencies, whose help he needed in forming a broad coalition government, and, at best, would be the deliverer of the lasting peace that so many people craved.

Some Palestinians immediately began to worry that Barak would only deliver more stonewalling. They were not alone. Not everyone in the U.S. government, particularly at the staff levels of the State Department and CIA, was rating

Barak's intentions for peace so generously. Since going at loggerheads with his self-declared mentor, Rabin, over the Oslo Accords, Barak had steadily espoused unilateral tactics like "separation," a logic premised on Israel's imposition of a solution upon the weaker Palestinians if they wouldn't accept Israel's terms. Many in the State Department considered this an approach that would render a lasting Arab-Israeli peace unlikely.[7]

One veteran intelligence professional, Melissa Boyle Mahle, who was the CIA's senior clandestine field operative assigned to Israel and Palestine from 1996 to 2001, reflected on the disconnect between the perception of Barak in Washington and the views held by most Palestinians:

> It's a misconception to say that the Palestinian street welcomed the election of Barak. There was a lot of pessimism already at that time. Netanyahu was not beloved on the Palestinian street. But I think that Netanyahu was a known quantity, and the pre-election statements of Barak and his performance prior to that led the Palestinians to conclude that he was not going to be a great peacenik. Indeed, one of the activities that Barak launched shortly thereafter was abandoning the Palestinian track for the Syrian track.[8]

Another veteran U.S. intelligence officer, who had been intimately involved in the Oslo process and was charged with assembling a leadership profile of Barak, was alarmed by the picture that emerged, and summarized this assessment to Washington via outgoing cables:

> Among Israeli intelligence officers, the election represented a contest between Bibi and Barak—the "hated" guy and the "idiot." One boyhood friend remarked that Barak is intelligent, but not as intelligent as he thinks. People within the military establishment are not very impressed with him—he would be due for a meeting at 9 A.M. and show up at 11 A.M.

> Barak is confident, arrogant, and prone to making decisions on his own, preferably without consulting others.[9]

After years of taking a keen interest in domestic politics in Israel—where he enjoyed tremendous popularity—Clinton understood that peace would not come unless Barak kept obstructionists out of his cabinet. With this in mind, the United States effectively stood the peace process down in order to give Barak the time to accomplish this goal. At least initially, the Palestinians would have to wait.

Forming his government would be a daunting task. The Likud Party, under the new leadership of hard-liner Ariel Sharon, gave Barak little choice with its demand to have ultimate veto authority over any permanent-status territorial concessions.[10] But without Likud the pickings were slim. While he enjoyed a landslide victory, Barak's Labor Party did not gain as many Knesset seats as expected. The majority of Israeli voters strongly supported Netanyahu's ouster, but there had been numerous divisions spanning a variety of issues. For example, there were tensions between religious and secular social policies, such as whether or not Orthodox believers should be exempt from military service and the amount of public funding for religious schools.

More troubling for Barak, there was deep public fragmentation over how to proceed with the peace process. He had promised that if he concluded a peace agreement with Syria, Lebanon, or the Palestinians, he would put any territorial concessions before the public for its approval. But there had been little public preparation, either within Israel or in the United States, on behalf of creating an independent Palestinian state or, in the case of Syria, fully relinquishing Israeli occupation of the Golan Heights.

As Israel's close ally, the United States also needed preparation. Such comprehensive moves would have required bipartisan U.S. Congressional backing at a time when Republicans, some of whom politically mirror the right-wing preferences of Israel's Likud Party, were in the majority. The persuasion of the U.S. president would be pivotal. But ever since Jimmy Carter daringly advocated the creation of a "Palestinian homeland," a move that provoked strong opposition from the powerful pro-Israel lobby and was seen as a symbol of Carter's maladroit political nature, little had been done to ready the U.S. public for the eventuality of a Palestinian state. No U.S. president, Democrat or Republican, had taken this step. And, to the detriment of peace, President Clinton would do so only in January 2001, when he had just two weeks left before the expiration of his final presidential term.

Clinton likely felt that he had done enough; he had undoubtedly gone further than any other U.S. president in recognizing the Palestinians and their leadership. He had hosted Arafat at the White House for the first time in history and did so many times thereafter; this was a gesture that gave important legitimacy to the Palestinian movement. He even made the first visit of a U.S. president to Palestine—to Gaza City, of all places—following the 1998 Wye River Agreement. But for all these improvements, including a certain degree of personal sympathy for the plight of the Palestinians, by the time of Barak's election, Clinton was still unwilling to expressly advocate the unstated Oslo endgame of an independent Palestinian state.

There were, of course, domestic U.S. political reasons for this. In 1998, a torrent of controversy had followed the remarks of his wife, Hillary, who stated before a group of Arab and Israeli teenagers, "I think that it will be in the long-term interests of the Middle East for Palestine to be a state."[11] The first lady's comments exceeded her husband's level of political comfort, as was made apparent by the White House press secretary's immediate clarification: "That view expressed personally by the first lady is not the view of the president." One year later, with Mrs. Clinton readying herself for the race to become a senatorial candidate in New York, a state that has a pro-Israel reputation stemming in part from its 12 percent Jewish vote, Republican New York City Mayor Rudolph Giuliani reminded voters of her comment and termed Hillary's endorsement of Palestinian statehood a "very big mistake."[12]

The chance that Clinton was going to rise to the occasion and declare the inevitability of Palestinian statehood before election season in November 2000 was nil. Though he did not have to face another election himself, Clinton saw the promotion of his wife's political future as a top priority (perhaps as a way to make amends for his dalliance with Monica Lewinsky). Clinton also channeled efforts—though at times unwanted—toward the presidential candidacy of his loyal partner, Al Gore, with whom he also wanted to repair relations after the Lewinsky scandal. If Hillary Clinton's 1998 statement on Palestine was used as a barometer, President Clinton could easily conclude that public remarks on taboo issues such as Palestinian statehood, the fate of Palestinian refugees, or the division of Jerusalem could be injurious to either campaign.

These circumstances late in Clinton's tenure limited his freedom of movement in Middle East negotiations precisely at a time that called for daring diplomacy and the shattering of taboos. It has often been speculated that Jimmy Carter endangered his chances at re-election in 1980 by alienating his pro-Israel constituencies; Clinton's acute sensitivity to electoral considerations—even when it was not his own candidacy that was at stake—meant that diplomatic judgment would, in the end, be sacrificed to political expediency.

• • •

**From Clinton's perspective,** though, the U.S. Congress and public had been a secondary consideration, given Barak's "take charge" commitment to lead Middle East peacemaking.

Barak was heralded everywhere for his unique qualifications: As Israeli historian Avi Shlaim wrote, Barak was neither a dove nor a hawk; he was what Israeli's call a *bitkhonist*, or a "security-ist." Barak had been firm in his conviction that he could use his security bona fides, as Israel's most decorated war hero, in order to unite his country toward a national consensus for peace.[13] He believed the only way to pursue negotiations on all fronts was from a position of strength, and it was believed that his straddling of the political fence would allow him to attract bipartisan support, both in the Knesset and the U.S. Congress.

Barak was a hybrid of right-wing and left-wing political persuasions, so when he assumed office, it was natural that he would try to forge some right-wing alliances, ostensibly in order to enable the left-wing platform of peace to be tabled. Gilead Sher, a trusted friend and confidant of Barak who would later become his chief negotiator with the Palestinians, described the rationale and tensions behind Barak's efforts:

> What I figure Barak tried to accomplish is the very broad coalition of parties from the National Religious Party on the right to Meretz on the left. There were seven parties that participated in the coalition and signed the platform of the newly elected government. And I believe it has to do with Barak's intention to pursue and exhaust every effort in order to achieve permanent status or at least try or attempt to achieve and conclude negotiations on permanent status.
>
> Now, in light of that, he knew that he would lose the political extremities along the way as he approached the crucial crossroads and the conclusion of the core issues. At the same time, we thought that such a large coalition would allow him to build national consensus over sensitive issues toward the referendum that would take place at the end of the process, once an agreement had been achieved.[14]

Barak needed sixty-one out of 120 Knesset seats for a majority, so a "deal with the devil" of some sort was necessary to form his government. By bringing in a wide range of odd bedfellows, including the pro-settler National Religious Party (NRP), the ultra-Orthodox Shas Party, and the Russian-Jewish Yisrael Ba'Aliyah Party, Barak managed to secure a robust majority of seventy-five seats.

Noticeably absent from his coalition were the Israeli-Arab ministers, who had amassed a notable ten seats by the time of Barak's election. This was for two reasons. First, Barak thought he could count on the "Arab vote" should a peace referendum be tabled. Second—a tangential but important reason that reflects the second-class treatment of Arab citizens within Israel—was that if Barak's government included Arab-Israeli Knesset members when a peace referendum came to a vote, the right wing would have a field day opposing the deal by labeling it as a fifth-column "Arab" plan.

Barak did what he thought was politically necessary and, on July 6, 1999, fifty days after the election, he presented his newly formed government after formally assuming office. After weeks of haggling, the disparate members of Barak's coalition agreed, in principle, to his mandate:

> Peace will not come unless it is based on four pillars—peace with Egypt, with Jordan, with Syria and Lebanon [counting as one], and with the Palestinians. Israel has signed peace accords with Egypt and with Jordan, leaving two remaining steps to a lasting peace in the region. These two assignments together—the reaching of a permanent agreement with the Palestinians and the achieving of peace with Syria and Lebanon–are equally vital and urgent in my eyes.[15]

By excluding Likud and including "lesser evil" right-wingers in his government, Barak faced an unenviable political challenge that would severely strain his peacemaking agenda. Even so, many of his dovish Labor supporters were surprised to find out that a little under half of his Cabinet officials were the same people appointed under Netanyahu's Likud government. The inclusion of the right-wing groups would eventually undermine him.

The pro-settler NRP, which has a notorious reputation for joining any coalition that will give it the most prestigious cabinet seats and the richest coffers for its special interests, was expected to stay loyal, as Sher explained, until ideological lines had been crossed—in particular, any permanent-status referendum calling for the dismantling of settlements. But for the short term, Barak planned to appease the party by allowing settlement-building to continue.

Barak appointed the head of NRP, Yitzhak Levy, to be the minister for housing and construction, a position that would give Levy ample opportunity to finance and strengthen settlement construction in the occupied territories. Upon joining Barak's government, Levy reassured his constituents that nothing would change, saying, "Barak said clearly that he won't freeze settlements" and that he would allow for the "natural, needed growth" of existing ones.[16] Barak gave the Ministry of Interior and Ministry of Absorption, which regulates and builds housing for Jews who immigrate to Israel, to Yisrael Ba'Aliyah's Natan Sharansky, the hard-line former Soviet dissident who is a vocal supporter of Jewish settlements, particularly in the Golan Heights.

Noticeably absent from the spotlight was preeminent Oslo endorser and Nobel Prize recipient Shimon Peres; this reflected the depth of Barak's disdain for the Oslo Accords and their architects. Barak allotted Peres a bland portfolio to keep him far away from the Ministry of Foreign Affairs, instead giving the appointment to David Levy, a former member of the Likud Party whom he expected to behave moderately. Yossi Beilin—who was closely aligned with Peres, had brokered Oslo, and was an advocate of negotiations with the Arabs—was also given an odd and distant appointment as justice minister. Equally unusual was the appointment of

Shlomo Ben Ami, a Labor official and former history professor, to the position of minister of internal security. As a testament to his own micromanaging, Barak reserved the Ministry of Defense portfolio for himself, which most in the IDF brass did not appreciate.

• • •

**Expectations among much** of the Israeli public were that the Palestinian track should be resolved in order to achieve real peace with the Arab and broader Muslim world, including Syria and Lebanon. But Barak marched straight toward his campaign commitment to withdraw Israeli troops from Lebanon within one year. Most Israelis who voted for him probably recognized, at least on some level, that doing so would require negotiations with Syria to ensure that they exerted their virtual control of southern Lebanon to promote Israel's border security. To placate the other parties—as well as the Israeli public and members of the U.S. negotiating team who were opposed to this notion—Barak expressed his commitment to work on all negotiating tracks, emphasizing that he understood the Palestinian track to be the Gordian knot at the heart of the broader Arab-Israeli conflict.

The Palestinians couldn't have agreed more. Indeed, they demanded action. Although Palestinian resistance groups continued to be kept at bay by Arafat's security forces, under Netanyahu's tenure, life for most Palestinians had been miserable. The declining Palestinian economy, combined with Israel's continued policy of provocative house demolitions, expropriation of Palestinian land, and settlement construction, made for a toxic, indeed explosive, atmosphere. Economic agreements negotiated under Oslo that were supposed to benefit the Palestinian people were never properly implemented. By 1999, the severe restrictions placed on movement of people and goods within the occupied territories, aside from provoking humiliation and anger, had eroded any gains the Palestinians might have enjoyed after the 1993 Oslo signing. These sobering realities were in plain view to everyone, and had far-reaching consequences.

As the Palestinian economy declined, so too did faith in the Oslo process. Toni Verstandig, a political appointee who served the Clinton administration as the deputy assistant secretary of state for Near East affairs, was responsible for handling the Arab-Israeli economic portfolio during the peace process. In what she terms Israeli "protectionism," Verstandig describes how successive Israeli governments spent the Oslo years invoking security as an excuse to keep economic hegemony over Palestinian life:

> Had we faithfully implemented agreements that had been reached, we would have had equity in the bank. We would have created support on the [Palestinian] street and we would have had the reserve when we needed it and the times were tough. We never fully—the *parties* never fully—implemented their water agreements. They never fully implemented their economic agreements.
>
> You had this unfortunate situation of security being used as an argument to adversely affect the movement of goods and people. Security is an aspect that everyone accepted, but it was made with such a broad sweep that it was quickly realized that it was just another excuse at protectionism. We never implemented. . . the *parties* never implemented—the Israel-Jordan economic agreements. That also hurt the Palestinians, because they couldn't have an open economic relationship with their Arab partners in Jordan.
>
> The bureaucracy in Israel is unbelievable! And it is a much more *protectionist*-driven bureaucracy than this vibrant free-market democracy that it truly is. So you have this huge governmental disconnect between a vibrant private sector—before the breakdown of peace, the second-largest listing on

> the NASDAQ—and a government full of protectionists not wanting to, for whatever good reason, give up an inch of an economic toehold.[17]

As the quality of Palestinian life declined, those Palestinians who questioned support for the Oslo process began to take aim at the Palestinian Authority leadership who had agreed to it. Palestinian intellectuals, many of whom never had confidence in Oslo, like the late Edward Said and Haydar Abdel Shafi, would be vindicated for their years of opposition. Said, who enjoyed wide respect and popularity as a public intellectual and scholar at Columbia University, leveled criticism at the PLO leadership for agreeing to Oslo's terms. He specifically called into question the Palestinian Authority's security cooperation to disarm resistance groups in the wake of Israel's continued expropriation of Palestinian land.[18]

Indeed, from the time Oslo took effect until June 1999, the Israeli government confiscated over 54,400 acres of Palestinian land in the occupied territories; 80 percent of this was done under the Netanyahu government.[19] As the population of Jewish settlers doubled during the Oslo period, Said pointed out that "for the first time in the twentieth century, an anti-colonial liberation movement has not only discarded its own considerable achievements but has made an agreement to cooperate with a military occupation before that occupation has ended."[20]

Six years after Oslo began, Arafat found himself surrounded with rising street-level dissatisfaction and growing political instability. Even his close advisers began questioning the wisdom in Oslo. Former PLO legal adviser Omar Dajani explains:

> Palestinian negotiators came to feel particularly burned by what they perceived as Israeli bad faith in interpreting the numerous ambiguous formulations in the Oslo agreements,

> which, *inter alia*, required the release of "prisoners" without stipulating how many, provided for Israeli redeployment from "West Bank territory" without indicating how much, and called for "free and normal" movement of Palestinian persons and goods "without derogating from Israel's security powers and responsibilities . . ."
>
> The rapid growth of Israeli settlements in the occupied territories elicited criticism of the PLO's failure to secure an explicit commitment to a settlement freeze; and the sporadic imposition of severe restrictions on Palestinian movement within the occupied territories, as well as into Israel and abroad, called into question the wisdom of the complex jurisdictional scheme established by the agreements and the overriding control reserved by Israel.[21]

There had been transgressions on both sides since the Oslo Accords began, primarily because the years of enmity had been artificially replaced with a document that relied on "good-faith implementation" by both sides. This formulation, which U.S. Middle East envoy Dennis Ross had introduced and insisted upon, gave the misimpression that the Palestinians had strength to bargain on equal terms, and thus not only carry out their own obligations but compel Israel to implement its half of the Oslo "land-for-peace" bargain. The "good-faith" formulation was quickly frustrated by the many interpretations of Oslo given by Israeli leaders who succeeded Rabin, as foreign-policy decisions were often left to the whims of domestic Israeli politics. Moreover, U.S. negotiator Ross, the primary arbiter of which side had acted in good faith, was viewed by the Palestinians as overwhelmingly biased toward Israel. In fact, he often did side with the Israelis.

But far worse for Arafat's popularity was how Israeli governments were able to convince the United States to allow it to delay implementation of its obligations. The 1995 Oslo II Agreement was in large part a renegotiation of the original

Oslo Agreement, in Israel's favor. Like Oslo II, the 1997 Hebron Protocol and the 1998 Wye River Agreement were further renegotiations in Israel's favor.

By 1999, the question on the minds of most Palestinians was whether Barak would be any different: Would he seek to implement the prior obligations or resort to the same strategy of diluting Israel's Oslo responsibilities?

Things were clearly different as Barak took office. The key argument frequently cited by Israeli politicians who sought to defend Oslo's breaches—whether it was refusing to hand over land for autonomous Palestinian rule or continuing with new settlement construction—was nearly always "security." The Israeli public, however, had voiced its disapproval of this approach when they cast their vote for Barak. In fact, those who supported negotiations were generally in agreement with the views held by professional members of U.S. and Israeli security and intelligence organizations, who advised Barak that the Israeli government would no longer be able to avoid confronting the hopes most important to the Palestinians—like the dismantling of Jewish settlements and a return of most of the Palestinian land occupied since the 1967 war.

The heads of Barak's intelligence services kept him abreast of the realities Oslo had produced for Palestinians. The fig leaf of security would be a hard case for Barak to make, especially with Israeli-Palestinian security cooperation yielding a lull in violence by groups like Hamas. Ami Ayalon, a retired admiral who served during this period as director of the Israeli domestic intelligence agency, Shin Bet, described why there was a golden era of security at the time of Barak's election:

> We had security. In the last twelve months before the Intifada [of September 2000] only one Israeli was killed as a result of terror. *One Israeli!* What was the reason? It was not because the Shin Bet was better. I was most of that time the director and I can tell you that the security organization of Israel today is much better and,

> in spite of the fact, we are losing many people almost every day! The answer was somewhere else. At least the analysis we made then—and I think this is the real answer—is that we saw correlation between support for the peace process among Palestinians and the terror policy of Hamas. The higher the support of the peace process, the Hamas attempts were lower—because you have to understand that Hamas will never fight against the Palestinian street. . . .
>
> And the second factor was the security policy of the Palestinian organizations. The moment that the Palestinian street supports the peace, they can fight Hamas without being perceived as our collaborators.[22]

The success on the security front was largely due to the Clinton administration's execution of a CIA covert action program aimed at training and equipping the Palestinian security apparatus to fight terror. While it was widely successful, former CIA officer Mahle, who described her role then as only "security liaison," began to see the same trend that Ayalon described:

> After the Wye River accords, you really started to see an erosion of public opinion in terms of what the Oslo process was bringing in terms of tangible improvement to Palestinian daily life. As a result of that, there started to be a drift on the street: the popularity of Arafat was dropping. . . . The street eventually abandoned support of the negotiated settlement period.[23]

The founder of the Palestinian Red Crescent Society, Dr. Haydar Abdel Shafi, who as a negotiator at the 1991 Middle East peace conference in Madrid had demonstrated his willingness to accept the Israeli state, is known for having privately and publicly counseled Arafat against Oslo because of its failure to stipulate removal of, or at the very least a hard freeze on, settlements. As someone who is still widely regarded as one of the wisest unofficial leaders in Palestine, it was moderates like Dr. Shafi—an octogenarian who had lived in Palestine since the days of British colonial rule—who consistently decried from his Gaza Strip home the hypocrisies of the Oslo Accords. He deplored the fact that while the PLO decided in 1988 to recognize Israel's right to exist, throughout the Oslo years it was evident that elements of the Israeli government were still implementing the goal of early Zionism: the appropriation of as much of Palestine for the Jewish state as possible.[24]

While Barak was forming his government, provocative settlement construction instigated under Netanyahu continued with the intention of rendering a final compromise impossible. Dr. Irving Moskowitz, an American Jew from Miami, met no resistance getting the outgoing Netanyahu cabinet to approve his million-dollar plans to construct 132 housing units in a Palestinian area of East Jerusalem. A spokesman for Moskowitz confirmed that the project was a message to Barak. Moskowitz defended his building, noting that it was in "complete harmony" with Barak's vision of an "eternally united Jerusalem under exclusive Jewish sovereignty."[25] Also, at the expense of nearby Palestinian villages, Netanyahu's outgoing defense minister approved construction to connect the mega-settlement of Ma'ale Adumim with portions of East Jerusalem.

So as to give Barak some time to get grounded, the U.S. State Department did little but declare the building a "provocative act by an outgoing government." The Palestinians waited to see how Barak would respond, knowing from their experience during the Oslo years that it was unlikely the United States would offer little more than rhetoric. In response to U.S. inaction on settlements, the Palestinian Authority began to openly criticize the most influential members of the U.S. negotiating team, who they believed were inadequately conveying their problems to President Clinton.

Their criticism was not without basis. Toni Verstandig

received the field reports on settlements back in Washington, and recalled how an opportunity to do business differently under Barak was put aside by Dennis Ross. Verstandig explained how the U.S. team handled the incoming reports on settlements, and why U.S. government inaction persisted:

> We met every day at 10 o'clock, and fought like tooth and nail. It wasn't that there was resistance. [But] there were factors that were brought into play . . . and we would argue about the particular press guidance language.
>
> Dennis was the most uncomfortable with the most direct approach, in terms of criticizing. I think he felt that we couldn't diminish our leverage with Israel if we came out and publicly criticized what he believed was catering to constituencies in Israel, because it would weaken that particular Israeli government, and that particular Israeli government—at the time—was pursuing peace and therefore we had to take into account all else that they were doing.[26]

The pleas of the Palestinians to stop settlement construction, often conveyed through by the reporting of CIA and State Department officers, nevertheless appeared to fall on deaf ears at the higher levels in Washington. In addition to conveying their concerns routinely to their U.S. counterparts on the ground, the Palestinians tried to alert the two most central policy figures, Ross and Martin Indyk, that the settlements were going to jeopardize the chances for a final-status agreement.

By 1999, this proved to be a daunting, if not useless, endeavor. The Palestinians pointed to the bias of Ross, charging that his affinity toward Israel was directly responsible for the lax U.S. policy. The credentials of Ross, including past associations both with the staunchly pro-Israel American Israel Public Affairs Committee (AIPAC) and as a policy analyst at the pro-Israel Washington Institute for Near East

Policy (WINEP), served to feed the common perception among Palestinian negotiators that he was, as the de facto Palestinian Foreign Minister Nabil Shaath put it, "more pro-Israeli than the Israelis."[27]

Ross made one of his first public endorsements on settlements while campaigning for the re-election of his previous boss, President George H.W. Bush. Speaking before members of San Francisco's Jewish community on April 22, 1992, Ross boasted as an "achievement" of Bush's Middle East foreign policy record that the Arabs "had not been able to make the formal freezing of settlements a precondition for the holding of talks."[28] If Ross had to moderate his views toward settlements at all upon becoming the central negotiating figure under Clinton, the legalistic lexicon of Oslo offered him an escape. Under Oslo's fine print, settlements would be dealt with as part of the final-status negotiations. Thus the United States was able to dodge a vigorous confrontation over settlements by miring themselves in renegotiation upon renegotiation during the interim period. Indeed, Oslo said nothing about settlement "dismantling" or "evacuation"; much less did it call for a cessation of construction during the interim years. Instead, settlements were made part of the long-term Oslo objectives under the following clause:

> It is understood that these [permanent status] negotiations shall cover remaining issues, including: Jerusalem, refugees, settlements, security arrangements, borders, relations and cooperation with other neighbors, and other issues of common interest.[29]

Those within the U.S. government who regularly fielded complaints on settlements dutifully reported their findings, but stressed that the onus was on Washington to carry out a policy change. From her years of experience as a liaison between Israeli and Palestinian intelligence services, Mahle opined that "the settlement issue, more than anything else, inflamed the street."[30]

There is a general consensus among State and CIA officials that the United States had an opportunity to do business differently after Barak's election. Even Israeli intelligence officials like Ami Ayalon hoped that, for the sake of maintaining a period of relative calm on both sides, U.S. policymakers would use the election of Barak as an opportunity to reverse their blasé attitude toward settlement growth. At least for Ayalon, the polls the Shin Bet relied upon sent an ominous message: By June 1999, a 63 percent majority of Palestinians did not trust the peaceful intentions of the Israeli people.[31]

## • THREE •

# *Leaning Toward Syria*

IN THE SUMMER of 1999, as far as most of the Mideast specialists in the Clinton administration were concerned, including Sandy Berger's NSC, it did not make sense to focus on anything but the deteriorating Israeli-Palestinian track.[1] But at the highest echelons of Albright's State Department, support had been slowly mounting for a broader, multilateral effort that matched Barak's Syria-first preferences. In a June 3, 1999, speech, Martin Indyk, who as assistant secretary for Near East affairs was crafting policy for the State Department, did his best to assuage Palestinian concerns. He stated:

> We do not fear this notion that one track will move ahead faster than other tracks. If we're moving ahead on all tracks we can create the positive dynamic that we once had in the peace process, in which progress on one track helps generate progress on another.[2]

Despite his public statements favoring progress on all negotiating tracks, in truth Indyk was the U.S. official who most strongly advocated a behind-the-scenes, single-focus,

Syria-first agenda. Indyk's rooted views on Syria extended back to his days as an analyst for the American Israel Public Affairs Committee (AIPAC).[3] After founding the AIPAC-sponsored Washington Institute for Near East Policy (WINEP) in the mid-1980s in partnership with future State Department colleague Dennis Ross, Indyk began to sell the Clinton campaign as early as 1992 on the advantages of Syria-first. Indyk recalled his rationale, which remains the same today:

> I have always seen the virtue—from an American point of view—of going with Syria-first. In terms of our strategic interests, a peace treaty with Syria would produce a peace treaty with Lebanon, would deal with the Hezbollah problem in southern Lebanon, and take the only remaining conventional Arab army out of the conflict with Israel.
>
> Syria was the beating heart of pan-Arabism. And once it made peace with Israel, all the other Arabs would have cover to normalize their relations. Iraq and Iran would have been seriously isolated once Syria was taken out of their potential nexus—Iran, because of the peace treaty between Israel and Lebanon, would have lost its toehold in there.
>
> And we would have been in a much better position *then* to work the Israeli-Palestinian track in a situation where Arafat would have to get serious about doing a deal for fear of being left high and dry. And the Israelis would be in a better position in which to do a deal.[4]

Indyk's policy arguments can be summarized in one line: it would be easier to force the Palestinians to submit to Barak's final-status terms after regional allies who offer resistance, like Syria, were taken out of the equation. Indyk had also seen the "virtue" in Syria-first well before he became a U.S. citizen in 1993. He individually sought to push this agenda with prior Israeli governments and, in a 1991 WINEP report, he spelled out the argument for why the United States should do the same:

> At a minimum, the U.S. needs to have its priorities clear. U.S. strategic interests would best be served by an agreement that reduced if not eliminated the chances for another Syrian-Israeli war. Who rules in Nablus [Palestine] is *not* a strategic priority for the U.S.[5]

The idea that the Palestinian question should not take priority as the core of the Arab-Israeli conflict was a personal agenda that Indyk carried with him into the U.S. government.[6] Once Clinton became president in 1993, Indyk, an Australian citizen who covered the Middle East as an intelligence officer in Australia's government, underwent expedited citizenship procedures in order to join the Clinton foreign policy team.[7] Just one week after becoming a U.S. citizen, Indyk was granted the nation's highest security clearances and thrust into the epicenter of U.S. national security policymaking with an appointment to the position of Middle East adviser to the president at the National Security Council.[8] During their first NSC strategy session on the Middle East, the president signed off on Indyk's rationale, deciding himself that his administration would promote the Syria-first strategy.[9]

Clinton later appointed Indyk as the first Jewish-American ambassador to Israel, in 1995. His appointment was an exception to the State Department's universally applied security practice of avoiding such ethnic appointments (it will not, for example, name a Chinese-American to become the U.S. ambassador to China; this policy is to ward off routine attempts by intelligence services to manipulate allegiances). As was evident in the case of Jonathan Pollard and numerous other still-classified instances of hostile Israeli-intelligence actions against the United States, the outward public ambience of friendly relations is misleading. As far as counterintelligence professionals were concerned, Indyk could have become a target for Israeli intelligence recruitment: He resided in Israel during the 1973 war and had even served a stint as a volunteer with Israeli civil authorities during that crisis.[10]

But despite the appearance problems the ambassadorship created for Indyk, who as an American Jew would be vulnerable to the sometimes anti-Semitic charges of "dual loyalty," he took little to no measures to either lower his profile or downplay his affinity for the Jewish state. In a 1998 AIPAC interview, he assured members of the U.S. pro-Israeli community that "evenhandedness is not in our lexicon."[11] This was a posture that, according to some of his State Department colleagues, gave him the hallway reputation as "a true Zionist."[12] His open support for the Israeli Labor Party would ultimately compromise his representational obligations as ambassador following Netanyahu's election.[13] Former ambassador to Israel Ned Walker recalled:

> Martin had been very supportive of Labor. I mean, that's why Netanyahu had a hard time dealing with Martin, because he had been so openly advocating Peres's election when Netanyahu won.[14]

Indeed, upon Netanyahu's election, Indyk was returned to Washington and named the assistant secretary of state for Near East affairs.

Barak was comfortable with Indyk and his longstanding Syria-first views. Prior to his first meeting with Arafat, Barak gave an interview in which he said—using the same logic Indyk espoused—that he saw the Palestinians as "the weakest of our adversaries." Dismissive of the Palestinians as a strategic adversary—which furthered the Palestinians' feeling of humiliation—Barak continued that "as a military threat they are ludicrous. They pose no military threat of any kind to Israel. The Syrians, however, are a source of conventional strength that can generate a major collision."[15]

By the summer of 1999, Indyk was in for a flattering surprise. He had worked closely with Barak on negotiations with Syria during the mid-1990s while Barak had been serving as chief of staff to Rabin.[16] Through the oblique and ultimately successful lobbying efforts of Barak's wife, Nava, who is a close friend of Indyk's wife, Jill, an Australian diplomat, President Clinton agreed that fall to again nominate Indyk as ambassador to Israel.

Their mutual elation was hardly concealed. Indyk then remarked that "it is not often that you get a second chance, and I believe with Prime Minister Barak's election, we now do have a second chance."[17] In his view, not only did the administration have a second chance to broker peace as Clinton wished, but the ambassadorship gave Indyk another chance to facilitate the process on the ground. From Israel he would be able to work again with Barak, this time the Labor prime minister, to prove the Syria-first strategy worthwhile.

• • •

**It became apparent** that the United States would follow this strategy, but it would first have to pass a pro forma muster with Clinton's lead Middle East envoy, Dennis Ross. Ross and Indyk, known for their years of friendship and fraternal commitment to promoting the interests of Israel, had diverged in their levels of influence upon entering U.S. government service. In many ways Indyk had lagged behind Ross's career advancement. Like Indyk, Ross had unabashedly championed exceedingly pro-Israeli policies as early as his first 1985 WINEP policy publication, when he called for the appointment of a "non-Arabist Special Middle East envoy" who would not "feel guilty about our relationship with Israel and our reluctance to force Israeli concessions."[18] Through his affiliation with the Republican Party, Ross first went on to espouse his ideology by securing a position as part of the Reagan administration's NSC Middle East team. He later advanced under the successor Bush administration to become director of the State Department's highly influential Policy Planning Division.

The 1992 election of Democratic Bill Clinton would normally have meant an end to Ross's appointment. But Ross's shrewd nurturing of connections ensured that his ability to guide Middle East policy would transcend domestic political boundaries, in no small part because of Indyk's own appointment within the Clinton administration, which enabled him to put in a good word on Ross's behalf.[19] As Clinton took in the recommendations of his new cabinet, including Indyk's Syria-first doctrine, he not only reviewed and approved the creation of a new State Department envoy position based on Ross's earlier WINEP paper; Clinton also selected Ross himself to fill the job. In the summer of 1993 Ross became the first "non-Arabist special Middle East envoy" to lead U.S. negotiations.

But following Barak's election and the excitement both Ross and Indyk shared at playing leading roles in concluding historic peace agreements before the end of their government service, what was once a subtle competition over who could best direct U.S. Mideast policy was transformed into a negative tension, particularly as Barak adopted Indyk's Syria-first strategy. Ross, who had become the ubiquitous face of Israeli-Palestinian negotiations, was uncertain over which direction to head and did not want to be the one to dampen Barak's enthusiasm, which Clinton fully shared.

Should Ross have used his position to resist the Indyk/Barak push regarding the Syrian track, his own centrality in the process could have brought the scorn of Barak and, in turn, put his own hard-won influence over the president in jeopardy. Ross apparently did not want to risk being viewed as a spoiler. These internal dynamics created an opening that any prime minister would seek to exploit. Barak would certainly do so.

It became all the more palatable for Ross to accept the new turn when, in late June 1999, an unusual exchange took place between Syrian President Hafez al-Assad and Barak. To everyone's disbelief, the two had exchanged sweet nothings through British journalist Patrick Seale. It began with Barak's pronouncement, before formally taking office:

> The only way to build a stable, comprehensive peace in the Middle East is through an agreement with Syria. My policy is to strengthen the security of Israel by putting an end to the conflict with Syria. I am truly excited to see if there is a possibility to conclude a "Peace of the Brave" with Syria.
>
> There is no doubt that President Asad has shaped the Syrian nation. His legacy is a strong, independent, and self-confident Syria—a Syria which, I believe, is very important for the stability of the Middle East. I see Syria as a pillar opposite us on the other side of the region.

Days later in Damascus, Asad reciprocated with extraordinary compliments:

> I have followed [Barak's] career and his statements. He seems to be a strong and honest man. As the election results show, he evidently has wide support. It is clear that he wants to achieve peace with Syria. He is moving forward at a well studied plan.[20]

• • •

**Before embarking on** his first symbolic visit as prime minister to neighboring Arab countries, Barak met with Arafat on July 11 at the Erez crossing, at the northernmost border of the Gaza Strip. To the displeasure of the Palestinians, Barak began his meeting by asking Arafat to consent to a delay of Israeli implementation of the recently signed 1998 Wye River Agreement while he pursued a fast track toward final-status negotiations. Arafat objected, insisting that the two must be done simultaneously—implementing Wye and beginning negotiations on the final status.[21] Despite his inability to secure assurances from Barak on Wye's implementation, Arafat decided to give him the benefit of the doubt, ending their first meeting on an upbeat note, calling Barak "a friend and a partner." Upon his return from the U.S., the two agreed to meet again and resume talks.[22]

On July 15, Barak arrived in the United States for an especially warm six-day visit, beginning in Washington. The president's wife, Hillary, had been off campaigning in New York that morning for her U.S. Senate bid, and Clinton and Barak were afforded a three-hour tête-à-tête in the family's private living room.[23] During this meeting, Barak formally notified Clinton that, for his government, a treaty with Syria would be more important, from the strategic point of view, than an accord with the Palestinians.[24]

Many within the State Department and NSC were skeptical of the Indyk-Barak push for Syria-first. Though Clinton had agreed to this strategy when Indyk originally presented it at the beginning of his administration, there had been nothing to show for it, since the Arabs and Israelis themselves were not willing to accept it. In fact, the Israelis and Palestinians had secretly concluded the Oslo Accords behind America's back. Then, when the United States tried to gain momentum again on the Syrian track, the Israelis went off and did a secret deal with Jordan, in 1994. Later, due to lack of trust between Netanyahu and the Clinton administration, official U.S. mediation with Syria stalled and instead focused on the Palestinians.

To allay Clinton's concern that a focus on Syria might further damage the worsening Palestine track, Barak gave Clinton his word that Israel would come through on all its agreements with the Palestinians—including the Wye Accord.[25] Clinton accepted Barak's assurances, and predicted for his own aides afterward that Barak would be "a leader who will be scrupulous in terms of living up to his obligations."[26]

On the first night of Barak's visit, he, Clinton, and their wives adjourned to Camp David, the president's official retreat nestled in the bucolic Catoctin Mountains of nearby Maryland. At the venue where the U.S. brokered the historic Israeli-Egyptian peace agreement in the summer of 1978, Barak whetted Clinton's appetite for peace with a history lesson. While touring the cabins where Egyptian leader Anwar al-Sadat and Israeli Prime Minister Menachem Begin stayed during their Nobel Prize-winning summit, Barak flattered Clinton by stressing the importance of U.S. presidential intervention, reminding him of how during the summit, President Jimmy Carter had been able to "bypass everyone and make things happen" when negotiations got bogged down.[27]

In an intimate discussion that lasted until almost 2 A.M., Barak confided to Clinton that he was prepared to "make painful compromises" for peace.[28] In the next few days, however, Barak brought along additional requests that he saw as necessary in order for him to succeed. Foremost, he wanted to modify U.S. diplomatic involvement in the process. He had publicly criticized the monitoring role of the CIA in Gaza as inappropriate,[29] preferring instead that the United States contribute to the process more "as a facilitator than as a kind of policeman, judge, and arbitrator at the same time."[30]

This was primarily a slam on the CIA's Tel Aviv station, which was assigned the controversial role of monitoring Israeli and Palestinian fulfillment of obligations. The president was familiar with the CIA's work, as many of the various breaches of the Wye River Agreement were reported directly to him via secret memorandum. One U.S. intelligence officer serving during the Netanyahu period lamented:

> I believe that both the Israelis and Palestinians were in breach of several agreements reached—including the Wye agreements. But I mostly fault the Israelis. In their culture, the Israelis will accept a deal, and then go into debate and delib-

eration afterward about whether they are going to live up to the terms of the deal. Culturally, this was a real problem.[31]

As intelligence officials complained that the president was not pressuring either side to live up to its obligations, the CIA became a judge without an enforcement capability—a political lightning rod that was struck by both sides. Barak wanted the CIA monitoring mechanism to end.

But underlying Barak's preference for less direct involvement was really a veiled criticism of Clinton's special Middle East coordinator, Dennis Ross, who, since 1993, had become the symbol of the "incrementalist" process, which was, in Barak's view, a step-by-step, "death-by-a-thousand-cuts" procedure. At the time, Ross suggested that he was "a bit taken aback and hurt" by Barak's public criticism of the "facilitator" role he was playing, but he responded with confidence that "when the work has to be done, it will be myself and Martin doing it."[32]

Barak also felt vindicated in his original opposition to the Oslo Accords, as he found the slow-moving, nuanced diplomatic process and its reliance on procedures like "confidence-building measures" troubling, particularly because of his belief that the concessions already made to the Palestinians had gone too far.[33] Using his penchant for metaphors in one of his first encounters with the UN special envoy to the Middle East, Terje Roed Larsen, who was a supporter of the Oslo process, Barak described it as "a very ugly dog," saying, "The tail is not ugly, the head is ugly, but you don't chop the head, you chop the tail, but not a bit every day." Barak felt there were good parts of Oslo, but he wanted to amend the agreement by discarding the parts he did not like.[34]

In private, more of Clinton's principal advisers were becoming concerned with Barak's new preferences, particularly as they were manifested in his efforts to "presidentialize" the process by demanding "direct, instant, and frequent access to the president." Barak had resisted the advances of lesser U.S. officials in the weeks leading up to his first Washington visit, even refusing to delegate real authority to his own subordinates for liaison. Such tactics, if continued, would, in effect, cut Ross—and Barak's own advisers—from the loop. Sharing this anxiety was Secretary Albright, who at the time submitted a confidential memorandum to the president with her own impression that Barak was "secretive and didn't have a large circle of aides who knew his mind."[35]

Barak was not against all American intervention—certainly not increased economic assistance. To reward Barak's peaceful rhetoric,[36] the Clinton administration, through Defense Secretary William Cohen, matched Barak's declared commitments by pledging the Pentagon's construction of a third $42 million Arrow missile battery for Israel's protection against medium-range missile threats.[37]

This came with Barak's announcement of an ambitious new plan to negotiate peace between Israel and Syria, Lebanon and Palestine within fifteen months—before the end of Clinton's presidency and even before the November 2000 election season kicked in.[38] The fifteen-month plan was great news for Clinton, who had watched the Oslo process ebb and flow throughout his time in office, and dreamed of concluding it on his watch. Some, particularly in Israel, began to probe the wisdom and manageability of pursuing all three tracks within Barak's own self-imposed timetables. But his spokeswoman, Merav Parsi Zadok, defended the rationale:

> In fifteen months we should know the results of all these plans. Firstly, there has to be flexibility on the part of the different parties. Secondly, there needs to be a U.S. will to invest in the process—politically, diplomatically and financially. And finally, there needs to be a realization that we are working within a time frame. Whoever holds back now, might find themselves out of the loop at the end![39]

For the Palestinians who suspected that Barak might try to play the Syria track off the Palestinian negotiations in a game of musical chairs, these words confirmed their suspicions. Clinton responded to Arafat with his own assurances over the fulfillment of Wye River:

> I told him that [Barak] was committed to working in partnership with Chairman Arafat and honoring any agreements that had been made to this point. I went out of my way not to describe Barak's proposals or to advocate or not advocate, but simply to say that I was convinced they were being made in complete good faith.[40]

Clinton accommodated Barak's high-level negotiating preferences[41] and allowed Barak to "drive the process."[42] This happened in part because he knew that if Barak's bold three-front approach succeeded, it would dwarf the two-front (Palestinian and Jordanian) efforts undertaken by Rabin. But the key advisers surrounding Clinton had also been confident in Barak's confidence. He was primarily backed by Ross, Albright, and Indyk. Indyk believed that the Syrian track was far more ripened, much less complex, and most likely to succeed. Ross, who was far more influential with the president than Indyk, also went along with this view.[43] A very senior State Department official concluded that the United States followed Barak on Syria because, "let's put it this way—Albright was persuaded that Barak knew what he was doing."[44] Secretary Albright later reflected on this inaccurate opinion she held of Barak:

> One of the things you have to understand is we were so pleased to see Barak, who was eager to do things. I think that one of the mistakes we made was to think that Barak—while he clearly was a military genius—had enough of a political strategic view on some of this.[45]

After spending his last night in Washington at an elegant White House gala with over 400 attendees,[46] Barak returned to Israel, carrying himself with the aplomb that comes only from the personal backing of the president of the United States. First on his agenda when he arrived home was an unavoidable meeting with Arafat. In order to carry out his ambitions with Syria, Barak needed to either do as he promised Clinton and honor Israel's prior Wye obligations on the Palestinian track or resort to the strategy of Netanyahu by browbeating the Palestinians into signing another agreement that watered down Israel's obligations. Barak knew that such a move would placate the right-wing, pro-settlement elements in his coalition and thus keep his political costs low while testing the waters on the Syrian track.

## • FOUR •

# *The Palestinians Accept a Bad-Faith Bargain*

**THE SUDDEN HEART** attack and death of Morocco's King Hassan II on July 23, 1999, was untimely for everyone. In a neighborhood where the newly created Jewish state had few friends, Morocco, under Hassan's leadership, had been among the first Arab nations to forge relations with Israel. He was an influential figure in Arab-Israeli negotiations, promoted Israeli-Palestinian dialogue as early as the late 1970s, and successfully intervened in helping to bring Egyptians and Israelis to the table at Camp David in 1978.[1]

One result of Hassan's years spent pioneering improved Arab relations with Israel was an especially close friendship with Shimon Peres. Peres's trust in Hassan was manifested in a rare form of Arab-Israeli cooperation on a particularly sensitive issue: the establishment of a joint Moroccan-Israeli committee on Jerusalem. Eulogizing the king before the Knesset, Peres lamented the loss of Hassan, who had delicately served as the "Muslim world's official keeper of Jerusalem." Peres remarked how Hassan had "navigated this role with care, and worked hard not to create any provocations," adding that he "put out fires and never lit them."[2] At least thirty kings, princes, and heads of state flocked to Rabat, the capital of Morocco, to pay tribute to King Hassan, who, after the recent death of a fellow peacemaker with Israel, Hussein of Jordan, was the longest-reigning Middle East leader.[3]

Despite Hassan's friendliness toward Israel, he held clout in the Arab and Muslim world, and his judgment was trusted on issues that inevitably affected the Israeli-Palestinian negotiations, like the status of the Haram al-Sharif/Temple Mount.[4] For the short-term efforts of Israeli-Palestinian negotiations, the funeral of King Hassan allowed for another postponement of Barak's scheduled meeting with Arafat to discuss implementation of Wye, as both leaders, and indeed many leaders throughout the Arab and Muslim world, traveled to Rabat to pay their final respects.

Ever resourceful, President Clinton sensed an opportunity to turn lemons into lemonade. Just one week before the funeral, Barak's security adviser, Danny Yatom, issued a statement saying that Israel was prepared to resume talks with Syria where they left off under Shimon Peres in 1996.[5] If Clinton could get Syria to agree to the same, the Syrian track could begin and save everyone a lot of time. After promising Barak during his Washington visit to communicate directly with Syrian President Hafez al-Assad on his behalf, Clinton pondered using the funeral as a chance to arrange an impromptu meeting between the two leaders. Later, the *New York Times* speculated that Clinton might broker a famous first handshake between the two seemingly intractable foes.[6]

Assad, a reclusive leader who rarely left Damascus, was scheduled to attend the king's funeral but canceled without explanation. The media attributed Assad's absence to irritation over Israeli Foreign Minister David Levy's open calls for a Syrian-Israeli bilateral meeting at the funeral.[7] But sources close to Asad saw this as only part of the picture. In addition to his longstanding commitment not to make peace with

Israel until Israel agreed to relinquish the Golan Heights, under occupation since 1967, Asad had long ago decided that he would not meet or shake hands with any Israeli prime minister short of a final peace agreement that restored Syrian territory. Asad would not break these pledges simply because of a funeral, so he decided to stay home; he felt the timing was exploitative and without preparation.[8]

Even without Asad's attendance, nearly a full quorum of influential Arab leaders arrived alongside the Israeli delegation, and the focus turned to the Israeli-Palestinian track. Clinton, Barak, and Arafat held a five-minute, though unproductive, trilateral meeting.[9] More substantive were the hallway discussions and pledges from some Arab countries, like Egypt and Jordan, which concretely offered their own direct diplomatic intervention. The work was divided. After consulting with both Clinton and Barak, King Abdullah II of Jordan departed for Damascus in order to help revive Syrian-Israeli discussions with Asad.[10] This left time for both Clinton and Barak to consult with Egyptian President Hosni Mubarak, who earlier had made several requests for his government to have a more active role in the Israeli-Palestinian talks.

Shortly after the funeral, on July 27, Arafat and Barak met for roughly two hours at a military base near the Erez crossing.[11] Arafat told Barak his people were becoming disillusioned, and he insisted that Barak produce more than peaceful rhetoric. Arafat pressed again for implementation of the Wye Agreement, which consisted of Israel's obligations to turn over 13 percent of West Bank land to Palestinian rule, to release political prisoners, to construct a new seaport, and to open a "safe passage" route connecting Hebron in the West Bank to Gaza.[12] Arafat reminded Barak of the Palestinians' continued implementation of their Wye River security obligations, and asked Barak, as a show of good faith, to stop settlement construction.[13]

Arafat foresaw that resolving final-status issues—some of

which are the most central to the hundred-year-old conflict—would take more time and focus than Barak thought, and that his people were incapable of waiting longer to see basic improvements in their lives.[14]

Barak continued to assure Arafat, "We are committed to Wye; we will implement Wye,"[15] and with that qualifier, Barak pressed Arafat for an additional two weeks to shore up a new timeline for Wye's implementation. In describing Arafat's choices, Barak commented that insisting on full implementation before final-status talks would be a "bumpy road." He added that "if they choose the main road, it will be smooth."[16] Despite all the U.S. effort that went into concluding the Wye Agreement, at a press conference on July 28, National Security Adviser Sandy Berger gave the impression of U.S. ambivalence, stating, "Over the next few weeks, I think we will have some decisions about whether we're going down the Wye road or whether or not we're going down a road that has some modifications."[17]

As the weaker bargaining party, the Palestinians had no real choice but to consider Barak's new proposal. Arafat was forewarned that this would likely include such disheartening provisions as only partial withdrawal of Israeli troops under Wye and then deferral of other provisions until final-status negotiations. To examine the question fully, Arafat assigned Saeb Erekat to work closely with Barak's negotiation adviser, Gilead Sher, a respected Israeli attorney.[18]

Arafat's strategic decision to consider Barak's proposal infuriated some of his own advisers, particularly Mohammed Dahlan, chief of Gaza Preventive Security, who was starting to look like an Israeli quisling while continuing to fulfill the Wye responsibilities of cracking down on militants. Dahlan, a fluent Hebrew speaker who is particularly knowledgeable about Israeli politics, was puzzled by the odd lack of cooperation from Prime Minister Barak when it came to implementing agreements negotiated under Likud Prime Minister Netanyahu. He said, "We understand it when we sign an agreement with the Labor Party and the Likud wants to change it, but not if Likud signs an agreement and Labor wants to change it!"[19]

Many inside Palestine were growing distrustful, including some of Arafat's own advisers, who saw Barak's reluctance to implement the Wye Agreement as indistinguishable from the deceitful tactics of Netanyahu.[20] On July 28, Dahlan and Erekat took their grievances to Egyptian adviser and Camp David I veteran Dr. Osama el-Baz.[21] As was agreed during the funeral of King Hassan, the Egyptian government intervened to see what help it could provide to break the impasse.

The major issue, it appeared, could be summed up by Barak's remarks during a meeting with members of his own cabinet. He was concerned that a further redeployment of troops, as called for under Wye, would be "more than the Israeli public could handle."[22] The issue of withdrawal is inextricably linked to settlements, and given the composition of his new cabinet, he felt it was far too early for him to confront the settlers.[23] As far as Barak was concerned, further redeployment might deplete the reservoir of political capital that he badly needed to conserve for a final-status agreement. He defended his position on security grounds, pointing out that "fully implementing the pullbacks would leave several Jewish settlements in the West Bank isolated between Palestinian-controlled areas."[24] Indeed, were the Israelis to abide by their Wye commitments, roughly fifteen Jewish settlements would be isolated in Palestinian territory.[25]

Barak met with Mubarak to explain his new version of implementation and ask for his help in swaying the Palestinians. After hearing Barak's plan, Mubarak agreed, offering that he saw "no problem with starting final-status talks before Wye is completely carried out." As for Barak's proposed new timetable, Mubarak remarked that it was "no problem" if it is "delayed two or three weeks."[26]

The Palestinians were upset, and to make matters worse, they could no longer count on Madeleine Albright's scheduled mid-August visit, which they had hoped would produce movement on Wye implementation. On August 9, Barak formally requested that she postpone her trip in order to provide more time for direct talks already under way.[27] Albright agreed and rescheduled, adhering to Barak's strong preference that the Americans not disrupt what he viewed as routine Israeli-Palestinian negotiations.[28]

In shuttles between Jerusalem, Tel Aviv, Gaza City, and Cairo, the Palestinians spent weeks in a frustrating process of renegotiating Wye. On August 23, Arafat openly renewed his request for Albright's intervention, telling reporters "the situation needs an external effort . . . in order to implement what has already been agreed upon before." The United States appeared indifferent to the request, and Israeli Foreign Minister David Levy scoffed that "there is no need for pressure nor the media dramatics that we are witnessing."[29]

As time wore on, more "flexibility" on the Palestinian side was achieved. September approached and it appeared as though Arafat was ready to capitulate and accept Barak's renegotiation of Wye. As Albright prepared to meet with Barak and Arafat to preside over an agreement, a crisis erupted over minutiae. The issue of prisoners, a provision of Wye that bore heavily on the good will between Arafat and Barak, took preeminence as mothers began marching all over the West Bank and Gaza demanding the release of their jailed sons, whom the Palestinians viewed as political prisoners jailed for resisting occupation. Under Wye, as many as 750 prisoners were promised for release. The kinds of prisoners to be released (i.e., "criminal" as opposed to "security" prisoners) had been left to a vague oral agreement between Clinton, Arafat, and Netanyahu. Barak was only willing to turn over 350.[30]

In advance of her arrival, Albright dispatched Dennis Ross, his deputy, Aaron Miller, and Martin Indyk to help clinch a deal so that the United States and Israel could turn their sights toward Syria. But at this point in the Oslo process, there was little trust between the Palestinians and Ross, and the parties stayed their course primarily because of the eleventh-hour mediation efforts of Osama el-Baz.[31] Ross busied himself with the Israelis, spending a full day drafting the text to be used in the renegotiation,[32] including language that would remove Arafat's ability, as he did in May, to threaten unilateral declaration of statehood should Israel renege on its implementation obligations once again.[33]

When Albright arrived on September 2, she announced, "It is only natural that while I am here I try to be of assistance. We are prepared to take whatever role is necessary."[34] Albright inserted herself at the homestretch of the talks, shuttling between Barak and Arafat, hoping for an agreement so she could keep her appointment with the Syrians and use a Palestinian-Israeli agreement as leverage.[35] But this was starting to worry the Palestinians, who were sensing that the U.S. motivation for helping the agreement was simply to enable Barak to turn his attention to the Syrian track.[36]

This, too, was the working assumption of several members of the U.S. negotiating team, some of whom were not convinced of Barak's intentions to pursue both tracks equally.[37] Nobody wanted to pursue the Syrian track more than Martin Indyk, but the Palestinian suspicion was becoming palpable, so he felt obligated to warn Barak of the harms of renegotiating Wye. During a rare heated exchange between Indyk and Barak—two longtime friends—Indyk criticized Barak for proposing the changes, instead arguing that Wye implementation should begin first, as the Palestinians viewed this as "a reliability test." Only after implementation began, Indyk argued, should the additional proposals be introduced. Barak silenced the discussion, invoked his authority, and told Indyk that he would "appreciate him speaking in a different manner."[38]

The U.S. went along. Barak was obstinate, and besides, Arafat was close to accepting his deal. After shuttling back and forth between Barak and Arafat and presenting the text that Ross and the Israelis prepared, Albright, speaking from

Arafat's Gaza offices, announced that an agreement to implement Wye had been reached.[39] Members of the U.S. team lauded the agreement as proof of what could be accomplished through more direct dialogue, unlike the Wye Agreement, which relied on heavy browbeating by the U.S. negotiating team. The new agreement had been brokered almost solely by the parties themselves, with outside help coming largely from the Egyptians. Not even Albright's intervention made much of a difference; she conceded that her role was that of neither mediator nor facilitator—"handmaiden" was the term she chose.[40]

The agreement—officially, the "Sharm el-Sheikh Memorandum on Implementation Timeline of Outstanding Commitments of Agreements Signed and the Resumption of Permanent Status Negotiations" (commonly referred to as "Sharm"), was mocked by commentators, with some critics calling it "an agreement to implement an agreement to implement an agreement . . ."[41] The Palestinians were dissatisfied, to say the least, after bargaining away what was already agreed upon the previous October under Netanyahu. Expressing this opinion before the signing ceremony began, Nabil Shaath, the de facto PLO foreign minister, downplayed Sharm as "not a big achievement—this is already about a year too late!"[42]

For Palestinians, the deal was somewhat sweetened with the inclusion of two very important documents. Though they are just beyond the four corners of the primary agreement, two "letters of assurance" would serve to allay increasing Palestinian concerns about Barak's continuation of settlement construction. On behalf of the United States, Albright wrote:

> In order for these negotiations to succeed on such an accelerated basis, it is essential to create the right environment. In this regard, as good-faith negotiations proceed, neither side should take unilateral actions that undermine this environment.

> We are conscious of your concerns about settlement activity. As President Clinton has written to you in the past, the United States knows how destructive settlement activity has been to the pursuit of Palestinian-Israeli peace.[43]

In its own independent addendum, the European Union backed the Palestinians with stronger language, stating:

> The European Union reiterates its call on both parties to refrain from activities which prejudge the outcome of final-status negotiations and from any activity contrary to international law, including settlement activity.[44]

In a September 4, 1999, convocation ceremony at the Egyptian resort town of Sharm el-Sheikh, Yasser Arafat and Ehud Barak signed the agreement while Secretary Albright, President Mubarak, and King Abdullah II served as smiling witnesses. Photographs were taken and optimism was projected. Speaking from Washington, President Clinton hailed the agreement, saying, "It shows that when both sides are willing to work together, their fundamental requirements can be met, confidence can be built, and the process can move forward."[45]

The gist of this agreement was as follows: Israel agreed to implement the second of three further redeployments, originally stipulated in the unfulfilled 1995 Oslo II Agreement, by further dividing the implementation into three incremental dates: on the following day, September 5, on November 15, and on January 20, 2000. By January 20, exclusive Israeli control over the West Bank was scheduled to be reduced from 72 percent to 59 percent, and the Palestinian Authority was to be given control of an additional 11 percent of the area.[46] On its prisoner obligations, Israel agreed to release a total of 350 prisoners, beginning September 5 with 200, and an additional 150 on October 8. Israel agreed to restart the "Interim

Committees" (dealing with economic issues and people-to-people exchanges) created at Wye but suspended since Barak took office. Safe-passage routes connecting Gaza with the West Bank were to be opened in phases, and a seaport was approved for construction, subject to Israeli oversight.[47] The sum total of the Sharm Agreement was narrowly focused on carrying out only the second further redeployment. It did, however, recognize the validity of the third further redeployment of Oslo II, and Sharm called for establishing a bilateral committee, called the Third Further Redeployment Committee, to discuss the areas to be transferred.

The determination in this agreement followed the fifteen-month timeline Barak set for all three tracks, and it gave the Palestinians two new benchmarks to look forward to, known by their acronyms as "FAPS" and "CAPS." It began with FAPS, or "Framework Agreement for Permanent Settlement," which called for the hammering out of a conceptual structure for final negotiations in just five months—by February 13, 2000. It next set an ambitious deadline for CAPS, or "Comprehensive Agreement for Permanent Settlement," i.e., a final end to the decades-old Israeli-Palestinian conflict, to be concluded no later than September 2000.

It appeared from the U.S. side that the Palestinians were appeased. While the ink was still drying on the Sharm Agreement, Secretary Albright and her entourage arrived in Damascus for a scheduled meeting with President Asad and his foreign minister, Farouk al-Shaara.[48] The Palestinian Authority, reluctant to engage in another signing ceremony that would bring little actual improvement to the daily lives of Palestinians, was at least able to secure an almost immediate, though small, Israeli military withdrawal and at least a nominal release of some political prisoners. Added contiguity and the quality of the land that Israel was to relinquish were important factors of Sharm. Should Barak turn out to be, as Netanyahu was with Wye, a scofflaw concerning Israeli obligations, some Palestinians believed that Arafat might be in a position to accrue more bargaining leverage with Clinton when the time came for final-status talks the following year.

The perception after Sharm was that Barak had won. He succeeded in bringing the Palestinians around to accepting a renegotiation of a prior agreement. From the Israeli perspective, the fact that the Palestinians were convinced to give up something they were lawfully entitled to was viewed as a good precedent for Barak's fifteen-month objective of reaching a final-status agreement. And as Barak had intended all along, the Sharm Agreement offered him the time needed to explore the terms of a Syrian-Israeli peace agreement, without giving up any political capital on the Palestinian track.

• PART TWO •

# BARAK OPTS FOR SYRIA FIRST

## • FIVE •

# *"Find Me a Way to Fudge It"*

**IN ORDER TO** make the strategy of Syria-first work, the United States team spent the fall of 1999 immersing themselves in groundwork, primarily by lubricating the friction points that had lain dormant during the Netanyahu years. A new dynamic was thrown into the mix under Barak, with his promise to withdraw from Lebanon no later than June 2000, and both Ross and Barak gave surety on Israel's intention, with or without a Syrian agreement, to do just that.[1]

This was a significant leverage point against Syria, which stations approximately 35,000 soldiers in Lebanon and acts as a power broker for the Lebanon-based Shiite resistance group Hezbollah. For many years, Hezbollah has been the only card the weaker Syrians could use to keep Israel uncomfortable with its occupation of the Golan Heights and southern Lebanon. In the face of Barak's planned unilateral withdrawal, Syria stood to lose its ability to encourage Hezbollah's proxy attacks against Israeli military forces within occupied Lebanon.

There were also high risks for Israel, should Barak make a

unilateral withdrawal without negotiation. One of them was that resistance groups within Palestine might see the withdrawal as a defeat of the Israeli military, take inspiration from it and themselves turn away from years of negotiations, once again embracing armed struggle as a way of ending Israel's occupation of the West Bank and Gaza Strip. At a strategic level, for Barak there was also the possibility that, absent an agreement with Syria to restrain Hezbollah, Hezbollah might shift its attacks from Israeli soldiers occupying Lebanon to civilian targets in northern Israel and Jewish settlers in the Golan Heights. This could easily provoke a retaliatory Israeli military strike on Syria proper, which had not occurred since 1974.[2]

The Syrians, Barak knew, have dilapidated Soviet military hardware that is no match for Israel's modern, nuclear-equipped forces. Barak publicly accused the Syrians of possessing chemical and biological weapons, which could potentially have escalated into a doomsday confrontation. American intelligence officers, who were aware of Syria's limited capabilities (it has far weaker bio-chem weapons capabilities than other Arab actors in the region, including Egypt), considered Barak's arguments dubious, particularly because Damascus knew that if it attempted to use such weapons it would be subject to a devastating—perhaps nuclear—counterattack. Nevertheless, Barak sought to guard against this possibility by putting Israeli military might on display; he ordered a provocative series of "war against Syria" maneuvers on the Golan Heights, within view of international observers who were reporting to Damascus.[3]

Next, in October 1999, Barak gave "priority-A" designation to new settlements in the Golan Heights, a significant economic bonus that encouraged additional settlement growth by providing for the highest level of government subsidy.[4] Just as it had been the customary practice on the Palestinian track, Barak used settlement expansion on the Golan Heights both as a form of obtaining negotiating leverage with Syria and as a means of reassuring right-wing supporters of his government.

Barak's saber-rattling and antagonistic settlement push did not deter Syria's readiness for peace. For Syria, peace with Israel is possible, and it boils down to a single element that rests on a simpler principle: Full Israeli withdrawal from the Golan Heights, and thus implementation of UN Security Council Resolution 242, which is based on the international legal principle embodied in Article 2 of the UN Charter, "no acquisition of territory by the use of force."

Only full-territorial withdrawal based on Resolution 242 had brought peace between Israel and Egypt in 1978 and Israel and Jordan in 1994.[5] Syria expects no less: Israel's full withdrawal and subsequent restoration of Syrian territory to the June 4, 1967, line, which was annexed by Israel in 1981 and is now home to a variety of wineries, ski resorts, and a population of roughly 17,000 settlers in thirty-three settlements.

Both Ross and Indyk viewed Syria's willingness to pursue restoration of its territory as major progress and as an improvement on the historical Syrian practice of conjoining its own grievances against Israel with the complex issues facing the Palestinians. Unlike other Arab governments that sought to curry relations with Israel or the United States, Asad had stayed the course of unity, standing watch as the stalwart defender of the cause of Arab nationalism.

Syria stopped measuring its case exclusively alongside Palestine in 1993, when, in Asad's view, Arafat went his own way and secretly signed the Oslo Accords to negotiate with Israel. From Asad's perspective, Oslo would not be defended by later generations of Palestinians, as it did not fulfill basic Palestinian rights.[6] Once Arafat abandoned Syria's side, Asad thenceforth defined comprehensive peace as pertaining only to Israel, Syria, and Lebanon.[7]

After he signed the Oslo Accords, Yitzhak Rabin knew that Syria could still play a spoiler role on the Israeli-Palestinian track. So, from late 1993 to early 1994, while the Israeli-

Jordanian agreement was looming, Rabin sent Asad signals of conciliation, resulting in an event commonly referred to in Arab-Israeli diplomatic vernacular as the "Rabin deposit."

On August 3, 1993, Rabin told U.S. Secretary of State Warren Christopher that "Israel is ready for full withdrawal from the Golan Heights provided its requirements on security and normalization are met." The United States recognized the seriousness of the offer, as full withdrawal would not only end hostilities between Israel and Syria but also pave the ground for normal relations between Syria and the United States, which views Syria (because of its support for Hezbollah) as a "state sponsor of terrorism." At the personal request of Rabin, Christopher promptly relayed this message to Asad the following day.[8] Asad was skeptical of the move until July 1994, when the Clinton administration provided him with confirmation that Rabin's reference to "full withdrawal" could indeed be construed as a withdrawal consistent with Resolution 242, specifically, to the June 4, 1967, line.[9]

For Syria, Rabin's acknowledgment and willingness to define the reference of withdrawal as the June 4, 1967, line was a landmark. During Clinton's first term, tripartite discussions on the basis of Rabin's deposit advanced. Barak, too, had contributed significantly to the talks, as Rabin's chief of staff and then his foreign minister. After Rabin's 1995 assassination, discussions premised on "the deposit" continued under his immediate successor, Shimon Peres. But like every other constructive measure regarding Middle East peace, progress came to a virtual halt during the 1996-1999 term of Netanyahu.[10]

• • •

**During Albright's first** move to jump-start the Syrian-Israeli talks following the Israeli-Palestinian Sharm signing on September 4, 1999, Syrian Foreign Minister Farouk al-Shaara relayed

Syria's sincere desire to conclude an agreement with Barak, remarking in a press conference:

> As far as Syria's position is concerned, we believe that Prime Minister Barak belongs to the school of Rabin and that he considers Rabin as his mentor and if he's going to follow his steps, we have the feeling that he is going to endorse what Rabin has deposited with President Clinton. When he does, Syria will be ready to resume the talks where they left off.[11]

Clinton had been told by his advisers that Barak was reluctant to deliver the Rabin deposit. But he wanted to do everything possible to get talks started. So, in true Clinton form, he told his advisers, "Find me a way to fudge it."[12]

What Albright proposed to Asad on Barak's behalf, was to resume official negotiations "with a promise to recognize at a later date the 'promissory note' that was deposited by Yitzak Rabin."[13] This approach was based on more than seventeen personal phone calls Clinton had with Assad and Barak during August, as he vacationed in Martha's Vineyard. At meetings later that month at the UN in New York and at the White House, the United States first pressed five points that Israel wanted Syria to agree to before giving recognition of the Rabin deposit. The points included security arrangements, normalization of relations, water arrangements, terms for Israeli withdrawal from Lebanon, and a timetable for implementation. Such a move, without a political guarantee by Barak that Israel would fulfill the Rabin deposit, was viewed by Syria as an unhelpful diversion. To avoid stalemate and pursue the Rabin deposit during Clinton's fading time in office, back-channel talks began and secret messages were passed from Shaara to Barak through the Jordanian, Omani, and French foreign ministries.

In order to streamline channels, Barak solicited the sole involvement of the United States, stating his fear that other countries might end up "burying the process instead of advancing it."[14] At the request of Israel, Dennis Ross set up three days of secret preliminary talks on August 26 between Uri Sagi, Barak's envoy to the Syrian talks, and Riad Daoudi, the legal adviser to the Syrian Ministry of Foreign Affairs.[15] At the official residence of the U.S. ambassador to Switzerland in Berne, Sagi and Daoudi focused on finding out the extent to which Barak recognized the Rabin deposit. In the presence of Ross, Daoudi gave assurances to Sagi of Syria's seriousness about making peace with Israel. Despite this, Sagi revealed that he was not authorized to give confirmation of the Rabin deposit's existence, ambiguously remarking that "if the deposit did exist, Barak would not withdraw it."[16] Nonetheless, the talks left Sagi with a feeling of optimism, and he immediately reported to Barak that "we have partners for peace. An accord is in sight."[17]

Ross coordinated additional meetings for Sagi and Daoudi in Washington on September 15, adding Yoel Zinger, who as a legal adviser to the Israeli military had contributed to Israeli-Egyptian peace and the Oslo Accords, and General Ibrahim Omar, who was Asad's head of military intelligence. Again, in the presence of Ross, who was accompanied by Martin Indyk, Robert Malley, and Aaron Miller, Daoudi emphasized Syria's commitment to reaching peace with Israel. Syria proved forthcoming again, agreeing to tackle all the other issues important to Israel, including normalization of relations, water, and security.

But to the Syrians' frustration, the Israelis were noncommittal about accepting the standard interpretation of the location of the June 4, 1967, line. In the Syrian view, it is a line that was precisely drafted by UN truce officials and clearly demarcated. Still, the Israelis gave a different interpretation, and Sagi, who was still unauthorized to discuss the Rabin deposit, was only able to weakly signal to Daoudi that "we are going to give you something, and it won't be the 1923 international boundary."[18] Without confirmation of the deposit, Daoudi felt the meeting ended poorly and without reaching a common understanding. But Sagi, after hearing reiterations of Syria's commitment to peace, felt even stronger that "peace with Syria is within arm's reach."[19]

Dissension arose within the Israeli team over how to proceed. Some, like Ami Ayalon and Gilead Sher, advised Barak not to become too involved in the Syrian track to the detriment of the Palestinian one. Looking back at Barak's choice, Sher lamented:

> I thought it was a mistake at the time. I told Barak that this is deviating from the real core problem of the Arab-Israeli conflict, which is the Israeli-Palestinian dispute, and that whether he would be successful or not on the Syrian track, the Palestinians would forever look at it as a humiliating, neglecting attitude, and it will make hard bargaining much more efficient from their side toward their constituencies and vis-à-vis the Israelis negotiators once the negotiations are resumed at the right pace.
>
> True, there was an official track of negotiations between Israelis and Palestinians all along the way, but it wasn't anything that was aimed at concluding an agreement on core issues—not until mid-April 2000 and immediately after the failure in Geneva [March 27, 2000].[20]

There were members of the U.S. negotiating team like Gemal Helal, policy adviser and Arabic translator for the president, who felt that negotiation with Syria first was "a big waste of time." Helal reflects that, within the State Department, "Indyk was almost the only one who wanted to follow this. To a certain extent, Ross went along with it."[21] Ross defended Barak's strategy at the time, stating "[Barak] has also said, much as we have said, that whatever is done on the Israeli-Syrian track does not come at the expense of the Israeli-Palestinian track."[22] Aaron Miller, Ross's deputy, felt that the Syria-first approach was a distraction from the more pressing issue of Palestine,[23] but Secretary Albright had previously warned Miller and Ross not to present either her or the president with differing views. As a result, Ross's seniority often trumped other dissenting policy recommendations,[24] though the decision ultimately rested with Clinton and Barak, who were, in the views of Miller and Helal, too optimistic that both tracks could be done.

The United States and Israel proceeded with Syria. As Shaara spent most of October and November recovering from open-heart surgery, communications moved the next channel up in a series of direct and sometimes lengthy phone calls between Clinton,[25] Sandy Berger, and Asad.[26] In an attempt to restart talks in November, Clinton sent Asad a letter of interrogatories, focused on the question, "If Israel meets your territorial demands, what will Syria be able to do for Israel in the area of security arrangements, diplomatic normalization, water, security along the Lebanese border, and a timetable for phasing in the aspects of the package?"[27] When Albright visited Asad in December to retrieve the answer, a breakthrough was made: Asad was willing to "respond favorably to the letter and start talks where they had left off" before Netanyahu's election in 1996.[28]

To "start talks where they had left off" was a form of constructive ambiguity, a diplomatic tactic of leaving contentious points vague in order to bring parties closer. It enabled each side to proceed based on its own interpretations of precisely where negotiations "left off." Unfortunately, Barak thought they fell short of the confidence-building measures he had sought from Syria in September with his five political demands conveyed by Clinton. To meet Barak halfway, Asad agreed to Albright's request that a high-level delegation be sent without delay, at the foreign ministerial level, to meet with Clinton and Barak in Washington.

Contrary to Syria's historical practice of not holding senior-level political negotiations without "payment"—in this case, without a firm Israeli commitment to the Rabin deposit—Asad gave in. This was, to be sure, viewed both in the United States and Syria as a major concession.[29] American negotiators, particularly Ross, were enthused by the move, which to them signaled a dramatic willingness on Asad's part to conclude an agreement.[30] Perhaps, they believed, a Syrian deal could be reached after all.

To construe the gesture as a political victory, Barak commented to his own party members:

> Four years ago as foreign minister, I saw and sat one person away from Farouk al-Shaara at lunch given by the king of Spain, but we couldn't speak with him. It was impossible to conduct a dialogue, and today we are able to conduct a dialogue.[31]

Political analysts in Israel, however, saw things differently. Even before his scheduled visit with Shaara, Barak was chided for agreeing to meet with Shaara, who was "only" a foreign minister. Israeli pundits predicted that "every word Barak speaks will be recorded in the Syrian mind as a promise. Every world that Shaara speaks will await Asad's final ruling."[32] And despite Barak's efforts to portray the peace efforts with Syria positively, in the absence of prior public preparation for peace, particularly among the Jewish settlers in the Golan—whose permanence was suggested and even encouraged by Barak's recent actions—Israeli domestic opposition came out strongly against concessions.

As Barak prepared to leave for Washington, he discovered that fully relinquishing the Golan Heights would, in fact, be more politically costly than he first believed. The chairman of the Likud Party, Ariel Sharon, called Barak's willingness to end the occupation of the Golan a "total surrender," and lambasted the Clinton administration, opining that, when it came to territorial compromise, the "American internal interests don't have a thing to do with vital Israeli interests."[33] For Barak, Sharon's assertions were particularly biting, as

Sharon had once considered Barak one of his favorite generals while Sharon served defense minister in the early 1980s.[34] When rumors circulated that Barak was willing to make good on the Rabin deposit, Sharon blasted him, claiming that the concessions were "dangerous" and "a big victory for Syria."

Barak was also unable to gain sympathy from influential elements within his own coalition government. His Interior Minister, Natan Sharansky, took part in a series of pro-settler rallies, including a massive demonstration in front of the Knesset, and threatened to withdraw from Barak's government should territorial concessions with Syria be made. Sharansky's Yisrael Ba'Aliyah Party represented recent Jewish immigrants from the former Soviet Union, many of whom had settled in the Golan. Sharansky harnessed their energy against peace by attacking Asad, whom he disparaged as "the darkest of any dictator," worse than any of the Soviet leaders during his years of captivity in the Siberian gulag.[35] Sharansky's rhetoric in explaining why he opposed peace with Syria remains the same today:

> The depth of our withdrawal from Syria will be at the depth of democracy there. I always say "I am ready to give them all the rights, *except the right to destroy me!*" And as long as they will not be able to destroy me, Syria must rebuild democracy![36]

Joining Sharansky in protest was Yitzhak Levy, Barak's minister of housing and chairman of the National Religious Party, which represents the overall settler movement. Levy likewise threatened to quit Barak's government, and stated to his supporters that "we cannot be partners, under any circumstances, to the uprooting of communities, or any withdrawal from the Golan."[37] Most imperiling to Barak's government was the anticipated opposition of Shas, the Orthodox Sephardic Party, which would, on the spiritual advice of its rabbi, likely use its powerful block-voting in opposition to peace with Syria, should such an agreement ever reach the stage of referendum.[38]

With right-wing settler groups able to dominate the Israeli discourse over returning the Golan, concern grew in several Israeli cities over the appearance of political graffiti that called for Barak's assassination.[39] Barak's Deputy Minister of Defense, Ephraim Sneh, publicly stated his "fear [of] violent activity by extremist elements," and others noted the similarity with conditions that preceded Rabin's 1995 assassination.[40]

But just as things seemed out of his political control, a surprise gesture was made: Barak's fractious cabinet closed ranks and symbolically stood behind him. They provided him with an upbeat send-off before he boarded the plane to Washington.[41] Hours after this show of solidarity, Barak arrived at Andrews Air Force Base on December 15. The Israeli delegation was confident that despite all the domestic hoopla, Barak was prepared to negotiate.[42]

The Clinton administration, too, was hopeful that Barak was ready to get serious. But Barak got cold feet at the last minute: Martin Indyk, who was summoned onto Barak's jet from the tarmac at Andrews, was the first to learn of the depth of Barak's political fears.[43] Not even Sagi, Barak's lead negotiator with Syria, was aware of his hesitation.[44] While still on the plane, Barak revealed to Indyk, the leading U.S. advocate of the Syrian negotiations, his change of heart. "I can't do it," he confessed. "My people won't understand. It's all too quick. I have to prepare my public for a full withdrawal from the Golan, and I have to take time."[45]

Barak's sudden backpedaling portended disaster. But for the U.S. team hosting the talks, the show had to go on. With shakiness, on December 16, just days before Christmas, the highest-level talks ever between Israel and Syria commenced with a televised media appearance in the White House Rose Garden. After crediting the meeting as a "new chapter in history," President Clinton invited his guests, Barak and Shaara, to address the press pool. Barak's opening comments were laconic but conciliatory, as he called for both negotiators to "put an end to the horrors of war."

Next to deliver, Shaara unfolded a prepared speech much longer than anyone had anticipated. He chided the media for providing empathetic coverage of the 17,000 Golan settlers who faced resettlement in the wake of an agreement, and spoke about the marginalized portrayal of the more than 400,000 Syrians who were forced to flee their homes after Israel's occupation began. His remarks, which for his U.S. hosts never seemed to end, gave a vituperative history lesson that, among other things, blamed Israel for provoking the 1967 war. Shaara harshly criticized Israel's occupation, stating, "For Syria, peace means the return of all its occupied land, while for Israel peace will mean the end of the Israelis' sense of fear; fear that is a result of the occupation."

Clinton and Barak were offended by Shaara's commentary, which they found crass, discordant, and less than conciliatory. But for Barak, Shaara's speech also offered welcome cover. Once the parties adjourned across the street to Blair House, where the talks were to take place, Barak raised Shaara's speech with Clinton as a reason to not show flexibility on territory, the Syrians' utmost concern. Barak feared that an already shaky Israeli public opinion would sense weakness should he reward the Syrians by returning their land.[46] With such a negative beginning, Clinton devoted his personal involvement to improving rapport. It worked, and as the hours passed, the atmosphere became positive and both parties spoke to their U.S. hosts very movingly about peace.[47]

The Israeli delegation, in addition to Barak and Sagi, also included military and intelligence professionals. They had fruitful and beneficial dialogue with their Syrian counterparts, giving particular emphasis to the areas of security. There were no media leaks, and some inroads were made.[48] Inside and away from the cameras, the U.S. negotiating team was able to guide the parties into an organized and structured agenda that narrowly defined the remaining problems under four specific realms: borders, water, normalization of relations, and security.[49]

After just two days of discussions, the parties broke with a surge of optimism and an announcement to meet again in two weeks at an undisclosed location in the United States. Barak, it turns out, was finally willing to give both the Syrians and Americans a commitment to the Rabin deposit.[50] As Albright had earlier promised Asad, Barak pledged to deliver the Israeli offer to withdraw to the June 4, 1967, line at the next round, in January 2000, when four committees, including a committee on borders, would convene and finally hammer out the details of implementation.[51]

Asad was elated and began to prepare his public to elicit popular support. Since he had been one of Israel's staunchest critics over the years, Asad knew that for there ever to be a handshake over a lasting peace agreement based on "full peace for full withdrawal," his public must be readied psychologically. While talks were under way at Blair House, Asad instructed government workers in Damascus to hang political banners calling for peace with Israel. Covered by an astonished Israeli press, and an even more surprised Syrian public, some of Asad's posters read: "We fought honorably. We negotiated honorably. We will make peace honorably." It was not only a reference to the dignified manner in which Asad was seeking peace with Israel, but also to the prideful way in which Asad viewed Syria's coming to terms with the existence of a Jewish state.[52]

Members of the U.S. and Israeli negotiating team interpreted the concessions Asad was willing to make—the sending of his foreign minister, the willingness to initially begin negotiations without a firm commitment to the Rabin deposit, and the various manifestations of peace—as an impressive confirmation that Asad was pining for a deal. The United States and Israel both sensed Syrian urgency based on four factors: that Asad appeared to be nearing the end of his life; the pressure of time constraints given the approaching end of President Clinton's tenure; the U.S. distraction of interests given the Palestinian track; and Barak's public commitment to withdraw from Lebanon the following summer. Unfortunately, all of this gave Barak, who liked to rely on his innate strategic judgment, a sense that he could exert even more bargaining leverage over Asad. Thus Barak began to theorize that Asad might perhaps relent on his firm territorial demands under the right conditions.[53]

Upon returning home from the Blair House talks, Barak found his domestic political problems growing, with right-wing constituents haggling over the smallest of diplomatic minutiae: At Blair House, Shaara had reiterated the Syrian preference to hold off from a public handshake until the final conclusion of a deal. When asked at the time, however, Barak gave the Israeli media the impression that a handshake did in fact take place inside, behind closed doors. The nonexistent handshake was covered for three days, until finally, upon returning home, Barak reversed his story on television.[54] The right-wing Likud faction hyped the absence of a handshake as a sign of disrespect and Syria's unwillingness to come to terms with Israel's existence. But Barak's handling of this episode was the least of his problems.

Rumblings within Barak's own government flared up again, particularly among the ultra-Orthodox Shas, which began threatening destabilization of his government by withdrawing from the coalition—a move that would leave him with a minority of just fifty-one out of 120 members. Advisers had warned Barak about inviting the ultra-Orthodox group into his "big-tent" coalition. As predicted, since joining, Shas had used blackmail tactics by conditioning its support on national items important to Barak with Barak's funding of its religious school system.[55]

Barak found the opposition formidable, and began to seek help from outside sources. To improve his unenviable situation, he turned to members of the same American team he employed during his campaign. The Labor Party again procured assistance through Clinton's public relations guru, James Carville, who had helped elect Barak and was father of the winning slogan used in Clinton's 1992 campaign, "It's the economy, stupid." In order to keep in touch with what the public was thinking, Barak, as if to emulate the political savvy of Clinton, began relying on and placing personal emphasis on the use of polls.

Barak's consultants also launched a PR offensive. Carville promoted Syrian-Israeli peace by floating new slogans like, "It's good for the economy, stupid," "It will bring the boys home" (referring to Israelis serving in southern Lebanon), and "It will isolate your real enemies" (i.e., Iran and Iraq).[56] Some of the efforts, which were viewed as imported White House propaganda, appeared to be taken too far. Members of the Knesset felt cheapened when provided with surveys claiming that an $18 billion U.S. cash transfer to Israel would lead to a 10 percent increase in Barak's chances of winning a majority vote in a land-for-peace referendum with Syria.[57]

Politically active members of right-wing American Jewish organizations also spoke out. They let it be known to Likud Party members that the Israeli Embassy in Washington had asked them to lobby their congressional representatives in support of financial subsidization of Israeli-Syrian peace.[58] The less-than-discreet efforts again drew the attention of Sharon and fellow Likudnik Silvan Shalom, who charged both Clinton and Barak with "buying" the hearts of Israelis as part of Clinton's ambition to win a Nobel Peace Prize before his term ended.[59] Seeking to harness U.S. opposition, Sharon went so far as to pen an op-ed in the *New York Times* attempting to convince Americans "why Israel must not give up the Golan."[60]

The results of Barak's last-minute PR efforts were mixed. Polls showing right-wing opposition to a Golan deal caused him to overcompensate. He dismissed positive reports showing that a Syrian peace agreement would be backed by senior members of the military establishment. Tel Aviv University's Jaffee Center for Strategic Studies, in its annual report authored by retired Israeli military officers, advocated what should have been a heartening conclusion: that the timing was right for Israel's full withdrawal from the Golan. The study, among other things, cited the overwhelming strength of the Israeli military and its ability to defend the pre-1967 borders as a reason to abdicate the burdens of the Golan occupation.[61]

As the millennium approached, Barak realized that he had to make a decision. Decisiveness had never been a problem for him as a military commander, but now, in a much different political world, he found himself cornered between competing ideologies. All the past efforts he had made to paint himself as one of Israel's most respected leaders were now coming to bear. Because the Syrians were meeting him halfway, a major decision lay just ahead. He knew that performance would be expected by the United States and others. Both Clinton and Barak realized that the next round would determine the legacies of both leaders. And for Barak, his commitment to full withdrawal would be a litmus test for how negotiations on other fronts could be expected to succeed.

# • SIX •

# *Showdown at Shepherdstown*

**ON THE EVE** of Barak's departure to Washington for the next set of negotiations with Syria, Uri Sagi spent an entire night reminding him of the strategic importance of concluding a Syrian peace deal. Sagi, himself a retired general who had fought on the Golan Heights during the 1967 war and had even commanded the prestigious Golani Brigade, assured Barak that he knew better than anyone what the stakes were.[1] But as they prepared to fly back to Washington, where Barak would be expected to table the Rabin deposit,[2] Barak expressed doubt to mask an underlying political stage fright. Despite all of Sagi's legwork, Barak was caving to the political pressure of the right wing. He told Sagi about another new poll, which showed that only 13 percent of Israeli respondents agreed to a total withdrawal.[3]

Sagi advised Barak not to attend the next round of talks after sensing that more groundwork needed to be prepared at the foreign ministerial rank. He proposed that Barak send David Levy, his foreign minister, to handle the discussions. But Barak, wishing to turn the Syrian negotiations into a series of events, decided that he should be the one to go. Reflecting later on his obstinacy, Sagi hypothesized that "Barak became afraid that David Levy might steal the political show."[4]

Barak brought with him a phalanx of military and security advisers, hoping that the Israeli public would feel that its security interests were in safe hands.[5] Accompanying Barak was Sagi, once a former head of Israeli military intelligence; Zvi Stauber, a former Israeli intelligence officer who had worked on negotiations with Jordanians, Palestinians and Syrians; and Amnon Lipkin-Shahak, the Israel Defense Forces chief of staff after Barak, who was also heavily involved in mid-1990s talks with both Syrians and Palestinians. David Levy, a Likud member, joined the group but played little role, as he speaks very poor English. In addition, Barak brought Elyakim Rubinstein, the attorney general.

Barak's spokesman, Gadi Baltiansky, was also present with media headlines, prepared for either outcome.[6] This was because members of the Israeli delegation truly did not know what to expect, in part because Barak had not made his own decision. The Israeli delegation was out of the loop because Barak had withheld the details of Sagi's back-channel negotiations with Syria, due to his own concerns about leaks to the media. Thus not every member of the delegation was able to weigh in confidently or with equal knowledge.

In contrast, the Syrian delegation was well-constructed and prepared. As the Israelis had done, the Syrians brought with them a number of military advisers, some of whom were former adversaries of Israel on the Golan battlefields in the 1967 and 1973 wars. Accompanying Shaara was Deputy Foreign Minister Majid Abu Saleh. Also present were Youssef Shakkour, the retired head of the Syrian army; Riad Daoudi and General Ibrahim Omar, both whom had interacted in prior back channels with Sagi; Walid Moallem, the former ambassador to the United States who had negotiated with Israel for many years in that capacity; Mikhael Wahbah, the

Syrian representative to the UN; Majed Daoud, a former director of the international water department; Bouthaina Shabban, a trusted aide and translator for President Asad; and Suleiman Serra, from the Syrian embassy in Geneva. The composition of the Syrian team was a balance between expertise and experience, as many had continuously negotiated with five Israeli governments since the 1991 Madrid conference.[7]

The parties arrived in Shepherdstown, West Virginia, on January 3, 2000, to begin their discussions. The State Department team, headed by Secretary Albright, Dennis Ross, Martin Indyk, Gemal Helal, Jonathan Schwartz, the deputy legal adviser to the Secretary of State, and Wendy Sherman, a principal officer and appointed adviser to Albright, would orchestrate the talks from a nearby conference center that had been rented out for their exclusive use. From the NSC, Sandy Berger, Bruce Riedel, and Rob Malley also partook. For secrecy reasons, Barak demanded that his U.S. hosts arrange the summit in the form of a vacuum; he insisted that cell phones be collected to curb media leaks. At the commencement of the talks, State Department spokesman Jamie Rubin met Barak's request to take things slow, and set public expectations exceedingly low. He remarked:

> I think it's fair to say that Charles Dickens's novel *Great Expectations* is not the novel that is being read by the negotiators and the working level officials. We do not expect to be able to achieve a core agreement in one round of negotiations.[8]

Indyk and Ross, now aware of Barak's political misgivings, sought to keep this from the Syrians, in hopes that Barak's cold feet would thaw. Blatant hints were dropped by Barak; had the Syrians been listening carefully, they would have seen his digression from the Blair House commitment to deliver on the Rabin deposit. In his departure speech on

January 3, Barak revealed that "nobody knows what the border line will be."[9] Barak convinced Sagi to try to make use of his perceived negotiating advantage, and arrived at Shepherdstown with a request for Clinton to postpone the convening of the committee on borders for the first two days, hoping that Syria, eager for a deal, might concede additional security assurances.[10]

Once discovered, Barak's opening tactic deeply damaged trust and hurt the feeling of good will among the Syrians, who had traveled to Shepherdstown after weeks of fasting and exhaustive preparation during the holy month of Ramadan. They had arrived quite prepared to sign a peace agreement ending all hostilities, and were hoping that peace would come amid their celebration of Eid Ramadan. After receiving assurances from Secretary Albright in December—and even from Barak himself at Blair House—that the Rabin deposit would be tabled, they were outraged to learn of his retrenchment only after arriving.[11]

President Clinton, the only person believed by the U.S. and Syrian teams to have sway with Barak, was called upon to intervene. Over the course of the next few days, Clinton shuttled the sixty-five-mile trek between Washington and Shepherdstown, holding over six private meetings in order to get Barak to authorize his delegation to assemble the borders committee.[12] His own frustration evident, Clinton resorted to "taking Barak to the woodshed," as Indyk described it, but was unable to loosen Barak's tight grip on the Rabin deposit.[13] Desperate, Clinton unavailingly spoke in private with Likud opponent Ariel Sharon, in an attempt to soothe Barak's political fears and win over the secret endorsement of his archrival.[14]

While Clinton attempted to cure Barak's indecisiveness, Shaara agreed, albeit grudgingly, to Clinton's request that Syria allow participation in the three other committees, on water, normalization of relations, and security. As happened at Blair, significant concessions were extracted by the Israelis, even though they had not shown the Syrians the prize for their efforts. Asad had authorized Shaara to accommodate Israel on all of its security concerns in exchange for withdrawal to the June 4, 1967, line. Shaara daringly exceeded this mandate—without the Rabin deposit—hoping that the U.S. and Israeli teams would catch on to their seriousness, and convince Barak to convene the committee on borders.

Meanwhile, on behalf of the Syrian government, Shaara agreed to reduce the size of the Syrian military along the border (as Egypt had done in the 1978 Camp David agreement), placing American and French—even Israeli—military observers within Syrian territory, and the placement of electronic censors all along the Golan, including radar sensors that would hang from balloons.[15] The Syrians also welcomed additional monitoring mechanisms, such as U.S. satellite imagery that would detect if either side was preparing hostile military action against the other.

With regard to normalization of relations (or "peaceful relations," as the Syrians prefer to call it), Syria abided by its stated premise of "full peace for full withdrawal," and agreed to extend full diplomatic relations, complete with functioning embassies, an exchange of ambassadors, an end to the economic boycott, and the establishment of commercial relations. Water, the Syrians posited, was a much simpler solution. If the Syrians had wished to contaminate, pollute, or construct an upstream dam that would alter water flowing downward to Lake Tiberias (also known as the Sea of Galilee), they could have done so at any time prior. Syria agreed that Israel could keep its use of the lake, which the Israelis use for nearly 40 percent of its total water freshwater resources,[16] and the Syrians reacted positively to the idea that the United States would fund desalinization plants to provide both sides an alternative supply.

Even with the progress being made by Syria, neither Clinton nor Albright—furious at this point—could get Barak to budge on delivering the Rabin deposit. Barak pleaded with

Clinton not too push things too fast toward an agreement, asking the consummate American politician to understand his domestic political concerns and his preference that prolonged negotiations take place so that the Israeli public would perceive its leader as "putting up a tough fight."[17] Ross, who was sympathetic to Barak's pronouncements on making concessions on both the Palestinian and Syrian tracks, saw how things were deteriorating and was guided by his belief that the United States shouldn't be "too tough" with Barak. Looking back on the errors in hindsight, Ross has delicately conceded that this was a mistake, but then turned defensive:

> We let [Barak] dictate too much of what was going to be possible and what we would do. We could have taken a tougher posture towards him in terms of just making it clear we wouldn't do certain things.
>
> The problem is that, here was a guy [Barak] who was prepared to make very far-reaching concessions. And it was, after all, *his concessions!* They weren't our concessions! So it's easy to say "we should have been tougher"; on the other hand, if you were too tough, then nothing might be possible and we would never even be able to explore what might be possible.[18]

To help clarify positions and move the parties forward, Ross and Indyk, with input from others, prepared a "draft peace treaty" in the form of a "non-paper,"[19] to be presented to both parties by the president. The draft treaty detailed very far-reaching Syrian concessions but was designed by the United States so that it was, as Indyk later put it, "basically silent to send pabulum on the question of Israeli withdrawal."[20] Barak, not yet wishing to acknowledge, as Rabin had, Israel's willingness to withdraw to the June 4 line, instead persuaded the U.S. team to try to advance an alternative withdrawal based on a map created by British and French colonial rulers during the days of Mandatory Palestine, called the 1923 International Boundary. If used, Israel would stand to gain proprietary rights over Lake Tiberias and thus over the scarce water resources it has controlled since 1967. And should they wish, Israel would then be in a position to deny Syrians the opportunity to "dip their toes in the lake," as the 1923 International Boundary buffers the shoreline with a ten-meter-wide strip of land.

For Syrians, this notion is regarded as wishful thinking, primarily because the language of UN Resolution 242 calls for "withdrawal of Israeli armed forces from territories occupied in the recent conflict," meaning withdrawal to the positions that were held on the eve of the Six-Day War. Their evidence in this regard is compelling and historically accepted by both sides—even the Israelis do not dispute that, before the outbreak of the 1967 war, the Syrians inhabited and controlled the northeastern beaches of the lake.

The Syrians viewed Barak's attempt to control the ten-meter strip as both a lack of seriousness and a form of Israeli avarice. For generations, the Syrians had used the windswept beaches along the lake as a recreational area for swimming and vacation; the idea that Israel would actually control the last ten meters of beach leading to the water was a torment that Hafez al-Assad would never accept. In his estimation, to relinquish what is guaranteed to Syria under international law and revert to a map created by illegitimate colonial rulers would not be consistent with his pledge of making a peace that Syria's future generations could defend.[21]

Barak's request to use the 1923 International Boundary would also require the United States to part ways with its own historical interpretation of Resolution 242, dating back to the months of tense debate leading up to its passage in November 1967. Part of the reason that 242 passed without the United States exercising its Security Council veto was that it kept the Israeli withdrawal clause vague, simply requiring "withdrawal . . . from territories." Since the definite article "the" preceding "territories" was absent, the

Israelis could use the vagueness to avoid fully withdrawing from all of the Arab land they occupied. The U.S. ambassador to the UN at the time, Arthur Goldberg, believed that vagueness when crafting the withdrawal clause was necessary, as it would promulgate a "land-for-peace" formula that would impel the Arab governments to recognize and negotiate with Israel. At that time, bilateral assurances were given by Israeli Foreign Minister Abba Eban that "Israel was not seeking territorial aggrandizement and had no 'colonial' aspirations."[22] Based on this premise, the United States agreed to advance the nonspecific language, placing Israel in a position of hegemony.

The British government, recovering in 1967 from its own Middle East colonial wounds, fought the proposed ambiguity. It recognized that the language could make Israel the de facto assignee of property rights on the land it occupied. Doubting Israel's claim that it did not have territorial ambition, Britain threatened to strike down the U.S.-sponsored language with its own Security Council veto. The United States and Britain overcame the impasse by agreeing to a clarification via a secret memorandum.

The existence of this classified agreement was kept hidden from public knowledge until the early 1990s, when the full text of it was leaked to and distributed by American historian Donald Neff. Unlike the language of 242, the premise of the U.S.-UK agreement was very unambiguous: The two countries agreed that 242 on the Egyptian and Syrian fronts would mean *full* withdrawal to the June 4, 1967, line in exchange for full peace.[23] History had shown that the United States was true to its agreement, as Camp David 1978 succeeded as a result of President Carter's principled stand beside the U.S.-UK interpretation. For their offer of full peace, Egypt received full Israeli withdrawal.

To abridge the call for withdrawal to the June 4 line was controversial, to say the least. Over the course of a few days, the nervous U.S. delegation tried to break the diplomatic logjam by winning Syrian flexibility on the principle Damascus valued most—withdrawal to the June 4 line. Despite the consensus of the intelligence community and professional Syria desk officers at the State Department who believed such a move would fail, the U.S. drafters decided to float a trial balloon on the border issue to buy Barak some time.

The drafters rationalized this course of action by trying to resuscitate a remark that was previously made by Shaara at Blair House. According to Albright:

> I can't tell you how much time we spent trying to figure out this whole issue of the "June 4 line." And one of the big deals at Blair House was that Shaara said, "there is no book in any library that actually says where the June 4 line is."[24]

In the Syrian view, the statement was made as Shaara was harmlessly attempting to overcome Barak's obstinacy during a discussion on the June 4, 1967, withdrawal. Whatever new interpretation the Americans might have construed, Shaara was fully confident that the Americans knew that he was well on record, as was Asad, by stating over and again that the June 4 line "certainly" means that Syrian sovereignty must be restored all the way to the waterline of Lake Tiberias.[25] Fatigued by the reality that Barak would simply not give in, Albright, Ross, and the drafters of the "draft peace treaty" flirted with a new position that could possibly give room for Barak's maneuver to retain a small portion of land sealing off the shores of Lake Tiberias from Syria.

On the morning of Friday, January 7, while seated around a cozy fireplace, President Clinton, accompanied by Albright and Berger, distributed confidential copies of the proposed U.S. draft to both Shaara and Barak. For Shaara, America's unwillingness to commit to full withdrawal was wholly unacceptable. Barak, who the Americans knew was trying to "slow-walk" the process, quickly requested that a few days be taken to study the paper, give individual feedback, then adjourn before coming back for a second round.[26] As the Israelis began observing the Sabbath that evening, and as Syria would be celebrating Eid Ramadan the following day, Clinton agreed with Barak and suggested to the Syrians that the parties return on Sunday prepared to give their comments.

In the interim, Albright convinced Barak and Shaara to step away from the caldron of decisions and spend some downtime touring her nearby farm and the local U.S. Civil War battlegrounds of Antietam and Harper's Ferry. Barak was enthusiastic about taking a break, and was attentive while receiving battlefield history lessons from the NSC's Bruce Riedel, who is an avid Civil War buff. Hoping that some breathing room would help the process along, Shaara accepted Albright's suggestion and adjourned to her rustic retreat.

At the close of the weekend a storm of controversy erupted when the London-based Arabic newspaper *Al-Hayat* published a leaked summary of the U.S. draft. The eyes of Arab readers went straight to the published U.S. understanding that Syria "does not object to taking into consideration the topographical nature of the terrain on each side of the border" and that "Syria recognizes that the line of June 4 is not a border and has not been marked out, and it therefore agrees to participate in the determination of this line." If Syria had accepted such a measure, it would have been a monumental concession and departure from the Arab negotiating standard of Resolution 242, as it would later open an advantageous door for Barak to edge away from the June 4 line and argue for border modifications under Israel's much-preferred 1923 International Boundary.

For Israelis, in particular those who found withdrawal from the Golan unacceptable, the leak forced them to confront the reality that Barak was really considering returning almost all of the Golan. But Barak's spokesman, Gadi Baltiansky, played down the suggestions of withdrawal and began to publicly pro mote Barak's unwillingness to convene the borders committee. He dismissed the many Syrian concessions that were made and reacted to the leak by assuring the Israeli press that "Israel would not present any concrete position on the border until it receives clarifications on security and normalization issues."[27] Foreign Minister David Levy also called the leaked text "theoretical," and assured the public that "on the issues of borders, nothing has been agreed."[28] Unnamed Israeli delegation members began to spin falsehoods before international television outlet CNN, and unattributed Israeli quotes soon appeared accusing Syria of intransigence, stating, "The Syrians, so far, have not delivered the goods."[29]

Later that evening, President Clinton met again with Shaara and Barak, this time over a farewell dinner of beef tenderloin and wine. The conversation was perfunctory. Barak, still unwilling to table the deposit, announced that he was obliged to return home to Israel for a few days. Shaara—at the peak of frustration, bitterness, and concern for his own political neck—also decided to return home and deliver Asad the bad news. As the last meeting adjourned, Clinton signaled to Shaara that he wasn't alone in his frustration. In the presence of Riad Daoudi, Clinton bluntly commented to Shaara that "if I knew that Barak was going to behave like this I would have never asked President Asad to send his foreign minister!"[30] In his memoirs, Clinton wrote, "to put it mildly, I was disappointed."[31] A very senior U.S. State Department official corroborated that Clinton wasn't the only one mad at Barak:

> [Madeleine Albright] was furious with Barak at Shepherdstown because he had specifically told us that he would put down the Rabin stuff when they were all together. He never did it because he was concerned about the polls. It was a missed opportunity.[32]

In *My Life,* Clinton makes it clear that Barak was less forthcoming than the Syrians:

> The Syrians came to Shepherdstown in a positive and flexible frame of mind, eager to make an agreement. By contrast, Barak, who had pushed hard for the tables, decided, apparently based on polling data, that he needed to slow-walk the process for a few days in order to convince the Israeli public that he was a tough negotiator. He wanted me to use my good relationship with Shaara and Asad to keep the Syrians happy while he said as little as possible during his self-imposed waiting period.[33]

The next day, without even a closing press conference, Barak and Shaara departed, with the only agreement being that they would return and continue on January 19. Both sides returned home to unpleasant scenes: Barak to a demonstration of over 100,000 right-wing Israelis who were against giving up the Golan; Shaara to an angry Hafez al-Assad, who was livid that Shaara had seemingly offered "full peace" without the sine qua non of "full withdrawal."

Matters took a turn for the worse on January 13, when, to the dismay of both U.S. and Syrian negotiators, the full text of the U.S. draft treaty was published in *Ha'aretz,* a prominent Israeli newspaper. Apart from listing nearly all the Syrian concessions that were made, the seven-page document showed, among other things, the "pabulum" that was drafted: that Israel recognizes neither "withdrawal" nor "the June 4, 1967, line." The Israeli position contained in the document was that there might be "relocation" and that such relocation would only apply to military personnel, thus giving the impression that civilians, i.e., the 17,000 Golan settlers, might in fact have a chance to stay put, though as subjects of Syrian rule. Newspapers everywhere pointed to Barak's political consultants as the probable source of the leaks, as it appeared to be an attempt by Barak to convince his right-wing constituents that he was not "selling out" their interests, and that he had, in fact, fought the good fight.[34]

Asad was deeply embarrassed by the leaks. Accusations began to circulate within Syria that Asad was giving up on

Syria's vital interests for the selfish sake of handing over power to his son, Bashar.[35] For a country where the government controls the media, Asad, convinced that Barak was not serious about concluding a deal, recalled the delegation in its entirety and severed all contact. In a lengthy phone conversation with Asad right after the leak, Clinton tried to convince him to resume contact with the Israelis and return his delegation.[36] But it was too late. The state-controlled radio in Syria gave the United States and Israel its response:

> We are now demanding a concrete review of the negotiations and that requires an undertaking by Israel to demarcate the border of June 4, 1967. An Israeli refusal on this issue will prevent any progress being achieved by any of the other working groups and so a third round of talks would be useless.[37]

When asked in public how he felt about Asad delaying the talks until further Israeli commitment, Barak would show a tough game face, commenting that "if it is not convenient for the Syrians to come now and they need time, then they should take the time. The delay does not bother us."[38]

• SEVEN •

# *Collapse of the Israeli-Syrian Track*

AS IT TURNED out, Barak's insouciance after Shepherdstown was all a bluff. He knew that, out of the narrow window of opportunity during Clinton's term, too much time and effort had already been spent on Syria. Barak adamantly wished to fulfill his campaign promise of withdrawing all Israeli troops from Lebanon, but it became clear to him that his public was not properly braced for peace with Syria. Not wishing to suffer the political blowback of being the party to shy away from peace, Barak needed something that would provide him with a graceful exit from the Syrian track.

Disappointed by the ending at Shepherdstown, Clinton, advised by Indyk, Barak, and Sagi that an Israeli-Syrian peace agreement could be reached, tried to convene one final summit. Ross, following the logic of others on the U.S. negotiating team, was increasingly interested in turning back to the Palestinian track. He reflected on the dilemma:

> We had missed the moment at Shepherdstown. That was the point. But we couldn't get Barak to get off of the Syrian track and focus on the Palestinians unless we could satisfy him

that we had done everything we could with Asad. And that's the real reason in the end we went back to Geneva [on March 27, 2000].[1]

As the lead negotiator, Ross had to bridge the differences in strategy between an Israeli prime minister—whose country Ross had always given the decisive advantage throughout many years of negotiating—and President Clinton, who genuinely believed a deal was possible but did not wish to do anything to exceed Barak's comfort level, supposedly because he was saving political capital for the Palestinian track. Realizing the latitude afforded him by Ross, Barak saw an opportunity to use his persuasive leverage over both Ross and Clinton, and thus succeeded in crafting a plan with Ross that would satisfy both his and Clinton's short-term political needs but—unfortunately for Syria—not Asad's.

The idea was to offer Asad something that anyone familiar with the details of the Arab-Israeli conflict knew he would outright refuse—something less than what was entitled to Syria based on Resolution 242 and the June 4, 1967, line. Though it would be an offer that would assuredly fail, it could be publicly touted, both among the right-wing hawks in Israel and the United States, as "generous" according to technical percentage points. The plan involved using the 1923 International Boundary—a notion that was rejected outright by Syria at earlier talks—and an additional 190 meters around Lake Tiberias (denying access to the water with a total buffer zone of 200 meters), thus allowing the Israelis to keep a military road to circumnavigate the lake. Also, Israel would seek to keep territory and control in the northern Golan on both banks of the Jordan River, well within the Syrian side of the June 4 line. As a quid pro quo, Israel would agree to drop its claim based on the 1923 International Boundary, which was drafted more than two decades before Israel was a state, to the Syrian village of al-Hamma, by agreeing to return a small sliver of mountainous land in the southern demilitarized zone. All told, the land swap Barak and Ross envisioned would actually exceed the percentage of territory guaranteed to Syria by Resolution 242, but would be based on *different* territory.

Ross had been forewarned many times by Asad and others that Syria would accept nothing other than what it was entitled to under Resolution 242—nothing more, nothing less. So too had Barak. There was no wavering on this principle. Walid Moallem, who negotiated this issue ad nauseam during his lengthy assignment as the Syrian ambassador to the United States, had this to say:

> In 1994, I went with Dennis Ross to Latakia [in Syria] to meet with President Asad at his [vacation] home. Asad said to Dennis, "I can't give up one inch of my territory. The Syrian people will not accept my agreement which will give them less than one inch of our territory."
>
> I met Barak in 1995 while he was at the chief-of-staff talks at Blair House, and I told him twenty-eight times within two hours about Israeli withdrawal to the June 4, 1967, line.
>
> Barak told me, "Why are you repeating this?" I said, "Because I want you to go to sleep and dream of this line!"[2]

When the United States floated the idea of the 1923 International Boundary at Shepherdstown, Riad Daoudi, Asad's legal adviser, warned Ross of the danger of this proposal:

> Don't present anything of this kind because you are going to have a real, *real* negative reaction with Asad, and your role as an intermediary in this process might be affected![3]

Ross, however, was not too concerned with the warnings, given his own reputation among State Department colleagues for having a personal disdain for Syria, and, in particular, a loathing for Asad.[4] Clinton, on the other hand, saw things differently and, impressed by his own powers of persuasion, thought the relationship he had built with Asad might be enough to convince the Syrian leader to accept what Ross explained as very minor changes.

As a politician, Clinton probably thought the offer would just have to suffice. The pressure built by the Israel lobby was starting to have an impact on Congress as groups like the hawkist Zionist Organization of America, sounded the alarm that a withdrawal from the Golan would mean "Israel will be left only with a piece of paper and the promises of an unreliable dictator."[5] The right-wing Jewish Institute for National Security Affairs also chimed in, circulating an advisory letter signed by over twenty retired U.S. military generals—as well as former CIA Director James Woolsey—which read, "The negotiations surrounding the Golan Heights have the potential to undermine regional security efforts that are important to the United States."[6]

Barak, Clinton, and Ross all knew that Asad would not attend any final meeting lest Clinton himself give strong assurances that the Rabin deposit would finally be tabled. Something had to be done, so Barak engaged in what Israelis call *hasbara,* or, roughly, "propaganda." Leaks appeared in Israeli newspapers. *Ha'aretz,* on February 28, reported that Barak told his cabinet:

> Yitzhak Rabin had given the Americans a commitment, which they passed on to the Syrians, that "If they fulfill Israel's demands, Israel will be ready to return the entire Golan." The Syrians "asked several times what the line was, and Rabin, following consultations and discussions, said it was the line of June 4, 1967."[7]

According to *Ha'aretz,* Barak went on to tell his cabinet that his government was not about to "to erase the past."

But indirectness was as far as Barak wanted things taken. When an unwitting Secretary Albright suggested that she make a trip to Damascus to outline the plan, Barak quickly rejected the idea. Barak wanted the discussion to be very abstract and discreet, in part because he did not want the secretary and her entourage bringing publicity to something he never intended to honor.[8]

The task to deliver this plan to Asad at a summit was thus left between Ross, the White House, and the NSC, where a two-pronged strategy was developed: direct calls from the president and the use of a highly trusted Arab emissary.

Following Shepherdstown, Clinton made several unsuccessful attempts by phone to convince Asad that Barak was serious about peace, without explicitly mentioning the June 4 line. Bouthaina Shabban recalled with clarity the following:

> I was the interpreter—and [Clinton] was saying to him, "I am going to India and I would like you to meet me in Europe," and President Asad said, "I'm in the middle of formulating a government. I can't do it now. What am I going to do in Geneva? What are we going to do?"
>
> [Clinton] said to him, "Your requests are met; you will be very happy." What was the request of President Asad? He announced one thousand times an Israeli withdrawal to the line of June 4, 1967. And [Clinton] said, "The deposit is in my pocket; your requests are met and you will be happy."[9]

Asad, perhaps mindful after the well-publicized Lewinsky scandal that Clinton had the ability to be coy with words, specifically asked Clinton to clarify that he could count on the U.S., on behalf of Barak, to deliver a withdrawal to the June 4 line. According to Shabban, Clinton responded, "I don't want to speak over the phone. But trust me: you will be happy."[10] According to one senior diplomat:

> It seemed to me that Asad really had confidence in Clinton. He would not make Clinton uncomfortable by asking and insisting that he give the specific details. Asad just wouldn't put a condition on a meeting with the American president.[11]

While Asad trusted Clinton, some members of his staff were quietly skeptical. But at this stage in world affairs, the word of the president of the United States was good enough for Asad.

What helped convince Asad was that, with Barak's blessing, Clinton enlisted the support of Prince Bandar bin Sultan, the Saudi ambassador to the United States. Bandar, who had successfully delivered innumerable secret messages between the two governments, going back to the early 1980s between Asad and the Reagan administration, had a longstanding trust with Asad.[12] One veteran U.S. intelligence official who participated described Bandar's influence as "tremendous." He said:

> There were plenty of qualified [U.S.] Foreign Service officers who could have made this trip. Clinton's selection of Bandar was purposeful. He was a very active mediator during the Oslo years, and [Clinton knew that he] could deliver Asad.[13]

After receiving Oval Office instructions on the weekend of March 18-19, 2000,[14] Bandar and his deputy, Rihab Massoud, listened to Clinton's instructions, which were premised as follows: "If I am able to pressure Barak into conceding the June 4, 1967 line, I'll call you and let you know that you can tell Asad to count on me satisfying his demands at a summit."[15] Knowing what this meant and not wishing to convey false assurances, Bandar pressed Clinton and received his explicit guarantee that such an interpretation would, in fact, mean a withdrawal to the June 4, 1967, line, and that Barak himself was endorsing this channel. Massoud made a contemporaneous note of Clinton's promise,[16] and neither Bandar nor Massoud asked any further questions: Like Asad, they believed that the word of the president of the United States carried weight.

Just days later, Bandar conveyed the message to Asad in Damascus, who replied with relief that he had spoken with Clinton over fifteen times, and that "Clinton knows what I want. God knows he knows what I want."[17] Asad was positive, and as a token to Barak, he promised to use the Syrian military forces to quiet Hezbollah on the Lebanese border while he awaited Clinton's word. Bandar passed the good news back to Berger, who at that time was accompanying the president in India. Shortly thereafter, a message was indirectly returned by a secure phone call from the NSC's Bruce Riedel, also in India with the president, to Rihab Massoud, who was in Saudi Arabia accompanying Bandar. Massoud recalled:

> Bruce Riedel was with them at that time. He called me personally and he said, "We have it [meaning that Clinton succeeded in getting the Rabin deposit from Barak]. Let's go for the summit!"[18]

Clinton's summit invitation was quickly offered, though such a moment had been a long time in the making. For years, Syria had remained in a technical state of war with Israel, and it had paid a big price for this. It appeared those days were finally coming to a close. Asad knew that peace with Israel would enable his country to modernize politically, economically, and socially. His strategic decision to seek full peace with Israel in exchange for full withdrawal would bring about a new era for Syria and would open his country to the friendship and support of the United States, leading his people toward a better future. Feeling on the brink of peace, Asad accepted and agreed to meet Clinton in Geneva.

On March 26, 2000, the Syrian delegation arrived at the Intercontinental Hotel in Geneva. They immediately began to prepare for the next morning's meeting. Word came through the State Department's protocol office that the United States wished to have a significantly larger meeting, with far more attendees. Unsurprisingly, the Syrians agreed and also enlarged its list of participants. There were two meetings scheduled. The first was to conclude and finalize the details of a historic Israeli-Syrian peace agreement. The second was a meeting that Asad had long awaited: improving bilateral U.S.-Syrian relations.

• • •

**The U.S. delegation**—including the staffs of Sandy Berger, Madeleine Albright, and the president—had just skipped across Asia in an exhausting trip. The president's plane, Air Force One, did not touch down in Geneva until roughly 2:30 A.M., and spirits were not high. While on the plane, Berger, who in the final year of Clinton's administration had become Albright's nemesis, suggested to her in passing that Ross was reporting on the peace process directly to him and the president, without informing her. Albright was livid. The White House staff was conscious of the tensions between the two, which would later become more visible, but did everything to keep the president shielded. One senior White House official candidly explained the broader problem:

> You would have to ask Dennis who he thought he worked for. I think Dennis thought he worked for the president, and not Madeleine. A lot of time and effort was spent on making sure that Madeleine didn't feel slighted.
>
> She wasn't at the president's right hand—that was Sandy. She wasn't the person the president asked—that was Sandy. To the extent that the president wanted to go deeper, Sandy in many cases was just a facilitator. He was the one who got the right person in front of the president at the right time.

> Frankly, the president was more interested in what Rob Malley [NSC staffer] had to say than what Madeleine had to say. He knew more about the Arab-Israeli conflict than Madeleine did. So he didn't really need his secretary of state. There were a lot of conversations that Sandy Berger had about how the White House would position things so as to enhance Madeleine's role.
>
> We were just in a weird spot in the administration. Everybody was beginning to think about, How [is] the world going to view me?[19]

Known for her strong personality and tough demeanor, Albright departed for the hotel and sent aides to awaken Ross, who had arrived just hours earlier. He had been preparing for the meeting and was also operating on very little sleep. Human frailties came into play. The one-sided shouting match that followed did not end until almost 5 A.M., and aides seriously doubted whether Ross or Albright would be able to get any sleep before the next day's important meeting.[20]

The same could not be said of the president. Though tired from his trip, Clinton was energized at the prospect of what he believed could be the conclusion of a deal. He had read intelligence reports that said Asad was in much worse physical shape than anything caused by jet lag,[21] including one report stating that Asad was weak from having recently undergone blood transfusions.

At 10:30 A.M. on March 27, the U.S. team assembled outside the hotel conference room. The staff advances had delicately set up this room, even requiring the president's valet to smuggle clandestinely bulky top-secret maps inside and away from the sea of reporters.[22] Albright, Ross, Berger, and Clinton all appeared and met with Asad and his entire delegation, which had emerged from the hotel elevators on time. Even though intelligence estimates from the State Department's Bureau of Intelligence and Research had forewarned the White House that a proposal offering anything less than a full withdrawal to the June 4 line was "not what Asad needed,"[23] Clinton and Albright both thought there was room to maneuver. They expected it to be a long day. Indyk, who was in Tel Aviv, remembered the source of their optimism:

> I don't believe the 200 meters around the lake would have stopped the deal in other circumstances, because Barak had indicated to us that he was going to be flexible on that and we had all sorts of other ways to deal with that. He indicated to the president in a phone call before the president left for Geneva that he was willing to do more than that.[24]

Ross knew what these further concessions might be, but acting on Barak's instruction, he wanted first to see Asad's reaction. After greeting Asad, standing for photos, and surveying the large assembly, Clinton immediately suggested to Asad that, for intimacy and efficiency, the delegations be narrowly pared down. This was Asad's preference, so he agreed. Clinton next asked that Secretary Albright remain. Asad agreed, and indicated that Shaara would remain also. Both agreed on the need for their translators, so Gemal Helal and Bouthaina Shabban remained. The final request caught Asad off guard: Clinton asked that Dennis Ross remain, because he had something to present. As they headed toward the room, Asad agreed to Ross's attendance without requesting as protocol that any additional delegates remain from his side, but he asked Clinton that Ross leave the room immediately after he presented his ideas, as Asad did not trust Ross. Clinton knew that over the years many Arab leaders had come to mistrust his special envoy, with his pro-Israel leanings. Not wishing to create any embarrassment, Clinton agreed to Asad's request.[25]

Only a handful of participants were in the room and privy to the actual conversation, though Sandy Berger and Rob Malley were able to eavesdrop on the conversation by hiding behind a nearby wooden partition. Madeleine Albright, who was in the room, recalled that:

> President Clinton began by thanking Asad for coming and acknowledging the physical difficulties the obviously ill leader faced. Asad replied, "I never get tired of seeing you." The president gave an abbreviated version of his "our children will thank us" speech . . . and said he was gratified that he had been able to earn the trust of Syria without losing the trust of Israel.[26]

According to Albright, Barak had given Clinton specific talking points which he insisted the president read word for word without deviation. Though Albright found this "patronizing" and "micromanaging," Clinton obeyed.[27] She stated:

> Then [Clinton] said that he wanted to make a formal presentation of what the Israelis were prepared to do. Asad replied, "Fine, I will not respond until you finish, but what about territory?"
>
> "The Israelis," said the president, "are prepared to withdraw fully to a *commonly agreed border.*"
>
> Asad said, "What do you mean by 'commonly agreed?'"[28]
>
> Asad reportedly followed up with the riposte, "Is this the line of June 4, 1967?"[29]

For Asad, what ensued looked like the routine of a charlatan who reveals a concealed trick. Ross quickly presented a map based on the 1923 International Boundary, which completely enveloped all of the shoreline and water to which Syria was entitled to under the June 4 line, including both banks of the Jordan River and the Lake Tiberias beachhead. It was all about water.

Clinton, prepared for this contingency and wanting to break out his personal relations and lawyering skills, tried to ignore what had become the elephant in the room. He tried to get through Barak's script: "Let me continue! Israel will retain sovereignty along Lake Tiberias and a strip of territory . . ."[30]

But Asad had tuned Clinton out, simply remarking, "The Israelis don't want peace! There's no point in continuing!" A brief debate ensued. Clinton attempted to rationalize Barak's offer, citing the "unsteadiness of Israeli public opinion" and Barak's "shaky parliamentary coalition." [31]

Thinking as a politician, Clinton excused his own trickery and Barak's disheartening offer by saying to Asad that "Without sovereignty over the lake, Barak will never be able to sell the agreement [to the Israeli public]!"[32] According to Asad's translator, Shabban:

> The issue was access to the water. Asad insisted on going back to the line of June 4 in which Syria had access to the water. The offer was to move Syria away from the water. The territory that was offered instead of water was a useless and rocky territory, and Asad knew it inch by inch.[33]

Though only twenty minutes had passed, the conversation abruptly ended in disaster. Ross did not leave the room, and when it was hinted that Barak was prepared to do more, Asad turned to Ross. Angry over the entire debacle and the impact it would have on future generations, Asad demanded, "I want to know what the Israelis have offered!"

"No!" Ross responded, appearing to be disappointed with what he would later bill as Asad's intransigence for not succumbing to his famed "incremental" tactic of using more time to produce further concessions.[34]

Clinton, who perhaps did not want to give the impression of anything less than total cohesion within his administration, did not weigh in. Ross, who was cranky and knew that the president would be upset, acted to perhaps divert Asad's anger and throw him off guard by alleging to him that "certain members of the Syrian delegation had previously approved of the map." Outraged, Asad turned to Shaara and asked him if it were true. Shaara denied this, and everyone began to note the shift in the ailing Asad's physical demeanor. Walid Moallem opined:

> Asad was very nervous—he felt he was cheated. I think that the Americans got some information that Asad was coming to the end of his life and wanted a deal, so they thought they could push a deal through that was less.[35]

As it appeared to everyone that the summit had failed, the U.S. negotiators listened as a vacant and withdrawn Asad began to wax nostalgic over the beaches where he used to barbecue and swim. Clinton, appearing not to understand the dimensions of the Arab-Israeli conflict and the importance that dignity has in Arab and Muslim culture, lightheartedly responded by offering what amounted to an Israeli swim pass. Clinton is reported to have said, "I'm sure the prime minister will give you permission to go swimming there again."[36]

As the meeting broke and the doors swung open, Asad exited the room, managing to conceal his anger only with a smirk. There was one brief, final encounter with Albright, who was not aware of Clinton and Berger's back-channel commitments regarding the Rabin deposit through Prince Bandar, and who, by all accounts, was exceptionally displeased with Asad's reaction. According to Shabban, Asad remarked to Albright:

> OK, now that we don't have any peace process to work on, let us work on Syrian-U.S. relations. You know we have more time now. [Albright] said to him, "President, don't be kidding. I don't think the U.S. would have good relations with Syria until Syria signs a peace agreement with Israel."[37]

• • •

**According to Albright,** at the close of Geneva, the Syrians pleaded with President Clinton not to cast blame on them for the failure. Clinton allegedly gave it momentary consideration, and with some irony, granted them only that "the world will judge."[38] Indeed, immediately afterward, the world began to judge Asad to be the reason for Geneva's failure, based on the initial spin and statements made by Clinton, Ross, and Barak.

It was President Clinton who started the momentum of blame against the Syrians—albeit vaguely—during a press conference the following day. Clinton said:

> I went to Switzerland to meet President Asad, to clarify to him what I thought the options were and to hear from him what his needs are. I asked him to come back to me with what he thought ought to be done. So the ball is in his court now, and I'm going to look forward to hearing from him, and we're going to talk about what else I can do, what else we can do together.[39]

Lamenting the failure of Geneva, Clinton, in keeping with the same practice after Shepherdstown of not criticizing Barak, instead conferred on him unconditional praise:

> I think [the Israelis] are making very serious efforts. And I think Prime Minister Barak would like to do this as quickly as he can. And I can tell you they have made very, very serious efforts on all tracks, and I think you will continue to see progress at least on the Palestinian track and, of course, I hope we'll have some progress on the Syrian one, as well—as well as in Lebanon.[40]

The following day in the Knesset, after Barak had just survived five votes of no confidence, Barak took Clinton's face-saving prevarications and, rather than quietly accept them and focus on the Palestinian track, began to blame Asad in order to maximize his own peacemaker image. Building on Clinton's statements, Barak added, "The positions have become clear, and the masks are off. Asad [is] not ready for the type of decisions that are necessary to reach a peace agreement."[41] Predictably, some of Barak's political problems abated, particularly with Shas and Yisrael Ba'Aliyah. Natan Sharansky sang Barak's praise for "not giving in to Asad," and Shas agreed to remain in his coalition government—at least for the time being.

To the Israeli left and center groups, which might have supported a full withdrawal from the Golan if presented by referendum, Barak handed them a new reality. Inching further from President Clinton's initial comments, Barak promoted a starker reason why Geneva failed: Peace, so long as Asad remained president, was impossible. Barak commented, "You need two to tango. We cannot change the Syrian leadership if it turns out it's not ripe for a peace agreement."[42] Barak's minister for internal security, Shlomo Ben Ami, who was considered one of the more left-leaning advisers, built on Barak's spin, telling Israeli radio listeners, "I've been saying for several years that there is no chance of reaching an accord with Syria—they have a North Korean mentality."[43] For those among the Israeli left who feared an escalation in Israeli-Syrian tensions and wanted to ensure that every possibility of making peace with Syria was exhausted, Barak's minister for Jerusalem affairs, Haim Ramon, assured that, "If, Heaven forbid, there is some kind of confrontation with Syria, the prime minister and all the leaders . . . can look in the eyes of the parents and the soldiers and say, 'We went above and beyond to reach peace, it didn't work out, *and not because of us*!'"[44]

But nothing could have further assured the Israeli public that their leadership was correct in placing blame on Syria than the corroboration quickly offered by Clinton just days afterward:

> I don't think it's enough to say: "I don't like your position. Come back and see me when I like your position." If [President Assad] disagrees with [Israel's] territorial proposal, which is quite significant, then there should be some other proposal, I think, coming from the Syrians.[45]

Ross arrived in Jerusalem immediately following the collapse in Geneva and would be quoted just weeks afterward promoting a new theory on what happened. According to the *New York Post*:

> U.S. envoy Dennis Ross and other Clinton aides believed Barak's offer would work and so the president invited Asad to Geneva. But Asad surprised Clinton by telling him that before the Six-Day War in 1967 he used to swim in the Sea of Galilee and would insist on returning to it.
>
> "We found Asad more intransigent than his own people," Ross told Barak in Jerusalem a day after Geneva. He said that from the U.S. point of view, the Israeli positions were "logical and understandable"—and that when the minutes of the Geneva summit are made public, the world will be surprised at why it was impossible to overcome gaps that were so slim.[46]

Though far less savvy in its use of media communications, the Syrian government tried to get its message out in the Israeli press. A quote from Syrian Foreign Minister Shaara in the *Jerusalem Post* read:

> What was proposed via Clinton [at Geneva] was control over the entire river and lake. This constitutes a retreat from Shepherdstown and from the Rabin deposit proper. There is an Israeli deposit with President Clinton in this regard. Ehud Barak acknowledged the existence of this deposit. We have American letters signed by President Clinton regarding the

> deposit. So why should we abandon it, and how can we agree to something else? Our position is clear and firm on this.[47]

As victims of Clinton's perfidious mediation, the Syrians began to lose hope. Signaling that he no longer trusted the U.S. mediation role, Asad called for the immediate intervention of the European Union.

Meanwhile, back in Washington, Albright continued to believe that Asad had missed an opportunity until she had an epiphany just days afterward during a dinner with Prince Bandar. Bandar, who listened patiently as Albright "complained" about Asad's reaction at Geneva, was chagrined to realize that Clinton and Berger had not shared *any* of the details of the Bandar back channel with Albright.[48]

The left hand had not known the actions of the right. So Bandar, a Saudi, became the first person to communicate to an astonished Secretary Albright his own role as a secret envoy on behalf of the U.S. president before the summit. He revealed to her the explicit assurances Clinton had given Bandar: that he would issue Asad the invitation only if Clinton were able to relay his assurances that Barak was willing to deliver the Rabin deposit, and that the NSC's Bruce Riedel had conveyed that message. According to a public interview Prince Bandar gave nearly three years later, Albright reacted with both profanity and shock, saying, "Son of a bitch! *That Sandy*. Now I understand why Asad looked so stupid to me."[49]

Not long afterward, the mantra of blaming Asad for the failed Geneva summit was woven into the American newspaper and editorial debates. Amos Perlmutter, a professor at American University in Washington, DC, editor of the *Journal of Strategic Studies,* and a columnist for the *Washington Times,* wrote in an opinion piece:

> Jane Perlez in the March 28 *New York Times* correctly reported that Mr. Asad was "immovable," and above all

"appeared to have come to Geneva with the misconception that Mr. Clinton was in a position to give him what he wanted from Israel."

The peripatetic dictator of Syria, the aging, rigid, Mr. Asad, has once again defied the American president. How many more times will the leader of the Free World, the only superpower, implore the anachronistic petty dictator of a minor and strategically insignificant country called Syria?

*The Washington Times* on March 29 reported Mr. Asad is seeking European Union intervention in the peace process. This is tantamount to saying he no longer considers President Clinton as a mediator. In fact, he is reported to have said Mr. Clinton is pro-Israeli. Then why did he invite the president to meet him in Geneva?[50]

Later, in the influential journal *Foreign Affairs*, Perlmutter disputed an article written by Henry Siegman, who concluded that Barak misread what kind of deal Asad would accept. Geneva failed, Perlmutter assured, because "most Israelis doubt that Asad wants peace and suspect he is angling for U.S. support to modernize his ailing army."[51] Other Barak backers, like Uri Dromi, head of the Israeli Democracy Institute in Jerusalem, drew on the old Abba Eban maxim in describing the Geneva summit as a Syrian missed opportunity. With an air of hubris—even ridicule—over Israel's ability to maintain its occupation and reap the literal fruits of the Golan, Dromi wrote in the *Boston Globe*:

American presidents, secretaries of state, and diplomats have all courted [Asad] for years. Arab leaders, mainly Egyptian President Hosni Mubarak, coax him to hop on the peace wagon and bring hope to the peoples of the Middle East. And what is his clever response? A cough and a spit in the

> face. Indeed, to borrow Abba Eban's immortal phrase, [Asad] never missed an opportunity to miss an opportunity.
>
> Peace with Israel might mean Israeli tourists, bringing with them the scent of freedom and democracy. Scary! Peace with Syria will probably have to be put on hold until Asad's successor takes over. In the meantime, Mr. Smart Guy can sit in Damascus and eat his heart out while we hold onto the Golan Heights and harvest its incredible grapes. I, for one, would never miss an opportunity to taste the great wines we make there.[52]

On May 23, 2000, the belief in Syrian culpability inevitably seeped into American presidential politics. Robert Zoellick, a foreign policy adviser[53] to presidential candidate George W. Bush, delivered a speech at an annual WINEP banquet in which he stated:

> I was deeply troubled as an American to see President Bill Clinton go to Geneva and get stiffed by Hafez al-Assad. Now, at times the United States gets stiffed—I understand that. But frankly, to be honest, that's one of the roles of a secretary of state, not the President of the United States. I was honestly surprised he went to that meeting without knowing what he was going to get. That's what Madeleine Albright's job was.[54]

Leon Fuerth, a national security adviser to Vice President Gore, who was rumored to be Gore's top candidate for secretary of state upon a possible November victory and who had extensive contact with Secretary Albright throughout the campaign, could not allow the Clinton administration to be trashed in his presence. In an attempt to rebut Zoellick, Fuerth put forward an altogether new theory: "What makes you think the president didn't know what was supposed to happen? What makes you think that it wasn't Asad who, for his own political reasons, flipped signals at the last moment, at the point of no return?"[55]

Later that same evening, in a speech before AIPAC's annual banquet, Gore must have picked up on Fuerth's suggestion. As if Asad had rejected an agreement that would have brought peace, Gore declared, "Syria may not choose to pursue peace for now. It is Syria's choice. But make no mistake: Syria has no right to pursue a course of conflict that denies peace to others!"[56]

Then-candidate Bush, who was not familiar enough with the details to comment, nevertheless felt comfortable in broadly criticizing Clinton's approach to the peace process. Before the AIPAC audience he observed only how, "in recent times, Washington has tried to make Israel conform to its own plans and timetables; but this is not the path to peace." He added, "Israel's adversaries should know that in my Administration, the special relations [with Israel] will continue if they cannot bring themselves to make true peace with the Jewish state."[57]

Richard Perle, a member of the WINEP board of advisers who was also a foreign policy and defense adviser to the Bush campaign, asserted pessimistically that Syria is "a country that supports terrorism. It's hard to imagine that [Asad] could ever become an instrument for peace."[58]

# • EIGHT •

# *The Truth About Geneva*

**NOT UNTIL OVER** a year after the collapse of the Syrian track negotiations, in the summer of 2001, did the first lone voice of dissent raise questions about the widespread notion of Syrian culpability. In writing on the deleterious effects of the U.S. and Israeli campaign launched against the Palestinians after the Camp David II summit, Robert Malley—who was described by his White House peers as the most knowledgeable NSC adviser on the Arab-Israeli conflict—revealed that Barak had brought the same bad-faith baggage from the Syria track of negotiations over to the Palestinian track. Malley, a French-born Jew who later became a U.S. citizen, graduated from Oxford and as a young attorney had held a prestigious clerkship on the U.S. Supreme Court. He described the following scene from Camp David II, where Clinton exploded at Barak for "retracting on his previous positions" with the Palestinians:

> In an extraordinary moment at Camp David, when Barak retracted some of his positions, the president confronted

him, expressing all his accumulated frustrations. "I can't go see Arafat with a retrenchment! You can sell it; there is no way I can. This is not real. This is not serious. I went to Shepherdstown [for the Israeli-Syrian negotiations] and was told nothing by you for four days. I went to Geneva [for the summit with Asad] and felt like a wooden Indian doing your bidding. I will not let it happen here!"[1]

Malley's criticism raised many eyebrows and produced several rebuttals, including one by Dennis Ross and another by Ehud Barak. Not surprisingly, Barak accused Malley of engaging in "pro-Palestinian propaganda" and later attributed Malley's criticisms as the work of "some low-level American player." He recalled the failures of the Syrian track far differently. By reiterating his prior description of events, even using some the same metaphors, Barak attributed the failure to the absence of a Syrian "partner" in peace:

> We were very close. It was very clear to me that it could be reached. We will leave no stone unturned on the way to peace, and if there is a partner, there will be a peace agreement. But at the same time, it takes two to tango. You cannot impose peace. One party can impose war on the other side, but no party can impose peace on the other side. If there will be no partner, at least we will know the reality, however painful or frustrating, and we will stand united and could expect honest people. This was the strategy. It was said loud and clear from then.
>
> Now, what really happened after Shepherdstown was that somehow Asad—and I now tell you my judgment—he found himself in declining health. He was aware of it. He was totally consumed by the need to ensure a succession process that will lead to power taken by his son Bashar, and it just consumed him.

> At a certain point, he kind of shaped an approach that said, "If Israel is ready to capitulate to all my basic demands—even before the negotiations open, as a precondition for opening the negotiations—I will be ready to consider it." But this is beyond what we [Israelis] can afford.[2]

As with any whistle-blower who alleges wrongdoing, Malley soon bore the brunt of political ostracism and anger from some of Clinton's more outspoken pro-Israel political appointees, including his direct boss Sandy Berger, who was furious that Malley would disclose the private comments of the president.[3] Others among the vanguard of blame rallied to Israel's defense. Ross corroborated Barak, with an apologetic account: "When we went to Geneva I had no expectation that it would be successful. I thought we had already missed the moment. We had missed the moment at Shepherdstown. That was the point—after Shepherdstown then, I think, Asad changed course."[4] Indyk, who was rumored within the State Department to have fallen out of favor with President Clinton for failing to make his theory of "Syria first" work, likely based his account on that of Ross who attended Geneva, stating similarly that:

> Barak was in a hurry, and so he formulated a proposal to Asad which included a commitment to full withdrawal to a line based on the line of June 4, 1967, with a request for control of 200 meters around Lake Tiberias. Now, you talk to different people and you get different answers. I was not at Geneva when the president presented that to Asad, so I only have second-hand reports.
>
> From what I was told, my conclusion is that Asad went to Geneva to say no. He was no longer prepared to do a deal with Israel. He was coming to the end of his life. He had one project left in him, which was to put his son in power—he did

not actually complete that job because he didn't get rid of all the old guard around him. But for Asad, I believe that at the time he decided he didn't have the strength and it was too risky to get into a deal with Israel. So when he was ready, Barak wasn't. When Barak was ready, he wasn't.[5]

President Clinton's chief of staff, John Podesta, who was privy to the conversations at Geneva and who admitted his limited foreign-policy expertise, recalled that "Asad was just blown away" by the scenario. Said Podesta, "This was not a negotiation! This was a . . . *here was a generous offer; give me the reaction!*" Podesta went on to explain that had Asad said, "I think if you draw the line over here a little differently," then "that might have been a basis for negotiation. But Asad was just . . . taken aback by the whole thing."[6] Albright promoted her own explanation of the failure:

> I think it failed because you had a stubborn President Asad on one side. And I do think that in many ways it was a Barak opening—I mean we had all kinds of ideas for this: That there could be a peace park. It would be, basically, a way to have an international thing. You know, we talked about it as the "Clinton peace park," or whatever. I mean I could understand it from both sides. The Israelis needed sovereignty to make sure that's their water supply, so they had to have it.
>
> The amazing part is I had gone [to the Golan Heights] in 1986 when I was still a professor at Georgetown, and you look at it and the Golan Heights are . . . they overlook Israel. And it's such a completely different strategic thing for them to be up there with their guns versus the Israelis being left on top. And you can understand why they needed the protection . . .
>
> I think he [Barak] couldn't [withdraw to the June 4, 1967, line]. He *did* need to have something. But they were—but we

> were going to make up, or they were going to make up for whatever small percentage of land he was going to lose in some other place.[7]

Advised by Ross on all matters relating to the peace process, Albright invoked an illogical security argument that disregarded Syria's full accommodation of Israel's security needs, even to the point of allowing the presence of international and Israeli military observers on Syrian territory. Despite the Syrian willingness to disarm the entire Golan and fill it with military observers and UN monitors, Albright favored the hawkish Israeli skepticism that no matter what, there would always be the possibility of a breach in which the Syrians would somehow gain a military advantage over Israel and, to quote Albright, get "up there with their guns."

Such rationalizations by members of the U.S. team reveal how it was not just Barak but also a narrow cadre of U.S. negotiators who were not prepared to help Israel let go of its occupation. Albright, chief among them, was perhaps conditioned by years of running the gantlet for defending the "unshakable" U.S.-Israeli alliance as the U.S. ambassador to the United Nations. In her memoirs, she writes:

> I did not approach the Middle East inflexibly except for one point. I had always believed that Israel was America's special ally and that we should do all we could to guarantee its security. Since Israel's victory in the 1967 Six-Day War, we helped Israel preserve regional military superiority so that its enemies couldn't destroy it. We provided generous help to Israel's partners in peace and endorsed the principle of land for peace embodied in UN Security Council Resolutions 242 and 338.[8]

If one is to believe that Albright followed this standard, here again it appeared that she could not have understood the security concessions offered by Syria, including Asad's willingness to continue leaving Israel's water sources undisturbed. Surely the 200 meters of land bordering the lake were not necessary to guarantee Israel's safety from a naval launch or a contamination raid of the lake (especially as the underground wells and overland tributaries leading to Lake Tiberias are well within Syria proper).

It seems, then, that given Syria's commitment to make full security concessions and the fact that it was highly unlikely that Syria—not known for loose internal policing—would allow saboteurs to surprise international monitors with a contamination attack and imperil Israeli's principal water source, Albright was insincere in saying that her support for Israel was only because of its "security."[9]

It turns out that Albright, like her heavily relied-upon adviser Dennis Ross, also felt that as the victors in its preemptive 1967 war, the Israelis were "reasonable" in holding out for a little additional land and, though not mentioned anywhere in Resolution 242, that they could also squeeze out the ability to keep all the water and beachfront while claiming it under the broad category of "security." Ross, who held tremendous influence over the president until Geneva, had Clinton, Albright, and others convinced that "support for Israel" should also mean strong allegiance to Barak's domestic political needs, and certainly no pressure on Israel to make concessions beyond Barak's level of comfort.

Despite having learned—in 2000, directly after Geneva—of the explicit assurances given to Asad by Prince Bandar on behalf of Clinton, Albright refused to amend the historical record with this information in interviews or in her best-selling autobiography, released in September 2003. In an interview in July 2003, she elaborated:

> I think Asad came—I don't know why . . . have you read the Bandar piece [in the March 23, 2003, *New Yorker*]?
>
> He [Asad] somehow had a different impression of what he was coming there to do—why, I don't know. . . . We get in there and

> the president—Barak gave the president kind of a "scenario," which I actually thought was kind of patronizing—micro managing—and that it was to present this idea. And the minute that Clinton kind of got finished with that then Asad asked a question about—the issue was that they would withdraw to a common boundary. And Asad says, "What do you mean a common boundary?" And, then it was . . . you know, when the president said, "Well, I want to talk to you about this."
>
> Then basically Asad said, "Well, if I'm not going to get it all back this is finished!" So Asad never even looked at what some of the ideas were that Clinton was presenting and—I don't know whether the mistake was going there at all—because I do think that there should have been something between putting the president in that position. But Barak basically always wanted Clinton out there, out front, saying that "Clinton's ability to present the case" or "knock heads together," or whatever . . .[10]

The general lack of coordination at the highest levels of the Clinton administration, coupled with reliance on the opinions of advisers like Ross and Indyk, was detrimental to the outcome of the negotiations. Albright expressed disbelief in Asad's refusal of the Geneva offer, saying, "It was just a strip [of land] that would have permitted some sense of security for the Israelis as far as the water was controlled. And so Asad basically gave up 99 percent of what he had for the 1 percent—or less than 1 percent—that he didn't have![11]

Albright would also marginalize the Palestinians' territorial rights—despite the fact that the Palestinians, unlike Asad, were even willing to consider some forfeiture of land based on an uneven ratio at negotiations later that year. Palestinian legal adviser Omar Dajani explained:

> We met in Washington to consider Israel's annexation of up to 2 percent of the West Bank, then U.S. Secretary of State

Madeleine Albright told them: "You say you need 98 percent of the West Bank. The Israelis say they need it to be 92 percent. The obvious compromise is 94 to 96 percent." A plea to the Secretary by Mohammed Dahlan not to reduce needs to bazaar-style bargaining fell on deaf ears.[12]

• • •

**To seasoned experts** of the Middle East conflict, the Clinton administration failed because it did not confront the Israeli leadership concerning their commitment to the process. William Quandt, a historian at the University of Virginia who gained his expertise through both academic study and public service as a former NSC staffer to President Jimmy Carter, compared the efforts of Carter and Clinton. Though Carter would later receive the Nobel Prize for U.S. mediation between Israelis and Egyptians—including his display of political courage in showing "tough love" for Israel by convincing Prime Minister Menachem Begin to give up the Egyptian Sinai—it was principled political advisers like Quandt who were a critical ingredient in making that summit a success.

When asked to offer his opinion on what the Clinton administration did wrong at Geneva, Quandt said:

> I think Clinton should have said to [Barak], "There is only one basis on which I am going to help you on that front: If you are willing to give back every square-inch of the Golan Heights, I will go and see Asad tomorrow and we'll have a deal next week. But I guarantee you—less than that, and we're not going to get a deal. I know the guy. If you are prepared to go that far then by all means, let's start with Syria. But let's not waste our time on the Syrian front if you're not prepared to go that far."
>
> I'm convinced that Clinton never had that conversation with him. Yet everyone who has dealt with Syria knows that while

> Hafez al-Assad was president, that was the sine qua non. Instead of doing that Clinton said, "Well, let's give it a try!" You know, Bill Clinton never met a problem he couldn't find a compromise to, and we wasted most of the first year on the Syrian front, and at the end we had nothing to show for it.[13]

When I raised this issue with Ross and Indyk, some contradictory accounts emerged. Ross contended that Clinton did not have a conversation—such as the one proposed by Quandt—with Barak.[14] But Indyk, then in Tel Aviv, believed that he did. Indyk stated:

> Yeah, there were lots of conversations with Barak. Barak knew he was going to have to give them all up. He was looking for cover to be able to sell it to the Israelis. That's why I say the 200 meters was an effective opening position. He indicated to the president in a phone call before the president left for Geneva that he was willing to do more than that.[15]

A former State Department political appointee who was directly involved believed that Ross was the only one who knew Barak's bottom lines:

> A meeting took place right after Geneva between Dennis Ross and Congressman [Sam] Gejdenson, who at the time was the ranking Democrat on the House International Relations Committee. Gejdenson, who was very pro-Israeli, specifically asked Dennis why Geneva failed. Ross told him that Barak had crafted a number of steps but they never got presented because Asad said "no." Gejdenson specifically pressed Ross on what happened, and asked, "Could you let me know what those steps were?"
>
> Dennis said, "I couldn't even lay out what the Israelis were willing to do, because the answer was no—and emphatically

no! I wasn't permitted to lay those out to Asad—he wouldn't even hear them!—and I won't lay them out for you."[16]

• • •

**Another participant and** observer of the negotiations is Gemal Helal, an influential State Department career professional who carries the deceivingly modest title of "Arabic translator to the president, national security advisor, and secretary of state." He has been an influential figure in advising President's Clinton and George W. Bush on U.S. foreign policy related to the Arab-Israeli conflict. As the only Arab-American who negotiated in several of the Oslo peace process venues, Helal's input has been solicited by his White House and State Department colleagues on policy matters far more important than Arabic translation.[17] Over the course of several meetings and phone interviews with me, Helal assessed his understanding of Barak and Clinton's failed mediation efforts at Geneva. The sticking point, according to Helal, is the prior historical implementations of Resolution 242 and the broader issue of whether a Syrian-Israeli peace can preclude a Palestinian-Israeli peace. According to Helal:

> Resolution 242 was an issue during the Syrian negotiations, which preceded Camp David II, as the Syrians wanted 100 percent of territories. For Syrians, all the land must be returned in exchange for peace. This is the basis for all agreements: It was applied in Egypt, [and] it worked for Jordan also [though a piece of territory was leased, and the part Israel controls is a leased territory]. In theory, Jordan also received 100 percent of their territory back. This theory was applied by Syria at Geneva.
>
> On the old [1923] maps and papers, Syrian territory goes between the last ten meters of borders, but there was no

> Israel on the map at the time. The border was never static; it was always shifting. On the eve of the 1967 war, the Syrians had control of the water line. They would fish and swim there. The Syrians wanted to go back to the lake, because they perceived it as their right. However, in regards to water, the rules of international law will dictate this. The water itself was an international issue, and the Syrians would be willing to work around it—but not the territories.

Helal also addressed Clinton's idea of creating a peace park in the area, and the reason it failed:

> An idea was posed to make it an international park, which was rebuked by the Syrians, and the Israelis came up with clever ideas. They wanted to swap land and territory in al-Hama, thus actually giving the Syrians 100 percent. The Syrians said no, based on, "I want *this* land."

Finally, Helal questioned the wisdom behind the policy advice Indyk gave to Clinton:

> [Indyk] believed that it didn't matter who rules in Ramallah: Syria is a strategic threat and they must reach an agreement. Martin misunderstood the nature of the Arab-Israeli conflict; that the Arab countries would sympathize more with the Palestinians and their plight than with their individual countries. Martin saw it more from "who has the chemical weapons, who could win the war." He saw it as the size and the threat of the Syrian army versus the Palestinians, who weren't as armed and could be controlled. He felt that if they could cut a deal with Syria then normalization with the Arab world would be rational.[18]

Another participant in the negotiations was Toni Verstandig. She understood the Syria-first rationale, but questioned U.S. implementation and dynamics of the policy—in particular, Barak's ability to heavily influence Clinton. She stated:

> I understood the rationale between emphasizing Syria first, mostly because the Syrian issues were far more compartmentalized and could be handled in some cases more easily. Whereas, while the Israeli-Palestinian track was definitely the core of the Arab-Israeli conflict, and a comprehensive peace could not be achieved without having achieved agreement on that track, they were far more complex issues because they were so intertwined with Israel. In terms of demographics, in terms of the land, the location of borders, the economic issues, water, you had this underpinning of a very intricate fabric that wasn't easily split—as [it] was with the Syrian issues. You *could* live with an Israel-Syria peace agreement in the context of a cold peace and it wouldn't have that much of an implication. You *couldn't* in the context of Palestinians.
>
> One of my concerns throughout was our lack of constancy. What I mean by that was [that] we responded too easily to the internal political dynamics of Israel. Which meant we shifted gears, oftentimes, whether it was on issues or approaches; which is what lead to Syria first versus Israeli-Palestine [first].

Verstandig assessed the factors that influenced the president most:

> Indyk was always consistent [on Syria-first]. I don't know that anybody else was consistent. [But] Clinton really took the lead more from the Israelis. He supported Indyk in terms of when we pushed, he was there. But Clinton was far more influenced by the dynamic between [himself] and the particular Israeli prime minister.

> Now, when he had a very close relationship with that prime minister, like Barak, he was more inclined to embrace Syria-first. . . . I think one of the lessons learned will be the damage done by the synergy between the tracks, and playing one off against the other. And whether we were merely accomplices or whether we were a driving force is really yet to be seen.[19]

Bruce Riedel, Clinton's senior director for Near East affairs at the NSC, who had given U.S. assurances to the Saudis that Clinton had succeeded in getting Barak to commit to the Rabin deposit, declined to discuss this issue. At the same time, he lamented the ultimate harm that the collapse of Geneva had, and what the United States could have done to make the Syrian track successful:

> Insufficient attention has been focused on the Syrian track in 2000 and how the failure of the Geneva summit was a major blow to Barak and Clinton and reduced Arafat's room for maneuver in the Arab world. In retrospect the U.S. should have pressured harder to get a deal with Syria and put down its own ideas about resolving the outstanding territorial issues on that front.[20]

Ned Walker, who rose through the ranks to become ambassador to Israel and assistant secretary of state for Near East affairs, was repeatedly used by the Clinton administration to convey messages on behalf of Clinton, in part because of his deep knowledge of the region and excellent personal relationships with Arab leaders. Walker, now retired, sees the failure of Geneva more broadly than Riedel:

> I'd say it was a major blow to Asad, Barak, and Clinton. I think Asad came thinking that a deal had been cut. He could come home a victor, have his son anointed, and there would

> be this smooth transition. And when he got to the summit—I was not there but I had been reported to by various people—that what he had expected, based on the messages he received from the administration—from Prince Bandar bin Sultan—that he had expected a 1967 border agreement. The minute he heard that wasn't what was coming out of Clinton's mouth—he just turned off.

Like Verstandig, Walker believed that, though it was something Indyk favored, when it came to Syria, Clinton took his marching orders from Barak:

> Nobody was telling Barak what to do. President Clinton was fully supportive of Barak. I don't think if anyone had stood up and said "this doesn't make sense," that anybody would have listened! Barak was just . . . he was in the driver's seat throughout this thing. He pushed for the Camp David thing. He set the timing of these things. He spent the six months or so on Syria, and it was only until after that collapse that he turned then to the Palestinian issue.

But no one was more influential with how the president carried out this policy than Dennis Ross. Walker described the internal arrangements:

> When Secretary Albright hired me [as assistant secretary for Near East affairs] she said, "I want you to stay out of the negotiations—that's Dennis's job. You're to handle everything else in the Middle East, where we have interests and so on." So the whole portfolio of Israeli-Arab was strictly housed in Dennis's shop. That's not to say that Dennis didn't keep me informed all the time—he did. I never felt like I was being cut out, but Secretary Albright made it clear who her negotiating team was. She said, "I've got one negotiator, that's Dennis, *and that's it*!"

With visible disappointment and frustration, Walker recalled the reason he believed Geneva failed. According to Walker, just before Geneva:

> Dennis went to Barak, and Barak told him he could make an adjustment on that [Syrian] front with a tradeoff of land—the total area [being] the same [that had been done at Jordan]. Basically, when Dennis went to Barak on that line, they thought that the thirty yards [sic] was inconsequential! It was a rounding error! And that because it would be compensated. . . . But Asad didn't care two hoots about the territory! He cared about the image, stature, and being able to say, "I got the same thing the Egyptians got in the Arab world with Camp David 1978," and the Jordanians too in 1994. He couldn't go home and say, "I got less."
>
> Clinton felt that was close enough to take it to Asad, and had misjudged what Asad was hearing. Now, to be fair to Clinton, I don't know quite what happened in this game of "whisper down the lane." But I think Bandar had a different impression of what Clinton had told him. And when Bandar conveyed it to Asad, Asad jumped on it. So you'll have to get Bandar on this one, but he feels that Asad was screwed and that he was screwed because he had heard one thing from Clinton and then delivered something else. He felt [that] he was burned by that. He didn't lie!

Walker also did not find plausible either Indyk's or Ross's belief that Asad went to Geneva to say no. Walker believes they hold this view:

> Because he [Asad] didn't say yes! Asad didn't go to Geneva to say no. He went there with a full deck of negotiators. He went there assuming he would be able to say yes. The problem was that Clinton-talking-to-Bandar was a different track than Dennis-talking-to-Barak.

And, I don't know whether Dennis ever got together with Bandar to figure out what happened, but I know something screwy happened in there. And the message that Asad was getting, which he thought was accurate, didn't work. According to Bandar, Clinton told him, "Look, tell Asad he can get what he needs." He can get what he needs! But . . . Clinton certainly saw it in terms of, "What's a little bit of territory here or there?" I mean, he didn't say he can get what he *wants*; he said he can get what he *needs*!

But I can guarantee you Dennis is dead wrong. Asad wouldn't have come to Geneva if he had thought there was no deal. I mean, what in the hell does he get out of it? What did Dennis say that he got out of it that he would do that? Asad has a lot of ways of saying no, and that's not one of them! I mean he says no by not showing up in the first place.

Perhaps believing that his criticism had gone too far, Walker backed off and attributed the inveigling of Asad to mere "confusion":

Dennis has some vested interest in this whole thing but the thing is, it wasn't his fault. I think he thought he had an extremely good deal . . .

It [the failure of Geneva] would have been predictable if we had known what in the hell everybody was doing. But I think there was an actual, genuine confusion. I don't think anybody was ill-willed, or trying to make a problem here. I think there was some confusion, and it happens in negotiations when you don't have direct conversation through principals or when you have intermediaries who are not your own people. I think it's a mistake to use somebody like Bandar in a case like that. And I don't mean anything against Bandar, but *he can't speak for the United States!*[21]

Walker also substantiated that if what President Clinton told Bandar or Asad was that he will "give him what he wants" or "will please him," Asad could have been expected to interpret that as an explicit withdrawal to the June 4, 1967, line. Walker said, "Yes, Asad was always clear on that."[22]

• • •

**If anything constructive** can emerge from the absence of peace between Israelis and Syrians or, for that matter, Americans and Syrians following Geneva, it is that, perhaps for the first time, the failure has brought some Israeli and Syrian negotiators to a point of agreement. Through separate interviews with Syrian negotiators Bouthaina Shabban, Walid Moallem, and Riad Daoudi, and Israeli negotiators Uri Sagi and Amnon Lipkin-Shahak, I have discovered that both sides are irritated with the prominent Barak-Clinton-Albright-Ross-Indyk version of events.

While discussing the failures of Camp David II on the Palestinian track, Israeli negotiator Lipkin-Shahak provoked the following question:

> Shepherdstown is a very good question for your next thesis. . . . Why didn't the Americans learn the lesson of Shepherdstown? Before Camp David II, the agreement with Syria was touchable. And then Barak at Shepherdstown got cold feet! Barak withdrew from something that was touchable then, because Barak made it understood to the Americans and to the Syrians [before at Blair House] that he will be willing to withdraw to the 4th of June line.

Like Ross and Indyk, Shahak believes that an opportunity was missed at Shepherdstown, but it wasn't because of the leak. He says, "In January 2000 it was clear after Shepherdstown that dialogue with Syria failed. It was not because of the leak. *The leak was not even an excuse.* The dialogue failed because I think that Barak understood that the Israelis are not yet ready to give up to Syria a presence on the Lake of Galilee."[23]

Uri Sagi, Barak's lead negotiator, concurred, adding that "one can assume that the Syrians could have understood that the [Rabin] deposit still exists. But the deposit wasn't the issue. Put it this way: if I were the Syrian president, Mr. Asad, I would have believed that the [Rabin] deposit was in [a] very safe pocket."[24]

These characterizations stand in stark contrast to Albright's description of Shepherdstown. When asked if Shepherdstown was a missed opportunity, she replied, "Not if Asad had wanted to make a decision." Unlike Albright, Sagi believes that Shepherdstown failed because "Barak . . . became afraid of not being able to convince the public opinion in our country—Israel—so he got not only cold shoulder but hesitant. This was a big change for Syria."

Moreover, Sagi had the following to say in response to Ross's statement that Asad went to Geneva to say no:

> No? Just the opposite! He came to say *yes.* In order to say no, he could have said so and stayed in Damascus! Dennis is wrong. Why, then, did he [Asad] order 135 rooms in the Intercontinental Hotel for his team? Why? What is the purpose of inviting so many people? I tend to disagree. There were two main failures: the first, Shepherdstown, the second, Geneva. Mainly because of the parties involved, and mostly because the Americans did not prepare properly.[25]

Sagi declined to expound further on what the United States did wrong. Walid Moaellem agrees with Sagi in principle. In response to Ross's quote, Moallem said:

> Dennis Ross is saying that he didn't prepare well. He knows he didn't prepare well. Otherwise, by God's sake, how can

> you bring two leaders to a summit beforehand to fail—unless you planned it to be a failure? If you advise a president to go and you know it will fail, is it honest to advise him to go? It was planned to be a summit failure so they could open the way for Barak to withdraw unilaterally from southern Lebanon. This was the essence of Geneva. What Dennis Ross said shows we came very near to the agreement. Asad went to Geneva ready for peace based on the assurances obtained by Clinton. Barak was reluctant; he was hesitant.

Though some Israelis were hesitant to specifically name the people they hold responsible, the Syrians had no qualms. Moallem further stated:

> Dennis is my friend and used to be my partner, but unfortunately, instead of pushing ahead to conclude the agreement to where we came very near, he was listening too much to what the Israelis want. If the polls in Israel tell Barak not to do this, Dennis would play the role to justify why Barak was not doing this.

Why would the parties now hold Ross individually responsible? Without being made privy to Walker's description of the internal State Department arrangements, Moallem indicated why Ross should bear responsibility:

> Dennis Ross was the coordinator, he told us he accepted it on the condition that nobody could advise Clinton on the peace process except him. [Just one week after he was appointed peace coordinator in 1993] he told me everything had to come through him. Dennis was responsible for the peace process. Dennis Ross was accompanying [the] talks with Israel since day one. He was aware of Rabin's deposit, about Peres's assurance, and Barak's assurance. In this region every inch of your territory is important. UN

> Security Council Resolution 242 speaks about the conflict in June 1967—from day one in the peace process Syria spoke of the June 4, 1967, line.[26]

In a separate interview Riad Daoudi agreed:

> Throughout the process, the only thing that Dennis was opposed to is what the Israelis were opposed to. A mediator has to listen to both sides and say objectively, "This is what you should do." But when you are favoring the position of one over the other—in meetings, information, whatever—it seems to us that all the time Dennis was playing the game on the other side on all negotiating tracks, including Palestine, and trying to favor Israel.[27]

Indyk's remark, which described the Geneva offer to allow Israel to keep the 200 meters as Barak's "effective opening position," also drew strong criticisms. Ned Walker responded, "Then it's *even more tragic* that the 'whisper down the lane' syndrome struck here!"[28] Moallem, in turn, said:

> We came to Shepherdstown on American assurances that Shepherdstown would become the last meeting on all the elements. Since Barak arrived, he asked Martin to come to [the] plane and said he couldn't. I learned of this in May 2002, when Martin told me what happened. He said he was going to write about it in his memoirs. . . . Nobody told us Barak's hesitation. Why didn't Martin Indyk convey this to Madeleine Albright or Clinton?[29]

As Bruce Riedel earlier alluded, the failure of the United States to pressure Barak harder in his moment of hesitation created the ultimate disaster. Sagi, who appears haunted by his own knowledge that Barak was willing to do more at Geneva, said:

> You know, these are still very specific, sensitive issues! They came down to ten meters. Not precisely to the water. [But] he was prepared to go beyond that. I prefer to keep it in my knowledge. He was prepared to go all the way. But eventually he got hesitation.[30]

Moallem expertly spotted what led to Barak's hesitation:

> Barak should have prepared his public. He tried to use it as a tactic to buy time or win an election. He should have looked to the future and not looked back to the past. This is how we understand peace. Speak of a just peace because it is just for both sides. Speak of a durable peace because it is durable for both sides![31]

• • •

**The frenetic pace** of negotiations that continued beyond Geneva until the last hours of Clinton's presidency in January 2001 brought no public reversal of the "blame Syria" story by any members of the Clinton administration. In fact, as will be explored in the following chapters, almost the identical scenario of blame would play out after the conclusion of the Israeli-Palestinian Camp David II summit, with far more tragic consequences.

• **PART THREE** •

# THE CAMP DAVID DISASTER

# • NINE •

# *Gathering Storm Clouds*

**AS THE SYRIAN** track headed toward failure, the Palestinian track was not going well either. Two problems, arising from a structural imbalance of the Oslo Accords, were precipitating a crisis. From the Palestinian perspective, perhaps the most significant problem was Israel's refusal to end construction of Jewish settlements in the West Bank and Gaza Strip. From the Israeli perspective, the most significant problem was Palestinian breaches concerning their security obligations stipulated by Oslo. Reflecting on Washington's lapse in this regard, Aaron Miller said, "We failed to understand the crisis of confidence in Oslo created by two factors: 1) Israeli settlement activity, and 2) Palestinian acquiescence in terror."[1]

For both Israel and Washington, Palestinian security breaches raised questions about the broader intentions of the Palestinians. The U.S. and Israeli complaints included: the Palestinian Authority's (PA) inability to ensure unconditionally that all Palestinians would forsake "armed struggle"; the PA's failure to eradicate opposition groups that provided this outlet, such as Hamas and Palestinian Islamic Jihad; the

PA's failure to ameliorate hostile Palestinian attitudes toward Israelis, commonly termed "incitement"; and the PA's "revolving door" security practice, which involved the repeated detention and release of those suspected of conducting armed resistance or terrorism against Israelis.

According to the Israeli and American interpretation of the Oslo Accords, these breaches were inexcusable. While technically correct, they can only be understood in the context of Oslo's asymmetrical bargain, heavily structured in favor of the Israelis. As the Oslo years wore on, the Palestinian public would increasingly come to regret that their leaders had committed to these terms. One cannot understand this structural imbalance without examining the circumstances immediately predating Oslo, and the motivating factors confronting the Palestine Liberation Organization, The PLO at that time.

• • •

**The 1993 Oslo** Declaration of Principles was the vehicle for Israeli recognition of the PLO's legitimacy. Before the secret Oslo negotiations, the Israelis had avoided dealing with Arafat's PLO. (Washington had begun desultory talks with the PLO in the years after its historic 1988 acceptance of the two-state solution, but no real progress had been made.) Armed struggle against Israel had been the PLO's raison d'être and, as the saying goes with tigers, the Israelis had little confidence that the PLO's exiled leadership, then living in Tunis, would ever change its stripes. So when the United States, after its victory in the 1991 Gulf War, fulfilled its promise to work toward a comprehensive solution to the Israeli-Palestinian conflict by convening the multilateral Madrid conference that fall, the United States and Israel first looked to non-PLO interlocutors as means to deliver an end to the first intifada, which had raged since late 1987. The United States acceded to Israel's insistence that the PLO would not be given official status as an attendant, and both the United States and Israel assumed that Palestinian negotiators from the occupied territories would be more pliable than PLO officials. But to their disappointment, the Palestinian delegates, including noted intellectuals Hanan Ashrawi, Hayder Abdel Shafi, and Faisal Husseini, proved too rigid in their demands. Foremost, as a condition to negotiating peace, the Palestinian negotiators insisted that Israel cease land confiscations and construction of Jewish settlements in the territories. The Palestinians also insisted that the Israelis end human rights violations and recognize and apply a bedrock international humanitarian legal standard—the Fourth Geneva Convention—which would require Israel to join the international consensus and acknowledge its status and responsibilities to the Palestinian people as an occupying power. The Palestinians also insisted on a complete end to the occupation of Gaza and the West Bank, in accordance with UN Security Council Resolution 242, and the right of Palestinians to national self-determination and, thus, statehood.[2]

The United States and Israel found this too bitter a pill to swallow. But fortunately from their perspective, by 1993 they found a willing interlocutor in the PLO's leading revolutionary, Yasser Arafat. Chastised for spending years in cushy Tunisian exile during the first intifada, a defining moment when the impoverished Palestinians rose up to resist the occupation, Arafat was increasingly distressed at the growing popularity and prominence of grass-roots leaders in the territories. He had spent his entire adult life ensuring his own centrality in the Palestinian leadership. Humiliated and reduced to receiving update phone calls from the Madrid delegation in 1991-92, he saw an opening to reassert the PLO's international standing—and perhaps, most importantly, his own—when the talks bogged down after Madrid, primarily because the United States and Israel refused to accept the key stipulations of the Palestinian negotiators.

By 1993, Arafat wanted to take the PLO back to center stage. When the Israelis decided to test the organization through a series of secret back channels in Norway, they were surprised and pleased to find the PLO less rigid in its demands. Recognition of the PLO as the leader of all Palestinians was far too tantalizing for Arafat, the Israelis discovered. Accordingly, the Israelis had little difficulty convincing the PLO to drop the Madrid team's basic demands.

In a critical concession, especially crucial to Israel, the PLO agreed that it would no longer insist on Israeli recognition that the Palestinian people are subjects of an occupation. Israelis had studiously avoided any mention of the term "occupation," in part because Israel had refused to recognize the applicability of the Fourth Geneva Convention to the West Bank/Gaza Strip, which would have further obliged them to abide by the convention's normative legal principles, including a prohibition on the expropriation of land. The absence of explicit convention guarantees in an Israeli-PLO agreement would be a huge political victory for the Israelis, and might well have been celebrated as vindication by the settlers, though few chose to interpret the accord so favorably.

Israelis deeply opposed to Oslo weren't the only skeptics. The momentary intoxication that followed the White House signing ceremony and the Rabin-Arafat handshake in September 1993 made many Palestinians hesitant. Though oft forgotten, Hanan Ashrawi—hardly considered a radical by anyone—expressed a key objection to Oslo at the moment of its signing:

> It's clear that the ones who initialed this agreement have not lived under occupation. You postponed the settlement issue and Jerusalem without even getting guarantees that Israel would not continue to create facts on the ground that would preempt and prejudge the final outcome. And what about human rights? There's a constituency at home, a people in captivity, whose rights must be protected and whose suffering must be alleviated. What about all our red lines? Territorial

> jurisdiction and integrity are negated in substance and the transfer of authority is purely functional. . . . At least you should have done something about Jerusalem, settlements and human rights! Strategic issues are fine, but we know the Israelis and we know that they will exploit their power as occupier to the hilt and by the time you get around to permanent status, Israel would have permanently altered realities on the ground.[3]

• • •

**Just before the** September 13, 1993, Oslo ceremony, in an exchange of letters on September 9, Prime Minister Rabin agreed to "recognize the PLO as the representative of the Palestinian people and commence negotiations in recognition of the legitimacy of the PLO" in return for Chairman Arafat's crucial commitment that the "PLO renounces the use of terrorism and other acts of violence."

In addition to reaffirming the PLO's commitment to a two-state solution and Resolution 242, Arafat's letter assured Rabin of his agreement to "assume responsibility over all PLO elements and personnel in order to assure their compliance, prevent violations, and discipline violators." Interestingly, it was a condition added not at the insistence of the Israelis but rather of Dennis Ross, who after being surprised by the deal struck in Norway convinced Secretary of State Warren Christopher to withhold critical U.S. support for Oslo on the condition that Arafat both renounce violence and suppress any Palestinians who engaged in violence.

Few would challenge Ross's hard-line approach toward Palestinian security obligations. Even Arafat himself understood that Oslo was heavily skewed toward Israel. As Israeli sociologist Baruch Kimmerling and American political scientist Joel Migdal point out, from the Israeli perspective of the Oslo bargain, immediate security guarantees were the single most cherished gain. They point out that security was "frontloaded" in the agreement, a benefit to the Israelis.[4] Oslo allowed the Israelis to gauge the PA's compliance. In return, the PLO was allowed to form the Palestinian Authority (a government with some autonomy but no independence), consolidate existing institutions to ensure security, and assume functional control of certain areas in the territories. It would be allowed to negotiate for the independent state it desired but was guaranteed nothing.

To comply with the critical Israeli security demands and establish the PA's bona fides, Arafat was allowed—indeed, encouraged—to establish a robust security apparatus. In keeping with the model most frequently used by authoritarian Arab regimes, he organized a complex web of security and intelligence organizations with an estimated 40,000 armed Palestinians, making the Palestinian Authority the second-largest employer in the occupied territories. Through over twenty different sub-level security organizations, including military intelligence and counterintelligence units specially tasked with ensuring strict patronage to Arafat, this bloated security apparatus became an extension of Arafat's personal authority.

These security organizations were under the umbrella of either of two categories. First, the Preventive Security Organization (PSO), which was bifurcated between the West Bank, under the leadership of Jibril Rajoub, and the Gaza Strip, under the leadership of Mohammed Dahlan. Second were the *mukhabarat,* or intelligence services, which fell under the overall leadership of Amin al-Hindi, though administration was delegated at local levels in accordance with complex, preexisting patronage arrangements.

While the CIA and Israeli intelligence gave the PSO/mukhabarat significant assistance and training in order to enable them to do their job, it became clear that the PA would never meet Israel's "zero tolerance" expectations concerning even the smallest security infractions. To the delight of the Israelis, the PSO/mukhabarat kept resistance

Jordan's King Hussein (center left) joins Yasser Arafat (far left), Bill Clinton, and Israeli Prime Minister Benjamin Netanyahu (far right) in an attempt to settle differences shortly before the King's death. (© PLO)

Clinton is visibly agitated as he tries to get some traction with Netanyahu and Arafat amid the Lewinsky scandal. (© PLO)

Arafat with Colin Powell in 1998. (© PLO)

Arafat and CIA Director George Tenet at the Wye River talks, fall 1998. (© PLO)

Clinton and Arafat looking despondent in the Oval Office following a private meeting. State Department translator Gemal Helal follows behind. (© PLO)

Before Ehud Barak announced that he had "exposed" Arafat's true face at Camp David, many U.S. politicians took pleasure at meeting the Palestinian president. Here Arafat poses with prominent U.S. senators, the late Paul Wellstone, Frank Lautenberg, and Joseph Lieberman, the latter of whom became Vice President Gore's running mate in the 2000 presidential election. PLO Washington representative Hassan Abdel-Rahman and Hanan Ashrawi are also present. (© PLO)

Arafat with Saudi Crown Prince Abdullah. Saudi ambassador to the United States and *éminence grise* Prince Bandar bin Sultan is visible between them. Bandar played an important role in the Syrian negotiations. (© PLO)

Clinton shaking Hafez al-Asad's hand at the Intercontinental Hotel in Geneva, just minutes before he surprised the Syrian president with Barak's regression from the "Rabin deposit." Both Ehud Barak and Clinton would later blame Asad for the failure to reach a Syrian-Israeli agreement. (© Hotel Intercontinental, Geneva)

The American team at the Geneva summit. From left to right: Clinton, Helal, Albright, Berger, Podesta, Ross, and Malley. (© Hotel Intercontinental, Geneva)

The Swedish prime minister's majestic residence in Harpsund, just outside Stockholm, where secret talks were held between Israelis and Palestinians in May 2000. (© Gidi Grinstein)

A rare glimpse at the Israeli and Palestinian negotiators at the secret Harpsund talks. (© Gidi Grinstein)

Shlomo Ben Ami and Abu Ala talk privately in Harpsund. Barak forbade his team from discussing Jerusalem there, but Ben Ami's colleagues say he did it anyway, off the record. (© Gidi Grinstein)

Members of Barak's delegation at Camp David. Seated from left: Yossi Ginosar, Shlomo Ben Ami, Amnon Lipkin-Shahak, Einat Gluska (secretary), and Ehud Barak. Standing from left: Gilead Sher, Gidi Grinstein, Shlomo Yanai, Danny Yatom, Dan Meridor. (© Gidi Grinstein)

The American team at Camp David. From the left, front: Sandy Berger, Dennis Ross, Aaron Miller (far left), Bruce Riedel, Maria Echaveste, Gemal Helal, Clinton (back to camera), Robert Malley, John Podesta, Madeleine Albright. (© Clinton Presidential Archive)

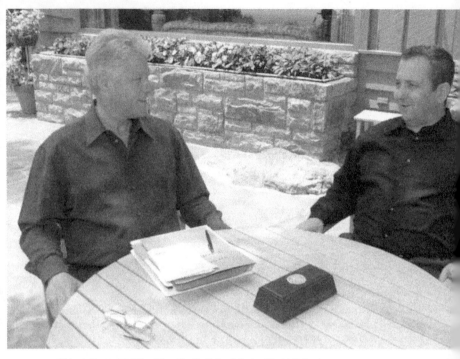

Clinton holds separate talks at Camp David with Barak (top) and Arafat (bottom).
(© Clinton Presidential Archives)

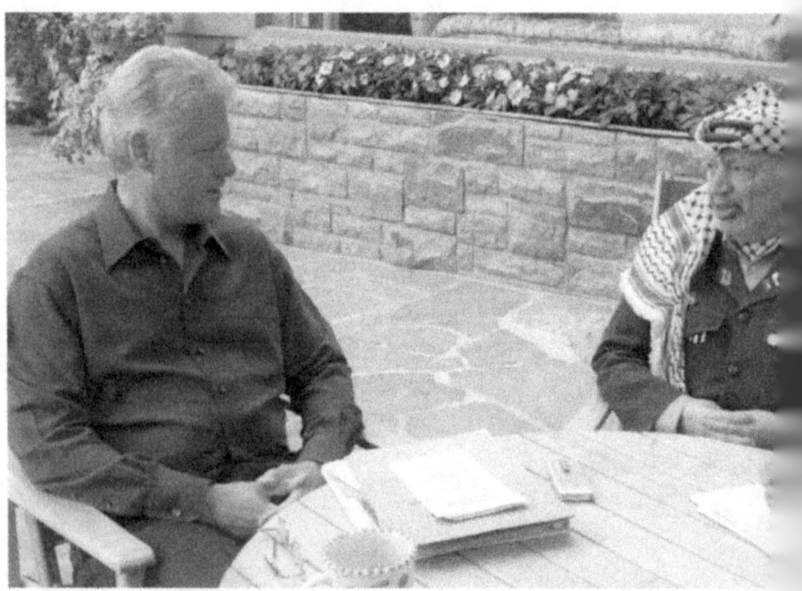

to occupation at a minimum, through heavy-handed and typically unlawful means—ranging from suppression of political protest and administrative detention of dissidents to torture and assassination—all to provide the environment demanded by Oslo for negotiations. However, as the settler population in the territories doubled, and as Jewish-only bypass roads began to crisscross the landscape, even as house demolitions and evictions continued—particularly in the Arab neighborhoods of Jerusalem—the PA's obligation to ensure total Palestinian forbearance on violent resistance would prove to be an unsustainable challenge.

The Israeli failure to deliver on the "backloaded" Palestinian benefits, including delay upon delay of interim withdrawals and final-status talks, stoked Palestinian skepticism regarding the wisdom of Oslo's bargain. The scathing criticism incurred by the PA for "giving up the store" on these rights while continuing to promote security cooperation dangerously undermined Arafat's fragile legitimacy. Even though the Americans and Israelis seldom focused on Arafat's political dire straits, as time wore on, it would make negotiating with him more difficult. Because of the rising unpopularity of the Oslo process, the PA was losing its ability to maintain grass-roots support. And as his own unpopularity increased, Arafat had to increase his rhetoric on issues of permanent status just to maintain his legitimacy.

These problems existed throughout the Oslo years but became especially bad in 1996, when Benjamin Netanyahu's "greater Jerusalem" settlement campaign was accelerated through the expropriation and settlement construction at Jabal Abu Ghneim, renamed Har Homa by the Israelis. It caught the attention of the CIA, charged with keeping its eye on grass-roots developments. Melissa Mahle remembered the Palestinian reaction:

> At that time, the settlement expansion that we were seeing in particular was the development of Har Homa and Abu

> Ghneim, which is the settlement just south of Jerusalem and just north of Bethlehem. This was a very hot issue and it almost scuttled the Hebron negotiations. It would be hard to say the settlements weren't an issue that was on the front burner. A campaign started that equated settlements with terrorism. There were banners that went up around Gaza and the West Bank at that time. There was a marked increase in anti-Americanism as well that was associated with all of this. It was very much *in your face*. . . . There was a great deal of concern about the direction that the process was going [in].[5]

Indeed, as Mahle observed, the mood toward Oslo among those responsible for delivering security increasingly grew foul. The Har Homa/Abu Ghneim fiasco became a landmark, as weeks of Palestinian riots and bloodshed were followed by yet more provocations, such as when Jewish-American millionaire Irving Moskowitz financed a new settlement project in the Mount of Olives/Ras al-Amud epicenter of Arab East Jerusalem just months afterward, resulting in the forcible eviction of several Palestinian families.

Washington's response to the PA's campaign to draw parity between both terrorist and settler infrastructures was decidedly negative, and sharp rebukes from Washington only increased despair among those Palestinians tasked with continually maintaining U.S.-Israeli security cooperation. Facing pressure from domestic Jewish constituencies in response to the Palestinian equation of settlements and terror, on August 6, 1997, President Clinton declared, "There is no parallel between bombs and bulldozers. You cannot draw a parallel." The Palestinians felt that Clinton didn't see how the settlements had actually become a recruitment tool for Islamist hard-liners and the enemies of Israeli-Palestinian peace.

To the ire of Palestinian security services, even during periods of violence, the issue of Jewish settlement construction was at best only on the margins of U.S. attention. Through word and deed, the Clinton administration kept its emphasis on eliminating Palestinian terror and violence. Domestic U.S. laws were enacted to reflect this commitment. In January 1995, Clinton declared a "national emergency" by issuing Executive Order 12947, placing a freeze on the assets of Palestinian (and some other) Islamic charities and organizations suspected of funding terror; he accused the groups of threatening "to disrupt the Middle East peace process." The United States also asserted control through its permanent-five membership on the United Nations Security Council. Washington cast the only veto on two separate Security Council resolutions that would have obligated Israel to cease construction of Har Homa. Reflecting worldwide outrage over U.S. obstructionism on Israel's behalf, the General Assembly later voted and passed a nonbinding resolution of censure, with an overwhelming 134-3 majority. To the detriment of its own global reputation, the United States stood beside Israel and the North Pacific island of Micronesia.

The Palestinians didn't see even the slightest U.S. effort to offer them legal protection. Nothing would stop the substantial U.S. investment in the settlement infrastructure: to the contrary, U.S. tax law even permitted the settlements and settlers to receive unlimited financing through tax-deductible, indirect subsidies by U.S. nonprofit charitable organizations. Increasingly, the PA grew incensed with the U.S. mediators for focusing only on preventing acts of violence against Israelis. Mohammed Dahlan described the crisis presented by Oslo's requirements:

> We consider settlements as terrorism—exactly as killing innocent Israelis and Palestinians. OK, I may understand what is happening in war times, but even in peace times they are taking our land and these are peaceful times! Even under Rabin, the Israelis did not stop settlements, nor under Peres. They were meeting with us during daytime, we were fighting with them against terrorism, and at night they were expanding their settlements. It was in front of the eyes of our people![6]

As Palestinians felt "buyer's remorse" as a result of the asymmetrical Oslo Accords, more and more of them began to reassert their right to resist. By 1999–2000, clashes between Israelis and Palestinians in the territories were a frequent occurrence. When settlers took over a house or proclaimed a right over Palestinian farmlands, Palestinians would arrive to confront the settlers, who were typically armed with more than stones. Violence would erupt. Often settlers would return later with IDF troops, who would again be greeted with stones, or even Molotov cocktails or gunfire. IDF bulldozers would raze the nearby buildings on "security grounds," which only heightened Palestinian rage.

Oslo's later iterations, including Wye (1998) and Sharm (1999), committed the Palestinians to such programs as the "collection of illegal weapons." But by the winter/spring of 2000, more and more evidence began to suggest that, even as Barak was neglecting the Palestinian track, repudiating his own interim withdrawal obligations and furiously building settlements, so too were PA leaders engaging in significant breaches of their own obligations, including the smuggling of prohibited weapons. By ignoring prohibitions under Oslo's secret security annex, Arafat allowed his forces to slowly resuscitate the armed struggle option. The CIA never believed these weapons were intended for terrorist organizations, but it was clear they were intended to equip the Palestinian security apparatus with a greater capability to fight, perhaps in an offensive mode despite Israel's superior firepower. This was a clear-cut violation: not only was the PA not turning over illegal weapons, it was arming itself to the teeth.

For Israelis, this raised concerns about the PA's overall intentions. As they saw it, when the PLO agreed to Oslo it had ceded the right to resist on behalf of all Palestinians. From the Palestinian perspective, the right to resist a belligerent occupation is guaranteed under the Fourth Geneva Convention's non-derogable First Additional Protocol.[7] According to their view—a view shared by many in the international community—customary international law precludes an occupying or occupied power from signing away these rights under any circumstances. Thus, though Oslo might have suggested otherwise, as far as many Palestinians were concerned, the right to resist occupation was never Arafat's to surrender.

Elyakim Rubinstein, a member of the Israeli Supreme Court who in 1999–2000 served as Barak's Attorney General, disagrees with the applicability of these rights, in no small part because Israel rejected the Additional Protocol. As the chief enforcer of Israeli law, Rubinstein articulated his view—reflecting the Israeli government position since 1967—that there is no situation in which the Palestinians can legitimately use violence, even in cases of self-defense, saying, "Look, there is no need to use force, for God's sake! There *is* a need to negotiate and finalize. . . . There are different ways to deal with it. But no need for force, because the courts are fair and the court many times will stop something." Rubinstein continued:

> Just to show you the way these issues are dealt with: When I was attorney general, I remember one Friday night, coming home from the synagogue, being at a dinner. Friday night, you know, is a day of rest. It has religious limitations and whatever. An attorney from my office came to see me. She said, "The military are agonizing whether they could demolish some building in a certain village, and they are there. Could you please look it up and see what is going on?" So we had all these kinds of . . . telephone discussions and conference discussions and all that, and finally . . . the decision was made and it was denied! And all I'm trying to say is that . . . these things are taken seriously![8]

It would be difficult to find a Palestinian who agreed with Rubinstein's characterization of the Israeli courts, which generally brought them little justice. The limitation of rights allowed to the Palestinians by Oslo highlights why more and more Palestinians came to view the Oslo document as fatally flawed. Israel became a party to the Fourth Geneva Convention in 1949, but government lawyers like Rubinstein claim that Israel has no obligation to follow the convention. "There was no occupation," said a dismissive Rubinstein, adding:

> The historic Israeli position since the 1960s—they have not changed—the legal position was set in 1967. We do not see it as an occupied territory because there was no recognized sovereignty there before 1948. No recognized sovereignty, so *no legal obligation.* On the other hand, we apply—and you can see U.S. applying—the humanitarian requests . . . or clauses—of this Fourth Convention. And in fact, all Palestinians have access to our Supreme Court.[9]

Curiously, a rare wavering on this position, at least by a sitting prime minister, occurred on May 25, 2003, when Ariel Sharon remarked, "You cannot like the word, but what is happening is an occupation—*to hold 3.5 million Palestinians under occupation.* I believe that is a terrible thing for Israel and for the Palestinians."[10] (Emphasis added.) Sharon quickly repudiated these comments, by his own admission due to Rubinstein's frantic warning about the serious legal consequences that could follow. Given Sharon's brutish legacy of trying to conquer a "greater Israel" at any cost, it's hard to imagine that this comment was anything other than a momentary lapse into truth-telling rather than a crisis of conscience.

• • •

**From the time** Barak formed his government in July 1999, the Palestinians bitterly complained to the United States and Israel that settlement activity—frequently accompanied by the eviction of Palestinian families and the razing of Palestinian homes—was ruining the spirit of peace. According to statistics by the Israeli group Peace Now, from the time Barak took office until December 1999, his government issued 3,196 new invitations to tender bids for settlement construction.[11] The rapid pace of construction helped to boost the Jewish settler population in the West Bank and Gaza Strip from 177,000 in 1999 to over 203,000 in 2000. Palestinians noted that Barak's settlement record even managed to surpass that of Netanyahu.[12] The seizure of Palestinian water and natural resources, coupled with construction of Jewish-only bypass roads, homes, and trailer parks—even provocative Israeli seaside beach condos within impoverished Gaza—aroused widespread Palestinian hostility toward the Israelis. Barak's settlement policy dashed hopes among those Palestinians who had listened to his siren song of peace at the time of his election.

Just days after the Sharm signing in September 1999, Barak made a well-publicized visit to the large West Bank settlement of Ma'ale Adumim, the same one the outgoing Netanyahu government approved for expansion, in what the State Department had termed "a provocative act by an outgoing government." Instead of bracing the settlers for the painful territorial compromise that lay ahead, Barak pledged that his government would help "strengthen" their presence.[13] "Every house you have built here," Barak told them, "is part of the state of Israel—forever—period!"[14] The settlers received Barak's rhetoric as a green light and made use of those members of Barak's cabinet who ardently supported the settlement agenda.[15]

The settlements have had a devastating effect on Palestinian society, particularly those that have been built near Palestinian farmland. To take just one example: While the Clinton Administration focused on preparing for back channels between Israel and Syria in September 1999, the Israeli government authorized the IDF to seal off 23,000 dunams of land belonging to the Palestinian villages of Beit Ula and Edna, west of Hebron, affecting hundreds of acres of fertile agricultural farmland used to sustain local Palestinians farmers.[16]

Though the bulk of settlements are in the West Bank, Barak's settlement policies also provocatively expanded them in the Gaza Strip, home to more than 1.2 million Palestinians crowded in an area just twice the size of Washington, DC. On September 16, under protection by IDF soldiers, Jewish settlers leveled twenty dunams of Palestinian land to the east of Rafah Mawasi in order to "expand it to the nearby Jewish settlement bloc of Gush Qatif."[17] In the three decades of Israel's occupation of Gaza, roughly 6,000 Israeli settlers had erected over nineteen colonies in one of the world's most densely populated areas. For the residents of Gaza, Israel's expropriation of land and the Jewish settler presence adds injury to the insults of a humiliating occupation. Even the Mediterranean Sea is not open, with Israeli warships and gunboats looming just off the surf in waters once used by Palestinian fishermen.

For the Palestinians of Gaza, the only thing "natural" about the growth of settlements is the incitement they represented. Even during the later stages of the Oslo process, in 1999, the Jewish settlers residing on confiscated Palestinian land faced demonstrations, riots, and threats of attack by angry Palestinians. The IDF bolstered its presence by providing protection at a rate of three soldiers for every four Jewish settlers.[18] The IDF presence furthered Palestinian feelings of frustration, humiliation, and rage.

There were other casualties of Barak's settlement expansion, including the Palestinians' plummeting confidence in U.S. mediation abilities. The letter of assurance attached to the Sharm Agreement, signed on behalf of the United States by Secretary of State Albright, proved unable to stop Barak's land grab. Political pressure mounted on Arafat, as he had publicly embraced both Barak and Clinton as his partners in peace. The Palestinian people called for action by their leadership, who they feared had lost touch with what they were experiencing.[19] On September 23, 1999, Yasser Arafat explained his predicament to the world in a speech before the UN General Assembly in New York:

> It is demanded that the Israeli government immediately and decisively cease all of its measures which violate international relations, law, and covenants and which destroy the chances for achieving peace. At the forefront of such activities and measures are the settlement activities and the confiscation of land, especially in al-Quds al-Sharif [Jerusalem] and its surroundings, the siege of the city of Bethlehem, and the rest of the Palestinian territories.
>
> The continuation of these settlement policies and practices severely diminishes the hopes and expectations generated by the signing of the Sharm al-Sheikh Memorandum and destroys prospects for the final settlement negotiations, which began on the 13th of September. The cessation of all such measures is needed so that we can, together with my new partner [Ehud] Barak, continue the march of the peace of the brave.

Arafat knew that he was preaching to the converted: Israel and the United States notwithstanding, there is a consensus among UN members, who back the position that all settlement activity is illegal under international law and a flagrant violation of Israel's obligations under the Fourth Geneva Convention, which states that "the occupying power shall not deport or transfer parts of its own civilian population into the territory it occupies."[20]

But the Palestinians knew that it was the United States that holds the greatest sway with Israel. Though the original Oslo Agreement was struck during secret Israeli-Palestinian backchannel negotiations with the aid of the Norwegian government, afterward the United States gradually boxed out other intermediaries. Washington's domination of the mediation process exacerbated the disagreement over settlement expansion. This has historically proved to be an area where Washington is politically uncomfortable; U.S. governments have for decades been unwilling to confront the powerful pro-Israel lobby. Toni Verstandig explains this dimension, which includes not only influential Jewish-American groups but also Christian evangelicals known as Christian Zionists:

> Settlements were an obstacle to peace, and that is the clear, honest truth. The other problem we have [with confronting settlements] is the domestic constituency here in America that is intimately linked in a very emotional way to that issue. And interestingly enough, linked even more in the context of the Christian right, who are every Sunday on the television raising money to support [settlements].[21]

As mentioned earlier, the fact that key U.S. negotiators were predisposed to side with the Israelis—especially on questions pertaining to settlements—only increased Palestinian mistrust of the whole process. The diplomats arousing the greatest suspicion among Palestinians, not surprisingly, were Dennis Ross and Martin Indyk. This had nothing to do with their being Jewish. On this topic, Nabil Shaath is candid:

> It's not a question of their religion, because Aaron Miller is Jewish, and Ambassador Kurtzer is Jewish, and the two were never suspected by the Palestinians of being partial, whereas Ambassadors Ross and Indyk were viewed by everybody as partial, biased, pro-Israel, and they sometimes defended Israel much more than the Israeli delegates did. In fact, we always thought that anything good about the peace process we got out of the Israelis when Dennis Ross was looking the other way.

> There was always closeness between at least some of the Israeli negotiators and some of the American negotiators. Obviously we're talking about a relationship of alliances that has existed for some time. Even though Mr. Clinton was really getting to see the issues in a different light and act more and more like a sponsor, mediator, and negotiator, we found that many people in his own delegation were so close to Israelis that sometimes they adopted positions that were more extreme than those of the Israelis."[22]

In a separate interview, Dahlan concurred:

> Dennis was saying about himself that "I am a conservative Jew." I have no complex with Jews. And, by the way, all the American team was Jews except for Clinton. But I have no complex toward that. *Absolutely* it has its effect or impact on the way of negotiations. I consider Dennis to be a professional negotiator. But my opinion is [that] Dennis . . . mentally . . . seemed one of the most dangerous persons in State![23]

Throughout the fall/winter of 1999-2000, CIA and State Department officers expressed serious concern about Barak's thriving settlement enterprise, but these worries were muted at staff-level meetings by Ross, who constantly argued that the United States needed to show empathy for Barak's internal political situation. As for policy meetings, one political appointee at State recalled, the settlements "were always a part of the debate, but never a major part of things. People were off talking on final agreement . . . settlements were always a marginal issue."[24]

If Washington had had an evenhanded ambassador in Israel, someone willing to at least take the Palestinian complaints seriously, the tensions could have been eased (though this probably would have heightened Barak's difficulties in holding his coalition together). But at least during the two periods when Indyk served in Tel Aviv (1995-97 and 2000-01), this was unlikely to occur. Like Ross, Indyk defended the one-sided U.S. policy. He reflected, "Basically what Barak told Clinton was, 'Look, we're going to do a deal in the next year and I need to conserve my political capital for that deal. If I confront the settlers now it will make it impossible for me to do a deal. It's much better if I confront the settlers *after* I have a deal and with the Israeli people behind me.' . . . That argument was accepted." When asked in hindsight if he should have pressed the settlement issue harder, Indyk, was adamant:

> No. I'm saying that *we accepted his argument.* Understand that the Palestinians we were negotiating with rarely made an issue about settlement expansion. It's not by coincidence that it wasn't in the Oslo Agreement—talking about settlement expansion. And Arafat himself—I can't remember a time when Arafat himself raised the issue. Saeb Erekat raised questions. But Arafat, Abu Mazen, Abu Ala—chief negotiators never made an issue out of settlements. They never made it an issue! In a sense, you know, it's not to say they didn't complain about it. But they never made it a "We can't negotiate without a settlement freeze" issue.[25]

Indyk's assertion that the PA's continued pursuit of dialogue through Oslo demonstrates that settlements were never "an issue" is an astounding claim—especially when one considers that the United States and Israel were emphatic that no realistic peaceful alternative outside of Oslo existed for Palestinians to obtain their freedom. Indyk's posture toward settlements highlights why PA negotiators began to view the U.S.-managed Oslo process as a mistake. Shaath comments:

> When you are talking about interim issues and not about the permanent-status issues, you sometimes give the impression that you give up on permanent issues. Settlements were a permanent-status issue. And that's why . . . to talk about it was

> only when the Israelis added yet another settlement, we blew up in the face and became very angry and made lots of protestation, and then the thing would calm down and we'd go back to other interim issues. But the importance of the settlement issues was never underestimated. In fact, I would say, that probably the settlement issue was the single most important destroyer of the Oslo agreement.[26]

Dahlan similarly viewed the State Department negotiators, particularly Ross, Indyk, and Albright, as especially unhelpful with settlements due to their own pro-Israeli bias and "advanced negative attitudes toward Palestinians." Years later, Dahlan was still raw with emotion over U.S. lack of concern about the issue:

> Dennis Ross was enlightened about the danger of these settlements more than 2,000 times! But he moved nothing with President Clinton. No one did anything—not Ross, not Albright, not President Clinton. The continuation of the settlements is the main factor that destroyed any kind of agreement.[27]

In disagreement with Indyk, CIA field operative Melissa Mahle, who was answerable to Indyk when he was ambassador, emphasized that she heard plenty about settlements from her place on the ground:

> I think that settlements were always an issue. They were certainly raised frequently to me as a reason why Palestinian security apparatuses had a difficult time taking certain kinds of actions because they felt the Palestinian street was against them. They didn't see the Oslo process and the constraints upon the Palestinian side being equally upheld by the Israeli side.[28]

Ambassador Walker, who rotated positions with Indyk, heard most of the arguments concerning settlements. As noted earlier, his inability to strengthen that policy was mitigated due to Albright's blanket assignment of the issue to Ross. Walker lamented:

> Nobody was pushing the settlements issue once Barak came in. We pushed it hard with Netanyahu with *limited* success. We had definitions of what constituted "expansion" and so on. Theoretically, those carried over. But everybody was so intent on negotiations that nobody wanted to rock the boat. It was first based on the desire to make the Syrian thing work, and then once the Palestinian side had started on the assumption that would be the overriding thing, the settlements wouldn't be an issue. So why create an irritant for Barak when he is in the process of negotiating away the very settlements you're complaining about? People weren't paying any real attention to the fact that more settlements were being created under Barak than under Netanyahu.[29]

Secretary Albright, now relatively free from the political constraints of once holding a cabinet-level post, fumbles to explain her own inaction. When asked if the Clinton administration played a hard enough role, she commented:

> No, no, we should have been much harder. . . . I think we should have been much tougher on settlements. . . . I'd be asked about them, and our guidance was basically to say they were very much a "complicating factor" in the negotiations. But that the. . . . you know, I don't think we'd come out and say they were illegal. But we *did* always say that they were a complicating factor and that they shouldn't be doing it. But we didn't come down hard enough on them.[30]

• • •

**In the 1999-2000** period, the United States and Israel gave kudos to the PSO/*mukhabarat* for their professional improvements and ability to keep terror in relative check. Aside from creating goodwill and high hopes for future coexistence, the relative safety afforded Israelis living in the pre–1967 borders increased tourism, trade, and investor confidence, resulting in an economic boom. But if there was any appreciation for the PA's efforts when Barak took office, the Palestinians were not seeing it.

Barak and Clinton's chief concern was that Palestinians' maintain the security status quo during the ten-month Syria adventure. While daily confrontations between Palestinians and Jewish settlers and IDF soldiers continued, the eyes of Israeli and U.S. diplomats were on the bigger security picture of Hamas and Palestinian Islamic Jihad; the havoc wrought by the former's 1996 quadruple bus bombings was a constant reminder to the United States of the necessity to keep pressure on the PA to deliver on its security obligations.

Memories of 1996 came flooding back just twenty-four hours following the Sharm signing when on September 5, 1999, two suicide car bombers detonated their charges in the coastal Israeli cities of Haifa and Netanya. The discovery of the culprits' Arab-Israeli identity—and the fact that only the bombers themselves were killed—prematurely gave Clinton, Barak, and Arafat some cause for relief. Initial fears that the bombers might have been from Palestinian Islamic Jihad, whose success in terror operations had diminished since Israeli intelligence assassinated its leader in Malta in 1995, ultimately proved correct. The PIJ's militant rhetoric had certainly increased in the wake of Arafat's agreement on yet another Oslo renegotiation. To be sure, the organization's ideology forbade recognition of a Jewish state under any circumstances. But its criticisms of the Oslo process, and of the PA's repeated concessions, were incisive. Just days following the Sharm signing, PIJ issued the following statement:

> The fact that after the recent "Wye-2" Agreement the [Palestinian] Authority is engaging in the so-called "final

> solution" talks when it secured only 5 percent of "area A" in the West Bank is a frightening concession by comparison even with the text of the Oslo Agreement, which states that, during the transition phase, the West Bank areas—with the exception of the settlements and Jerusalem—should come under the self-rule authority.
>
> This means upholding in advance Ehud Barak's no's and the Zionist Labor Party's action plan, squandering more of the Palestinian people's rights, and reaffirming the occupation's control over security and over Palestinian land. It also exposes the PNA's false claims with regard to national dialogue which did not strengthen the negotiators but instead forced them to make further concessions."[31]

In comparison to Hamas, which has played an important political and social function through its vast network of mosques, schools, charities, and hospitals, as well as having a military wing to engage in terrorist operations, PIJ had a much smaller membership and profile. For the United States, Israel, and PLO, the PIJ was a high-value target in part because it consisted of true believers in the most radical Islamist ideology but also because its operations were coordinated and financed from abroad by the avowed enemy states of Iran and, to a lesser extent, Syria. PIJ's compartmentalization of operational information made it especially difficult to penetrate. But through years of Israeli assassinations, jointly coordinated and conducted by Israeli-Palestinian security teams at times with intelligence leads provided by the CIA, the elimination and containment of PIJ operations proved moderately successful.

Neither elimination nor containment could work in the case of Hamas, an acronym for Harakat al-Muqawama al-Islamiya (Islamic Resistance Movement). During the first intifada (1987-93), Hamas gained prominence by partially filling the PLO's leadership vacuum, deeply interweaving its social function into the Palestinian political landscape, particularly in the Gaza Strip. Hamas offered Palestinians subsistence through religious schooling, orphanages, medical services, and social activities, as well as the advice and guidance of its spiritual leader, Sheik Ahmed Yassin. Hamas's political wing was recognized as legitimate by many, including the European Union, until intense U.S. pressure encouraged a reversal in 2003.

Like PIJ, Hamas was unequivocally opposed to territorial partition with Israel (though that position would soften somewhat). During the Oslo years, as the PA failed to deliver on the struggle for Palestinian freedom, Hamas sought to offset Israel's overwhelming military superiority through terrorist bombings against Israeli civilians. These operations were carried out by the organization's military wing, the Izz al-Din al-Qassam Brigade, whose growing popularity in convincing the population that armed struggle was necessary to deliver freedom greatly complicated the way in which the PA could approach the organization.

The PA leadership had to confront the reality of Hamas's potentially destabilizing challenge. As far as the Israelis were concerned, Oslo required the annihilation of armed opposition groups by any means necessary. But at least some U.S. negotiators concede in hindsight (and only off-record) the unlikelihood of this requirement: There is virtually no precedent in the history of conflict resolution of total disarmament of opposition groups as long as military occupation and continuation of hostilities by the dominant side persists. Even Barak publicly recognized this conundrum by demonstrating understanding of armed Palestinian resistance in a 1998 interview. Causing enormous domestic outrage during the initial stages of his campaign, Barak revealed that, were he born a Palestinian, "at the right age, at some stage I would have entered one of the terror organizations and have fought from there, and later certainly have tried to influence from within the political system."[32] No U.S. politician or negotiator could have made such an admission. It certainly gives credence to the view that total PA disbandment of armed resistance groups was unrealistic, especially when checkpoints, house demolitions, land confiscations, and the settlement enterprise persisted, denying Palestinians their life, liberty, and property.

Some within the career ranks of the U.S. government understood the political realities confronting Arafat—that he didn't have enough public backing to crush Hamas, and that if he attempted to do so it would tear apart the PLO. These analysts further understood the rationale behind his desire to co-opt Hamas's political wing. Others at the political level, like Toni Verstandig, saw the approach as foolhardy, in part because they believed Hamas was "as much opposed to Arafat and undermining Arafat and toppling him as they are a respective Israeli government. Arafat has yet to understand that dynamic."[33] Except in dire circumstances—notably, the PA's ruthless repression of Hamas after the bus bombings in 1996, undertaken by Arafat in part because his legitimacy to negotiate as the leader of Palestinians was in peril—the PA preferred cooptation to confrontation. According to Mahle:

> I think if you look at the historical development, the record will show that after the bus bombing campaign in 1995-96, there was a crackdown by the Palestinian Authority against extremists—not just Islamic extremists—but extremists across the board. That was really a substantive crackdown. Hundreds were detained and thrown into Palestinian prisons. And at that moment in time, the Palestinian Authority was able to do that because there was a perception on the Palestinian street that the bus bombing campaign had eroded the ability of the Palestinian Authority to negotiate with the Israeli government and achieve the national agenda. There was sympathy growing toward greater activism on the part of the Palestinian Authority. So there was a crackdown.

> And then slowly we saw a gradual release of the vast majority of those people detained in those large roundups because the Palestinian Authority had . . . a different perception of their role when compared to the perception of the Israeli-security services. And that was [that] the Palestinian Authority saw their role as a nation-building of their security services. So it was not their intent to *criminalize* the resistance against Israeli occupation. It was their intent instead to contain and co-opt the elements that were resisting in a way that was inconsistent with the desires of the Palestinian Authority. So the Palestinian Authority—and there was support on the street for this—was able to, through a series of actions of selective arrests, detentions, and then release, pursue a policy of co-optation of the extremist opposition. And they pursued that policy from 1996 on.[34]

As Hamas became more and more discontented with what it viewed as Israel's use of Oslo to legitimize the occupation, its rhetoric against Arafat steepened. Following Barak's election, Arafat's efforts to convene political dialogue with opposition parties, including Hamas, were embarrassingly dismissed.[35] Hamas gained sympathy when it railed against Arafat for capitulating to Barak over the renegotiation of Wye, also for pointing out the corruptions of Arafat and the PA, and blaming him whenever the Israelis failed to fulfill their side of Oslo's many agreements.

While the focus on Syria sidelined the Palestinians, Arafat's realities with Hamas soon became Barak's. On November 7, 1999, on the eve of convening the delayed Israeli-Palestinian FAPS negotiations, Hamas attempted to derail the talks by exploding a pipe bomb in the coastal city of Netanya, wounding twenty-one Israelis. The attack followed an earlier Hamas leaflet, which forewarned the arrival of a "distinctive escalation" in response to Barak's continued settlement drive.[36] Even so, IDF Chief of Staff Shaul Mofaz advised Barak that the Palestinians were doing better to fight terror, though he noted they "could do more when it came to collecting weapons, reducing the police force, and controlling incitement."[37]

The PA strongly condemned the attack and put its security cooperation into overdrive. In December, the Preventive Security Organization raided a West Bank Hamas hideout in Hebron, discovering a massive cache of explosives planned for use by the Izz al-Din al-Qassam Brigade.[38] Roundups of Hamas and PIJ fugitives were also conducted, and the debriefings concluded that Hamas was clearly gearing up its terrorist activities to compensate for what Arafat had failed to deliver. An additional bombing in the Tel Aviv suburb of Hadera on January 17, 2000, which struck a group of elderly Israelis sitting at a park bench, wounding twenty-two, gave further evidence that the Oslo security arrangements were wearing thin.[39]

From the Israeli perspective, these attacks continued because the PA's policy of co-optation had failed. The U.S. and Israel thought Arafat would balk anytime these groups applied even moderate political pressure. There was no better evidence of this than the "revolving-door" policy used by Arafat in handling those suspected by Israel, the United States, and even the Palestinian security services of involvement in either armed resistance or terror. The PSO would release prisoners upon receipt of weak guarantees that they would cease and desist in the future. Arafat sometimes claimed political necessity, such as when Barak failed to come through with the agreed release of the second group of prisoners required by Sharm in November 1999, but as far as the Israelis and the United States were concerned, this was inexcusable; the Israelis believed the PA was continuing to allow the terrorist infrastructure to grow.

Arafat tried to straddle the fence, moving swiftly against elements engaged in "military operations" (a code word for Palestinian terror against civilians) but at the same time encouraging resistance to occupation. But this only worsened his standing with his U.S. and Israeli counterparts. Even Gemal Helal, the only Arab-American member of the U.S. negotiating team, who is considered even by the Palestinians to be exceptionally fair, was strongly disappointed with the PLO's lackluster co-optation policy:

> The Palestinians never fulfilled their part. For eight or nine years all they did was whine and complain. Hamas and Palestinian Islamic Jihad always threatened Israel, said that they did not believe in Resolutions 242 and 338, and yet the Palestinians were in bed with both of these groups! Also, the Palestinians never educated their people on coexisting with Israel. For eight years they were supposed to collect their weapons—they never did. The Palestinians were also supposed to outlaw people who call for the destruction of Israel—they never did. I think that this was because Arafat wanted to have the "armed struggle option." He always wanted to ride the tiger of Palestinian anger.[40]

Whether it was giving fiery speeches calling for the Palestinians to resist occupation or releasing recidivist security violators, Arafat was making it clear that the PA's fulfillment of Israel's security demands was contingent on Israeli fulfillment of Palestinian demands regarding settlements, prisoners, and so forth. Many U.S. and Israeli critics of Oslo began to charge Arafat with using the agreement as a cloak to regroup and rebuild a more formidable resistance front. Meanwhile, the Palestinian street could sense that Hanan Ashrawi's prediction was right: Israel was exploiting its power as occupier to expand settlements, which would render final-status terms unacceptable. So Palestinians supported Arafat's breaching of security as a way to mitigate the damages he had incurred from the beginning of the peace process.

• • •

**While the United** States took no action to veto Barak's settlement drive, from October to November 1999, some 700 Palestinians of the Mount Hebron area were expelled from their homes in anticipation of the scheduled Sharm redeployment. Astoundingly, the IDF military court justified the forced evictions on the grounds that the Sharm redeployment would force it to withdraw from nearby military training areas. Eviction notices were posted to make way for additional firing zones that would "not endanger the lives of the local residents."[41]

Barak tried to quiet the criticism of settlements by playing a shell game: arbitrarily declaring some settlements "illegal outposts," he diverted pressure away from new settlements by ordering the removal of others deemed illegal. On November 10, 1999, Barak sent troops to remove twelve "wildcat" mobile homes deep in the West Bank, an outpost the settlers called Havat Maon, or Maon Farm. In a bit of carefully orchestrated playacting, the Barak government ensured that it was widely covered by the media. The images of hysterical settlers resisting the IDF's removal (though primarily without violence) had a deep effect on the Israeli public, who imagined much worse taking place if the IDF attempted to dismantle the settler infrastructure on a grander scale. Barak might have believed this tactic would allow him to save the coalition supporting permanent-status concessions, but it backfired, primarily because the televised images of the outpost removals—with their images of civil conflict—scared the Israeli public.

To signal to the Palestinians that the United States was not becoming neglectful, President Clinton met with both Barak and Arafat to commemorate the November anniversary of the Nobel Prize awards to Rabin, Peres, and Arafat in Oslo. The commemoration opened with a memorial for Yitzak Rabin. Barak said, "I vow to you, Yitzhak, a soldier who fell in the battle for peace, that we are determined to give your death a meaning by following your legacy." Contrary to Barak's request to Arafat that he not make any "aggressive" statements,[42] Arafat used the forum to again voice his concern, in the presence of Clinton, about Barak's continued settlement building. Arafat remarked, "In spite of our happiness with the start of implementation of the [Sharm] memorandum, we feel great concern over this destructive danger posed by the Israeli policy of settlements to the peace process, which has barely started to recuperate."[43] Also in Oslo, Nabil Shaath said, "The settlements inflame our public, symbolizing the perpetual nature of conquest, rather than its termination."[44]

Barak was reported as saying to Arafat afterward, "What do you care about the building permits that we issued? They have no meaning if we reach an agreement on the date that we set. After all, a new neighborhood cannot be built in three months." As became usual, in comments to reporters afterward, Barak defended the settlements by assuring that a final-status agreement was within reach, and that as prime minister he was compelled to uphold Israeli law.[45]

Only on rare occasions did Barak's application of Israeli law cut in favor of the Palestinians, and it was usually only on the symbolic level. One such case involved the dispute over the memorial of Baruch Goldstein. For years following the 1994 homicidal rampage of this Brooklyn-born settler, who in a hail of gunfire killed twenty-nine Palestinians inside Hebron's Ibrahimi Mosque (before himself being killed by Palestinians), Hebron attracted legions of radical settlers paying homage to a shrine erected in honor of Goldstein. This ritual of the radical settlers symbolized their defiance of Oslo's ostensible requirement that most settlers would have to return to Israel's pre-1967 boundaries. Hebron, the second-largest city in the West Bank (home to 140,000 Palestinians and, under Oslo's subsequent arrangements, 450 Jewish settlers given refuge in a 20 percent chunk of the city under IDF control), had long been a friction point. Radical Jews making pilgrimages to areas in and around Hebron, particularly the adjacent settlement Kiryat Arba, then the second-largest West Bank colony with 6,500 Jewish settlers, resulted in frequent clashes with local Palestinian residents.

On December 29, 1999, Barak's government struck the settlers a symbolic blow, complying with a Supreme Court decision handed down after a long, protracted legal fight by demolishing Goldstein's shrine.[46] The razing, however symbolic, was viewed as a shot across the bow to the settlers and a sign of worse to come. At that time, the Israeli media widely reported the concerns of Leah Rabin, who, reminding Barak of the fate of her husband, cautioned him that forcefully confronting radical Jewish settlers could cost him his life. While co-opting lesser-evil settlers by allowing them to build in other areas, Barak's challenge to the radical settlers was an attempt to build his image as a courageous peacenik in the mold of Rabin.

Unfortunately for the Palestinians, such acts were enough for the Americans, who were distracted. As the Syria track came to a close, American media coverage of Barak's settlement drive was scant. The Israeli media, nonplussed by the jarring diplomatic turns Barak had taken with Syria, nonetheless kept up its reportage on the settlements, as did most non-U.S. newspapers. A February 2000 article by Agence France-Presse covered the "little details" of settlements, which the U.S. government and media ignored:

> Israeli soldiers forcibly removed dozens of Palestinians Monday from the caves where they were living near this southern West Bank town, dumping their belongings on to the roadside, witnesses said. The army cleared out the homes of seventeen Palestinian families, who like many poor shepherds and olive farmers in the area lived in caverns dug into the rocks on this windswept outcrop of the occupied West Bank. Witnesses said the soldiers loaded the Palestinians' personal

effects, young children, and a few women onto trucks and deposited them on a road outside of a nearby town.

The men, however, refused to abandon their now-empty homes in the tiny hamlet of Jamba near the Susya Jewish settlement, unwilling to be transported with their families and possessions to a road near the village of Tawani. Israel state radio reported that two Palestinian men were arrested after they violently resisted their expulsion. The Israeli army declined to comment on the ejection.

As for the mobile homes at Maon Farm that Barak had earlier ordered dismantled—which gathered significant U.S. attention—AFP reported the telling postscript:

Scores of Palestinian residents in this area have been kicked out of their homes since November, when Prime Minister Ehud Barak ordered an illegal Jewish settlement outpost of Havat Maon be dismantled. One week after Havat Maon was taken apart, the Israeli army declared the area around it a military zone and began pushing out local Palestinian residents, who complained that their removal was designed to appease the settlers.[47]

## • TEN •

# *Roadblocks and Reversals*

DENNIS ROSS'S SLOW-MOVING, incrementalist mediation of the Israeli-Palestinian track was wearing out its welcome, particularly after the Sharm Agreement was signed. As Indyk had predicted, the Palestinians viewed Barak's honest fulfillment of this agreement as necessary not only to improve daily living conditions for Palestinians but also to establish a reserve of trust during the fall/winter of 1999-2000, which could later be drawn upon when confronting the thornier final-status issues. This could have worked in theory. But for Palestinians, the deceitful manner with which Barak and his U.S. promoters handled the interim Sharm Agreement did irreversible harm to the prospects of a final-status agreement.

Barak did comply with the first stage of implementation, beginning on September 5 with a timely execution of the first of three increments contained in the second further redeployment (or "Second FRD," in diplomatic shorthand). The first groups of prisoners were released, and droves of Palestinians made use of a long-awaited safe passage route between Gaza and the West Bank. International workers were allowed to begin construction of a seaport in Gaza, crucial to economic growth for all Palestinians.

But the scheduled November 15, 1999, deadline for the second increment of the Second FRD fizzled when Barak, in keeping with his preference for making moves that were cost-free on the domestic front, offered instead to withdraw from territory that was virtually unpopulated. Arafat rejected the proposal as an affront to the spirit of good faith, pointing out that it would bring no tangible improvements for Palestinians. Barak also went back on his agreement to release Palestinians who were imprisoned for acts committed before the signing of Oslo. Though consumed with Syria, the United States gestured cosmetically by dispatching Dennis Ross, who carried out multiple shuttle visits.[1] When Ross found that he was unable to secure Palestinian acquiescence in Barak's attempt to finagle his interim obligations, he dismissed Arafat's grievances, preferring instead to leave the parties to their own devices. Ross rationalized this indifference by saying, "The most important issue is resolving the permanent status questions and producing a framework agreement by the middle of February. If you look at the implementation of the Sharm Agreement, this is not the first problem that has cropped up. There is an implementation mechanism. They have solved problems before, and I expect that they will solve problems again."[2] For Palestinians, Ross's remarks were proof that the United States had chosen to minimize the importance of Israel's obligations on interim withdrawals. What they received instead was yet another promise that a final-status solution was imminent.

Only after time-consuming haggling was the second increment of the Second FRD carried out, on January 6, 2000, almost two months late. To the disappointment of the Palestinians, the 5 percent turnover of land involved only remote desert areas outside the city of Jericho; embarrassingly, it ended up including the area Arafat refused back in November. As a sweetener for agreeing to these areas—

which would alleviate some pressure by the Palestinians as he left for Shepherdstown—Barak secretly indicated he would allow Arafat greater influence in choosing the land in question for the final increment of Sharm's Second FRD, which he guaranteed would take place on January 20.

Weeks later, when Syrian talks were suspended following the leak at Shepherdstown, the Palestinians were expecting Barak to honor his obligation. That was not to be the case either; when Barak met with Arafat, he revealed his plans for yet another postponement. And, in a move that had been predicted by Palestinian skeptics, Barak signaled his intention to scrap altogether the Third FRD, which Israel had agreed to in the Oslo II, Wye, and Sharm agreements. "There's no point going ahead with it," said Barak. "We'll talk about it during the negotiations on the [permanent] status."[3] Though this further reduced Arafat's ability to keep his constituents believing in the Oslo process, the Israeli practice of ignoring Arafat's political realities was nothing new.

• • •

**Barak and Ross** had urged the Palestinians to concentrate on the permanent-status front. But the efforts to draft a Framework Agreement on Permanent Status (FAPS) between September 13, 1999, and the Sharm deadline date of February 13, 2000, proved fruitless. Arafat promptly assigned the FAPS portfolio to his Minister of Culture and Information, Yasser Abed Rabbo. But Barak, citing internal political divisions, would not put forward an Israeli delegation until November. He originally wanted Gilead Sher to lead these discussions, but Attorney General Elyakim Rubinstein challenged the legality of the appointment, pointing out that Sher was a member of neither the government nor Barak's cabinet. Rubinstein insisted that Sher first recuse himself of all ties to his prestigious law firm.[4] Rubinstein had not opposed a similar arrangement between

Netanyahu and his unofficial envoy, Yitzhak Mohlo, but nevertheless it cost the negotiations two crucial months before Barak finally named Oded Eran, a fluent Arabic speaker who had recently been ambassador to Jordan.

Once assembled, neither delegation took the other seriously. Each expressed concerns over the other's level of empowerment and ability to deliver. The Israelis viewed Rabbo as a firebrand given to making long speeches, who showed little flexibility on any of the core issues. They saw Rabbo's selection as little more than a political platform for Palestinians to rail against Barak's declarations on Jerusalem, settlements, refugees, and borders. There was just as much skepticism by the Palestinians. Historically, most serious Israeli negotiators had come from the military, intelligence, or political echelons. This was no less true of Barak's government. Palestinians viewed the latecomer Eran, a career bureaucrat from the Ministry of Foreign Affairs, as a second-choice candidate after Sher, not close to Barak.

In addition, the Palestinians were put off by the fact that the bulk of the U.S. and Israeli diplomatic energy was devoted to negotiations with Syria. Although both the United States and Israel acknowledged the Palestinian issue as being at the core of the Arab-Israeli conflict, they nevertheless proceeded with Syria, a country whose leader had never softened his rigid position on territorial issues. Thus Barak appeared willing to reward Hafez al-Assad's inflexibility on territorial issues even as he responded to Palestinian concessions with stonewalling.

Just in case the Palestinian negotiators were hopeful that the Israelis would offer them something parallel to what they had offered Syria—i.e., the Rabin deposit, or Israel's stated willingness to withdraw to the June 4, 1967, line—Barak decided to let them down early. In early November, reports appeared in the U.S. and Israeli press alleging that Barak presented Clinton with an outline in which Israel would recognize only "a Palestinian entity in nearly *half* of the West

Bank."[5] Shortly thereafter, while both Barak and Arafat were attending a conference in Paris, Barak proclaimed, "It's clear that Resolution 242 has a different meaning when it comes to countries like Egypt, or Syria, for that matter." An Israeli Ministry of Foreign Affairs spokesman further articulated his position, saying, "Since Barak has said that he will not withdraw to 1967 boundaries, and will keep most Jewish settlements in the West Bank and Gaza Strip in territorial blocks under Israeli sovereignty, he clearly does not view Resolution 242 as applicable to all the West Bank."[6]

Barak's comments might have been intended for domestic consumption, but they had a disastrous effect on the fledgling permanent-status talks. Despite the inclusion of Resolution 242 in every peace agreement signed by Israel with the Palestinians, including the original Oslo Accords, Oslo II, Wye River, and the recent Sharm Agreement, Barak's hard-line position that it would not be the basis for discussions over the West Bank and Gaza Strip undermined the efforts of both negotiating teams to establish goodwill. Moreover, it mired the initial FAPS meetings in stormy legal debates. Internal Palestinian memoranda of the permanent-status talks from November to December indicate that Palestinian discussions with Israelis focused on trying to walk them back from Barak's statements to the previously agreed international legal framework. According to one document, dated December 21, 1999, the Palestinians made little headway:

> The Israelis were seeking to shift discussion entirely away from legal rights and obligations . . . [and] engaged in legal discussions only superficially and tried at every opportunity either to dismiss international law as subject to dual interpretations or to encourage "more practical" solutions to the permanent status issues.

> The Israeli side . . . reiterated that Palestine was not mentioned in 242 and that the Palestinian peoplehood had not

received international recognition in 1967. When pressed regarding the legal status of the West Bank and Gaza Strip, the Israeli side refused to acknowledge any Palestinian right to the West Bank/Gaza, stating the issue would be discussed in negotiations. Further, the Israeli side refused to acknowledge that the Fourth Geneva Convention is applicable, arguing that Israel is not a belligerent occupant.

The Palestinians concluded:

The Israeli side is seeking to shift discussion away from legal rights and obligations. The Israeli side appears hesitant to use the term "annexation" when discussing the establishment of Israeli sovereignty over Palestinian territory. The Israeli side's proposals reflect Israel's maximalist position, not its actual demands. When asked whether they genuinely believed that these proposals would secure peace in the region, they appeared almost embarrassed about them and suggested that they were negotiable.

• • •

**Even if Barak** had been forthcoming at this stage or had built a reserve of trust, it is unclear whether the Palestinians would have been ready to proceed to the next stage. Though many among the senior PLO leadership, including Arafat, were eager to begin discussions over permanent-status issues, including topics that had long been considered taboo—Jerusalem, security, refugees, and borders—the truth is that they, too, were sticking to maximalist positions. This was in part because during the Netanyahu years and even well into Barak's term, the Palestinians were unable to come to internal agreement on these questions.

To be sure, the failures to prepare were derivative of the hardships resulting from Israel's longstanding military occupation. Ned Walker, then serving as the assistant secretary of state for Near East affairs at the State Department, points out that one of the crucial mistakes of the U.S. and Israeli negotiators at this time was their belief that the Palestinians had the capacity and resources to get their own house in order. Walker recalled:

> We thought of it as an equal negotiation between equal partners—a state and a state, or the heads of a state/heads of a state. It's not that way at all. The Palestinian Authority is not a state. They don't have the foundation of a state. They don't have the clout in the inter-Arab [world]. They're always out with their hat out asking for donations. They're always a *demandeur* in the Arab ranks—so they don't have stature.[7]

But not all of the fault could be shouldered by the United States and Israel. At the beginning of 1999, there were hardly any Palestinian lawyers representing the PA in negotiations; this was an astounding deficiency, given the complexity of issues and the impact any results would have on the lives of future generations of Palestinians. Mahmoud Abbas, known by his patronymic, Abu Mazen, held a law degree but had never practiced as an attorney. Many within the PA leadership, including Arafat, had disrupted their university education years earlier, when they devoted their lives to becoming revolutionaries in the PLO. Improvising became a signature trait, even at crucial stages of diplomacy: Palestinians would often arrive at complex negotiations with little but scribbled notes and scratch pads. Their preparation was no match for the Israelis, who were well-funded and well-organized. Israeli delegations usually comprised legal advisers, academic strategists, and professionals from the military and intelligence echelons. As one veteran observer of these discussions described, the PA often showed up at meetings still trying to define their rock-bottom positions, while the Israelis sat patiently with laptop computers and CD-ROMs containing well-developed, intricate plans and fallback positions for each scenario.[8]

When the time to put forward a definitive Palestinian position on final-status issues appeared on the horizon, the Palestinians realized the need to improve their own competencey. A scramble ensued to assemble a professional staff of international legal experts from the ranks of the Palestinian diaspora who could draft legal positions matching those of their Israeli counterparts. In the summer of 1999, the European Union agreed to fund the London-based Adam Smith Institute to provide the PA negotiators with legal guidance. Initially, the contract provided three legal advisers tasked with creating the Negotiation Support Unit. The NSU ultimately became a staff of six young, erudite consultants, many carrying Ivy League law degrees. These advisers spent the fall of 1999 in their new jobs hurriedly trying to prepare the PA for the fast-track permanent-status timeline.

As they settled in to life in the occupied territories, these advisers discovered the depth of the PLO's organizational dysfunction. Former PA legal adviser Omar Dajani quickly discovered the constraints imposed by Arafat's refusal to delegate decision-making power. According to Dajani, Arafat's insistence on having overlapping bureaucracies within the PA—all reporting directly to him—created "weak institutions and a competitive, internally divided leadership." This was all part of Arafat's abysmal, micro-management style. He wanted to have his hand in everything—whether signing vacation requests or peace treaties—so as to ensure obsequious loyalty among Palestinian officials, especially those not personally close to him. According to Dajani, this encouraged the hoarding of information.[9]

Like the PLO leadership, the legal advisers quickly found themselves sidetracked. Arguments with Israel over fulfillment of Sharm quickly stymied their ability to focus on permanent status (this was further complicated by Barak's decision to allow continued expropriation of Palestinian land, discussed earlier, which further detracted from preparation).

Moreover, the legal advisers would find themselves starting from scratch. Throughout the Oslo years, both the United States and Israelis dissuaded the PA from discussing what the unspoken Palestinians state might include. Nabil Shaath, who at the time served as the minister of international planning and cooperation, highlights what the Palestinians viewed as Dennis Ross's insulting refusal to address this issue, saying, "We avoided talking about permanent status all through the Oslo process. The Americans wouldn't want us to talk about anything permanent. I remember the ruckus I made when I talked about Palestine and Jerusalem. 'Don't talk about *Palestine,* talk about Palestinian things . . . *not* about Palestine.' And so, I'd say, 'Oh, the weather in *Palestine* is very good; I just came from *Palestine,* why don't you come visit us in *Palestine*?' And I'd say, "Now what would you call this?"

Washington's refusal to address final-status issues during interim negotiations caused foreboding among the Palestinians. They feared the United States would assume that, because of the PA practice of allowing for renegotiation upon renegotiation of interim agreements—only yielding tiny Israeli withdrawals—the United States would misjudge basic Palestinian demands at the final-status stage. Shaath explained:

> The Americans . . . knew we would be seeking a state, but the territorial aspect of that state they underestimated greatly. They saw us sometimes bargaining for 2 percent, 3 percent, further redeployment, and they thought that "OK, we asked for 40 percent and on the second further redeployment we got only 13, so maybe the Palestinian will do the same on the permanent settlement." In the interim agreements, it was a cumulative process. Anything you add you don't lose the right to ask for more at the next stage. At the permanent status, it's not cumulative—it's *subtractive.* Anything you give up

you never have the chance to talk about again, and I think the Americans missed that miserably.[10]

Simply put, the Palestinians knew that any land recovered during the interim phases of Oslo would not have to be renegotiated later at final-status talks. This was also why they were reluctant to begin final-status talks before the Israelis had fulfilled all their obligations on interim withdrawals. They knew the legalistic U.S. and Israeli negotiators would use this as a new starting point and force the Palestinians to bargain over land they should have already received.

• • •

**At least for** the moment, the Palestinians would dismiss Barak's rhetoric about not fulfilling the Third FRD, which even Netanyahu had agreed to complete. Popular confidence in the Palestinian leadership was so low that Arafat had to have something to take back to his people to keep them believing in his original Oslo commitment. For Palestinians, the key issue in January 2000 was Barak's failure to fulfill the final increment of Sharm's Third FRD. As was the case with all previous withdrawals, the area in question was small, totaling a 6.1 percent transfer of land from Area B (where Palestinians were responsible for civil but not security control), over to Area A (Palestinian civil and security control). Thus, after seven years of laborious negotiations under Oslo, this 6.1 percent transfer would raise the total of Area A to a mere 18.1 percent of the West Bank and Gaza Strip, with the combined Areas A and B totaling a paltry 41 percent of the territories. The rest of the territory was still Area C, under full Israeli civil and security control.

With Arafat's own political stability in jeopardy, on January 17, he asked for and received a meeting with Barak to quietly press for his performance on the final increment of Sharm's Second FRD. At Barak's home, Arafat demanded "payment" for the unabated settlement construction and interim Israeli breaches, requesting that the 6.1 percent withdrawal include the upgrading of Abu Dis, Azariyya, and Ram, three Arab villages on the outskirts of Jerusalem, from Area B status to Area A. According to Indyk, the United States understood Arafat's village request as something "he could show as a symbolic achievement," noting that "Barak agreed to do that."[11]

For Arafat, full Palestinian control over Abu Dis further cemented the Palestinian linkage to Arab East Jerusalem; from Abu Dis, the Palestinians have an unfettered view of the Haram al-Sharif's golden Dome of the Rock, an important site in the Islamic faith adjacent to the Al-Aqsa Mosque, Islam's third-holiest site. The turnover would signal Israeli seriousness on the final-status front by removing Abu Dis from having to be negotiated later during the final-status discussions on Jerusalem. For Palestinians, Abu Dis would be recognized as a final-status foothold for Arab East Jerusalem and not, as some Israelis had dreamed, become the endgame Palestinian capital, which Barak had to have known that Arafat, as well as the entire Arab and Muslim world, would reject outright.

Given that his full attention was still on Syria, Barak's promise to turn over an area that touched on the outskirts of Jerusalem—however slight—presented him, quite prematurely, with a new set of domestic political problems. Responding to the press reports of a full return of Abu Dis, Likud Party leaders, including Ariel Sharon and Jerusalem Mayor Ehud Olmert, waged a "fight for Jerusalem" and established a formal headquarters to organize an opposition campaign.[12] Of foremost concern to some Likud members, many of whom opposed any Palestinian state, was the notion that Barak's plan to "give away" Abu Dis at this stage would foreclose the possibility of later presenting this village as the future Palestinian capital. This arrived at a bad time for Barak, who was then under attack by Sharon after reports surfaced that Barak had been interviewed by members of the attorney general's office as part of a criminal inquiry into the campaign finance practices of his political party, One Israel, through its overseas nonprofit connections.[13] After spending time negotiating with Barak's delegation at Shepherdstown, Attorney General Rubinstein announced a criminal investigation of Barak and of his brother-in-law and cabinet secretary, Yitzhak Herzog, which further weakened Barak's ability to corral his seriously divided government.

Even though Barak agreed to return Abu Dis, raising Palestinian expectations, he reasserted an earlier argument, rejected by Arafat, to link Israel's fulfillment of the final increment of the Sharm Second FRD with the successful conclusion of FAPS, the latter of which neither side had seriously worked on and which thus stood little chance of conclusion by February 13.[14] To buy more time for the Syria talks, Barak requested that the interim January 20 deadline be extended a few more weeks. In a pattern that would later metastasize on a much grander scale, Arafat refused while Barak acted unilaterally.

Days later, Arafat took his protest to the White House. At a meeting with Clinton on January 20, he demanded U.S. assurances that all aspects of the Sharm Agreement would be fulfilled. Still riveted by the possibility of concluding a deal with Syria and perhaps even commiserating with Barak for having fallen under investigation, Clinton offered a press statement only reaffirming his commitment to the broader final-status picture, resorting to the earlier proclamations by Ross that the issues "have to be worked out between the two sides" and that neither side would be able to get all it wanted.

Though Clinton maintained that comprehensive Israeli-Palestinian peace was just around the corner, the Palestinians hardly shared this assessment. Aware of U.S. indifference to his own political realities, Arafat unavailingly sought the involvement of new interlocutors, especially those who had months earlier provided assurances to the PA regarding

Sharon. He raised his concerns with Egyptian President Mubarak, EU's Middle East envoy Miguel Moratinos, and EU's foreign policy head Javier Solana, as a means to leverage Barak. Knowing he had succeeded in co-opting the United States in his pursuit of Syrian negotiations, Barak fended off non-U.S. involvement by separately engaging Arab actors, including Mubarak and Jordan's King Abdullah II. Indeed, nothing concrete emerged from Arafat's moves or Barak's countermoves except for yet more delays.

The torrent of Likud criticism over Abu Dis became too much for Barak to bear. He signaled to the Palestinians—clumsily, through the Israeli press—not to expect Abu Dis as part of the final increment of the Second FRD.[15] The Palestinian response to the announcement, even from optimists like Saeb Erekat, was predictably negative. Erekat said:

> I do not know what Mr. Barak is trying to do. With whom is he negotiating? Whenever a critical voice emanates in Israel we find that statements come out from the Israeli government in a way that is not befitting to the peace process. We said that these mutual concerns have been met. We frankly say that when agreement is reached on something, we do not need to hear denial or confirmation from any quarter.[16]

At a conference in Switzerland on January 28, Arafat angrily denounced Barak's "bottleneck of procrastination, unilateral delaying tactics, and minimalist implementation that threatens the whole process."[17]

In a meeting at Gaza's Erez crossing on February 4, Barak presented Arafat a map that did not include Abu Dis or any of the previously agreed Palestinian villages near the periphery of East Jerusalem. Once again, Barak was still unwilling to entertain discussion over the completion of the Wye River's Third FRD.[18] Perhaps contrary to what Barak had expected after witnessing Arafat capitulate first in the renegotiation of Wye, and later in the second increment of Sharm's Second FRD (initially refusing, then ultimately accepting, the same territory months later), a sullen Arafat refused. Further, he suspended all negotiations with the Israelis, including FAPS, until Barak lived up to his word. As the meeting ended, it was clear to observers that relations between the two were poor. As Barak walked Arafat to his motorcade, the only semblance of civility was in an artificial handshake, after the jeering request of photographers.[19]

Most maddening to the Palestinians was the cavalier way in which Barak dismissed the hardships they faced, especially as a result of continued settlement expansion. Arafat was thus pressured to do something to make Barak take him seriously. The suspension of FAPS was a tactical maneuver to center international attention—especially that of the Americans—on Barak's bad faith. In the short term, Arafat's move would work.

• • •

**In Israel, the** passing of the February 13 deadline without a FAPS did not go unnoticed. Polls conducted in early February 2000 indicated that a "majority of Israelis favor giving up Arab neighborhoods in Jerusalem for the sake of a peace agreement" with Palestinians.[20] The growing concerns over the stalled Palestinian track highlighted a disconnect between Barak and his constituencies. The PA leadership, often as observant of Israeli public opinion as their own, sensed Barak's vulnerability and began to sharpen their own rhetorical swords. Ahmed Qurei, the speaker of the Palestinian parliament and a close adviser to Arafat, said, "We will convert Zone B to a Zone A area. Consequently, we will deploy Palestinian forces to the borders of Zone A."[21]

The comment by Qurei, also known by his patronymic, Abu Ala, only fed Barak's political difficulties by raising the specter of violent confrontation. Taking it as a veiled threat,

Interior Minister Shlomo Ben Ami reminded, "The Palestinians understand that in unilateral steps, Israel is stronger," and he admonished the PA to be more cautious in their statements and not "add a war of words to the existing political disagreements."[22]

But there was more disquiet from Arafat, who—echoing his démarche from the previous year—publicly announced that he would declare statehood by September 13, with or without an agreement with Israel. Although Arafat didn't know it, there were people within the Israeli security establishment, including Ami Ayalon, head of the Shin Bet, and Shaul Mofaz, the IDF chief of staff, quietly pressing Barak to drop the Syria track and focus on the Palestinians.

At the operational levels of the Israeli military and intelligence establishment, the tough Palestinian talk was taken seriously. The indicators on the Palestinian street suggested an alarming lack of faith in Barak and little expectation that a settlement would be reached within the ambitious timeline Barak once promised. These warnings, combined with intelligence reports of continued weapons smuggling and, worse, actions ordered by Arafat like the release of eighteen Hamas detainees on March 11, which he labeled a "goodwill gesture," were ominous.[23]

In anticipation, the IDF dusted off "Operation Field of Thorns," a 1996 contingency plan to swiftly reconquer the autonomous Palestinian territories should disturbances break out.[24] The IDF knew it would have overwhelming superiority, but the Israelis nevertheless had new factors to consider. Foremost was the professional training the Palestinians forces had received from the CIA. Although this was mostly limited to intelligence and bodyguard work, some Palestinians received military training in Jordan, Iraq, and Tunisia. Barak began to regret this training, but also the growing strength of Hamas and the prolific black-market arms trade between the Palestinian opposition and militias and radical Jewish settlers. The clashes between the Israelis and Palestinians in September 1996, after Netanyahu opened the Hasmonean Tunnels for excavation beneath the Dome of the Rock, killing fifteen Israelis and more than seventy Palestinians, evoked dread about what could happen if more fighting broke out. The Palestinians had only increased their capacity to resist.

Though Likud took the opportunity to snipe at Barak for his handling of the Palestinian track (for different reasons), more problems began to emerge among Barak's inner cabinet. Amnon Lipkin-Shahak, an integral figure who at the time was trying to repair the damaged Israeli-Syrian track, publicly criticized Barak for "humiliating" the Palestinians, adding that the Palestinians should have at least received one of the villages promised.[25] Former Israeli Prime Minister Shimon Peres, who had been kept away from the negotiations, voiced equal concern over the Syria focus, adding that he was much more confident a deal could be struck with the Palestinians.[26] Even Interior Minister Ben Ami, as well as Finance Minister Avraham Shohat, opined that, unlike the Syrians, the Palestinians were more "ripe" to make peace.

It seemed the United States got the message. As Barak pushed Clinton for one last stab with the Syrians in late February/early March 2000, the United States persuaded Barak that a Clinton-Asad summit would only be explored pending movement on the Palestinian track. For Barak, this meant he would have to implement the final increment of the Second FRD as a way to reopen the FAPS discussions. After multiple shuttle visits within the region in late February/early March, Ross found both sides entrenched. So far none of the Americans had been able to force Barak's hand, either with Syria or the Palestinians, and U.S. mediation efforts reflected a submission to Barak's obstinacy. Rather than press Barak for performance, Ross offered the Palestinians a confusing compromise formula; as far as the Palestinians were concerned, he was offering yet more of the same incrementalist slop.

Yossi Ginosar, an *éminence grise* for Barak who had spent years developing secret relations with the PLO leadership, was angry with the prime minister over his treatment of the Palestinians. Ginosar, a former Shin Bet official who had lost his son to the Israeli-Palestinian conflict years earlier, succeeded in convincing Barak to honor his commitment by recalibrating the return of all three villages: two could be counted on for April 23 and the last on May 23. He also convinced Barak to recommit to the Third FRD, to be executed by June 23 with renewed assurances that it would happen with or without the conclusion of FAPS (rescheduled from the missed February 13 deadline to May 23). The Palestinians could select the 6.1 percent from an area of 13 percent, not the 10 percent originally suggested by Ross. Moreover, Barak agreed to fulfill other stalled aspects of Sharm, including a release of Palestinian prisoners before the March 20 celebration by Muslims of Eid al-Adha; a pledge to make an effort to reimburse the Palestinians for illegitimately withheld value-added taxes; and an opening of the northern safe-passage route between Gaza and the West Bank, which had been placed on hold. In return, the Palestinians agreed to resume the FAPS negotiations in Washington, weeks later.[27] The Palestinians thus accepted what in essence was yet another renegotiation of a prior binding agreement.

Ross, Barak, and Arafat concluded this footnote to prior Oslo agreements on March 8 in Ramallah, but only after a noteworthy diversion from the norm. Assenting to the Palestinians' request—trust between Arafat and Barak was nonexistent and the Palestinians had demanded an external guarantor—the United States agreed that Clinton himself would affix his personal imprimatur to the March 8 deal, formally making the United States responsible for the amendments should Barak again renege.

• • •

**Before Barak could** make good on the March 8 amendment and upgrade the 6.1 percent of Area B to Area A responsibility, he had to fight first within his cabinet and then among the broader Knesset for their approval. Three cabinet ministers, including Yitzhak Levy of the NRP and Natan Sharansky of Yisrael Ba'Aliya, voted to reject it, though it eventually passed muster.[28] It was an even tougher sell on the floor of the Knesset, mainly because of the inclusion of the Palestinian village of Anata, which the settler lobby referred to by its biblical name of Anathoth. Despite the understanding among most right-wing Knesset members that Anata, a Palestinian village already in Area B and surrounded by two Jewish settlements on the northern edge of East Jerusalem, would be turned over to the Palestinians as part of a final-status agreement, some members alleged heresy at the proposed return, calling Barak's attention to Jewish scripture, which read, "God told the prophet Jeremiah to purchase the land in Anathoth."[29]

As he reacted in other scenarios—whether on the Syrian or Palestinian front—Barak caved. Meron Benvenisti, a former deputy mayor of Jerusalem, criticized this backing down on the Anata issue as a "missed opportunity," reasoning that with final-status talks on the horizon, it would be wise for the Israeli prime minister to "start preparing Israeli public opinion for compromise." It likewise infuriated the Palestinians, as Saeb Erekat wondered aloud in response, "How will we discuss the real Jerusalem if they cannot agree to Anata?"[30]

On March 20, Israel made its final withdrawal of the Second Sharm FRD, without Anata or other villages adjoining "greater Jerusalem," and only after facing protests from settlers, who feared the withdrawal would leave their homes isolated within the Palestinians areas. The areas upgraded to full PA control included villages near Ramallah, Bethlehem, Hebron, and Jenin.[31] There were some major disappointments, such as the fact that Barak handed over just fifteen prisoners rather than the more than one hundred requested (out of an estimated 1,600 total).[32] The release of prisoners was a volatile issue for the Palestinian public, and Israel's refusal to comply with earlier agreements on this issue heightened popular mistrust and fury. But the forward movement had been enough to get Arafat back in the game. In compliance with his obligation, he authorized a delegation to travel to Washington to restart the FAPS discussions.

Clinton and Barak, consumed with the upcoming summit in Geneva, had averted a full-blown crisis and, with even the mildest movement on the Palestinian track, would be able to hint to Asad that there were other games in town. The Palestinians, holding their breath in expectation of a full Israeli-Syrian peace, were hoping for a positive outcome. It would be, after all, a good precedent to have Syria join the ranks of Egypt and Jordan, as full restoration of occupied territory might indenture Barak to do likewise for Palestinians.

## • ELEVEN •

# *A Dose of False Hope*

THERE WERE MYRIAD problems facing Clinton as he returned home from the failed Geneva summit on March 27, 2000. He had been told by Martin Indyk and Dennis Ross that the proposal put forward by Barak was good; moreover, his advisers had hinted that the Syrians were willing to entertain something less than full territorial restoration. Ross and Indyk were wrong on both counts.

Clinton's State and NSC teams were bitter about the Syrian failure. Dissatisfaction by the White House and NSC turned into a desire for accountability; increasingly, questions were raised about Ross and Indyk and, to a lesser degree, Secretary Albright concerning their overall handling of the peace process. Those at staff levels of the State Department became aware of Clinton's unhappiness—clearly evident even to Egyptian President Mubarak's visiting delegation. Rumors abounded that Indyk, now less prominent though still sitting as ambassador in Tel Aviv, would be asked to resign.[1] After all, Indyk was the Syria-first brainchild.

Indyk was not alone in the hot seat. Asad, Arafat, the Palestinians, and even Barak had complained to Clinton about Ross at various stages during the previous year, leading Sandy Berger and his NSC staff to take a more direct role than ever before. To be sure, criticisms of Ross from the Arabs were nothing new, and were viewed as coming with the job, while occasional complaints by Israelis throughout his lengthy tenure bolstered his claim to impartiality.

But Clinton did not like to fail, and the criticism from all sides of Ross's poor preparation and doubts about his ability to conclude the Oslo process led to fleeting White House deliberations over whether or not he should go. One senior Clinton White House official explained:

> Part of what the problem was with people like Dennis . . . instead of being a broker—instead of facilitating the parties making a deal—they started doing it as if they were the principal [or] the President himself. And the truth is that we needed new blood; we needed fresh eyes. The U.S. should have been—and needs to be—an honest broker. But if after several years they feel you have taken one side, you're not effective! . . . There were some who said he should be replaced.[2]

Unfortunately, at this late stage in the game, removing Ross might cost more than keeping him; it would signal disharmony and likely have detracted even further from the remaining chances for an agreement. His knowledge of the Arab-Israeli negotiations was unparalleled in the U.S. government. Moreover, if Ross left, Albright would be expected to assume the portfolio, but she was clearly unable to manage the situation on her own, having little expertise on the topic. To her own frustration, she had become excessively reliant on Ross.[3]

Ross himself certainly didn't seem to be aware of his precarious position. For example, in the spring of 2000 he took a notorious stance on Israel's proposed billion-dollar sale to

China of advanced Phalcon radar technology, a system that closely paralleled the sophisticated U.S.-made AWACS technology, which the United States had exported to the Israeli air force earlier on the condition that Israel would not export it to anyone else without U.S. permission. It was widely argued that, were Barak to sell the Phalcon to China, U.S. troops would be vulnerable in the event of a showdown with Beijing. That China's possession of the Phalcon would imperil the strategic U.S. alliance with Taiwan was apparently not a concern to either Barak or Ross. But they nevertheless persisted with the deal, annoying Clinton administration cabinet officials, including then Defense Secretary William Cohen, and the U.S. Congress, whose opposition to the sale was so airtight that threats were made against Israel's future foreign-aid requests. Members of Congress harshly criticized Barak at a time when they were factoring substantial U.S. grants as part of an incentive to conclude a Syrian-Israeli peace (by some accounts, a staggering $17 billion); as the Israelis and Palestinians reached the final-status stages, additional U.S. grants would be considered.

According to one State official, Ross had the gumption to keep pressing the issue even when it became clear no one was for it, unabashedly pleading, "You have to do the sale—we gave them our word!" This drew the ire of those within the NSC, particularly Mara Rudman, the NSC chief of staff. Rudman went so far as to directly accuse Ross of being insubordinate to the president.[4]

As Clinton and Barak held more direct exchanges, often resulting in substantive debriefings within the White House and NSC only, Ross increasingly sought to preserve his role by hoarding information he collected from his own contacts. As an unashamed supporter of Israel's security interests, Ross was paranoid about possible final-status "concessions" by Israel, especially as others, including the president, were discussing these items more frequently without his participation. A colleague of Ross at State described the situation:

> In the last year, [Ross] began pushing people outside and away—especially if they weren't like-minded with regard to Israel. He would do things like give solo briefings to the secretary (before he would normally do this with Indyk). But as he was pushing people out, he himself started getting pushed out. Dennis assumed he knew more about the issue than anyone else, and when he felt close to getting a deal, it became evident to everyone that his more pro-Israeli feelings were coming out. As we came very close to the time to do a deal, Dennis became very nervous about the Israelis' position on the potential deal.

The same State official continued:

> Arafat always complained to us that his message wasn't getting through to the president. He couldn't stand Dennis. The White House would even call to inquire with the Near East Affairs Division at State. NEA responded that Dennis was handling all of Arafat's correspondence—on his personal computer. No one said anything about this, even despite the fact that it was all classified and on his personal computer . . . Ross was handling all correspondence coming from the Palestinians. All of the papers that the PLO sent went right from Nick Rasmussen's desk [Ross's assistant] to Dennis, and once there, he wouldn't let anyone see them. When it became clear that Dennis didn't want anyone to see those documents from the Palestinians, the president and Sandy Berger decided to cut Dennis from the negotiations.[5]

To be fair, Ross did not hoard information only to maintain his position in the bureaucracy. Ned Walker recalls that while he was serving as ambassador to Israel during Netanyahu's term, Ross gave explicit instructions not to keep any official record of Arab-Israeli negotiations in order to avoid leaks.[6] Walker, who thought Ross did this in part to keep the information for his own use, lamented the confusion it created during later attempts to review progress or mistakes.[7] But more problematic, the processing of this information by Ross and Indyk on their personal computers left both open to eavesdropping, well within the technical capabilities of common computer hackers and most intelligence services, including Israel's.

• • •

**Many within the** NSC and State, including Sandy Berger and Aaron Miller, expressed their concern about the harm of the Syria-first policy directly to the president; these officials saw the collapse of the Geneva talks as a logical point to redouble efforts on the Palestinians track. But for domestic political reasons, the president's time was quickly receding. A peace agreement would almost certainly require additional funding from the United States, which would require legislative approval. But Congress went into recess in August, and after Labor Day the election season would begin, making serious negotiations difficult or impossible. American diplomats were fully aware that the Palestinians were despondent that final-status issues had not yet begun. Those serving the Clinton administration saw that a full-charge-ahead with the Palestinians would be needed immediately.

Unfortunately, Barak's immediate concern was still not the Palestinians. Incredibly, he still hoped Asad would respond positively to the Geneva offer. And whether he did or not, Barak intended to make good on his campaign pledge to withdraw IDF troops from Lebanon by June, a move he knew would be a political victory for him at home. American diplomats hoped that a properly executed Lebanon withdrawal would strengthen Barak's coalition, thus enabling him to be more forthcoming with the Palestinians.

The State Department, and particularly the U.S. mission to the United Nations, energetically lobbied Security Council members on Israel's behalf for a clean bill of health should the IDF end the twenty-two-year occupation of southern Lebanon. Ever since the IDF seized a strip of territory there in 1978 to repel PLO attacks on northern Israel (Israel had seized far more territory in its 1982 invasion), both the Security Council and the General Assembly had issued resolution upon resolution calling for Israel's total withdrawal. The standard was Security Council Resolution 425 of 1978, which called for Israel to "withdraw all forces from Lebanon and respect its sovereignty."

This was on Barak's agenda when, following the Geneva collapse, he made an urgent appeal to visit the president to win support for his plans on both the Lebanese and Palestinian tracks. During a meeting with Clinton at the White House on April 11, Barak revealed his plan for a final settlement, which would nonetheless postpone discussion of Jerusalem, even as Israel annexed or retained for an extended period roughly one-third of the occupied territories.

In total, Barak's scheme would be unacceptable to any Arab. A plan that called for outright annexation or continued Israeli occupation of one-third of Palestinian land in the territories was something the Palestinian people would never accept, much less be grounds for an "end of conflict." As was the case with their denial of Syria's basic demands and entitlement under international law, the Americans were callous to these realities. It is improbable that Berger, Albright, or Clinton pointed out these difficulties to Barak during their separate meetings with him. Several Israelis within Barak's innermost circle saw problems with his fundamental outlook. Regrettably, they too would do nothing to nip it in the bud. Shlomo Ben Ami recalled:

> In one of our first meetings, Barak showed me a map that included the Jordan Rift Valley and was a kind of very beefed-up Allon Plan [formulated by Israeli Labor Party leader Yigal Allon in 1967, soon after Israel conquered the territories, this plan called for Israeli annexation of roughly

> 50 percent of the West Bank, with the rest either returned to Jordan or allowed some form of autonomy]. He was proud of the fact that his map would leave Israel with about a third of the territory. If I remember right, he gave the Palestinians only 66 percent of the land. Ehud was convinced that the map was extremely logical. He had a kind of patronizing, wishful-thinking, naive approach, telling me enthusiastically, "Look, this is a state; to all intents and purposes it looks like a state."
>
> At that point, I didn't argue with him. I didn't tell him to throw the map into the garbage or to turn it into a kite. But later, in the wake of advance talks with the Palestinians and internal clarifications, he understood that it was impossible to present a map like that publicly.[8]

At a press conference following the Clinton-Barak meeting, the focus of discussion was all about Lebanon, Syria, and, to a lesser extent, the Phalcon sale to China. When asked of his satisfaction over Barak's handling of the interim Sharm withdrawals, Clinton said, "I think you should wait and see what happens in the next few weeks," no doubt referring to his conviction that Barak would not let him down on the March 8 three-village transfer agreement. Barak added, "We have a variety of ideas to discuss about how to move to give new momentum and energy to the Palestinian track in order to live up to the time line that we have set, together with Chairman Arafat."[9]

Both Clinton and Arafat would be in for a letdown. Barak's management of his unwieldy coalition government left much to be desired, but it was especially wanting in the normal consultative and preparatory sessions expected from any prime minister before peacemaking with the Arabs.

Within a ten-month period, Barak had flirted with a total withdrawal from the Golan Heights and an end to fifty years of conflict with Syria. He had also announced his intention to fully withdrawal from Lebanon and bring an end to that quagmire. He knew a Lebanon withdrawal would be generally popular with the Israeli public (if not with many in the military), as Israelis felt no emotional or religious connection to Lebanese territory. Many questioned the death of Israeli soldiers in a seemingly endless occupation and draining war against the increasingly effective insurgency of Hezbollah, the Shiite guerrilla movement. By mid-April, Barak was announcing what had been speculated all along in the Israeli press: his intention to upgrade Abu Dis to full Palestinian control.

Barak had been taking the Israeli public through a dizzying round of proposals; while both he and his American supporters felt that they were bold and courageous, cracks were beginning to form in his coalition. In keeping with the law of unintended consequences, the new coalition troubles began with something seemingly unrelated. In April, the ultra-Orthodox Shas Party (recall that the party held a robust seventeen out of sixty-one seats in the Knesset, and were thus a powerful force in Barak's coalition) demanded that the government fund its religious school curriculum. This would have been a tough sell to most Israeli governments, but it stood little chance of succeeding given that it required the approval of Education Minister Yossi Sarid, the leader of Meretz, a vehemently secular party holding ten seats. Sarid opposed Shas's request on principle. But Barak needed the support of Shas in order to make delivery on the April 23 village transfers.

Sensing a problem, Barak privately requested Arafat's cooperation in delaying the village upgrades until May 1. Once again, Arafat agreed to Barak's request for a delay based on the excuse of domestic political turmoil. The details and dates of the March 8 agreement had been kept secret, but even so, erosion of Arafat's political base over the village debate was alarming.

But there were other problems within Barak's coalition.

Natan Sharansky of Yisrael Ba'Aliya and Yitzhak Levy of the NRP, who had resisted ceding any of the Golan to Syria, renewed their heartache over doing the same with the Palestinians. Both threatened to withdraw their parties from Barak's coalition in order to scupper the village upgrade. The loss of these two parties would have spelled the end of his coalition, and was yet another reminder of the bad choices Barak had made in forming his government. As Gilead Sher had noted, Barak and his close allies always expected the extremist factions of his coalition to withdraw their support as final-status discussions began; it wouldn't have mattered at that point, they believed, because a peace agreement would be promptly tabled as a referendum in the public domain. But the threatened departure of Yisrael Ba'Aliya and the NRP over interim-status issues—well before final-status agreements were even discussed—left Barak with two options, bad and worse: either call for early elections (and quite possibly lose) or form a national unity government, inevitably requiring overtures to Sharon's Likud Party. Sensing these vulnerabilities, Shas held stronger than ever to its demand for the school funding—an extortion of Barak, in essence, hinging money for Shas's religious schools upon fulfillment of negotiated foreign policy agreements with the Palestinians, and even with Clinton. As May 1 approached, the issues between Shas and Meretz were still not sorted out, and the Knesset went into recess until May 15, requiring additional delay.

• • •

**On March 22,** the Palestinian people received a small morale boost when Pope John Paul II made a historic visit to the West Bank. During a visit with Arafat in Bethlehem, at a time when the Palestinians felt all but forgotten, the Pope offered some commiseration, saying, "No one can ignore how much the Palestinian people have had to suffer in recent decades. Your torment is before the eyes of the world, and it has gone on too long."[10] The visit caused great controversy in Israel, particularly as the Pontiff made a detour from Bethlehem to the nearby Palestinian refugee camp of Dheisheh, where he lamented the living conditions of Palestinians as "deplorable" and "barely tolerable," observing that "above all, you bear the sad memories of what you were forced to leave behind." In his parting remarks, the Pope pleaded, "Dear brothers and sisters, dear refugees, do not think that your present condition makes you any less important in God's eyes! Never forget your dignity as his children!"[11]

Despite these papal sympathies, Palestinians made little headway toward realizing their goal of freedom. Arafat had agreed to restart the final-status talks on March 21, and again on April 7, dispatching Saeb Erekat and Yasser Abed Rabbo to Bolling Air Force Base to hold meetings with Oded Eran and other Israelis. The talks turned out to be "brainstorm sessions," pabulum to stall the Palestinians. Reflecting on these meetings, Erekat commented, "The Israelis weren't even mandated to discuss the final-status issues. We had some brainstorming sessions on all issues, but it was obvious it was a seminar. Oded Eran knew that. It was very obvious. Even the Americans who were there [Rob Malley, Aaron Miller, and Dennis Ross] said it was because of the 'other mistress' [Syria]."[12]

Arafat's political situation was deteriorating even further, primarily because of the growth of settlements and the delay in release of Palestinian prisoners. In April, Barak announced plans to allow for the construction of over 200 homes for settlers in the Golan. As one Israeli official warned, "More projects will be approved as the prospects recede for a land-for-peace trade with Damascus."[13] Logic might have suggested that Barak was venting the pressure valve with the Golan settlers in order to ready their counterparts in the West Bank and Gaza Strip for compromises. But his actions left no evidence of this. He continued building more "facts on the ground" in the occupied Palestinian territories in an attempt to co-opt the settler infrastructure. Barak delivered a letter to the 450 Jewish settlers of Hebron on April 1 that read, "On the occasion of the thirty-second anniversary of the renewal of the Jewish community of Hebron, I am happy to convey to the entire community blessings of success and shalom." The endorsement was denounced by Palestinians and members of the Israeli peace camp alike. Gideon Levy of the daily *Ha'aretz* editorialized:

> What good wishes can be sent to them? The wish that they continue to be an obstacle to peace? That they continue to brutalize their neighbors? And why does Barak have to congratulate them? And with his other hand he builds: Another twelve Jewish families, we are informed, will join the fifty-four families who already live in Hebron. That is just what the peace process and Hebron alike need: Another few dozen people to overturn the carts of Palestinians in the market, and all with the blessing of the prime minister of change.
> Did Barak ever see the bags of feces and stones that the settler children and their parents throw from the balconies of their homes at the market below? Was it to such people that he sent his good wishes? Is it really necessary to strengthen this violent group? At least Barak's declared predecessor and mentor, Yitzhak Rabin, condemned this dubious enterprise verbally ("a serious mistake"), even if he did not lift a finger to remove it. Barak, on the other hand, sends his congratulations.[14]

Barak also permitted construction in large settlements adjacent to Palestinian villages, which he promised to retain in Israel's future borders. To take just one example, the IDF destroyed five homes and uprooted over 150 olive trees in the Palestinian villages of al-Issawiyeh and Anata (just outside East Jerusalem in Area B area) after being rezoned as "government property" in order to facilitate plans for the expansion of nearby Ma'ale Adumim. When Palestinians moved in days later to rebuild from the rubble, the IDF response was to level an additional six homes.[15] Barak allowed the Israeli government to continue the expansion of Ma'ale Adumim, and 174 construction tenders were issued to legalize that goal.

In response to these developments, Ghassan Khatib, a Palestinian intellectual and former member of the 1991 Madrid delegation, wrote an article titled, "End the Cease-Fire." A Delphic forecast, it is worth quoting in full:

> It is useful to remember two things. One is that the entire conflict between Israelis and Palestinians is about land. The long history of fights, wars and resistance have been about Palestinians trying to defend their land and prevent the Zionists from seizing it.
>
> Second is that the terms of reference of this peace process and articles in signed agreements like the original Declaration of Principles stipulate that neither party may undertake unilateral actions that prejudice the issues to be negotiated.
>
> The Israelis are continuing the war as viciously as ever. Daily they take more land from Palestine. The Palestinians once countered this Israeli aggression by resisting and fighting back in wars or guerrilla fights or diplomatic battles against Israel, as well as inciting the Arab masses and governments to boycott Israel.
>
> But this struggle has stopped. It has been replaced by cooperation with Israel against those who try to resist Israeli aggression over land. It has also been replaced by Palestinian efforts to encourage Arabs to end the boycott of Israel and to contribute to Arab-Israeli joint activities and projects that most Arab people consider unnecessary.
>
> The tragedy is that while Israel unilaterally continues the war, the Palestinian side is unilaterally ceasing fire. This is adding

> negatively to the imbalance between the two sides in terms of power and action. Israel, therefore, is enjoying having its cake and eating it, too. The only way to stop this is if the Palestinian side offers Israel one of two options: either we both cease fire, i.e., Israel stops its settlement expansion policy or that peace negotiations should not be the only type of relationship between the Palestinians and the Israelis.[16]

Statements like these—not originating from Hamas but rather from a respected university professor—were naturally taken seriously by the Shin Bet and CIA. So, too, were the polling data collected by the Palestinian Research Center. Its April 2000 polls confirmed the extent to which the Palestinian street had united in its disgust at Barak and the actions by his pro-settler cabinet ministers. The trust of the Palestinian people was at its nadir: Just 13 percent believed in Barak's government, while 77 percent opposed it. Support for Arafat had also declined to its lowest point since 1994 (34 percent), as had the popularity of his political party, Fatah, while support for Hamas increased from 10 to 15 percent between the months of February and April, as Barak dragged his feet.[17]

Had Barak not ignored the "smaller" obligations under Sharm, such as the release of Palestinian prisoners, he could have indirectly shored up Arafat's political power vis-à-vis that of the Islamists. Within Israeli prisons, the integration of young Palestinians into politics had become part of life under military occupation. Those who were arrested by the Israelis for common security infractions, such as throwing rocks at occupation soldiers and demonstrating at checkpoints, could typically expect to spend up to six months in administrative detention. Often these youths would pledge their allegiances to a group not only to get through the ordeal, which often included coercive interrogation techniques (i.e., involving "moderate physical pressure," or tactics chronicled by a plethora of human rights groups as outright torture).[18] They also joined to establish important political alliances upon their release. After release, their time spent "on the outside" was an important gauge of character, almost as important as their time spent inside brokering alliances. Many towns in the West Bank and Gaza Strip had prisoners' clubs to express solidarity for those still in detention.

In the case of Fatah (created by Arafat and a group of his advisers in 1959, it has always been the largest faction in the PLO), those prisoners willing to join the *tanzim*, Fatah's grassroots organizational arm created in 1995 to offset the growing anti-PA factions waging war against the Oslo process, meant more bodies willing to pledge their allegiance to Arafat and thus support the PA and its promotion of Oslo. Several of Fatah's current leaders, among them Mohammed Dahlan, had advanced to senior positions in the PLO and PA based on their Israeli jail experiences during the first intifada as militants in the Fatah Hawks.[19] From the Israeli perspective, recruitment by Fatah was far preferable to recruitment by the Islamist groups. But Barak's stinginess on the release of prisoners, along with his practice of tightening the occupation through house demolitions and settlement construction, actually fostered recruitment by activist groups unalterably opposed to Oslo; the festering prisoner issue thus became a source of the violence that was to come.

The Shin Bet made an effort to reverse Arafat's troubling decline in popularity, recognizing that Israeli security depended on it. In April, it recommended that Barak release all prisoners affiliated with Fatah and continue to detain those with loyalties to Hamas or Islamic Jihad.[20] Barak dismissed their advice, even as pressure from the Palestinian street continued to build.

April 17, declared "Palestinian Prisoner Day," marked a series of low-intensity brushes between Palestinian and IDF forces, with massive prison riots in Israel and hunger strikes by detainees.[21] On the outside, several groups launched demonstrations and marches on Israeli checkpoints, some of them resulting in stone-throwing against IDF forces, who responded with rubber-coated steel munitions or, in some cases, live rounds. Hundreds of university students began the demonstrations in Bethlehem; weeks later, a much larger group launched similar protests in Ramallah, Jerusalem, and Gaza, the latter gaining the attendance of Hamas spiritual leader Sheik Ahmed Yassin.

• • •

**By the beginning** of May it was clear that the FAPS discussions between Eran and Erekat/Abed Rabbo had made little progress. There appeared little chance of concluding a FAPS by the agreed date of May 23. Barak, focused on the Lebanon pullout, had already announced publicly that the Palestinians would need to wait. "Once the public internalizes the fact that I am sincere," Barak reassured, "they will show a great capacity for understanding the matter of missed deadlines."[22]

After boredom at Bolling, the Palestinians would meet again with the Israelis on May 4, this time at a beautiful Red Sea resort in the Israeli coastal city of Eilat. Ross, Miller, Helal, and Schwartz attended from State, along with Rob Malley from the NSC. They hoped to convince the Palestinians that, with Syria out of the way, they were no longer considered "the other woman." In Eilat, the first semblance of final-status talks finally began. But as a result of how things were maneuvered there, by both Barak and Ross, the meeting only served to deepen Palestinian frustration.

The Palestinians had spent weeks entertaining bland issues like "state-to-state" relations, which didn't define what a Palestinian state would look like but rather how cordial the relations would be, and they were becoming restive. At Eilat, they insisted upon real negotiations, demanding that at least one of the final-status issues be opened for discussion. In an interview with Charles Enderlin, a veteran French journalist based in Jerusalem, Oded Eran recalled the talks, which opened with a Palestinian concession:

> We were having endless discussion on the question of the border between the two states. The Palestinians were saying, "Obviously, in accordance with Resolution 242, it's the line of 1967." I asked them, "And what about Jerusalem? There are large Jewish areas on the other side of the 1967 line." They answered clearly and warmly that those areas could remain under Israeli sovereignty within the framework of an agreement . . .
>
> I went to see Ehud Barak at midnight, in Tel Aviv, to tell him it was time for me to submit a map of the final status to the Palestinians. He agreed, and I was authorized to present a map, without any names whatsoever, dividing the West Bank into three sectors. Sixty-six percent would be immediately transferred to the Palestinians within the framework of the accord, 20 percent would be annexed by Israel, and 14 percent would remain under Israeli control for an indefinite period.[23]

This was even more insulting to the Palestinians than the formula Barak's people had presented to the Americans a few weeks earlier. Instead of moving toward a more realistic territorial proposal, the map Barak approved for Eran demonstrated a retrenchment from his April ideas: He lowered the areas proposed for indefinite Israeli occupation from 22 percent to 14 percent, while raising the areas for Israeli annexation from 12 percent to 20 percent. Despite Shlomo Ben Ami's earlier hope that Barak would not make those "patronizing, wishful-thinking, naive" territorial ideas public, he nevertheless proceeded with it as a trial balloon through Eran; he was not one of Barak's political advisers and therefore could be burned. Needless to say, the proposal to carve the West Bank into Barak's percentages provoked an outburst from Abed Rabbo and Dahlan, who stormed out of the room shouting curses in Hebrew, Arabic, and English.[24] Omar Dajani, one of the Palestinian legal advisers, stayed behind to study the map. He later said, "The map was outrageous, and we were thinking [they] couldn't be serious! All of the Jordan Valley was taken out. There were these massive settlement blocs, like little blue islands—including Hebron! We said, 'You think you're gonna keep Hebron?'"[25]

Perhaps the defining moment of this meeting was the raw display of arrogance by Ross, who fumed about the walkout, pretending to be personally insulted. He then threatened to leave himself.

To be sure, the Palestinians wanted to please President Clinton and thus hoped that with a good report card from Ross, the president's constructive involvement would later materialize. But in their opinion, based on what they saw at Eilat, Ross had only served to act as an extra negotiator for the Israelis and an apologist for Barak's plans to sustain the occupation.

After seven years as the lead Middle East envoy for the United States, Ross was still nowhere near the most basic understanding of what the Palestinians would consider minimally acceptable regarding territory. While the stronger Israelis held a full deck of cards to play (they had been successfully whittling down the 100 percent of West Bank and Gaza Strip territory to accommodate interim obligations), the interim process for Palestinians had thus far meant surrendering their hope on what the Americans, particularly Ross, would manage to get them. As the talks switched from interim to final-status, that model would no longer serve Palestinian needs. As the occupying power with control over the very thing the Palestinians wanted—a state—the Israelis would naturally have to be more forthcoming; this could only occur if the central mediator stood between both parties and demonstrated a willingness to "swing elbows." With

Barak, Ross was unwilling to do this, though even if he had tried it is less than clear it would have worked, especially given the personal relationship between Clinton and Barak and the precedent set by the Syrian track, where Clinton displayed an unwillingness to push the Israeli leader beyond his comfort level. Naturally, the Israeli prime minister felt emboldened to exploit the circumstances. Rather than join the Palestinians and express incredulity at the unrealistic maps Barak presented, Ross wanted to stick to process, still believing he could move the sides closer, using tactics like "conditioning" and "incrementalism" to bring the Palestinians around to Israel's demands. But Ross's model had become obsolete, even dreaded. Martin Indyk gently conceded how the incrementalist approach had expired even before Barak took office:

> You have to remember what the situation was at the time. Both sides had become disillusioned with the incrementalist approach. Dennis Ross's approach—this is not his fault—but Dennis Ross's approach had meant that we spent a year and a half working up the Wye Agreement which was simply an implementation agreement of an agreement that had already been struck. And then instead of being implemented—Bibi's government came down![26]

Even with this poor beginning, the Palestinians proved forthcoming. Arafat had been closely monitoring developments, and he wanted to see if his goodwill would be matched. For starters, as Eran described, the Palestinians recognized the historic Jewish roots in Jerusalem, demonstrating important flexibility toward them by offering to cede some Jewish portions of Jerusalem within the Palestinian areas of the Green Line. But they would also put forward an idea that other Arab states had refused—including Egypt, Jordan, and Syria—by signaling their willingness to consider land swaps. For the first time, the Palestinians entertained the notion of an Israeli annexation of up to 4 percent of the West Bank—provided Israel was willing to exchange land from within its 1967 borders at a one-to-one ratio. Yet for both these important moves, the Palestinians still had nothing to take back to Arafat, save for some promises that the villages would be coming, and Barak's touching commitment that he might someday even allow them a state.

• • •

**The official-channel** FAPS negotiations between Eran and Erekat/Abed Rabbo were all but meaningless. For Palestinians, the map Barak had authorized reflected not intent to reach peace but rather to legitimize the vision of Yigal Allon or of Ariel Sharon, who in 1991 put forward an idea with similar percentages, which would effectively cut the West Bank into three cantons to preserve Jewish settlements.[27] But the failure generated new ideas from Arafat's circle of advisers, led by Abu Mazen, who began to generate steam for resurrecting an approach that had proved integral in concluding the original Oslo Agreement. Unofficial back channels between Israelis and Palestinians who were politically aligned to their respective governments but not official representatives had moved mountains in the past, on both smaller, softer issues as well as in hypothetical discussions over the harder issues of final status, through an informal tactic known in Arab-Israeli diplomatic vernacular as "Track II diplomacy."[28] Clearly Barak was hesitant to deliver final-status ideas through the official "Track I" channels, comprising Israeli Ministry of Foreign Affairs civil servants and Arafat's own hodgepodge; Saeb Erekat was a spokesman who too often gave his feedback to the press, while Abed-Rabbo was less close to Arafat (not even a member of Fatah), and likewise would bloviate in public against Barak, particularly after Eilat.

There was a sense among Palestinians that, after the

unpleasant exchanges at Eilat, more intimacy would be needed to explore these difficult topics, if nothing more than to assuage Barak's political fears while giving both sides the opportunity to tease out ideas with a measure of deniability. Initially, as the Track I FAPS talks were bogged down, Barak had taken a stab at secret Track I diplomacy, by tasking two of his cabinet advisers, Amnon Lipkin-Shahak and Shlomo Ben Ami, to covertly engage two central PLO figures, Abu Mazen and Abu Ala, both of whom were personally close to Arafat.

It was a step in the right direction, but Barak was still unwilling to empower Shahak and Ben Ami with an official mandate. Shahak, a no-nonsense negotiator who was trusted by the Palestinians, was trusted by Barak as well but had also been a political rival (Shahak had been a candidate in the 1999 elections for prime minister). Like Barak, Shahak had an impressive military record. He was unafraid to tell Barak candidly of his displeasure with Barak's handling of the peace process, having done just that in the preceding months of negotiations on the Syria track, and their relations since the failure at Geneva had been tense. Shahak's partner on the Palestinian side was the judicious Abu Mazen, a veteran within the senior core of the PLO leadership who commanded a great deal of respect, including that of Arafat himself, but was nonetheless known for not being afraid to lock horns with Arafat. But in these secret talks, the only test of wills was between Shahak, Abu Mazen, and the Israeli prime minister. After wisely reasoning that Barak was still not comfortable with the secret Track I arrangements, like the Eran/Abed Rabbo talks, Shahak and Abu Mazen united in their refusal to dignify Barak's games. Shahak described the situation:

> He asked Shlomo Ben Ami and myself to go and talk to Abu Mazen and Abu Ala. It seems to me that this dialogue—after three or four meetings—was leading nowhere because there was no agenda on the table. I withdrew from this dialogue.

> Abu Mazen withdrew from the dialogue, and practically the dialogue came to an end. Barak didn't want a team; he wanted one or two persons to continue the dialogue. Shlomo Ben Ami and Abu Ala continued and then Gilead Sher joined Shlomo.[29]

Indeed, after sitting on the sidelines since he helped broker Sharm in September, Gilead Sher was brought back in April, having been assigned an important role in the negotiations as Barak's personal adviser. After being asked to join Ben Ami, Sher describes the scene as he found it, saying, "After the . . . 'general principles' exchange between Amnon Lipkin-Shahak and Shlomo Ben Ami from our side, and Abu Mazen and Abu Ala from the other side, there was a need to establish a more concrete and solution-oriented track, not continue discussing the spheres of general principles and then nothing in concrete terms."[30] With Shahak out of the picture, Barak signaled to Sher that he wanted the secret channels to continue.

Fortunately, the Palestinians had already been thinking more or less along the same lines, albeit through a different approach, and had even taken the initiative so they could begin. Abu Mazen, hoping to replicate the confidential environment of dialogue that had given birth to the original Oslo Agreement and subsequent unofficial discussions, requested the help of the Swedish government in establishing an informal and nonbinding Track II channel.

It began on March 7, 2000, during a meeting in Stockholm between Abu Mazen and Anna Lindh,[31] the gracefully poised Swedish foreign minister who had always extended her strong encouragement to the cause of Middle East peace. From Lindh, Abu Mazen's proposal made its way to Swedish Prime Minister Goran Persson, also a committed peace process supporter. Persson's Chief of Staff, Par Nuder, tells how Abu Mazen had identified "two London-based academics" as his representatives for these talks; when Nuder forwarded this proposal to Barak, the Israeli prime minister insisted on "either 'real' negotiations with Abu Mazen, Abu Ala, or Mohammed Dahlan—or nothing."[32] Barak realized that Abu Mazen's "London-based academics" were a reference to Ahmed Khalidi and Hussein Agha, two Oxford-trained political analysts and Fatah activists with "easy access" to the senior PLO leadership but holding no official status themselves.[33] Abu Mazen had mentored these two before in their Track II discussions with Israeli intellectuals throughout the 1990s.

But Barak's take on Track II was different; he had secretly sent Sher as a non-official to meet with Khalidi and Agha in London back in November 1999, until, by a fluke, their one-day discussions were conjectured by an Israeli journalist, Aluf Benn, resulting in Abu Mazen's cancellation of the channel (Abu Mazen did not want to undercut Abed Rabbo and the official FAPS negotiators). In general, Barak was constitutionally opposed to surrendering control over anything, but ever since the experiment, and given that the negotiations were approaching a later hour, he was hesitant about dealings with non-officials: The last thing Barak wanted was a repetition of the Israeli experience following the 1991 Madrid summit, when his side had been faced with razor-sharp non-official Palestinian negotiators like Hayder Abdel Shafi and Hanan Ashrawi, who had held steady in their demand that discussions be grounded in Resolution 242 and international law.

Nuder promised to make further attempts to convince Barak's office of Abu Mazen's good intentions; he wanted a round of preparatory talks between serious, though unofficial, negotiators on a lower level than his own. According to Nuder, after some delay Barak let him know in early May that the Israelis were ready, "But one thing surprised us: all of a sudden, Abu Mazen and the two Londoners were out of the picture. Instead, the Palestinians would be represented by Abu Ala and Hassan Asfur. Swedish diplomats foresaw problems, especially taking into account the frosty relations between Abu Mazen and Hassan Asfur."[34]

Nuder thought he had succeeded, but at Barak's insistence, the dynamics of Abu Mazen's original Track II concept had morphed into another round of secret Track I. Moreover, the composition of the Palestinian team—without Abu Mazen—was akin to placing a powder keg underneath the volatile intra-PLO rivalries. Like Barak, the disunity within Arafat's own government was almost as volatile.

Asfur had an especially acrimonious relationship with Abu Mazen. Asfur had once been Abu Mazen's chief of staff, but the two had fallen out over issues following the 1998 Wye agreement, which led, at one point, to demonstrations outside Abu Mazen's Gaza Strip villa. Dahlan failed to quell the situation, which included rock-throwing, and Abu Mazen was crestfallen to learn that Asfur was among those leading the crowd. Abu Mazen had not returned to Gaza since that episode, and in the period afterward, anything touched by either Dahlan or Asfur was naturally frustrated by Abu Mazen's spite.[35] Even though Asfur would be paired with Abu Ala, a senior PLO leader who hailed from the same pre-1948 generation as Abu Mazen and Arafat, for Abu Mazen, the very fact that Asfur would be holding potentially binding official, albeit secret, talks over the most sensitive core issues, particularly refugees, was a serious problem.

Once again, Arafat's cultivation of internal rivalries would undermine the very thing he wanted: a serious effort to reach a final-status agreement. The Israelis were aware of these tensions, so they must have felt that the situation could work to their advantage (divide and conquer). Should the talks collapse, it would likely be with the Palestinians falling on their own sword.

• • •

**After several preparatory** sessions in Jerusalem, Shlomo Ben Ami, Gilead Sher, Abu Ala (and his younger son), and Hassan Asfur were spirited to one of Sweden's most secure destinations: the prime minister's official residence in Harpsund.

The negotiators were awestruck by the majestic landscape, with its deep blue lakes and crisp air. The extreme northern latitude facilitated an atmosphere of nonstop negotiations: day became night and night became day, as the sun would set at one in the morning and rise again just an hour later. Moreover, the Swedes would prove to be excellent hosts; they did not seek to insert themselves in the talks, nor did they offer anything more than a venue.

Barak gave a very limited mandate to Ben Ami and Sher, insisting that only the issues of territory, borders, refugees, and security be addressed. Barak insisted that there be no mention of Jerusalem, even though it was a core issue of the conflict inextricably linked to the others.

During their first weekend meetings, May 12–15, the negotiators went first to the issues of territory and refugees, and working out the modalities for how the channel would operate.

On territory, the Israelis tabled a map that, despite its lowballing, was nonetheless an improvement from Eilat. According to descriptions of the figures presented at Harpsund by Ben Ami and Sher, 76.6 percent of the territory would immediately become part of the Palestinian state (up from the Eilat proposal of 66 percent); 10.1 percent would continue to be occupied for a period of twenty years by IDF forces, for "security reasons" (as opposed to the originally suggested 14 percent); while the remaining 13.3 percent would be outright annexed by Israel (down from 20 percent).[36]

Ben Ami, who would later describe the map in misleading percentiles as "12-88," basically used the same calculus as Barak: Notwithstanding Israel's offer of a twenty-year continued military occupation of Palestinian areas, particularly along the Jordan River Valley, and annexation of large swaths of Jewish settlements, particularly Gush Etzion, Ariel, and others in or outside of Jerusalem, the Palestinians would nevertheless have an entity to call a state. According to Ben Ami, at Harpsund the Israelis rejected the breakthrough Palestinian idea of an exchange of territory as earlier suggested in Eilat, insisting that, in his own words, "our concept was that the West Bank and Gaza Strip were the sand table within which all the problems had to be resolved."[37]

For the Palestinians, this was a severe limitation. In their view, they had made their biggest concessions when they agreed in 1988 to accept Resolution 242. By accepting that principle, they had relinquished their claim to 78 percent of historic, pre-1948 Palestine. Negotiations under Oslo had since centered on the remaining 22 percent, based primarily on the cease-fire lines drawn in 1949. From the Palestinian point of view, nearly all of their concessions had been made: they were not about to accept 76 percent of the remaining 22 percent. Abu Ala, ever disbelieving of this offer, even remarked to Ben Ami, "Shlomo, take the map away. *What percentage do you really mean?*"[38]

For both sides, the issue of refugees was equally difficult. In 1948, up to 800,000 Palestinians (about 83 percent of the population then) became refugees at the birth of Jewish state; added by an additional 235,000 Palestinians following the 1967 war.[39] According to statistics by the UN Relief and Works Agency for Palestinian Refugees, a UN organ created to administer basic services to these refugees, there were more than four million Palestinian refugees in 2000, many living in camps in neighboring countries.

Discussions over the fate of refugees touched at the core of the conflict for Israelis and Palestinians alike. For Israelis, any demand for redress was considered an attack on the state's legitimacy. For Palestinians, a refusal to acknowledge the injustice of the 1948 expulsion, and thus the right of return, was considered a rejection of their very identity. Furthermore, it would entail an abrogation of UN General Assembly Resolution 194 of December 1948, an international right providing for their lawful return, which had been reasserted in the UN numerous times by overwhelming majorities, with the United States among them. But as far as the Israelis were concerned, because Egypt, Jordan, Syria, and a quorum of Arab states rejected the UN partition plan of 1947, laid out in Security Council Resolution 181, and then attacked Israel after its declaration of independence in May 1948, Israel was justified in standing up to the international community by refusing to recognize the refugees' right of return.

In Harpsund, after more than a half-century of deadlock, Palestinian delegates listened as—for the first time under an officially held dialogue—Ben Ami and Sher offered Israel's proposed solution: Refugees would be given the option of resettlement in either Arab countries, the proposed Palestinian state, or willing countries outside the Arab world, such as the United States and Canada. The figures to be allowed for "family reunification" to Israel proper were extremely low—according to Ben Ami, just 10,000 to 15,000, and would only be absorbed over a period of many years, subject to Israel's sovereign discretion.[40]

Israel's ideas on both territory and refugees were rejected outright by Abu Ala and Asfur for their inadequacy,[41] but nevertheless, through all the gut-wrenching debates that transpired, after months of delays since Barak had taken office, important taboos were at least being discussed directly by high-level negotiators. Sher, making use of his legal skills, brought important organization to the talks, and began to draft serious "non-papers" as the discussions progressed.

Yet for all the seriousness of these discussions, two developments would seriously hamper their effectiveness. First, the talks were leaked to an Israeli journalist just one day after they commenced. In Palestine, a firestorm of controversy followed, since other Palestinian negotiators in the front channel felt blindsided. Yasser Abed Rabbo took to the airwaves to condemn this external dialogue and promptly tendered his resignation as the lead FAPS negotiator.[42] Criticisms in the Palestinian press began to emerge that these negotiators were selling out on core issues—just as they had done with the original Oslo Accords—drawing the considerable concern of both Abu Ala and Asfur. Gilead Sher recalled the impact this had on everyone, but especially on Abu Ala:

> This leak worried the four of us negotiators, and we started accusing each other. From that moment on, the senior Palestinian negotiator, Abu Ala, practically stopped negotiating [and] became furious, literally feeling a threat to his life. Here you are: you are miles away from home, stuck for the weekend with an angry, senior back-channel negotiator whose identity has been exposed, and you absolutely must produce results, because time is running out.[43]

The natural suspect for the leak, Abu Mazen, had opposed the channel all along, and to this day he draws the strongest suspicion among American and Israeli negotiators, though certainly the leak could have come from others, including Barak's team, either as a result of its own infighting or because of failure to limit the discussions through secure means. Dennis Ross certainly blamed Abu Mazen, but also Arafat, saying, "I'm not persuaded it wasn't Arafat, indirectly. Arafat let others know—including Abu Mazen—because he knew that they would leak it, and I think it sent a message that there wouldn't be a private channel."[44]

The second problem with this first round at Harpsund stemmed circuitously from the decision by Ross to "drop in" on the meeting, and the shift in dialogue promulgated by the conclusions drawn afterward by both him and Miller upon their return to the United States. How the Americans made their way to Harpsund is still unclear, though both sides had provided them with updates on their progress. Why Ross felt his involvement was needed is also unclear. Sher was not opposed to an American visit, but recalled, "It was an American suggestion to spend a couple of hours with us on their way to the region. We didn't really need help then, everything was going just fine."

Upon the May 14 arrival of the five-member U.S. team, including Ross, Miller, Helal, Schwartz, and Malley, Ross asked for an update on the accomplishments, requesting breakout sessions with each of the participants.[45] Everyone was impressed, but more importantly, despite their disagreements in the past, both Ross and Miller were buoyant. Miller explained:

> My role was to assume that now, freed from the Syrian track, we could concentrate on the big thing. That made me incredibly energized. That also made me a victim of my own enthusiasm. What President Clinton should have seen was . . . Mr. President, use every hour of your last months, and you might be able to press on! Instead, we vacillated between August and September [1999]. Interested in low-level negotiations, we shifted to interim agreements—Sharm—then we shifted again to final-status talks and parameters, which was doomed.[46]

Looking back on his brief visit to Harpsund, Miller acknowledged:

> It was a disappointment for the Palestinians, it gave a false sense of confidence to the Israelis, and it was leaked. Some on the U.S. negotiating team mis-analyzed what happened. It gave me a sense of what could happen, and I was wrong. The leaks did not impede the later negotiations.[47]

Optimism over how much the talks had actually progressed was apparently shared by neither Malley nor Helal. Malley commented, "We were not as optimistic—we saw it as an important stage, but not as a breakthrough,"[48] while Helal was more critical:

> The Israelis completely misinterpreted [Harpsund]. They came up with an interpretation that was so rosy, and they wanted to understand only what they wanted to understand.

> They would interpret things in their own way, which had nothing to do with reality, especially with regard to the right-of-return issues.
>
> Arafat or no Arafat, every negotiator will have some limitations in their delegations, because those limitations reflect their wiggle room in Resolutions 242 and 338. Most flexibility shown was on the territorial swap. . . . There was little on the territories, and little on the right of return. At Stockholm, Jerusalem was never discussed because the Israelis were not authorized by Barak. This was because Barak wanted to be politically in a situation to deny that he was talking about Jerusalem. It's stupid to believe they can tackle major issues by not addressing Jerusalem. It was misleading—an absolute delusion—this notion that an Israeli prime minister was going to settle the issue without Jerusalem.[49]

It's uncertain whether the reservations held by Helal or Malley ever surfaced at these discussions or whether they made their way into the official reporting back in Washington. One thing was for certain—the leader of the U.S. team, Dennis Ross, was more than enthused. At a final group meeting before the negotiators were scheduled to depart, Ross said, "During these few days, you guys made the most significant step *ever* toward permanent peace between Israelis and Palestinians."[50] Nuder heard similar feedback from Ross, and recalled the direction it was heading. He commented, "Dennis Ross said to me 'I haven't seen anything as good as this.' Personally I think the bilateral negotiation should have continued longer. *But*—both Shlomo Ben Ami and Abu Ala were under severe domestic pressure from back home after the secret channel was uncovered. My personal impression was that the Israelis and the Americans were much more eager to have a summit than the Palestinians."[51]

From this point forward, the dialogue between Americans

and Israelis over how to make up for the delays and lost time would fundamentally change. As the parties returned to the Middle East on May 15, a day commemorated annually in Palestine as al-Nakba, or "the catastrophe," marking the creation of the State of Israel in 1948 and the birth of the refugee problem, the U.S. and Israeli negotiators were about to witness firsthand how disconnected their formulations were to the Palestinian street, which they had more or less ignored in the preceding months. It was not the first time they made such a miscalculation, nor would it be the last.

• TWELVE •

# The Decision to Go for Broke

ON MAY 15, 2000, Israeli and Palestinian negotiators left Harpsund's placid setting to confront an ugly reality upon their return. The pot of frustration that had been bubbling since Barak took office boiled over in the worst flash of Israeli-Palestinian violence since the "tunnel intifada" of 1996. The spark that ignited these violent clashes—the prisoner issue—was confusing to those not attuned to Palestinian politics. In truth, what triggered the spontaneous mini-uprising that May, later described by Aaron Miller as a "dress rehearsal" for the eruption of the second intifada the following September,[1] was neither conceived in a vacuum nor rehearsed.

Underlying these events was a caustic blend of internal Palestinian conflict combined with street-level anger at Barak's negotiating tricks, particularly on the interim issues, which Arafat appeared to have accepted. The PLO and Fatah—the dominant political bodies that sold the Oslo Accords—had placed their credibility on the line when they assured their constituencies that the best vehicle for achieving Palestinian freedom was peaceful negotiation. Nothing in the preceding years, however, had substantiated their claims, nor did the slow-going final-status talks give even the slightest promise that an acceptable outcome would follow.

Adding to the ugly mood on the Palestinian street were developments in neighboring Lebanon. Barak had planned on a full Israeli withdrawal in July, but he decided to do it sooner, in May. The withdrawal deeply affected grassroots Palestinian activists, who listened to the armed-struggle urgings of Hezbollah Secretary General Sheik Hassan Nasrallah, who in February of that year predicted that the Palestinians could "expect to suffer a disappointment in their negotiations for a permanent status" with Israel.[2] Nasrallah knew how to speak to the hearts of Palestinians, and he could back up his tough talk with action: Hezbollah succeeded in expelling Israel from Lebanon while not once backing down from its strategy of armed struggle or its political demands.

The example of Hezbollah's success proved a weakening factor for Arafat and his PLO/Fatah cronies, who were looking all the more foolish as they continued to defend the strategy of peaceful dialogue. Marwan Barghouti, who aside from Arafat was Fatah's most important West Bank leader—and considered by many to be a potential successor to Arafat in the event of statehood—sought to manage the rising street-level contempt for the Palestinian Authority and for Arafat. Barghouti used the Nakba Day demonstrations both to flex his own street muscle with the dejected Palestinian constituencies and upstage Arafat, and to remind the Israelis that the occupying power could no longer ignore its negotiated commitments (something Arafat would not necessarily have opposed).[3] Between April and May, masses of Palestinians, mostly students, took to the streets to protest Barak's refusal to release prisoners, at times throwing rocks at IDF troops and their fortified positions near West Bank settlements and checkpoints. Barghouti's legions of angry Fatah followers, along with Hamas activists—each seeking to outdo the other—not only threw rocks at IDF soldiers and Jewish settlers traveling on settler access roads but rolled burning tires and heaved Molotov cocktails at IDF fortifications.

On May 15, after weeks of skirmishes and brush-ups with IDF troops, the demos finally came to a head at a hilltop in al-Bireh, just north of Ramallah. It was a scene like so many others in the preceding days, with Israeli troops and Palestinian military policemen staring each other down. Beneath them, the Nakba Day demonstrators raged.[4] The Palestinian security forces, who saw the crowds engaging in what they viewed as legitimate expressions of frustration, watched as IDF troops responded to stones and Molotov cocktails with tear-gas canisters, rubber-coated bullets and, as one *New York Times* reporter observed, live ammunition.[5] The Palestinian policemen faced a dilemma: Should they preserve their own dignity and protect the Palestinian people, or avoid confrontation with the IDF forces, with whom they had for years collaborated but in recent times grown to despise? The outcome was an exchange of gunfire that lasted for hours, making rumors of peacemaking in Sweden sound all the more outlandish.

Barak called Arafat that evening, demanding that he restore calm; similar messages were passed from the White House.[6] Earlier that very day, as it turned out, Barak had finally managed to slip approval for the three village upgrades through the Knesset, with several abstentions from within his coalition, including Shas, despite his proclamations that the village of Abu Dis, not East Jerusalem, would become the future Palestinian capital. Until the eruption of violence, it had looked as though President Clinton would be able to breathe a sigh of relief, having affixed his personal assurances to the March 8 agreement.

The violence in the occupied territories made Barak reconsider. He was encouraged in no small part by the massive televised protests that evening of tens of thousands of right-wing Israelis congregated in Zion Square to listen to the familiar vitriol of Ariel Sharon, who declared, "The government has bowed to the Palestinian rioters. On the day they shoot, it is handing them territory."[7]

Just as Farouk al-Shaara's Blair House speech gave Barak the excuse to escape his Rabin-deposit assurances in the Syria negotiations, so too did the Palestinian demonstrators help Barak evade his March 8 village-upgrade commitment. He told Arafat he was putting the deal on indefinite hold, though given Barak's track record, it is less than likely that either Arafat or Barghouti were completely shocked.

Similar live-fire exchanges took place in the Gaza Strip between demonstrators and IDF forces protecting the perimeter around the Jewish settlement of Netzarim, though the clashes tapered off after several days. The decision by some Palestinian security officers to defend themselves and their people—against IDF troops positioned in occupied Palestinian land—brought home the reality of what might occur should negotiations fail to reach a final-status agreement. More importantly, for those Israelis planning for confrontation, it also renewed a debate over Arafat's ability to control not only the street demonstrators but even his own security establishment. Similar clashes had taken place on Nakba Day in May 1998, in which nine Palestinians were killed. But the May 2000 demonstrations, which left six Palestinians dead and over 1,500 injured, had also managed to inflict pain on the Israelis: Though there were no Israeli fatalities, forty IDF troops were wounded, some from bullets that had traveled down Palestinian barrels of Oslo-provided weapons.

Israeli hostility toward the Palestinians worsened, with supporters of peace feeling betrayed. From the Israeli perspective, their leader was preparing to table an agreement to pave the way for peaceful coexistence, and violence was the thanks they received. The intent of the PA was further called into question, as it appeared the Palestinian security services were unable to deliver on Oslo's requirements by preventing terrorism and other acts of violence; even more alarming, there was strong evidence that at least some personnel directly participated in the gun battles.

Shaul Mofaz, the IDF chief of staff, made a public revelation that same week, candidly disclosing that he had been close to quelling the disorder with U.S.-supplied Apache helicopter gunships, which were armed with missiles and large-caliber uranium-depleted rounds.[8] Such an asymmetrical escalation might have prematurely ended the negotiations at that point. But Mofaz's bellicosity expressed tensions throughout the IDF, which was increasingly fearful that war—not peace—was around the corner, and that spontaneous violence would erupt not only in the occupied territories but also along Israel's northern flank in the wake of Barak's withdrawal from Lebanon.

At an April 27 briefing on the Lebanon withdrawal, both the head of IDF military intelligence, Major General Amos Malka, and the head of the IDF Intelligence Research Division, Brigadier General Amos Gilad, gave Barak an apocalyptic report. They believed terror attacks would only increase should he withdraw from Lebanon, particularly in the absence of a negotiated agreement with Syria. Mofaz backed these assessments, likewise fearing a wider confrontation, perhaps with Syria.[9] But they were unable to convince Barak to change his mind; he had already earned the important support of President Clinton and Secretary Albright, who were working hard on his behalf to rally international support and hoping to get the withdrawal out of the way in order to focus on the Palestinian track. Barak was fearful that Hezbollah might prove the IDF predictions correct, but given his own tattered political standing, he decided that keeping his campaign promise was more important. The IDF assessments were naturally reported in the Israeli media, causing considerable alarm. But public sentiment was tilted the other way; indeed, it had been building ever since a rash of Israeli military casualities in 1997, when a helicopter accident killed seventy-three IDF soldiers, followed months afterward by the deaths of eleven elite commandos during a naval raid in a Lebanese town. A large movement lobbying for Israeli withdrawal, called the "Four Mothers," emerged afterward; its dedicated membership included the parents of IDF soldiers stationed in Lebanon.

Had the Lebanon withdrawal taken place at another time—especially after a conclusive deal with either Syria or the Palestinians—and with careful planning, there is little doubt it would have been seen as both a strengthening of Israel's strategic interests and a contribution to the lessening of regional tensions. Instead, in the immediate aftermath of the disastrous failure of the Syrian track and with limited time remaining to conclude a final-status settlement with the Palestinians, the withdrawal sent ripples through the regional power balance, further destabilizing Arafat's political standing.

In the week preceding the withdrawal, the IDF had to deal with innumerable logistical challenges. There was manpower to return, of course, and equipment to either remove or destroy. But perhaps the most difficult problem was how to deal with the transfer of power or possible decommissioning of the South Lebanon Army (SLA), a 6,500 member force composed predominantly of Lebanese Christians co-opted by the Israelis in the 1970s to fight the PLO and, later, to help maintain Israel's occupation while fighting Hezbollah. Initially, the IDF planned to hand over to the SLA the military outposts in its 440 square-mile "security zone." But ten days before, Sheik Nasrallah threatened to unleash his organization on the SLA and "enter every agent's home and slaughter him in his bed."[10]

On May 20, the IDF nevertheless pulled out.[11] But the following day, unorganized masses of Lebanese civilians unexpectedly descended on the SLA positions. Unwilling to use force to push the demonstrators back, the SLA folded, making a hasty retreat to the Israeli border crossing. Hezbollah seized the moment, and organized even larger masses to push deeper toward the Israeli border, overrunning the remaining SLA/Israeli positions and firing weapons on the last waves of retreating forces. The IDF, under Barak's close supervision from a nearby post in northern Israel, offered a relatively gentle response, no doubt seeking merely to prevent Hezbollah's advance from reaching Israel proper.

Though Hezbollah failed to produce IDF casualties, the televised images of national celebration in Lebanon, coupled with the accelerated IDF retreat and the long lines of over 6,000 SLA refugees and their families seeking refuge in Israel, heightened the controversy there. At least one major newspaper carried the headline "Day of Humiliation" in reference to the impetuously executed withdrawal, while the right wing assailed Barak for "running away" and displaying weakness.[12] The sentiment of most Israelis—one poll indicated that 75 percent approved the withdrawal—was that Barak had put an end to a quagmire that had become Israel's Vietnam.[13]

At least momentarily, Barak was able to bask in the satisfaction of having fulfilled a major campaign promise. But in the aftermath of the withdrawal, the response of both the Palestinian street and the Israeli military were a matter of concern for both the CIA and State Department officials closely monitoring the scene.[14] Palestinians celebrating the withdrawal took to the streets in Gaza; some placards read, "Lebanon Today, Palestine Tomorrow!" Toni Verstandig laments the impact it had for IDF troops who continued to pull duty in the Palestinian territories:

> The Palestinians, and, ironically, enough of the Israeli military were both adversely affected by that withdrawal. The Israeli military saw their military leave with their heads lowered, and the Palestinians said, "Wait a minute, Hezbollah got everything they wanted without negotiating an inch, and we don't have the June 4, 1967 borders—we have 80 percent of a West Bank that is carved up . . ."[15]

Verstandig concluded that the Lebanon withdrawal was "a very negative factor" that would influence the debate over whether or not Clinton should bring Barak and Arafat together for a summit—if only in order to ease the threat of further violence.

• • •

**The negotiations in** Harpsund briefly restarted, but after cycling through six draft non-papers, Ben Ami and Sher were still unable to offer compromises that came anywhere close to what the Palestinians had envisioned. The Israelis, for their part, rejected the Palestinian proposal to allow Israeli retention of settlement blocs in exchange for swaps of land from Israel proper. As for Jerusalem, Barak so strictly forbade discussion of it that when he discovered Ben Ami and Sher had left the "Jerusalem" clause blank on the last draft non-paper, he ordered its removal, revealing his anxiety over even a reference to the word.[16] (A high-level non-U.S. diplomat present at the talks subsequently told me that in sidebar discussions neither the Palestinians nor the Israelis would accept the other's sovereignty over the Temple Mount/Haram al-Sharif. But the sides did agree that Jewish neighborhoods in Jerusalem could remain under Israeli sovereignty and Arab neighborhoods under Palestinian sovereignty.)

Both sides, no longer having the secrecy they so badly needed, and facing intense domestic scrutiny following the leak about a secret channel, agreed to take the Swedish channel back to the Middle East. There were additional meetings, the last one held in Tel Aviv in mid-June, but once it became clear to the Israelis that they had exhausted Barak's mandates—both sides twiddled their thumbs while exchanging family stories—it came to an end.

The blowback from the Swedish channel leak would continue to frustrate discussions; after ineffectually dancing around the complicated Jerusalem issue, phantom reports surfaced in the Israeli and Arab media, prompting belligerent avowals from both sides, with the Israelis asserting that Jerusalem is "the most red of the red lines" that Barak "won't cross," and Arafat petulantly responding that "Jerusalem is the single most important element . . . and Jerusalem will be the capital of the Palestinians state whether they like it or not. And if they don't, they can drink from the Dead Sea!"[17]

In Israel, media leaks alleged that the negotiators in Sweden had been willing to divide Jerusalem, which Barak denied, while rumors of a possible withdrawal ranging from 66-95 percent of the territories sent Jewish settler groups into a rage. At least one of the settler leaders threatened Barak's assassination should he agree to evacuate settlements.[18] Rabin's violent death was once again projected onto Barak, who discounted his own safety even as Israeli security beefed up its protection.

At the same time that Barak was outwardly proclaiming Israel's strong desire for peaceful coexistence and a negotiated solution, he was listening to the military's insistence that he plan for a unilateral disengagement from the Palestinians, whereby IDF forces would reposition themselves around Jewish settlements to create new "defensive" borders. The chief advocate of this military strategy was IDF Deputy Chief of Staff Uzi Dayan, who urged Barak to consider the disengagement route as "a safety net to Camp David." He describes the exchanges he had with Barak:

> I asked him, "What are we going to do if we fail to reach an agreement at Camp David?" I asked him whether he was certain or sure that he's going to reach an agreement, and he said, "No, I don't know." . . . He was very confident that if there was no agreement, the Israelis would understand that we walked the extra mile, with everything possible. I said, "Look, don't think that the rabbits in this laboratory will be so appeased when the experiment succeeds but the whole laboratory goes into flames." And then we started to work out

> unilateral disengagement. And I said, "OK, if we can't achieve such an agreement, let's go and do what is good for Israel and the whole region and let's disengage from the Palestinians even if we don't have a partner.[19]

Thus, Dayan (the nephew of legendary Israeli Defense Minister Moshe Dayan), working together with Barak's Deputy Defense Minister, Ephraim Sneh, formed committees to explore contingency plans, which entailed confronting the innumerable logistical, legal, and foreign policy challenges in the event a summit failed, or if the Palestinians issued a unilateral declaration of independence that September. The Israelis knew the United States would object to the latter move. But they deeply feared that the international community, where Israel was highly unpopular, might immediately recognize Palestinian statehood. So, in addition to preparing for an Israeli-Palestinian summit, members of Barak's government, including Gilead Sher, began to take part in the Defense Ministry's secret planning.[20]

• • •

**By June 2000,** the Clinton administration was facing a crossroads in the negotiations. For Arafat, the turn of events in Lebanon would place a new strain on his ability to negotiate on the final-status front. He needed Barak's fulfillment on the interim issues to raise his credibility; his negotiators would be seen as weak if they entertained any further final-status compromises. Clinton, who had given his word to Arafat that Barak would fulfill his obligations, risked damaging his own standing with the Palestinians. Clinton understood that if the stalemate continued any longer, he would miss the opportunity of concluding a deal before the end of his presidency.

Barak appeared to have little difficulty convincing the United States that fulfillment on the turnover of villages might undo his coalition and end the peace process. At least one senior Israeli negotiator close to Barak did not share this assessment, noting that the village transfer "had been an ordeal anyway" and it was "a mistake for Barak not to do so . . . politically, he could have done it." Further strengthening Barak's plans to renege on his interim obligations was the upcoming June 23 date for completing the Third FRD, which he likewise defended breaching on the grounds that it would be political suicide if he carried it out. Barak was increasingly urging Clinton to convene a summit, where all the issues could be resolved. Barak began building his case with Washington, telling U.S. officials that the Palestinians "had not moved an inch" even as "his negotiators reached the end of their compromises."[21]

The Nakba Day demonstrations confirmed the sense among all camps that the issues would need to be resolved soon. This sentiment was buttressed all the more by the U.S. media, which had been taking a keener interest in the status of negotiations. Increasingly, the media began to portray a Camp David-style summit as the remedy to all Arafat's accumulating grievances with Barak.

At least to some extent, it appeared that Clinton bought into this rhetoric, which Barak clearly wanted. The United States slowly began to accede to Barak's scheme of dismissing outright the interim obligations in order to launch straight into a comprehensive deal. On June 1, following a short meeting with Barak in Portugal, Clinton went so far as to say, "This is tough work. But, actually, it is within view now." In truth, however, the administration fully understood the huge gaps between the sides. Unable to bring them any closer through direct dialogue—Arafat wouldn't budge without Barak's fulfillment of the interim agreements, while Barak sought to push it all to the side—Clinton decided to go with Barak's summit designs, and would spend the remainder of the month cajoling the Palestinians to agree.

Albright visited Arafat and Barak in early June, making little progress. Days later, on June 10, news from Damascus of the death of Hafez al-Assad from natural causes meant the

Israeli-Syrian track would not be restarted until his son, Bashar al-Assad, had time to establish himself, which everyone predicted would take many months, if not years. American diplomatic energy would be focused on deciding whom to send to the funeral; even though Clinton had attended the funeral of a former Japanese prime minister a week earlier, he awkwardly sent Albright in his stead.

• • •

**With few alternatives,** the front-channel FAPS negotiators convened on June 12 at Andrews Air Force Base in Maryland. This time, the Palestinian delegation was more unified—Abu Ala and Asfur were joined by Erekat, Dahlan, and Mohammed Rashid. But because Barak was still unwilling to comply with his obligations regarding the three villages, the prisoners, and the Wye River Third FRD that he'd promised a year earlier, Arafat ordered the delegation to discuss nothing other than the "generics," linking Barak's fulfillment of these to the final-status issues, which the United States clearly wanted to explore further.[22] In reaction to the deadlock, Aaron Miller briefed the Israelis, pointing out the following:

> The president is going to offer Arafat two options: directly negotiate the framework accord or the third redeployment—that is, a new interim accord.
>
> If Arafat chooses this latter option, the president will lose interest in it. Bill Clinton is approaching the end of his presidency, and he isn't going to waste his prestige and his time negotiating an interim accord. If Arafat decides to go ahead in the direction of the framework accord, then the president will commit himself to the negotiations.[23]

The United States had hoped Barak would come through with a badly needed confidence-building measure—fulfillment of Israel's Sharm obligations—to remove at least one legitimate complaint Arafat was sure to raise in his upcoming White House meeting. Should that occur, they were gaming, Arafat might be more willing to appear at a summit, perhaps even tolerating Barak's plans to dismiss the Third FRD the following week, which everyone but the Palestinians expected.

But Barak, appearing to sense that Clinton, too, was interested in holding a summit, had something else in mind. One the eve of Arafat's visit, the Palestinians received more insults: Barak announced he would release just three prisoners out of the remaining 250, while he confirmed his intention to breach Israel's Third FRD commitment, which the United States had painfully extracted from Netanyahu at Wye River in 1998. The Palestinians reacted with outrage. In a CNN media interview, Erekat said, "We will not allow its delay for even one minute," while in response to the prisoner hoax, which Barak had spun as "goodwill gestures," Erekat steamed, "We don't want goodwill gestures from the Israelis! All we want from Israel is to implement the agreements. They can keep their goodwill gestures for themselves!"[24]

On June 15, Arafat arrived in Washington in an especially bitter mood—certainly not with the disposition any president would have liked, given Barak's momentous request to bring all parties to a summit, which the Palestinians felt was far too premature. At a White House press conference before adjourning inside, Clinton told reporters, "I want to finish the job, and I'd like to see it finished on time." Not surprisingly, once the parties—which included Arafat, Erekat, Clinton, and Berger—were alone, the Palestinians opened up with their many grievances, which Clinton appeared to understand and share. Arafat is reported to have told Clinton the following:

> Mr. President, no negotiation can succeed without total adherence to the agreements already concluded. This is why I'm reminding you of the importance of the third

> redeployment, which, I may add, is mentioned in all the agreements reached up to now, agreements you countersigned [as witness]. . . . In these circumstances, what the Israelis want to negotiate with me in the framework of the permanent status isn't in accordance with the agreements. That's bad faith on their part. . . .

Arafat then laid out for Clinton his own forthcoming ideas for bridging the final-status gaps: that Jerusalem had to be the capital of two states, and that he was willing to discuss the idea of an open city. With regard to the question of territory, Resolution 242 and, thus, the 1967 line had to be the basis of discussions, though the Palestinians were certainly willing to discuss minor alterations. He continued:

> On the refugee issue, yes, there's Resolution 194, but we have to find a happy medium between the Israelis' demographic worries and our own concerns. . . .
>
> With regard to settlements, you are aware, Mr. President, of their destructive influence on the peace process (you've said that yourself), especially around Jerusalem and Bethlehem. For the Palestinians, the fact that the settlement policy as a fait accompli is still continuing means there's no more hope. It poisons the peace process. Mr. President, the settlements are at the root of the whole problem. . . .
>
> I think Barak has decided to put us in the position of the guilty party, and I need your promise that, wherever we go with the negotiations, you won't shift the blame for failure onto us and won't back us into a corner.

Clinton then made an important promise which he would later break, saying, "I promise you that under no circumstances will I place the blame for failure on you."[25]

Shortly afterward, Ross joined Clinton and Arafat in the

Oval Office, where yet another negative exchange took place—in the presence of the president—between an Arab leader and Ross. After accusing Ross of always taking Barak's side, Arafat was finally convinced to continue FAPS talks a few weeks longer, on the basis that if they didn't succeed Clinton would support a significant FRD. And the president once again promised Arafat—without any caveat or qualification, according to Malley, who was also present—that the Palestinians wouldn't be blamed if a summit failed.[26]

• • •

**That summer, the** deep disdain for Ross on the part of the Palestinians was no longer a matter of speculation within the Clinton administration. The president, through Secretary Albright, had to put forward a response to an explosive Congressional bill, known as the "Jerusalem Embassy Act of 1995," which sought to move the U.S. Embassy in Israel from Tel Aviv to Jerusalem, hence giving the latter official U.S. recognition as the Israeli capital. To be sure, such an act would have seriously undermined negotiations at this most critical juncture, not the least because it would accept Israel's unilateral annexation of Jerusalem following the 1967 war, which had since been declared illegal by a large majority of countries, including the United States.

Up to that point, Clinton had issued multiple executive waivers to keep the act at bay. The State Department had routinely argued the necessity of the waiver before Congress, on the grounds that compliance would pose a threat to U.S. national security interests vis-à-vis the ongoing Middle East peace process. In late 1999, when Congress tried to insert language to revise the act in order to eliminate Clinton's waiver authority, it was Ross who led the charge the other way.[27] Ross was furious to discover that Sandy Berger had been managing the politically dicey issue directly with Congress and the pro-Israeli lobby groups, including

AIPAC, without first seeking his blessing, and he sought to convince his colleagues otherwise.

The consensus within the State Department to oppose the legislation was strong—even Martin Indyk felt it was a bad idea—but Ross, whose son had been working as an intern for Al Gore's future running mate, Senator Joe Lieberman, a co-sponsor of the act, nevertheless forged ahead against the wishes of the president, even commenting at one meeting with words to the effect of, "If the two sides can work other things out, I just don't see why we can't move the embassy to Jerusalem." One State official who was present during the awkward moment recalls how "jaws dropped in the room," after which he was harshly criticized. Ross, who reacted with eye-rolling arrogance, acted unimpressed with the opinions until Jon Schwartz, using his sharp legal wit, quickly took him to task.[28] Ross was clearly outmatched and, to his own chagrin, President Clinton pressed ahead with the waiver, issuing it again on June 18, 2000.

The damage to Ross's reputation was no longer confined to Foggy Bottom's inner corridors. These internal workings were not known to the Palestinians, but as discussions over a summit progressed, they converged with multiple Palestinian expressions of a loss of confidence in Ross, citing a variety of reasons to almost anyone who would listen, including Congressional staffers and other State Department officials.[29] It was later reported that Arafat raised this issue directly with Clinton himself before the Camp David summit, asking that he no longer employ Ross as U.S. mediator.[30]

• • •

**As Arafat left** the White House, a swarm of journalists recorded his gloomy assessment, "Mr. Barak, up to this moment, lacks a desire to work with us in order to achieve a comprehensive lasting peace in the region." In response to Barak's decision to release only three prisoners, Arafat exclaimed, "That's an insult!"

After Arafat's meeting earlier that day, Ben Ami, Sher, and his young legal assistant, Gidi Grinstein, were received at the White House by Sandy Berger for consultations. Berger, whom they observed to be especially influential with Clinton, laid out the conditions under which the United States would call a summit, which they would report back home to Barak. Sher related:

> I met with Sandy Berger . . . he's a brilliant chap . . . far more brilliant than all the rest of the group. Really someone who was . . . very close to the president personally, he was a friend. Intelligent. Not afraid of saying what he thought, both to Barak and to Arafat.
>
> I reported to him the outcome of the Swedish track in the context of the Israeli government desire to see a summit taking place during the summer, before the air expires. And I remember Sandy telling me, "Listen, Gilead. There's only *one* condition for a summit to take place and for me to go to the president and tell him, 'Summon the parties!' And this is that I would be affirmatively convinced that this summit will succeed eventually. . . . I don't need guarantees. Yes, I need you to concede a couple of things, to do some confidence-building measures, et cetera. But once I am convinced that there is good chance—no, not good chance, that this summit won't fail—I will go to the president and ask him to summon the parties."[31]

As they joined the departing Palestinian delegation at Andrews Air Force Base, where Arafat was waiting for his plane (which the air force had grounded due to a fierce lightning storm), Shlomo Ben Ami would have some extra time to go over Barak's positions with Arafat. But the

Palestinian leader, fed up with Barak's political moves, was only interested in getting on board his plane. After shouting complaints to virtually every aide within earshot, he found solace in a nearby VIP lounge, where he sat slumped on a couch, oblivious to the commercial on a big-screen television booming some prophetic hip-hop lyrics, "It takes two to make a thing go right!"

• • •

**In the wake** of Arafat's meeting with Clinton and further Barak/Clinton telephone conversations, U.S. negotiators decided to try to rebuild trust between Arafat and Barak. In order to give shuttle diplomacy one last chance, President Clinton dispatched Albright to the region in order gauge how bilateral discussions were progressing. In the interim, both Ben Ami and Sher, convinced that Arafat was not adequately informed on the progress they believed was made in Sweden, which he termed the "bad channel" instead of the back channel, decided to offer him a personal briefing.

On June 25, a dinner was arranged for them at a home in Nablus, where Arafat was joined by his senior advisers, including Erekat, Abu Mazen, and Abu Ala. Arafat listened to their presentation, pointing out the bothersome gaps on both the refugee and Jerusalem issues, and stressing the need for more preparation.[32] He would at least make one formal concession to the Israelis that they could report back to Barak, putting forth his agreement to concede some areas of Jerusalem to the Jewish state. According to Ben Ami's version of the Nablus meeting:

> The only thing was a promise Arafat gave us, that the Western Wall and Jewish Quarter were ours. He talked at length about how he remembered himself playing with Jewish children by the Western Wall in the 1930s, so he knows that the Wall is ours.

> But on the question of refugees, there was something of a regression in the period between Stockholm and Camp David. Abu Mazen persuaded Abu Ala not to get into any discussion of numbers, but to stick to the principle of right of return.[33]

On June 27, Albright arrived in Jerusalem following an exhausting spree through European and Asian capitals, only to become a witness to more of Barak's unfolding domestic troubles. His failure to consult with his own cabinet over the projected final-status offers finally caught up with him, accelerating the disintegration of his coalition as rumors of a summit spread. Both the National Religious Party and Yisrael Ba'Aliya threatened to quit. Feeling kept in the dark, and with fears that a summit would fail, Natan Sharansky delivered Barak a letter on June 23, spelling out his intention to leave the coalition. Years later, an impassioned Sharansky maintained he was right:

> He proposed me to go with him. Instead of this, I gave him the letter about my resignation. And I told him, "Ehud, Ehud! There is absolutely no chance that you will bring us peace. You will bring us war—you will see! You will bring us war by your proposals!"[34]

Barak's political morass only seemed to deepen upon Albright's June 27 arrival. Before meeting with her, David Levy, leader of the two-seat Gesher Party, went public with his opposition to Barak's summit designs. Ironically, Levy expressed an apprehension similar to that of the Palestinians; that is, he believed the summit would fail, but Israel would catch all the blame:

> The talks with the Palestinians did not achieve any breakthrough. Israel gave a lot without receiving anything in exchange because of the way the negotiations were handled.

> We are in such a situation that should a summit be held, Israel would be asked for 90 percent of the West Bank and if we did not agree, we would be blamed for failure.[35]

After a perfunctory visit with Barak the following day, Albright reiterated to journalists that in any case, the call for a summit would be neither Barak's nor Arafat's to make. President Clinton would decide the issue after taking into consideration Albright's findings when she returned to Washington.[36]

With this dismal beginning, Albright arrived in Ramallah, perhaps hoping to receive some grain of optimism. But upon arriving at the Muqata, Arafat's official headquarters and residence, she got only more disappointment. The Palestinians were still enraged over Barak's various breaches and wanted nothing to do with a hurried-up summit, which they sensed Barak was plotting in order to blame them. Nabil Shaath recalled Arafat's discussions with Albright:

> She first tried to persuade President Arafat that the best course is to go to the summit and try to utilize the interest and the presence of the president of the United States to achieve success. President Arafat succeeded in convincing her that time is needed to prepare for a summit. President Arafat at first thought that we needed a couple of months of intensive effort, and then he said, "OK, maybe two weeks. And during these two weeks we'll really make an effort at getting preparation and covering some topics so that we won't start from zero and we'll have a better chance of success." Albright accepted and she said that she was going to persuade the president on the next day to follow that course.[37]

Dahlan and Erekat, also in attendance, both separately stated that they felt Albright had been convinced of the poor situation on the ground, and that the timing wasn't right to invite the parties to a Camp David summit. Erekat described how he succeeded in convincing Ross, who accompanied Albright, that more time was needed for preparation:

> The agreement we reached was that the summit was premature and that we needed three to four weeks for further negotiations. And it was agreed...to begin no later than the third or fourth of July . . . a pre-negotiation to the summit. We were going to try to do it in Washington.[38]

While Albright and Arafat were meeting inside, news emerged that Barak had gone public with a reaffirmation of his "four no's," his red lines on all the core issues. After the meeting, Albright and Arafat stepped outside into the dusty afternoon breeze, where reporters and news crews jostled each other to see if a summit would be announced. Naturally, a reporter asked for Albright's reaction to Barak's latest démarche, which she deflected. Arafat, however, appeared to be nearing the melting point; he remonstrated as if addressing the entire world, "Why did he fully implement 425 in South Lebanon? And why did he implement 242 on the Egyptian track and on the Jordanian track? Even on the Syrian track there was an agreement related to the return of all the land and the removal of the settlements!"

Albright returned to Jerusalem for a final press conference with Barak before returning home. Tuned in to their television sets, the Palestinians watched as Barak promised reporters that "the substantial negotiations will begin only if and when there will be a summit meeting." For Palestinians, that meant pre-negotiation of the core issues were off the table, which they felt had been agreed to hours earlier. Moreover, it meant that a summit was sure to be called, despite Arafat's appeals to the contrary, since the Clinton administration was unlikely to turn its back on Barak's "substantial negotiations" pledge. Once again, Washington had double-crossed the Palestinians. Albright explained:

> There was no question that Barak wanted a summit. We were running out of time. There we were in the summer and we were all going to be out of office. And Barak kept thinking that we had done as much as we could in the various back-channel things and various other meetings and it was essential to have a summit for the same reason it was with Asad—you know, we needed "the pressure of a summit" to get it done.
>
> There is also no question that Arafat did not want a summit. And partially he did not want a summit because he was fed up with the amount of time that had been lost over going the Syrian track, you know, you had been "slow-slow, now you are rush-rush." He was just objecting on the basic fact that he wasn't in charge of the schedule.
>
> I think that we all came down to the fact that we understood that there was a risk in having the summit, but that it was very hard to say no to an Israeli Prime Minister who wanted to make peace and that there was not a lot of other time to have it. So, I went along with it . . .[39]

Before departing Israel, the U.S. delegation was at least kind enough to send a heads-up to the Muqata, which Arafat's closest aide and confidant, Nabil Abu Rudeineh, described, saying, "They went to meet Barak, and they phoned us from the airport telling us that Barak 'needs a summit right now, without preparation,' adding 'we'll solve everything there at Camp David.'"[40]

Ross would later assail the merits of the Palestinian claims that more time was needed for preparation. He dismissed this argument, based on his own understanding of Arafat:

> This is part of the revisionism; part of the mythology that he needed time. If he was going to use the time, that's fine, he needed time. But he wasn't going to use the time! His mind worked in terms of September 13, which was the Sharm

> Agreement a year before, which had designated as a target date for reaching a permanent-status agreement. No way he thought he was going to have to make decisions two months before that. This is a guy who, whenever he makes a decision, he doesn't like to make decisions! He . . . he's a decision *avoider*; he's not a decision *maker*. So when is he going to make a decision? He's going to make a decision one second to midnight. And we weren't at one second to midnight! In his mind it was about five in the evening. Why would he make a decision then?[41]

• • •

**Over the Fourth** of July weekend, Clinton convened his advisers at Camp David, where he bunkered down to make one of the most important decisions of his presidency. As an outgoing president, he did not want to be remembered for brokering a string of close calls or summit failures. Both he and Barak were seeking advancement to the Super Bowl of summits, yet the fumbling of his teammate, Barak, at the earlier Shepherdstown and Geneva summits had thus far created a disappointing 0-2 record.

There were many factors to consider. Clinton surely had an appreciation of the importance of publicly preparing constituencies prior to tabling any political item. As he evaluated the odds of success, he could have clearly deduced that in the previous months Barak had only hardened his positions in public. The Palestinians, because of all the disappointments of the Oslo period, and because of Arafat's foul mood resulting from Barak's recent breaches, were both unwilling and unable to discuss more compromises. They continued to hold to maximalist positions.

The media's portrayal of the issues at stake, often in flashy soundbites or glib newspaper editorials, bore directly on the mood of the U.S. public—the guide of any politician, most certainly Clinton. As the discussions over a summit began to increase, the media spin accelerated. There was no greater advocate of holding a Camp David summit than influential *New York Times* columnist and Middle East specialist Thomas Friedman, who implored the Clinton administration to do just that throughout May and June, even conjecturing what he believed the parties surely knew a final offer would look like. On May 2, Friedman wrote:

> Don't kid yourself—we're approaching the moment of truth here, and for both Israelis and Palestinians it could be a moment of civil war.
>
> . . . Israelis and Palestinians know exactly what the outlines of their deal will be: The Palestinians will get back 90 percent of the West Bank and Gaza for their own state, and Israel will keep 10 percent—the 10 percent of the West Bank where 80 percent of the Israeli settlers live.
>
> Mr. Barak is also moving toward giving Yasir Arafat, the Palestinian leader, full control of the Palestinian village of Abu Dis, which is just outside the boundary of Jerusalem and could serve as the foundation for the Palestinians' own capital in the Jerusalem area—without Israel's having to redivide the city in any way. That means preparing Palestinians for . . . having their own Jerusalem—which they can call by Jerusalem's Arabic name, Al Quds—in Abu Dis, rather than in the old, eastern half of the city.
>
> This is not a test. This is the real deal. Completing it and implementing it are going to be wrenching experiences for both societies. Not doing so will be a disaster.[42]

Friedman, a Pulitzer Prize-winning journalist with years of experience in the Middle East, was highly regarded, particularly because of the relationships he had forged with politicians and diplomats in the region. He also had access to many members of the Clinton administration, and is close personal friends with both Miller and Ross, having founded with the latter a conservative synagogue, Kol Shalom, near their Bethesda, Maryland, residences. On May 23, as the talks in Stockholm concluded, Friedman laid out Barak's strictures as the only reasonable, sane solution. Couched in middle-of-the-road reasonableness, Friedman wrote:

> So many Israelis are shocked at news leaks suggesting that a final deal with the Palestinians will require Israel to give up 90 to 92 percent of the West Bank, not 60 or 75, which was the working assumption all these years. Many Israelis are going to be shocked to hear that despite their insistence on retaining a united Jerusalem, the Palestinians will have their own administrative capital on the outskirts, in Abu Dis, with some access to and oversight of Palestinian areas in East Jerusalem.
>
> As for the Palestinians, after 30 years of declaring that they will not cede to Israel one inch of the West Bank, they will be ceding 8 to 10 percent, on which 80 percent of the Jewish settlers live; Jerusalem will remain the unified capital of Israel, and, while there will be a symbolic return of some Palestinian refugees to pre-1967 Israel, it will only be symbolic. . . . Without these compromises, there will be no deal.[43]

Friedman was not alone in purveying extremely misleading and dangerous information and, not incidentally, setting up the Palestinians for blame if they rejected these "reasonable" parameters. Many U.S. journalists, such as columnist Jim Hoagland, opined that peace would come only if the Palestinians abandoned Resolution 242. He wrote, "A true peace agreement will not resurrect June 4, 1967. It will bury that date by reflecting all that has changed since."[44] Apparently lost on Hoagland was the irony of his demand that the Palestinians now dismiss the same UN resolution Washington had insisted for years the PLO publicly affirm before the United States would agree to negotiate with the organization. Hoagland's phrase about "all that has changed since" was clearly a code word for what the United States wanted the Palestinians to accept, to allow for Barak's plans to annex large West Bank settlements, which official U.S. policy had all along officially condemned but silently tolerated.

Given that the venue of the summit was in the United States, in the weeks leading up to it the United States became a public relations battleground for Barak, as right-wing American Jewish groups were already operating full throttle, with full-page ads criticizing Barak's negotiating outlines.[45] For his part, Barak understood that the support of the American Jewish community was central to his ability to reach an agreement or, in the event of a summit failure, shield Israel from criticism.

Barak deputized Yossi Alpher, a former Mossad officer and Oslo supporter, to work with Yoram Ben-Zeev, a Foreign Ministry official serving as deputy director of North American affairs, in order to rally American Jewish support. Alpher says he traveled to major U.S. cities, helping to "write the next day's editorial in the main newspaper, welcoming Israelis and Palestinians to Camp David and wishing them success." Moreover, he met with hard-line Jews who, in Alpher's view, "tended as a matter of course to be more hawkish on Israel's behalf than Israelis were." Among them was Richard Perle, a close adviser to presidential candidate George W. Bush. Perle promised Alpher that "no peace agreement would be acceptable if Barak gave Arafat a foothold in Jerusalem" and that if such a settlement came to pass he would "personally advise Bush to condemn the agreement."[46] As the summit got under way, the Bush campaign would distance itself from Perle's comment, which Perle insisted was only "made in passing." Through reporters, Bush offered Clinton his "best" as he tried to broker Middle East peace.[47]

On the eve of Clinton's decision to call a summit, Friedman, in his typically punchy style, penned one last op-ed to sum up his views:

> This is the season for deciding, and President Clinton should usher it in by summoning the Israeli and Palestinian leaders to Camp David for one last cards-on-the-table, in-your-face, put-up-or-shut-up summit to finally, finally put an end to this conflict.
>
> There is only one way to find out whether that chasm can ever be bridged, and that is by bringing together a U.S. president like Bill Clinton, who is trusted by all the parties; an Israeli leader like Ehud Barak, who understands what Israel will have to give for a secure peace; and Yasir Arafat, who has the stature, the interest in his dying days, to make the hard concessions for his own people. If these three leaders can't close the deal, no one can, and we need to know that now.
>
> You can have it now or after a lot more bloodshed, but it's not going to change. So let's try now. If you summon them, they will come; if they come, they will compromise; if they compromise enough—maybe you'll have a deal. The only people who would criticize Bill Clinton for trying and failing would be those who either don't want a deal or hate him to begin with. . . . So just do it.[48]

• • •

**"Going for broke"** became the catchphrase used to describe Clinton's call to convene Camp David II. Nothing could have been more ill suited, given the risks of failure. As the past four years have tragically demonstrated, both Palestinians and Israelis had an enormous amount to lose. There was also much at stake for both Clinton, in terms of his legacy, and, far more importantly, the future of U.S. national security interests throughout the Arab and Muslim world. Failure could have ominous consequences, given the rising popularity of terrorist groups such as al-Qaeda, which frequently railed against the United States for, among other reasons, its bias toward Israel and disregard for the interests of Palestinians.

Richard Clarke, who served as a special assistant to President Clinton as the National Security Council's national coordinator for security and counterterrorism, revealed in his controversial 2004 memoirs that an Israeli-Palestinian agreement had become the "one last major national security initiative" for the NSC, since "if we could achieve a Middle East peace, much of the popular support for al-Qaeda and much of the hatred for America would evaporate overnight."[49]

There were, unfortunately, other considerations for Clinton to ponder, both as a husband and human being, and as one of the most adroit politicians of his time. To bring the most sensitive Israeli-Palestinian issues to a head is always a substantial risk, but it would be especially so during the home-stretch campaign efforts of his wife, Hillary Rodham Clinton, in her bid for a New York Senate seat, and his Vice President, Al Gore, who was running for the presidency. Both Hillary and Gore faced ribbing from their opponents over the Jerusalem issue, with Hillary's opponent, New York Representative Rick Lazio, urging that the U.S. Embassy be moved from Tel Aviv to Jerusalem,[50] while presidential candidate Bush promised, "As soon as I take office I will begin the process of moving the U.S. ambassador to the city Israel has chosen as its capital."[51] In June 2000, Hillary faced ugly jeers while marching in a parade down Fifth Avenue in New York, as right-wing Jews and supporters of Lazio held signs that read, "Clinton kisses Arafat."[52] According to polls taken that summer, Hillary's relations with the Jewish community in New York were lagging below 50 percent.[53] Once the summit was under way, her relations with Jewish voters would continue to cause considerable angst. Amid charges that Hillary had uttered an anti-Semitic slur more than twenty-years earlier, the president came to her defense, taking the unusual step of breaking from the negotiations for an exclusive *New York Daily News* interview.

Al Gore would soon be counting on a strong performance at the upcoming Democratic National Convention, which, according to Dennis Ross, factored heavily in Clinton's decision. He related:

> The reason I recommended going was because the president made it clear that this was the last period at which he would do a summit. . . . After that, in August . . . you had the Republican convention first, then you had the Democratic one. And once the political season began, in the president's eyes, it would look as if he was trying to absorb the political space that his period of successors would be competing for. And he wasn't going to do that. Given the choice of having no summit versus having a summit—in my mind—it was worth the risk.
>
> The risk being that we wouldn't succeed but understanding as well that the consequence of *not* having a summit meant we would never know. You would lose the moment. Plus, Barak was saying he couldn't last longer. It was kind of a paradox because if his government fell he became a minority government when he went to Camp David.[54]

Clinton's Chief of Staff, John Podesta, related a less political understanding of Clinton's July 4 deliberations:

> I think that the president had faith that Barak, at the end of the day, could envision a future for the two sides that was positive and that would lead him to be able to take the tough decisions. If you remember there was a September 13 deadline, which is an Oslo deadline, right? I think that people thought that the shit was going to hit the fan.

> Maybe that was wrong, but I think there was a sense by both the Americans and Israelis that that was something of a real date. I think that [Clinton] thought that Barak was ready to make real decisions for peace. I think he thought that Arafat, who I think he had gotten to know, was never going to be ready until you actually put him in the room and that you might never know.[55]

• • •

**On July 5,** Clinton phoned both Barak and Arafat to issue the Camp David summit invitations. Barak quickly accepted. With Arafat, an affirmative response took some measure of coercive preparation, which the United States passed through Egyptian President Hosni Mubarak, to ensure that Arafat would not embarrass Clinton with a refusal.[56] Arafat was reluctant to dampen the president's enthusiasm or tell him no, and with repeated assurances that they would not be blamed in the event of failure, the Palestinians believed, at best, that Camp David might result in some progress, which they could then build on with additional negotiations or summits.

Unfortunately, the Palestinians were seriously misreading the intentions of both Clinton and Barak, who wanted a single, "pressure-cooker" summit to produce the coveted final agreement, leaving the remaining months to gain domestic and Congressional/Knesset support, with a formal signing ceremony taking place sometime near Clinton's remaining weeks as president. This did not make sense even to optimists like Aaron Miller, who, throughout his life as a student, historian, and negotiator of Arab-Israeli peacemaking, had not believed a single summit could work. Before the invitations, Miller tried to float the "series of summits" notion with Albright. But his suggestion was quickly shot down in a way that left no room for further debate. A rueful Miller even lamented that when he raised it, "she almost threw me out of the office!"[57]

Similar attempts were made by Saeb Erekat on July 9, who arrived in Washington in advance of the larger Palestinian delegation. His memory of this visit still haunts him:

> We warned them. I went to Albright in advance with Abu Ala and Hassan Asfur at the State Department for a dinner. And [from the Israeli side] there was Shlomo Ben Ami, Gilead Sher, and General Shlomo Yanai. I said to Albright, "Madeleine, please don't make it sound like a one-time summit. Don't make it sound like people should expect white smoke from Camp David. We're not ready. You're not ready. The Israelis are not ready. Unless you want to blame it on us, this will backfire! Make a series of summits. Don't tell Palestinians and Israelis that it's either/or. Don't tell Palestinians and Israelis that they should expect white smoke.
>
> I was blamed for being that honest. . . . "Oh, the Palestinians came not wanting an agreement because Saeb Erekat said so and so and so." I wanted more than this, I told them. You have a difficult situation on the ground. The lack of further redeployment; the lack of release of prisoners; the lack of economic situation; the lack of hope—it's a pressure-cooker situation. It will explode! I don't know when it will explode, but it will explode! . . . Some Americans said later, "Oh, they were planning the intifada!" You know? We knew it was coming—we knew it was coming! All of us knew![58]

• • •

**In the days** preceding Camp David, the president was reported to have devoted significant amounts of time studying in preparation, going over the smallest of substantive details with his closest advisers. Many parallels were made to the Carter administration's Nobel Laureate-winning 1978 Camp David summit between Israelis and Egyptians, and it appears Clinton attempted to learn those details as a guide for the difficult weeks ahead.

Martin Indyk prepared a classified briefing on Camp David I for Clinton, summarizing how a determined President Carter (who, like Clinton, was a Southern Baptist and a Democrat) had managed the risks involved, dramatically producing the groundbreaking agreement.[59] One might assume that it would have been easier for Clinton to receive a direct tutorial from Carter himself. Indyk laments that this was just not realistic, particularly because "there was a lot of friction" between them, and that the "White House viewed [Carter] as kind of a freelancer," particularly when it came to the Middle East.[60]

This is not to suggest that Clinton was disinterested in the lessons that could be learned from Carter's experience. Clinton read several chapters of William Quandt's seminal book *Camp David*, which documented the Carter administration's efforts to forge peace between two implacable foes, Egyptian President Anwar Sadat and Israeli Prime Minister Menachem Begin (Quandt had been director of Middle East affairs at the National Security Council during the Carter administration). Inside those pages, Clinton might have noticed some superficial similarities: Carter first presided over years of intensive negotiations, and a summit became necessary once Begin and Sadat felt they could go no further. Clinton should have noted how at Camp David I, Carter and his advisers convinced Begin, a rigid Likud Party member and ardent, lifelong proponent of a Greater Israel, to make a full territorial withdrawal from the occupied Egyptian Sinai—including the dismantling of Jewish settlements built there since 1967—in exchange for Sadat's pledge for full peace and security guarantees.

There were also stark contrasts for Clinton to consider. Unlike Begin and Sadat, neither Barak nor Arafat had the political strength to ensure that their compromises would not be overturned back home (though, to be sure, Sadat would pay the ultimate price for signing a peace treaty with Israel, when the Jihad group assassinated him during a military parade in 1981). This was particularly true for Barak, as just before his arrival, several members of his coalition deserted him as a result of his refusal to make clear his "non-negotiable points." Natan Sharansky's Yisrael Ba'Aliya was the first to go, while the NRP and Shas followed suit. Even his Foreign Minister, David Levy, resigned, leaving Barak with a seriously weakened minority government.

There were also preparatory moves by Carter that Clinton no longer had the luxury of making. For example, at early stages of Israeli-Egyptian negotiations—and not just in empty rhetoric—Carter's stance on Resolution 242 and the June 4, 1967, line, at least in regard to Egypt and Israel, was unwavering. Most important, he reiterated at every possible chance that Resolution 242 would be his guiding beacon in any possible compromise. Though both Egyptians and Israelis were pining for a deal, the Israelis nevertheless passed direct messages to Carter that "it would be futile to seek a declaration of principles on 242" from Begin.[61] (Begin had, in fact, resigned from Israel's national unity government in 1970 because Prime Minister Golda Meir publicly accepted Resolution 242 "in all its parts."[62]) But Carter was undeterred. Before issuing the summit invitations, which were kept out of public view as closely guarded secrets, he dispatched Vice President Walter Mondale, with whom he was very close, to convey this message in the most open possible forum.

In a carefully worded speech before the Knesset on July 2, 1978, Mondale articulated the U.S. reaffirmation of Resolution 242, stating, "In the Sinai, Israel has proposed a peace treaty in which there would be negotiated withdrawal and security would be achieved while relinquishing claims to territory. This approach can be applied in the West Bank and Gaza."[63] Mondale was initially reluctant to make such a commitment, particularly given his own future presidential aspirations. But his personal bond with Carter was strong, so he took the plunge. This conditioning of the Israeli public would give Begin crucial cover at Camp David when the defining moment for peace appeared. To be sure, there were many detractors, as there would be later to intimidate Barak, Clinton, and the entire Oslo process. According to Quandt, after leaving the Knesset podium Mondale was confronted by none other than Ariel Sharon, who accused him and the U.S. government of "sowing the seeds for war by overpressuring Israel and overpromising the Arabs."[64]

Despite the seven years of Oslo negotiations, by the summer of 2000, it was apparent to many U.S. observers of the conflict that conditions were still not ripe for a successful Israeli-Palestinian summit à la Camp David, 1978. For the Palestinians, the chief problem was not the idea of signing a full and comprehensive peace with Israel, including security guarantees, but that Barak, since taking office and many times thereafter, had made clear his intention to dismiss Resolution 242, and thus that the June 4, 1967, line would not be the baseline for discussions. Even worse, the United States did not challenge this. Unlike Sadat, Arafat had already pledged his willingness to accept Israel before the summit—as early as 1988, in fact—and the cessation of the first intifada during the Oslo years left him little bargaining power, while Barak, like Begin, managed to continue military occupation over the land in question.

Taking a firm line on 242 would have been difficult for Clinton because, to the detriment of peace, the historical U.S. position on 242—specifically as it applied to the West Bank and Gaza Strip—was that the June 4, 1967, line was not an internationally recognized border but an armistice line, with some scope for minor adjustments. Once Egypt abandoned its caretaker role over the Gaza Strip following the Camp David Accords in 1978, and once Jordan announced in 1988 it was no longer seeking to control the West Bank, the Palestinians were left to fend for the territories themselves, which the Israelis managed to populate with some

200,000 Jewish settlers—400,000 if illegally annexed East Jerusalem is taken into account. These "facts on the ground" were a conscious strategy to undermine the official U.S. position that only minor border changes could be accepted.

Barak's hypothetical discussions of returning 66-88 percent of the occupied Palestinian territories were difficult to square with the official U.S. position. It was an issue for Carter even before the Camp David 1978 signing, when Begin tried to thwart Carter's painstaking attempts to establish a firmer policy against Jewish settlements in the West Bank and Gaza Strip (which Begin insisted on calling Judea and Samaria). The result after Camp David I was that the territorial issues of the West Bank and Gaza Strip were shelved.

After inheriting these problems, Clinton could have used the original Camp David Accord as cover, as it contained a stipulation that the United States would be a full partner in seeking a fair solution to the Palestinian question, even mentioning reaffirmations that Resolution 242 applies to all of Israel's neighbors in future negotiations as well as other legal guidelines, like the UN Charter's important Article 2, which prohibits UN members from "acquisition of territory by use of force."

Twenty-two years later, these problems would remain for Clinton to address, but they had been made all the more difficult by the passage of time and the steady erosion of the U.S. position on Israeli settlements, particularly after the Oslo Accords were signed. The failure to keep U.S. policy firmly rooted in Resolution 242 would present Clinton with a most serious challenge as he sought to bridge the gaps on competing territorial claims. Even more difficult were the complexities of Jerusalem and the refugees' right of return. These complications were not present in the Egyptian-Israeli negotiations.

• • •

**In 1991, the** quasi-governmental U.S. Institute of Peace convened a three-day summit in Washington, D.C., to review the diplomatic history of the Arab-Israeli negotiations, focusing directly on the period after the 1967 war. The result of this meeting was the publication of a study titled *Making Peace Among Arabs and Israelis: Lessons from Fifty Years of Negotiating Experience.* Some of the authors of this early study include, ironically, future Camp David 2000 negotiators Martin Indyk and Aaron Miller.

According to the USIP study, the following highlights should be used by U.S. negotiators in order to ensure successful mediation:

- Successful mediation requires tedious, prolonged pre-negotiation to narrow the agenda, and identify informally the general outlines of an eventual agreement. Should formal negotiations succeed, both sides must believe that they can produce an acceptable agreement; if they do not, entering into formal negotiations may pose unacceptable political risks.
- Choose a venue for negotiations that is conducive to unpressured, informal discussions among participants when they are not in formal negotiating sessions. The settings should be sufficiently isolated to prevent unfettered media access to the negotiators.
- Keep in mind that leverage or "pressure" is of little or no value until the negotiating process is well advanced and the parties can "smell" agreement. Only when they fear losing a good deal that is within reach can a careful use of pressure facilitate the "end game." Pressure tactics are of no use, and are likely to be self-defeating, in the pre-negotiation phase.
- Do not become involved in internal Israeli politics regardless of how tempting the prospect might appear. Deal straightforwardly with the government

in office and focus on the prime minister as the ultimate source of decision making.

- Try to base the mediating process on already accepted negotiating guidelines—for example, Security Council resolutions 242 and 338 and the Camp David Agreement. Avoid creating broad new frameworks with untested or unfamiliar elements or terminology.
- Avoid public rejection of U.S. ideas or proposals; such a rejection could preclude reintroducing any of these ideas in a different context. Yesterday's rejected ideas can be, and often has been, part of tomorrow's accepted plan.

As the following chapters will demonstrate, the Camp David 2000 summit was almost destined to fail, as it violated almost every known guideline on how to conduct high-stakes summit negotiations. The consequences of failure would be momentous.

• THIRTEEN •

# Camp David 2000

AT CAMP DAVID on July 11, 2000, the United States convened a summit to resolve, once and for all, one of the most momentous conflicts of the twentieth century. The conflict involved a struggle between two nationalities for land and power, as most wars do, but it also involved, on both a symbolic and material level, issues that are central to the self-definition of the three great monotheistic traditions, Judaism, Islam and Christianity. A resolution to this conflict would require a resolution to the struggle over who would control Jerusalem, a holy city for all three religions, home to the Temple Mount for Jews, the Church of the Holy Sepulcher for Christians, and the Haram al-Sharif for Muslims, all of which lie in an area occupied by Israel since 1967 and illegally annexed in 1980.

President Clinton would assume these heavy burdens and be expected, perhaps unfairly, to bring finality to the corollaries of two great injustices: namely, Christian Europe's persecution of its Jewish population, culminating in the extermination of six million Jews during the Holocaust, and the concurrent creation of a Jewish haven in Palestine that trampled on the rights of the indigenous Palestinians, who, like other peoples throughout history, including the American Indians, had had the misfortune of standing in the way of another people's settlement and conquest.

Outside the confines of the president's official retreat in the deep woods of Maryland's Catoctin Mountains, the world below held its breath as decisions were being made about the future of the Middle East. Finding a solution to bridge the differences was the most unenviable task a leader could confront; for this reason Clinton deliberately set low expectations. But there was nothing he could say or do, once the decision had been made to convene a summit, that would undermine the dreams held by so many—whether it be Palestinians living in miserable refugee camps or Jews seeking an end to Israel's long confrontation with its Arab neighbors—that maybe, just maybe, the elusive peace would be discovered in Maryland, and later find its way to the peoples of the Holy Land.

• • •

**Camp David is** one of the most secure installations in the U.S. government arsenal. At all times, but especially during the summit, concentric rings of security provide its occupants with the utmost protection: the outer layers with local police and deputy sheriffs, Secret Service agents, and high-tech surveillance equipment and fences; the inner layers with heavily armed, infantry-trained Marines and a variety of Praetorian guards from multiple federal agencies charged with both protecting the leaders from physical harm or embarrassment and preserving the secrecy of what happens inside from the outside world's unwelcome penetration.

Drawing from the lessons of Shepherdstown and other venues sabotaged by leaks from the participants, the Camp David ground rules were an attempt to create as total a media blackout as possible. Joe Lockhart, the White House spokesman, along with Richard Boucher, the State Department spokesman, served as the gatekeepers of information between their guests and the outside world. They spent their days and nights crafting and vetting the blandest talking points, which they delivered twice a day at an elementary school turned mega-media center just down the hill from the retreat. There were the standard precautionary measures: Cameras and recording devices were prohibited. Cell phones were also ruled out, but even for those who succeeded in smuggling them onto the Camp David ground, they rarely seemed to work. Special phones inside the cabins enabled both Ehud Barak and Yasser Arafat to make outgoing calls after obtaining U.S. military authorization. Both sides were left to the honor system, which was kept believable by the presumption of sophisticated eavesdropping equipment. (In fact, both the Israeli and Palestinian delegations assumed that the United States had bugged the facilities; because of this, sensitive discussions requiring secrecy were usually conducted during walks in the woods.)

The delegates assumed their quarters in cabins named after trees found in the local area. Aspen, the most spacious cabin, which boasts a backyard terrace overlooking the verdant Maryland slopes and pastures, was reserved for Clinton. In an attempt to summon the positive mood of the 1978 Camp David summit, Barak was assigned to Dogwood, the lodge used by Egyptian President Anwar Sadat, while Arafat was given Birch—slightly closer to Clinton's, a subtle goodwill sign designed to ease Arafat's fear of entrapment—which had been used by Israeli Prime Minister Menachem Begin.

The cabin space at Camp David was tight, and the officials who made it there were presumed to be among the fittest, having survived a diplomatic version of Darwinian selection, whether by virtue of their personal relations with the respective leaders, professional capacity, intellectual merit, or a combination of all three.

Almost everyone Barak included with him held impressive legal, military, and intelligence credentials: Gilead Sher, an IDF colonel and lawyer assigned as "chairman of the negotiating team"; Shlomo Ben Ami, who in light of David Levy's resignation assumed the role of foreign minister as well as that of minister of internal security; Amnon Lipkin-Shahak; Danny Yatom, who had earlier served with Barak in the elite commando unit Sayeret Matkal and who later went on to become the head of Mossad, Israel's spy agency, and then Barak's chief of staff/senior security adviser; Shlomo Yanai, a retired IDF major general and military adviser; Dan Meridor, a former Likud Party member who headed the Centrist Party within Barak's coalition and also chaired the Knesset's foreign affairs and defense committee (Meridor was one of the opposition types cultivated by Barak; like Barak, he had opposed the Oslo Accords and was against fully relinquishing the Golan Heights); and Attorney General Elyakim Rubinstein, the only person in the compound who, as a young adviser to Begin, had participated in the original 1978 summit. Unofficial participants who frequently joined in included Yossi Ginosar, who acted in his usual capacity as a go-between with Palestinians; Israel Hasson, a former deputy director of Israel's General Security Service, or Shin Bet; and Gidi Grinstein, a young attorney with a law and economics background who is especially close to Sher and who acted as a secretary/note taker for the entire summit.

The core Palestinian negotiators alongside Arafat included the key players in Arafat's political circle, both "old guard" and "young guard" alike: Abu Mazen (Mahmoud Abbas), the secretary general of the PLO; Abu Ala (Ahmed Qurei), a core Fatah member and speaker of the Palestinian Parliament; Yasser Abed Rabbo, the minister of information and culture; Nabil Shaath, the minister of planning and international cooperation (a. k. a. foreign minister);[1] Saeb Erekat, the minister of local government and spokesman; Hassan Asfur, who headed the newly created Negotiations Affairs Department; Akram Hanieh, a newcomer to the negotiations and a well-respected journalist and political adviser to Arafat; Youssef Abdullah, Arafat's personal bodyguard, who played no negotiating role; Mohammed Dahlan, the chief of preventive security for Gaza; Mohammed Rashid, an ethnic Kurd and business partner of Arafat's who assumed responsibility for economic issues; and Nabil Abu Rudeineh, Arafat's loyal chief of staff, who handles everything from the president's personal correspondence to his scheduling of late-afternoon naps.

Both sides brought support staff and specialists. For Palestinians, the bulk of these individuals were attorneys from the Negotiation Support Unit (NSU) who, along with their Israeli counterparts, would negotiate "softer issues" like water, economics, and state-to-state relations at an obscure Federal Emergency Management Agency firefighting facility seven miles away in the town of Emmitsburg (by the summit's start, the senior Palestinian leadership had begun taking more interest in the legal opinions prepared by the NSU). Both delegations were allowed to bring just twelve official participants. With the exception of Ghaith al-Omari, a Jordanian with a law degree from Georgetown University, only a limited number of these advisers were allowed sporadic visits for quick debriefings or strategy meetings, which even then required special permission from the Americans on a limited, case-by-case basis. Their frequent screening away from Camp David, most often by Dennis Ross, had a damaging effect on the Palestinian team's abilities to put forward timely legal arguments and responses.

The ability of the Israeli team, which included the sitting Israeli attorney general and several respected lawyers, to provide a variety of drafts, arguments, and position papers proved a clear advantage, though it could also be a curse. The American hosts would take great pleasure at their professional approach, but at times there was "over-lawyering," which invited both setbacks and a hardening of positions even more restrictive than Barak's red lines. This was particularly true whenever Rubinstein was involved, whose reputation for being risk-averse conflicted with the very idea of a high-stakes summit.

There was a quasi-official specialized Israeli team that, in hindsight, arguably served one of Barak's most important summit purposes. The Israelis developed an intricate media/public relations plan, which can only be understood in the context of Barak's broader summit goals. An Israeli negotiator involved in every aspect of the summit told how it worked:

> We had a twofold objective. The guiding principle was for Israel not to capitulate in any conflict with the Palestinians, which by all intelligence estimates, we believed was coming. In order to keep this principle, Barak understood we would have to do two things. First, we would have to maintain internal unity. Second, we would have to sustain our international legitimacy.
>
> Barak thought that our ability to wage conflict with the Palestinians and not lose would be conditioned on those two things. So it was extremely important to him that the articulation of the summit made clear who came forward and on what issues and so forth.
>
> This is why he made it clear he went very far. He thought the summit would end and Israel would be accused of "not offering a set of conditions acceptable for the Palestinians," and they would blame Israel for the collapse of the Oslo process.
>
> It's a mindset issue as well: Barak constantly suspected that Arafat would never go the distance of ending the conflict, providing a finality of claims, recognizing the Jewishness of Israel, and so on. For Arafat, the interim agreement was his wet dream; he wanted another Israeli withdrawal, with no clarity whatsoever for the endgame, which would become the next endgame for the next set of demands. This is why we

> would push so hard on the finality of claims. In Barak's view, Arafat was a wolf dressed as a sheep: only if you challenge him to end the conflict will you expose [the fact that] he is not willing to end the conflict.[2]

Outside the Camp David fastness, an intricate cell of Israeli media spin doctors checked into local hotels, ready to activate Barak's plans, which meant, of course, defeating the American media blackout by providing real-time spin to well-placed Israeli, American, and European journalists. The central individual Barak relied on was Eldad Yaniv, the head of the Ministry of Foreign Affairs Information Department, who along with Barak's former army bureau chief, Yoni Koren, kept in frequent contact with Barak.[3] Staffers from the Israeli Embassy with full diplomatic credentials and privileges were able to shuttle information through diplomatic pouches to and from the Camp David facility with an inviolability that could not be challenged. Moreover, Barak brought with him encrypted communications equipment that, when it worked, allowed him to talk securely with his PR team in Israel, including Moshe Gaon and Tal Zilberstein,[4] the latter of whom was employed by Stan Greenberg, the powerhouse pollster employed by both Barak and Clinton who was concurrently managing the presidential campaign of Vice President Al Gore.

The Palestinians, with far less media sophistication and resources, had few options available to them should they have elected to break the rules—which, by all accounts, they tried to do. The handful of staffers from the PLO Mission to the United States were accredited with little more than a tax-free purchase card, much less the largess of full diplomatic privileges, and they had almost no access to the Camp David grounds. The Palestinian spokesperson was Hassen Abdul Rahman, the PLO representative to Washington, though at times he appeared to have less information than most Israeli journalists.

The American officials who made it to Camp David were winners of a politically loaded internal debate. Dennis Ross, for example, initially handled preparation of the list of participants until higher powers took over after he attempted to exclude one of Albright's closest advisers, Wendy Sherman. The contentious nature of the selection process, imperfect to say the least, resulted in the rejection of noted experts within the State Department, like Ambassador Ned Walker. As one of State's top "Arabists," Walker would have brought to bear his credentials of having lived and served his entire diplomatic career in the Middle East, including Israel. So, too, would Ron Schlicher, a career diplomat who had spent his career in the Middle East and was due to become consul general in Jerusalem. Ross kept them out in favor of John Herbst, to whom he was very close. Gemal Helal, an Egyptian-born Coptic Christian, was the only American official at Camp David who spoke Arabic or had ever lived in the Arab Middle East.

There were fifteen official U.S. participants, including the president. State Department officials included Albright, Ross, Miller, Indyk, Herbst (then serving as the consul general in Jerusalem), Verstandig, and Helal. Additional desk officers and staff assistants would be on hand for each of these individuals, while others busied themselves with the discussions at Emmitsburg. There were additional attendees at the talks who provided important staff work while the senior U.S. leadership sealed itself off from the outside world. Albright still had an entire department to manage, and she relied on her inner team, including her chief of staff, deputy chief of staff, press aide, and counselor to put out day-to-day fires.

The White House team was divided between the National Security Council and the political team. But as the summit proceeded, the lines between those responsible for the substantive negotiating issues and those protecting the president's political interests became blurred. Their collective team included Sandy Berger, who aside from being the national security adviser was a trusted confidant of Clinton since their days together at Oxford; John Podesta, the president's chief of staff; Maria Echaveste, the deputy chief of staff; Joe Lockhart, an assistant to the president and spokesman; Bruce Riedel, a former CIA official who served Clinton as a special assistant and as the NSC's senior director for Near East and South Asian affairs; and Robert Malley, who served as special assistant to the president for Arab-Israeli affairs and director for Near East and South Asian affairs.

The only American component not made public, in keeping with tradition, was Director of Central Intelligence George Tenet and his small staff of intelligence advisers, who joined the talks at a later stage.

• • •

**On the afternoon** of the opening day, Arafat and Barak walked together to the Laurel conference room, where the summit would officially commence, showing convivial spirits as the press pool snapped pictures of them playfully sparring over who would enter the door first. Once inside, over twenty-one negotiators convened around a long, rectangular table to hear President Clinton deliver what was no ordinary "history is in the making" speech.[5] Clinton underscored the difficulties that lay ahead, and he promised to stay as long as necessary to reach an agreement. There was one caveat: quite wisely, the White House wanted neither the President nor his enthusiasm to be taken for granted. They made it clear to both sides that Clinton would have to leave by July 19 to make the long flight to Okinawa, Japan, where his attendance at the G-8 summit—his final one as U.S. president—was expected. The Okinawa trip, designed as a sort of bookend to the talks, was counted on to help sharpen the focus of both sides.[6] And should they reach an agreement within those eight days, Clinton told them, he would exert all his powers to reward the parties with hefty financial contributions.[7]

Not to be outdone, Secretary Albright scheduled a trip for July 18 to London for meetings with European leaders. Albright's trip would never materialize, and as the days progressed, other negotiators from the National Security Council assumed a more central role that made her threat of departure less and less worrisome.

One of the most obvious issues Clinton had to deal with included finding a strategy to bridge the deep misgivings between Barak and Arafat. Both lugged plenty of baggage with them. The Palestinians had been hardened as a result of the disappointing Oslo experience; worse, their mistrust was not directed only at the Israelis. Quite fresh in their minds were the letters of assurance delivered by Albright at the signing of Sharm, subsequently ignored; the president's commitment to the March 8 village agreement, since reneged on; and Barak's baneful settlement drive, which, according to Amnon Lipkin-Shahak, had already done irreparable damage to the way Palestinians viewed their American hosts:

> It would have helped the Americans to be more trusted by the Palestinians. The Palestinians lost their trust through time. They look at the Americans as an Israeli agent. But they had no other choice. They could go nowhere. They understood that only the U.S. can really bring them somewhere.
>
> But I think the settlement case is a very good example of some Palestinian expectations—the Americans always told them they would never accept Israeli ongoing construction in the territories, and suddenly when Barak is talking with them they witness the ongoing Israeli efforts. And they blamed the Americans for it, not us.[8]

Perhaps aloof to this perspective, some White House advisers believed Clinton's personal style would mend relations. As Joe Lockhart put it:

> With Clinton, he not only knew the substance; he not only was a good negotiator and pusher and prodder and cajoler and schmoozer—all the things you need—but most importantly, he was able to talk politics with Barak like an Israeli; he was able to talk politics with Arafat like a Palestinian; he was able to talk politics with King Hussein like he was Jordanian. It was because he completely understood. He'd get a little information, he'd read his briefing book, and he'd immediately understand what the politics were and he'd see the deal. It wasn't only "Here's what makes sense; here's what they'll agree to," it was, "Here's what you'll be able to sell."[9]

Having lost his Knesset majority upon his arrival, Barak was in an especially foul mood. For Clinton, having a "here's what you'll be able to sell" political approach would do little to convince Barak to overcome his oft-reiterated negotiating red lines, particularly since he had been unable to sell his own coalition on the summit. Clinton, who hated personal confrontation and wanted to avoid one with Barak, offered him especially strong support, which, unfortunately, would prematurely foreclose possibilities at the earliest summit stages. There appeared to be little resistance among some of Clinton's advisers; at least some appeared to endorse it. Ross recalled why:

> The President was basically reluctant to say no to Barak. And here again, I come back to this: it may have been wrong but it was understandable. I mean, Barak was the guy who was taking the big leaps! Barak was the guy who was going to confront a terrible political reality at home when he did this! Barak was the guy who had enormous courage to do it! All of this was the way Clinton saw it.
>
> And, by the way, Clinton knew Barak's political reality. It's because his pollsters were also Barak's pollsters. And they kept him informed of what the polls in Israel look like. So it's

> hard for someone like Clinton, who was such an intuitive politician, to *not* put himself in the shoes of the guy who had this problem.[10]

Clinton's close identification with Barak's political risks became apparent to Palestinians during one of the first Clinton-Arafat meetings. Arafat opened by revealing to Clinton what was very close to his own bottom-line position on two of the most loaded core issues: refugees and Jerusalem. Arafat asked for Barak's recognition, in principle, of the right of return first before discussing "the practical details," while on Jerusalem, he remarked, perhaps too blithely, "It's really simple: East Jerusalem is ours; West Jerusalem is for the Israelis."[11] Thus far, Clinton had been unwilling to have a similar conversation with Barak. But it did not stop him from responding to Arafat, "Israel will never give up sovereignty over East Jerusalem. . . . Barak has a lot of problems when it comes to Jerusalem. He can't go backward."[12]

Here again the Palestinians saw that Clinton was unwilling to reconsider his abandonment of Arab legal entitlements, because of domestic Israeli politics that were beyond their control. By this time the Palestinians had gathered all the details from their Syrian colleagues regarding why that track had failed. For Palestinians, the American president's mindset was essentially unaltered, despite the fact that it had not served him well at the doomed Geneva summit.

In Clinton they saw negotiating blinders that suggested some form of Israeli co-optation, particularly when he floated the notion to Arafat of forgoing Palestinian sovereignty over East Jerusalem in exchange for Israel's relinquishing of claims to a buffer zone on the Western border with Jordan.[13] Naturally Arafat rejected these premises. The Palestinians' suspicion of their American host grew as they wondered why Clinton's aides, who they presumed had prepared him, would allow the president to believe such gambits stood a chance of succeeding.

• • •

**In fact, although** the American negotiators might not have realized it, the events of the following days marked an outright surrender of summit control to the Israelis. It materialized when the time came to use one of the key negotiating tools that made Camp David 1978 work: the presentation of an American negotiating draft. William Quandt, who as a young NSC staffer took part in Camp David I in 1978, explained the essentials, which he also conveyed to the Clinton administration when consulted in the weeks before the summit:

> I've considered one of the key innovations that we used at Camp David I the idea of a simple negotiating text, which we would put forward as our best judgment of what would work. The text was constantly subject to revision. We'd talk to one side about it, then the next side, and it was kind of an attrition process. . . . We had twenty-three drafts. By the time we got to the end, we kind of wore them down on all the little stuff . . . and the one or two issues that they really cared about were in sharp focus, and everything else had been agreed upon. I was just quite surprised that that technique was totally not explored [at Camp David 2000].[14]

By the third day at the summit, on July 13, both sides were believed to be withholding in the discussions in anticipation of a U.S. draft. But the Americans couldn't start the drafting process until they had at least a presumption of what the final compromise would entail. And since they would not firmly lay down Resolution 242 as the summit standard, they lacked clear red lines of their own. Barak was to fill this vacuum with his own red lines.

Though Clinton had been given promises of "bold ideas" from Barak, both the president and his team had yet to determine what Barak's rock-bottom needs were. As Malley later wrote, on Jerusalem they knew only what Barak claimed he could not accept: "Palestinian sovereignty over any part of East Jerusalem other than a purely symbolic "foothold." On territory, Barak revealed that if Arafat asked for 95 percent of the West Bank "there would be no deal."[15]

From the political perspective, John Podesta recalled that even for Americans, the core issues could not be discussed in advance because "people wouldn't entertain it as a subject."[16] On the issue of territory the Palestinians saw evidence that most of the Americans—even those perceived to be moderately fair—were still nowhere near acceptance of their legal entitlements under Resolution 242 and the June 4, 1967, line. Nabil Shaath recounted:

> When we started talking about permanent status I engaged Aaron Miller—whom I like more than others—and I said, "Aaron, I hope you are not really underestimating the territorial issue." And he said, "No, no, no, we're not!" I said, "What do you mean you're not. . . . What percentage do you think the Palestinians will settle with in the territorial issue?" And he said, "Seventy percent?" I said, "Aaron, you're miserably misinformed. Nothing less than 100 percent, plus or minus a few percentages for swap on a one-to-one basis . . . if you think we're going to accept *anything* less than one hundred percent, you're kidding." He was shocked.[17]

Like Jimmy Carter at Camp David I, Clinton played a central role in the drafting process. At Camp David 1978, after mastering all the details and considering the input of his staff, Carter devoted much time in writing the first draft himself, laying out purely American principles as guidelines for the summit. Clinton, by all accounts a quick study and brilliant generator of ideas, had a strong legal background, never a liability in such negotiations. In the pre-summit days, aides recalled that he immersed himself in the final-status issues like a grad student, even learning the names of neighborhoods and streets in

Jerusalem. Clinton, along with his State and NSC teams, had little problem evincing a characteristic cocksureness.

Though politics was considered Clinton's strongest asset, it worked against the negotiations at the earliest summit stages. Once he made the decision to produce a draft, he left Camp David to attend an NAACP convention in Baltimore. His delegation of the drafting process to others might have protected him politically in the event both sides rejected it, but only the president could forcefully repel criticisms from the Israelis and Palestinians. Instead, his drafters had to shoulder those incalculable stresses alone.

Notwithstanding this downward assignment, Clinton rightfully expected his own delegation to have mastered all the details. At least in the eyes of Israeli and Palestinian negotiators, the staffers Clinton relied on, particularly the ones from State who had negotiated well before the Oslo process started, arrived at the summit as victims to their years of focusing on "process" rather than the finer details that would be explored at Oslo's inevitable conclusion. One Israeli negotiator offered his general impression:

> The American team didn't know the substance. It is one thing to know the principles of an agreement, and another to master the details. If you don't have a rich, sophisticated understanding of the issue, when you are confronted by reality you are left paralyzed. Whereas, if you have a very rich understanding, you're going to be able to be creative, always willing to adapt and compromise.[18]

Indeed, as Aaron Miller later agreed, "The Israelis and Palestinians came very prepared to Camp David—the problem was, we didn't."[19]

There was an exceptionally short learning curve for the American team. Consensus-building during this process was all the more challenging when, for the first time, the drafters had to come to an agreement on the Israeli and Palestinian wants versus needs on each of the issues. Their discussions were "extra virgin"; on top of that, in keeping with Clinton's wishes, they had to err in the direction of Barak's red lines.

Proceeding cautiously, they virtually duplicated the provisions put forward in a copy of the sixth and final framework agreement non-paper from Harpsund they had obtained, which neither Barak nor Arafat had accepted (Arafat had rejected it in large part because the non-paper made no reference to Jerusalem).

In addition to these problems and mistakes, the American claim to be an honest broker was further undermined when Ross, along with Miller, Malley, and Schwartz, assumed the enabling role for Clinton's toleration of Barak's subversive practices. Ross and his team gave a sneak preview of the American draft to members of the Israeli delegation, including Ben Ami, Rubinstein, Sher, Shahak, and Gidi Grinstein.[20]

The whole gesture backfired when the draft was revealed to Barak. Ever the micro-manager, Barak, in a meeting with Albright, had the following reaction: "I must see it. Maybe my negotiators will make a mistake. I have to let you know whether I can accept or reject it." After learning of Barak's suspicion upon his return, Clinton invited Barak to Aspen, where he agreed to share with him the first draft. According to one witness, Barak was so bothered by what the Americans appeared willing to propose that he came down on Clinton "like a ton of bricks." Even before the Palestinians made their review, Barak issued what would become the first summit rejection.[21] Albright gave her general impression:

> President Clinton was supposed to sit down—did sit down—with Barak and Arafat, to kind of get them in the mood for what we were doing. And then Barak, in exactly the way he had done at Shepherdstown—he's the one who wanted us to do this—and then he didn't like the paper. He also didn't trust his own negotiators! . . . And so it immediately kind of

> got off track by this foot-dragging on Barak's part, and irritation on Arafat's part for being there in the first place and the fact that Barak was in, you know, such a bad mood when he got there. So the mistrust between the two of them was evident practically immediately.[22]

According to Albright, the President did not want to "corner" Barak. Thus, at Barak's request the Americans made further modifications to the draft, supplanting American principles with hypothetical, nonbinding terms in the form of bracketed language, represented by "I's" and P's", which had been used (without success) at Shepherdstown and also in the direct negotiations at Harpsund. In addition to the I's and P's, the Americans put forward "alternative possible solutions," marked "ALT."

The first sign that the draft held virtually no American weight was the posting of disclaimer upon disclaimer. Among them:

> . . . The paper does not represent a U.S. position.
>
> It is in the form of a draft FAPS but does not include all the issues the parties may wish to include . . . nor does it address each issue with the degree of specificity that the parties may desire.
>
> The I: and P: language is only a U.S. estimation based on discussions with the parties and is not intended to bind or prejudice the positions of the parties.

For example, Article III of the draft, which addresses "Borders, Settlements, and Territorial Arrangements," listed the following ideas:

> 2. In the area of the Gaza Strip the border will be the June 4, 1967 line.

3. In the area of the West Bank,

(a) the western border of the Palestinian state [I: will be delineated taking into account the 1967 lines, the realities on the ground and the strategic needs of Israel] [P: will be the June 4, 1967, line]

ALT 1: The western border of the Palestinian State will be based on the 1967 lines with agreed modifications to reflect, inter alia, demographic realities and strategic concerns of the parties.

(c) the remainder of the West Bank [P: will be under Palestinian sovereignty] [I: will include limited territories under Israeli control for security purposes for an agreed period at the end of which they will be divided between the two states on an agreed ratio of 7:1 (or 8:1) for the Palestinian State].

4. Neither Israeli settlers nor Palestinians will be required to leave their communities as a result of the establishment of the final borders. Those who choose to remain in areas in which they are not citizens [P: will be subject to local law] [I: will be able to maintain their collective communal identity]

The most controversial part of the draft, Article VI, dealt with the most important issue of Jerusalem:

4. The Jerusalem municipal area will host the national capitals of both Israel and the Palestinian State.

At 1 A.M. on July 14, the Israeli delegation made a cursory review of the second iteration. Shortly thereafter, the wrath of Barak came down hard. Despite all disclaimers as not representing a U.S. position, the sentence on Jerusalem appeared without brackets, striking panic in Barak that Palestinians would interpret it as a green light to divide Jerusalem, which not only violated his own red lines but seemed to disregard his designs for a Palestinian capital in Abu Dis. Ross, who was standing in the prime minister's cabin, took the brunt of Barak's vituperation. The Palestinians, he knew, would be expecting their draft from the president soon. Not wanting to upset Barak, Ross capitulated, making an impromptu correction with his own pen, crossing out the word "municipal area," adding a caret before "Jerusalem," and adding the words "expanded area of."

Despite having participated along with Malley and Schwartz in converting the first iteration into the bracketed second-iteration style Barak preferred, Ross had underestimated what Barak's resistance would be. Amid criticisms over the slapdash changes he made, Ross first defended his actions to others on his team as not wanting to "prejudge the outcome" for Israelis. Later he would accuse Malley and Schwartz of making the changes behind his back—completely inconsistent with the slow, deliberate, and legalistic nature of career bureaucrat Jon Schwartz, much less Rob Malley, also a lawyer with a cautious approach.

But the Jerusalem language was not the only unilateral "correction" Ross made on behalf of the Americans. Barak also objected to the preambular language regarding Resolution 242, which read:

> REITERATING their commitment to United Nations Security Council Resolution 242 and 338 and confirming their understanding that the FAPS is based upon and will lead to the implementation of Resolutions 242 and 338 between them;

Seeking to get the Palestinians away from the idea of having Resolution 242 as the negotiating standard, Barak likewise convinced Ross, not a lawyer, to make another change, so that it read:

> REITERATING their commitment to United Nations Security Council Resolution 242 and 338 and confirming their understanding that the FAPS is the basis for their implementation and will lead to the implementation of Resolutions 242 and 338 between them;

This crucial but subtle distinction would allow Barak to hold to his earlier claim that a settlement would fulfill 242, even if it was not based on 242. Despite Ross's remarkable efforts, neither of these accessions were enough for Barak, who responded with another rejection.[23]

Needless to say, the Palestinians did not react favorably when they finally received their copy, an hour later. Ross's handwritten changes on Jerusalem did not go over well; the same held true with the undermining of Resolutions 242 and 338. Other American principles caused them just as many problems, such as the retreat from Resolution 242's baseline principle that the June 4, 1967, line applied to all occupied territories, not just the Gaza Strip but the entire West Bank (the Israelis had made it clear from the beginning of the talks that they were willing to withdraw entirely from Gaza as part of an agreement). There was widespread anger among the Palestinians, and not only from Arafat. Abu Mazen and Abu Ala both went through the roof, as did the younger negotiators, who felt the summit hosts were attempting to dilute their rights from the outset.[24]

For Palestinians, there was no conceivable way the Americans could have listed these principles as "estimations based on discussions with the parties," unless the only parties they really listened to were the Israelis. At 2:30 A.M. on July 14, Erekat and Abu Ala met with Albright and Ross and formally rejected the document. This, unfortunately, would become a recurring summit theme. Ross openly admitted to Erekat what he had done afterward,[25] which Arafat reportedly described as an "Israeli trick," confirming his fears that the summit was one great U.S.-Israeli conspiracy.[26]

Both sides were furious, and for the first time at the summit, the Americans managed to unite Israelis and Palestinians in disdain for the hosts' sloppy handling of the negotiations. Both felt the U.S. draft was created in haste; as a result, both had tainted impressions of the American mediation abilities for the remainder of the summit. Akram Hanieh later wrote, "It was a bad paper by any standard and made clear the fact that the American peace team had deliberately distorted the Palestinian positions to President Clinton, enabling them to make bridging proposals that suited them."[27] Similarly, Gilead Sher said, "The first American document that landed on our desks was a cut-and-paste document of quite a lousy quality. It had a lot of mistakes in it and a lot of loopholes."[28]

Unfortunately, the wrong lessons were learned from this misstep: as a matter of summit procedure, virtually all the American ideas would henceforth be conveyed through oral presentation, which Barak had preferred all along. But such verbal commitments could hardly satisfy the complexity of the issue involved. Even though the first American draft was flawed, the worst mistake was to abandon this drafting process altogether. With its abandonment, multidimensional core items were reduced to bazaar-style haggling, subjected to the inherent frailties embodied in each negotiator's understanding of the English language, note-taking ability, and memory, at times selective.

The document presented became little more than a record for the historical archive. Tragically, it was the only draft the Americans formally presented to both sides during the entire summit.

• • •

**After four days** in isolation, everyone was unhappy, and the prospects of finding an agreement were bleak. Clinton was trying to find a way to move the parties forward. Those considered by the White House to be part of the State Department team, including Albright, Ross, Miller, and Indyk (lumped in for a range of issues going back to Syria), were counted on to manage and direct the administering of the summit. When the drafting process was stunted, the White House and NSC staff, increasingly protective of the president and not wanting a repeat of Shepherdstown, began probing the State team for its fallback plans and alternate strategies.

Some from the highest levels of the State team even began to rethink the wisdom of convening a summit, despite the fact that they were already there. Maria Echaveste, who as deputy chief of staff described her role as "making the trains run on time" for the president, described what she believes was Albright's summit indecision: "She went back and forth. On the one hand I think she was the strong voice saying we should meet, but then as things started blowing up, she said on several occasions to me that 'We shouldn't have done this! We should have waited! The Palestinians weren't ready!' "[29]

Albright, with some shock, offered the following defense:

> [Echaveste] was there from a political perspective and she really was not that familiar with the details. . . . Part of the thing was that the White House—the NSC—is the one that kept switching the signals. Dennis, who really knew more about this than anybody else, had a process that he wanted to follow out. And when Sandy [Berger] kept switching the signals on it, I think it threw everybody kind of off kilter.

According to Albright, "When the first three days at Camp David didn't work, with one paper here and one paper there and all of that—the disagreements over that created disagreements within our own teams."[30]

As they reassessed what to do, Berger focused heavily on the weight of time—by several accounts, far more than Ross, who preferred to stick to process. Among all sides, Ross had been the face associated with the draft presentation. Given that it produced immediate rejection, Berger was a forceful voice advocating a move beyond the draft method, which he might have thought was too slow to produce an agreement within the next five days, before the president's scheduled departure. Some Israelis overheard the arguments that followed—so loud it carried through to the other cabins. The general impression was that "some of them thought the United States should be much more aggressive about putting forth a set of agreements and sticking to it; while others thought it was a mistake to put the credibility of the president on the line for the [sake of more] process."[31] The seeds of dissent between the NSC and State teams were sprouting at the worst possible moment.

• • •

**The dispositions of** both Israelis and Palestinians needed to be improved, so Clinton sent word to everyone that the U.S. draft was no longer on the table. A new approach was needed. Some in the Palestinian delegation, like Erekat, felt strongly that more progress could be made working directly with the Israelis.[32] So, at Arafat's suggestion,[33] Clinton directed the parties to begin negotiating in three separate groups: borders and security, Jerusalem, and refugees.

On the Israeli team, negotiators Sher and Shahak expressed concern to Barak that they still had not had an open and candid discussion among themselves to arrive at what the true red lines were, particularly on Jerusalem. In the presence of Barak and the entire Israeli team, Shahak openly began to challenge the wisdom of "fighting to the end on everything"; too hard a bargain would foreclose the possibility and benefits of peace, and Shahak even took to challenging the morality of the prime minister's calls for annexing most settlements: "Three hundred thousand non-Jewish Russians have been absorbed into Israel in the last few years," Shahak said, according to Sher. "Is that moral?" Barak appeared to want none of the discussion, offering vaguely that "we have genuine, internal red lines, which each of us knows."[34]

Palestinians were more open in their willingness to discuss areas for compromise. But absent an initial recognition by Israel of the principles of Resolution 242, 338, and 194, they were less than willing to discuss possible tradeoffs.

There were, of course, exceptions. On one of the first evenings at Camp David, Erekat offered what Israelis interpreted as an important concession on the topic of Jerusalem. Dan Meridor recalled Erekat's words: "We cannot allow that East Jerusalem would not be under our sovereignty—*at least the Arab parts.*"[35] For Meridor, himself the most hawkish negotiator on Barak's team, this signaled hope that the illegally built settlements in areas of greater Jerusalem, particularly in Ma'ale Adumim, which together included more than 150,000 Jews, would be available for conversion to Israeli sovereignty.

For Palestinians, such a diversion from the June 4, 1967, line as narrowly applied to portions of East Jerusalem merited discussion so long as it was understood that sovereignty would be granted over the Arab neighborhoods of Jerusalem and, most importantly, only should Israel forgo its insistence on sovereignty over the Old City's Haram al-Sharif/Temple Mount. These were important developments, considering that it was the first time the Israelis were allowed to discuss the topic with their Palestinian partners. But since a compromise on the Jewish Quarter of East Jerusalem had been proposed by Arafat a month earlier, during his meeting in Nablus with Ben Ami and Sher—without any reciprocal tradeoff—Erekat's move was all but accepted as a given. Perhaps hoping the Palestinians just might accept a capital for their state in Abu Dis, Clinton, after joining the initial Jerusalem discussions with both Israelis and Palestinians, repeated the same slogan on Barak's behalf: "I know Barak cannot give up on Jerusalem."[36]

• • •

**Because the Americans** did not stick to the terms of reference used in all prior negotiations between Israelis and Palestinians, namely Resolution 242, Camp David became for the Palestinians more a test of wills with the American hosts than a summit to negotiate with Israelis. In one of the first committee meetings on borders, Ben Ami told both the Americans and Palestinians that Israel would be unable to accept the June 4, 1967, line as a basis for discussions for fear that if an agreement was not reached, the Palestinians would be able to walk away with the commitment in pocket (such as what Rabin had given Asad). The American motives for agreeing to this approach, according to Ben Ami, were slightly different, as Clinton wished to preserve Barak's option to keep "80 percent of the settlers in sovereign Israeli territory."[37]

During a borders meeting on July 16, the Clinton-Barak push to drop the June 4, 1967, line resulted in an episode that not only devalued the objectivity of President Clinton in the eyes of the Palestinians but resulted in the president's discrediting of Abu Ala, a central Palestinian negotiator. It began when the Palestinians reacted to the first and only map the Israelis presented at Camp David. With high expectations that new proposals were going to be made, the Palestinians were angered to see the same map that had been presented at Harpsund, which reflected 10 percent of the West Bank under continued indefinite occupation and 14 percent annexed by Israel, leaving 76 percent of the territory for the proposed Palestinian state. According to Helal, the president asked Abu Ala to use a blank map—literally—to put forward a Palestinian counterproposal.[38] Instead, Abu Ala demanded an Israeli commitment to negotiate on the basis of the June 4, 1967, line. After investing lots of time on Barak's behalf at other venues where this Arab refrain resulted in no deal, Clinton went postal:

> Sir, I know you'd like the whole map to be yellow. But that's not possible. This isn't the Security Council here. This isn't the UN General Assembly. If you want to give a lecture, go over there and don't make me waste my time. I'm the president of the United States. I'm ready to pack my bags and leave. I also risk losing a lot here. You're obstructing the negotiation. You're not acting in good faith.[39]

Helal, believing the president could no longer afford to treat anyone with kid gloves, later revealed that it was he who had advised Clinton to react in the manner he did. Indeed, Albright later described the blowup as though it were lifted from a script: "Having made his point, he motioned to me and we strode dramatically out—at precisely the moment a downpour began. It was either get wet or forfeit the drama of our exit, so we went and got drenched." While intervening acts of God might have been enough to cool the president down, his explosion was a turning point, according to Gilead Sher:

> The shouts could be heard in every room of the lodge. Abu Ala, white as a sheet, left the room, very hurt. This was a critical moment, with far greater implications than could be initially gauged. Abu Ala lost all faith then in the honest, unbiased brokerage of the United States, and thenceforth would repeatedly claim that the Americans were inclined to accept Israel's positions without considering the Palestinians.[40]

According to Ben Ami, Abu Ala was so afflicted by the American president's scolding that he was nearly reduced to a vegetative state: "From that moment, almost the only thing he did at Camp David was drive around the lawns in a golf cart."[41] Martin Indyk, a harsh critic of the Palestinians at Camp David, concedes that Clinton's outburst cast the Palestinians into further summit paranoia:

> Abu Mazen was already against the process because he thought it was designed to screw him. Now Abu Ala was alienated because the President humiliated him. And so you had a kind of critical mass of Arafat's advisers against doing anything, and Arafat himself [who] thought he was getting trapped. And he got more and more paranoid when Barak wouldn't deal with him, so you had a pretty disastrous kind of dynamic developing. [42]

Most Palestinians at Camp David seemed to understand that it would be useless to compete with Barak in trying to bring Clinton and his delegation closer to their positions. The U.S.-Israeli alliance seemed unbreakable and, at least with some individuals, religious. Yossi Beilin, a dovish adviser whom Barak did not bring with him to Camp David, had recently written of the American negotiating team during the Oslo period, "This was a team decidedly dominated by Jews, proving that Bill Clinton was not afraid of making such appointments.... I don't know if the composition of the team was a cause of concern to our Arab counterparts; I must admit we found it reassuring, although we were aware that the positions taken would not automatically be pro-Israeli."[43] Indeed, at Camp David, Jewish-Americans made up nearly two-thirds of the U.S. negotiating team. Some Israelis concede that, had the demographics been stacked the other way—with two-third Arab-Americans—they would have been unnerved.

Most members of the U.S. team had little familiarity, much less cultural intimacy, with the Arab and Muslim world—certainly far less than most members of the Israeli team. This became evident in little matters, such as when the Israelis invited Arafat to attend a Shabbat eve dinner on July 14. This was nothing new for Palestinians: Fridays are a special day of prayer to both Jews and Muslims, and throughout the years of close negotiations between Israelis and Palestinians, many religious occasions were observed. For some reason, Clinton nonetheless felt compelled to enlighten Arafat beforehand on religious sensitivities and the saying of the kiddush blessing.[44] Arafat had to explain that he knew the ritual well.

Awkward moments like these made Palestinians nervous, particularly when they affected discussions on Jerusalem. For example, during one of the Jerusalem sessions attended by the Americans, Sandy Berger requested of the Palestinians, at Barak's suggestion, that Jews be allowed to pray within the Waqf, the Islamic religious trust that maintains the holy grounds within the Haram al-Sharif.[45] Such a notion disregarded the arrangements both sides have generally respected: Jews and non-Muslims are forbidden from praying at the Al-Aqsa Mosque. Arafat, confused that the Americans would raise an idea that only the most extremist Jews would support, thus had to provide a history lesson, reminding them that "after the occupation of Jerusalem in 1967, Moshe Dayan, whom the Israelis consider a hero, forbade Jews from setting foot in the Haram."[46] Immense dangers were associated with upsetting the status quo, and the Palestinians surmised the fingerprints of Barak, who, obsessed with what he could or could not sell on Jerusalem back home, might allege religious intolerance as a way to sabotage the talks and blame the Palestinians.[47]

The Americans and, to a lesser extent, the Israelis felt immovable cultural barriers when dealing with senior Palestinian leaders Arafat, Abu Mazen, and Abu Ala. Ross, perhaps defensive over the repeated criticism made against him by Arafat, increasingly depicted Arafat as the most intransigent summit obstacle while seeing hope in "small groups of Palestinians who were working with the Israelis and with us to do a deal."[48] Just as he explained the failure at Geneva by portraying Asad as obstinate while claiming that Shaara and Daoudi had shown more "flexibility," so, too, would Ross seek to do the same with Arafat and his younger group of advisers.

The small group Ross and others referred to consisted primarily of Mohammed Dahlan, Mohammed Rashid, Hassan Asfur, and, to a lesser extent, Saeb Erekat. A senior State

Department official likewise endorsed Ross's move to "divide and conquer," stating that "Abu Ala and Abu Mazen were not helpful, and Dahlan and Mohammed Rashid were." Believing these two would be "more forthcoming," the Americans increasingly courted them by trying "to do negotiations at a lower level, to see if some of the underbrush could be cut out."[49] John Podesta recalled why this happened, only recognizing later that it had been a major mistake:

> I think it was partly conscious and partly subconscious. It was conscious in the sense that the younger guys had more *capacity* to deal. The subconscious part was that the younger guys were more *simpatico*, if you will . . . .[50]

Dahlan recognized that his comparative youth and ability to speak Hebrew (even a little bit of English) was an advantage as far as his Israeli and American counterparts were concerned. But he had all along sensed danger that the Americans would confuse his personal traits and capabilities with their own delusions of "flexibility," especially on core issues. He often took to reminding them, "Look, on the serious issues there is no flexibility." Dahlan went on to explain that, while he would keep an open mind on tangential issues, there would be no deviation from the core issues, in which the Palestinians were united. Sensing the problems this would create within his own team, Dahlan naturally took to Arafat's defense, pointing out what he viewed as the Americans' dismissive attitude toward Arafat's flexibility: "Arafat is the most flexible person in the Palestinian leadership! . . . No one could ever dare or deny . . . when President Arafat acknowledged Resolution 242. It simply gives the Israelis 78 percent of the land of historical Palestine!" Dahlan vehemently recounted what he viewed as Arafat's mistaken "flexibility" over the years, particularly regarding the repeated watering down of Israeli obligations during Oslo.[51]

In the Americans' eagerness to conclude a deal, the focus on presumed internal differences among the Palestinians was based on the hope that at some point they would pressure Arafat into accepting their envisioned compromise; alternatively, it might lead to an end run around Arafat, perhaps even provoking a mini-coup within the Palestinian hierarchy that would result in agreement. In the end, there was little to show for all these maneuvers. In fact, it stoked even more suspicion within the Palestinian team, resulting in more negotiation gridlock and dissension that at one point resulted in an actual fistfight between Abed Rabbo and Asfur.

• • •

**Though it wasn't** recognized at the time by the delegations, some of the committee meetings were making significant first steps in discussing taboo issues, particularly regarding refugees. At various points these talks were held between Israelis most ardently opposed to the right of return, including Elyakim Rubinstein and Dan Meridor, and Palestinians who were perceived by Americans and Israelis as being the most rigidly principled, including Nabil Shaath and Abu Mazen, although some of their colleagues privately say the exact opposite is true. To be sure, the Israeli side had regressed from its earlier ideas at Stockholm, according to Ben Ami, because they felt with "flexibility on the territorial issue—that the peace would not stand or fall on [the refugee] issue."[52] Regardless, these four negotiators were not involved in Stockholm, and to a certain extent both sides represented the types of Israelis and Palestinians who would ultimately have to endorse any compromise.

These talks were over fifty years in the making, and though some, like Meridor and Abu Mazen, had debated the topic with each other privately as early as 1997,[53] Camp David was the first time they had negotiated the issue in the context of a

U.S.-mediated effort to reach a workable solution. Sharing the sentiment of countless other Israelis, Meridor related how the refugee issue was perceived by Israelis, and how this related to their own experiences as refugees from Europe:

> We sat with the Palestinians on refugees for five, six, seven meetings, for several hours each. It was very interesting—very good, but very, very deep. You could see, in most moralistic terms, two narratives colliding . . . . It's narrative: it's to say, for me, Dan Meridor, the return of Jerusalem to Israel is a historic justice in the most sublime sense—on a historic basis, a human basis . . . after what had happened [to the Jews in Europe]. To me, there is nothing more just that was done in human history than this. And we did it! We never took the land from people who owned it. The Arabs never owned Palestine. For years there were Arabs there, there were Turks there. They never made Jerusalem their capital.
>
> So I saw people there. It doesn't seem like my parents—I say it very personal, but it's not a personal thing—who made their way to Palestine . . . leaving Europe and going through the embarrassment to this land, as if they did something awful, like a crime—taking away a land that belonged to Palestinians, in their perception.

Meridor knew that any refugee compromise would take a long time to condition both publics, definitely more time than the eight days set aside. Even so, he concluded what he believed would be necessary:

> It's the most sensitive, the most touching, the most emotional, religious involvement. There's a constituency for this—it's a million or a half a million or two million—whatever people, some of whom were kept for sixty years in the refugee camps. Promised, time after time, that they will eventually go home. So I say to you, or I say to my people, I will tell the Israelis—

the Jews—"We fellow Jews cannot get all the land. Why? Because we have here three or four million Palestinians who don't want to live under us. We've been forced on them, and we don't want them to be part of us anyway. We want to stay a democracy. There is no way."

. . . I say to [the Palestinians]: "You . . . say to your people, 'All the land is ours—Haifa, Tel Aviv, all is ours.' But there are Jews. Five million Jews, and we need to live with them." This is reality. So we should have all of it but the cantons. So we retain power, we have a part of it since the first time. And all our aspirations will be realized in that as safe. You Arabs who lost your home or were expelled or ran away or whatever, you want to return to the land you will be in the land—in the part that is called Palestine. Not in the part that is called Israel, because you can't go to your home anyway because your home is now not in existence anymore—inhabited by Jews for sixty years or something.[54]

Malley, who attended most of the refugee talks, noted that Palestinians were not asking for a full right of return. What they wanted was recognition of the right of return *in principle,* after which they would agree "to take into account Israel's interest." For the Palestinian negotiators, this was a gigantic concession—indeed, it was one that they knew was considered thoroughly unconscionable to a great many of their own people. But to the Israelis it was unreassuringly, indeed threateningly, vague, and constituted a dangerous legal loophole. As an American looking for a compromise, Malley described the difficulty:

It's hard, because [once the principle of return is recognized,] why should it be 10,000, 20,000, 30,000, 40,000, 50,000? There is no logical break point, unless you're prepared to say—which the Israelis said—no right of return to Israel at all, and let Israelis do family reunification, which is

> where we headed. But it is very hard for the Palestinians to basically agree we're giving [the Israelis] one principle completely, whereas on all the other ones, there's some flexibility, some nuance, some compromise.[55]

After Camp David some Palestinians conceded, off the record, that Arafat had been willing to accept a limited right of return, in all likelihood within the symbolic strictures of "family reunification" entertained at Stockholm, so long as the Palestinians received recognition of that right and a viable state with Palestinian sovereignty over East Jerusalem and the Haram al-Sharif/Temple Mount. With those compromises in hand, Arafat would be in a strengthened position to go to the Al Aqsa Mosque and address the entire Palestinian diaspora: "There is no reason to go live in Israel now. Come home and help us build the state we have!"[56]

Unfortunately, Barak did not come to Camp David seeking the necessary tradeoff by delivering a full restoration, or even close to a full restoration, of the June 4, 1967, line, much less Palestinian sovereignty over the Haram al-Sharif/Temple Mount. As negotiations approached the second week, these issues were far too underdeveloped. The best the Americans could hope for was to bring the parties closer.

At least initially, the Americans did not feel Barak had come ready to negotiate, particularly considering the lack of civility he accorded Arafat throughout their few summit exchanges. There was no better example of this than on the evening of July 16, when Clinton convened Arafat and Barak for a dinner. Throughout the meal, Barak said almost nothing to Arafat, who looked humiliated. Israelis later excused Barak's behavior as a personality quirk. But there was no denying they had earlier used the argument of poor personal relations as a reason for not making negotiating concessions with the Syrians at Blair House and Shepherdstown. Gemal Helal made the connection:

> Right before Camp David, Barak kept saying that this is the time to sit down and get to it. But in reality, they never sat down and got to it! Except for one dinner, this never happened, and even at dinner you could not discuss.
>
> The point was to go because of the leaders. Once there, however, Barak locked himself up in the room. He didn't have one single gathering with Arafat except for tea with the condition to not discuss things of substance. Barak didn't play the role he said he wanted to play, which was to sit down and look Arafat in the eye.
>
> He did the same damn thing with the Syrians at Shepherdstown. I described him to Clinton by giving him the nickname "the runaway bride." Barak is the runaway bride.[57]

Sandy Berger later disclosed his frustration with Barak to Sher, saying that Barak, in his opinion, had "pressured" Clinton to do the summit but once there had refused to show "required flexibility." Berger went so far as to tell Sher that he intended to switch his summit role and become "the president's watchdog."[58]

To steer a new course, Clinton asked for the cooperation of both Arafat and Barak in presenting two negotiators each, without letting the rest of the delegation know, to engage in marathon discussion on all the issues.[59] It was to be a simulation exercise, and whatever was to be discussed would be completely protected and nonbinding.

Thus from just after midnight until noontime on July 17, Ben Ami, Sher, Dahlan, and Erekat found themselves under lock and key at the Laurel conference center with strict orders that they could not leave or talk with others on the outside. It was an artificial pressure cooker, but at this stage the Americans were running out of ideas on how to get both sides to reveal their bottom lines. Perhaps feeling the pressure from the hosts, the

Israelis brought forward several ideas the Americans noted as progress. According to Ben Ami:

> For the first time, we put forward a proposal about Jerusalem. The proposal was that the outer envelope of Arab neighborhoods in the city would be under Palestinian sovereignty, the inner envelope would be under functional autonomy, the Old City under a special regime, and the Temple Mount under a perpetual Palestinian trusteeship. Clinton was very pleased with our proposal. Ehud also thought we had taken a courageous step—that was before he made his own courageous decisions—and it was a form of a breakthrough that extricated the process from its impasse.[60]

The Israelis also improved on territorial issues, moving down the areas for annexation from 14 to 12 percent; reserving 10 percent of the West Bank along the Jordan Valley for long-term occupation under a lease arrangement of twelve to thirty more years. While land leasing terms did work well in the Israeli-Jordanian peace agreement, in light of the cumulative Palestinian Oslo experience, the Israeli leasing terms were always accompanied by the proviso that the handover of land to Palestinians would be on the "basis of mutual agreement," meaning it would almost never be honored. This would raise the net Palestinian areas (including the Jordan Valley areas under continued Israeli control) to 88 percent.[61] This figure, of course, did not factor in the areas Israel presumed it could annex, such as territorial waters of the Dead Sea; the area known as "No Man's Land," near the Latrun salient northwest of Jerusalem; and portions of post-1967 East Jerusalem, which altogether totaled 5 percent of the land.[62] Nor did it take into consideration the break in territorial contiguity created by the more than sixty Jewish settlements and access roads the Israelis wanted to remain within the proposed Palestinian state, under some sort of vaguely specified autonomy.[63]

In exchange for this offer, the Israelis wanted the Palestinians to agree to a total "end of conflict" agreement, eliminating all past, present, and future claims, which prompted one of the more colorful moments during the exhausting morning hours. Ghaith al-Omari, one of the young Palestinian legal advisers, was allowed to the talks along with Gidi Grinstein and Israel Hasson from the Israeli side. Ben Ami, seriously sleep-deprived by that point, criticized Omari regarding the Dahlan/Erekat skittishness over the "end of conflict" demands. Omari, less exhausted and thinking critically about the unknown damages and expenses associated with reclaiming land, lost or damaged property, and the undoing of the settlement infrastructure, replied, "Obviously, we haven't discussed our compensation for the years of occupation." Grinstein understood Omari's good intentions but could not hold back Ben Ami, who went berserk. The Israelis at the summit began to suspect the Palestinians were planning massive lawsuits, so they dug their heels in further.

Despite everything, the Americans were trying to miss the trees and see the forest. Having learned afterward that the Israelis had agreed to share functional control of the Haram al-Sharif/Temple Mount while retaining overall sovereignty—something the Americans wouldn't have dared propose before the Israelis—their summit outlook turned optimistic. The Palestinians, who advised the President in a letter that without a commitment to international resolutions there would be no agreement, did not share the same sentiment.[64]

• • •

**For both Clinton** and Barak, domestic realities were affecting the summit. In Israel, more than 150,000 demonstrators gathered at Rabin Square in Tel Aviv to protest the talks. Ariel Sharon, who had organized the rally with Natan Sharansky and others, had the following message for Barak:

> Before us, to my regret, and I say it with sorrow, is a prime minister who threatens his people with terrorism, with war, with an intifada, and enlists world leaders, ministers, and political activists to join in his threats. . . . A responsible, experienced prime minister would limit himself to one sentence. He would say: 'Israel is strong. You have been warned.' That is how a strong, self-respecting country behaves. . . . Barak's peace is a mistaken and a bad peace, a peace of the moment. We must speak about what Arafat will give up. I want to hear from Camp David that Arafat has given up East Jerusalem and the Old City; that he gave up the Jordan Valley; the airspace over Judea and Samaria. I don't want to hear, and I'm sure you don't want to hear, all the time only about Israel making concessions![65]

Clinton, meanwhile, had to break from the negotiations in order to come to the defense of his wife, Hillary, who was accused of making an anti-Semitic remark nearly three decades earlier. The *New York Daily News* sensationalized the rumor, so Clinton phoned its chairman, Mortimer Zuckerman (also the president of the Zionist Organization of America), who agreed to allow an interview. Clinton's response:

> She might have called [a former campaign manager] a bastard—I wouldn't rule that out. She's never claimed that she was pure on profanity. But I've never heard her tell a joke with an ethnic connotation. She's so fanatic about it. She can't tell an ethnic joke—it's not in her. Every Jew in America is nervous about the Middle East, and this comes out at this time . . . . [The Lazio campaign knows] if they have to go head to head with her on stature, on accomplishment and on her record, they lose. So the only thing they have left is character assassination.[66]

Regarding the summit progress, Clinton remarked,

> I would be totally misleading if I said I had an inkling that a deal is at hand. That's just not true. But we're slogging. God, it's hard. It's like nothing I've ever dealt with—all the negotiations with the Irish, all the stuff I've done with the Palestinians before this and with the Israelis, the Balkans at Dayton.[67]

With the domestic political risks painfully evident, Clinton was in no mood to hear the Palestinians dismiss the latest proposals of Ben Ami and Sher. Arafat, however, remained determined to assert sovereignty over East Jerusalem, including the Haram al-Sharif/Temple Mount.

At a meeting on the evening of July 17 at Aspen, Arafat made an astounding relegation of the territorial issue to President Clinton. In exchange for guarantees that there would be a fair solution to the refugee question, no Israeli presence on the border with Jordan, and full Palestinian sovereignty over East Jerusalem—except for the Jewish neighborhoods, which he had conceded earlier—Arafat told Clinton he would be willing to leave the issue of territorial percentages to Clinton's judgment. Within an hour the Israelis knew what had been offered, as Dan Meridor divulged:

> There was a breakthrough meeting between them—the Americans and the Palestinians—in which Clinton allegedly said to Arafat, "Barak wants 10 percent of the land . . . I think I can take him down to 8 percent. And I ask you, Mr. Arafat, to leave it to me to finalize this."
>
> The response of Arafat, as I was told immediately after it happened by Dennis [Ross] or Martin [Indyk], was that Arafat had said, "I want a swap in exchange of land." Not saying "No," saying "A swap!" He was *not* insisting on the exact 1967 line . . . . Clinton said to him, "The swap can only be symbolic." . . . [Ross and Indyk] saw it as a great breakthrough, because we see we are without an agreement regarding the

> borders. And I said immediately, no way! I was against any swap, I have to admit.

Meridor further explained how the Americans revealed to him their proposal to bridge the differences on territorial percentages:

> I asked, "What did you have in mind by the swaps?" And the response to me was, "[We] wanted to give you 9 percent, not the ten percent you wanted, and take from [Israel] 1 percent." This is what I heard with my own ears from the American negotiators. I said no way! . . . The Israelis would not agree to this, I know that.[68]

With foreknowledge over what Clinton was going to propose on territory, Barak cleverly adapted his stance on that issue by repackaging it in a way he knew in advance would be welcomed.

• • •

**On July 17, in** a marathon session from 1 P.M. that day until 6 A.M. the next, Barak and his team finally began their internal wrangling to see what they could live with. Ben Ami and Sher had broken the taboo on Jerusalem the night before, and it was time for Barak to gauge how others would react. The discussions were described by some Israelis as especially long and difficult. Many members of the team were risk averse, but at least four said Barak should be more forthcoming. Some Israelis thought that, while they would not agree to Palestinian sovereignty over the Haram al-Sharif/Temple Mount, they also would not force the issue of keeping it under Israeli sovereignty. Barak made clear to all his belief that "no Israeli Prime Minister can give up the Temple Mount." As the hours passed, it became evident that almost no one thought it wise to keep insisting on Israeli sovereignty over the Arab neighborhoods of East Jerusalem. Even Rubinstein managed to change his mind, at one point uttering, "There is no way to have Israeli control over the Palestinian populated areas of Jerusalem."[69]

Just after midnight on July 18, these important talks were interrupted when Barak, who was enjoying a dish of peanuts, managed to get one lodged in his throat, rendering him unable to breathe. Gidi Grinstein, working in an adjoining room, recalled first hearing coughs, then pats on the back, voices with a serious tone, finally a secretary's pleas to call for a doctor. By the time Grinstein walked into the room, the prime minister was barely standing, with his hand in the air. Amid the panic, Grinstein, the youngest member of the delegation, grabbed the prime minister like a rag doll and with one forceful thrust of the Heimlich maneuver was able to save the day. Everyone was unsettled, including Grinstein, but after the momentary rush of bodyguards, Marines, and the president's own physician, it was all back to business.

To interrupt what appeared to Palestinians as Barak's self-imposed exile to avoid negotiations, Clinton went over to Barak's cabin to check on his health and carry the momentum of Arafat's latest offer. The advances made during the internal Israeli discussions—described by one Israeli as ones that "could only be done by a person with balls the size of Barak's"—would not be passed along to Clinton, at least initially. The prime minister, in a negotiating construct that Malley would later characterize as the "false bottom" approach, purported that Sher and Ben Ami had taken him beyond the ends of his elasticity. For Clinton, it was more evidence of the pussyfooting he had grown weary of in the weeks before the summit. Still dour over Barak's refusal to honor the March 8 commitments, which, in Clinton's own words, had caused the Palestinians to view him as a false prophet, the president was out of patience. According to Malley, Clinton let loose with "all his cumulative frustrations":

> I can't go see Arafat with a retrenchment! You can sell it; there is no way I can. This is not real. This is not serious. I went to Shepherdstown [for the Israeli-Syrian negotiations] and was told nothing by you for four days. I went to Geneva [for the summit with Asad] and felt like a wooden Indian doing your bidding. I will not let it happen here!"[70]

Since Clinton was scheduled to leave the following day for Okinawa and there was no agreement in sight, he proposed to Barak either ending the summit or brokering a limited agreement.[72] Some on the American team, particularly from State, supported this approach, believing it a mistake to do anything otherwise. But in the end, both Barak and Clinton wanted to return home with the coveted "end of conflict" grand bargain.

At this point in the talks, given the impasse on big issues, the American team figured the best thing would be to move the talks forward by reaching agreement on smaller details first, which might build momentum toward agreement on the more difficult issues. Whether in committee meetings or discussions among the leaders, Clinton's ability to do this was greatly frustrated by his own team's poor administrative handling of the summit, aggravated further by internal divisions and disunity between Albright's State team and Berger's White House/NSC team.

The importance of summit staff work was central to the success of Camp David 1978. William Quandt reflected how this dynamic helped facilitate President Carter:

> We had a pretty good support team for the president who had worked together for quite a long time and knew each other well. What that meant was that we were pretty good at doing quick staff-work and there weren't a lot of internal divisions. We would tend to produce reasonably coherent and agreed positions, and at the end of the day it was still up to the President to either accept them or not accept them.

The dangers of having a divided summit staff, Quandt said, was that the "staff can screw you up."[72]

Indeed, at the Camp David 2000 summit, State team members were frustrated at what they saw as the White House/NSC team's usurping of the negotiations. Many of them had been preparing for this summit their entire adult lives, but as Indyk explained, the political jockeying, which at times left him out, gave way to what he considered a dysfunctional situation:

> The way things were structured at Camp David was completely—instead of Dennis going with the president to the meetings with the principals or Barak, it was the president and an NSC note taker, because if Dennis was going to go with the president, then it also required Sandy and Madeleine to go—plus a note taker—plus a translator. So instead of one-on-one plus note takers, translators, you would end up with five of them, and therefore I think this was just a real problem.
>
> . . . You had all these other people who were kibitzing the president—advising the president—a cacophony of voices . . . . So there was the president, Sandy, Madeleine, Rob Malley, Bruce Riedel, John Podesta, Maria Echaveste and Dennis. Dennis is just one voice who only had a partial readout to what exactly happened. And so I think it was just a very dysfunctional time.

The summit had taken this form, Indyk believed, because "it was a White House show; this was history being made!" Indyk further maintained that some people who had no experience dealing with Arab-Israeli issues and were in the talks for purely political reasons affected the quality of what the United States could present:

> There were a lot of cooks in the kitchen that didn't know anything about what they were doing. In terms of the people

> who were in the room around the president, you had the president, Sandy Berger, and Madeleine Albright. You had John Podesta—as the chief of staff—you had his deputy, Maria Echaveste....[73]

Dennis Ross could not have agreed more. With a slight degree of arrogance, he gave his view of the role he was supposed to play:

> I was in a better position than they were because I would get a fuller debrief. I'd get a reading of all the notes by the note taker because right afterwards, you see, the debriefs were kept only to me, Madeleine, and Sandy. So I actually was in a pretty good position to know.
>
> But the real problem I think was . . . the fact is the president, as good and as knowledgeable as he was, is not a negotiator, whereas I knew these guys inside and out because I lived with them. On every single one of these issues I had fought through with them over time. So you didn't have the benefit of me fighting through in a meeting, with one side or the other, when they would come up with their particular approach. And that I think was a mistake.
>
> It was also true that maybe because the stakes were even higher, Sandy and Madeleine also wanted to be in, and what Martin said was right. You would suddenly go from—you had a group as opposed to just the two of us.[74]

But as far as the White House/NSC team was concerned, the State team was inefficiently managing the president's time, which inevitably diminished the procedural aspects of the summit. Echaveste observed:

> There were times they were not prepared. By "they" I mean the State Department and Dennis and Madeleine. Initially they were

making the plan—"OK, this is what we are going to do today"—as we went along. We would get together in the morning. It always started because the protocol office wanted to know, "OK, are we having lunch together today? Are we going to sit separately?" . . . [Protocol offices] couldn't get any traction from Dennis and Madeleine, because they didn't have a plan.

The Clinton administration had commonly been criticized for its informality and its graduate-school style of handling policy debates. But at Camp David this approach was taken to the point of diminishing the president's role, which Echaveste objected to:

There were times, especially at the beginning, when it was like [Clinton] was sitting there as one of the staff people figuring out how this should run. That's not what the president should be doing! So we had to really push. He shouldn't have to be sitting there with Dennis and Rob and Bruce and Madeleine and Sandy—let's not forget Sandy. That was a huge tension between Sandy and Madeleine as to who was sort of orchestrating the pace of the discussions and what's being discussed.[75]

Toni Verstandig, who was considered part of the State team led by Ross, acknowledged the administrative problems and internal power struggles:

I don't think we were prepared going into the meetings as well as we should have. I am a structured, detail-oriented person. I don't think we did the kind of paper preparation, "ganging-up," "this happens and then you do this; this is the fallback." It was very loosy-goosy, because that's Dennis and that's the way Dennis liked to run things.

The cooks in the kitchen—it's not so much the numbers at meetings, but numbers at a particular meeting. You would

> have Sandy Berger, Madeleine Albright, the political people, you know . . . Maria Echaveste, Podesta, and there were a lot of cooks in the kitchen. . . . The pendulum would go from Madeleine to Sandy. You had too many poo-bahs; you had too many chiefs![76]

In the view of some Israelis, the internal American problems portended disaster. Sher and Grinstein went so far as to lobby their hosts to start locking in points of agreement. Where gaps remained, they encouraged the Americans to lay down their own formulation and crack heads as a way to move through disagreements. Instead, their hosts kept waiting for a breakthrough, without properly locking in the advances that had been made. Though Barak professed that he wanted nothing committed to paper, his own team recognized that, should the summit collapse, their achievements might perish and that positions on all sides might even harden. What they did not realize was how closely the Americans would take Barak's lead on every aspect of the summit.

The Americans who shuttled in and out of different meetings relied mostly on their memory to report progress to others, which left them vulnerable to mistakes or charges of unfairness in the event that an issue later became a point of contention. Verstandig would later reflect:

> I wish we had had a more formal structure. That doesn't mean in a bureaucratic sense. But that means that notes were taken and kept for review; a more formal record of meetings. Dennis was the only one who had them, and they were his personal, chicken-scratch notes. Had we done more complete brainstorming and research we would have been able to push the process along.[77]

• • •

**Just before dawn** on July 18, Clinton had a private conversation with Barak in which many believed he finally heard Barak's bottom lines. At least on territory, Barak's ideas mirrored precisely what Ross had earlier signaled as an acceptable American figure: Israeli annexation of 9 percent of the West Bank in exchange for a 1 percent swap of Israeli land to be added to the Gaza Strip. In addition, Barak wanted continued Israeli occupation over 15-20 percent of the West Bank border with Jordan for twelve years. Refugees would be given a yet-to-be-defined "satisfactory solution." On Jerusalem, most of the outer neighborhoods would fall under Palestinian sovereignty, while the inner neighborhoods would fall under an Oslo-type juridical scheme that accorded Palestinians certain municipal responsibilities, such as security patrols and trash collection, without having actual sovereignty.

All of this, however, was to be overshadowed as Barak put down his ace of spades: Palestinians would be granted sovereignty over the Christian and Muslim quarters of the Old City, with guaranteed custodianship—but not sovereignty—over the Haram al-Sharif/Temple Mount.

Reactions within the U.S. team were a mixture of optimism and pessimism. Albright, judging by the fact that Arafat would be able to claim a capital in East Jerusalem, saw Barak's offer as "both far reaching and brave."[78] Ben Ami recalled:

> I remember walking in the fields with Martin Indyk that night and both of us saying that Ehud was nuts. We didn't understand how he could even have thought of agreeing. Afterward I wrote in my diary that everyone thinks that Amnon [Lipkin-] Shahak and I are pushing Barak to the left, but the truth is that he was the one who pushed us leftward. At that stage—this was the start of the second week of the meeting—he was far more courageous than we were. Truly courageous. Clinton told me a few times: "I have never met such a courageous person."[79]

Others from the American team, like Gemal Helal, knew full well the proposal stood no chance of being accepted by either the Palestinians or the broader Arab and Muslim world. As Malley would later argue, Barak's offer was just one of many that were too often "greeted with unwarranted enthusiasm" based on the "distance Israel had gone, rather than the distance that remained."[80] The most important summit reaction, however, was from President Clinton, who had begun considering delaying his trip to Japan to see if the proposal could fly. Amnon Lipkin-Shahak observed:

> The Americans wanted an agreement—no doubt about it. The Americans really appreciated what Barak did, because Barak, for the first time in the history of Israel—Rabin didn't put Jerusalem on the table for discussions, Peres didn't do it, for sure not Netanyahu—and not even Barak before he was elected! I think that Clinton was really surprised by the generosity of Barak about Jerusalem. I think that the American team never dreamed that Barak would put on the table such an offer about Jerusalem.[81]

• • •

**Not far away,** in Emmitsburg, Maryland, the best and brightest Israeli and Palestinian experts were haggling over important economic and civil affairs issues. Toni Verstandig, who surveyed the progress, sent news to everyone that an agreement between the leaders was imminent. A sense of urgency was injected into the discussions, as two Israeli and Palestinian water experts furiously worked on a hallway chalkboard, arguing back and forth like competing mathematicians. Verstandig, perhaps impatient from watching the exhausting bartering process, stepped between the two and said, "I'm not going to allow these piddly issues to be a stumbling block to a peace agreement!" With that, witnesses recalled, she took the eraser, wiped off the formulations, and with a piece of chalk drew an elongated dollar sign. After slamming the chalk down and facing the group, her words would leave them speechless: "Just tell me how much!"

Even when word got back that a deal was not so imminent after all, the Emmitsburg talks persisted. But after sensing that the American facilitator would rather buy peace than negotiate it, the value of presenting well-prepared arguments seemed less important. Boredom reigned, and with all the action elsewhere, even the bodyguards looked hard for amusement. While showcasing evasive driving maneuvers in the parking lot outside, one special agent managed to flip his vehicle upside down, creating quite a scene.

• • •

**On the afternoon** of July 18 Clinton decided to present what Barak had earlier revealed to him under the guise of "American ideas." To assuage Barak's paranoia that Arafat, who might not see it as far-reaching enough, would attempt to pocket the proposal to divide Jerusalem's neighborhoods in the event the summit failed, they were conveyed as talking points to Arafat, who took notes. Given Ross's indirect assurances on the territorial swap of 9:1, there was some truth to the description of that part of the deal as American. But Arafat, ever suspicious and far less enthused, could not hold back on interrupting the President. "These are Israeli ideas," he said. "I received them unofficially from the Israeli delegation two hours ago."[82]

To be sure, the form of Clinton's presentation was bothersome for Arafat. But not as much as the substance, which he rejected outright. Arafat reportedly responded by saying, "I'm not about to have Israeli occupation replaced with Israeli sovereignty."[83]

Word of Arafat's rejection quickly reached Barak, who took the liberty of advising Clinton that the "American" proposals on Jerusalem no longer stood. Barak convinced

Clinton to remove them from the American ideas. Clinton's subsequent attempts to get Ben Ami to resurrect the idea were to no avail.[84]

On the evening of July 18 the Israelis and Americans prepared a proposal that would have the UN Security Council bestow diplomatic/embassy status for Palestinians over the property of the Haram al-Sharif/Temple Mount. The Americans knew they would face little difficulty passing such a vote through the permanent five Security Council members. But they would first need the important approval of the newly anointed King Muhammad VI of Morocco, who inherited his father's role as Jerusalem caretaker under the umbrella of the Organization of the Islamic Conference's Jerusalem Committee. While this was a creative way to leave Israelis with ultimate sovereignty over the Haram al-Sharif/Temple Mount, the Palestinians would not construe it as fulfilling their legal rights. More importantly, the entire Muslim world, including almost sixty member states within the OIC, would be even more unlikely to accept Israeli sovereignty over the Haram al-Sharif/Temple Mount than Arafat.

During a chance encounter with the president at the cafeteria, Mohammed Dahlan got a sense from Clinton that a new idea was in the works. His gut made him worry. Fearful that the summit would end by blaming Arafat and, by default, the entire Palestinian cause, Dahlan believed his reputation as one of the more flexible Palestinians might convince Clinton to run it by him first; if Dahlan found it unacceptable, then it certainly would not fly with Arafat. Clinton agreed, and soon Ross and Helal presented it to him in private. Dahlan recalled that he was the first Palestinian to reject it, even pleading with Ross, "If you show this initiative to President Arafat, the whole summit will explode tomorrow morning!" Feeling reassured that his point had been made, Dahlan felt less worried that Arafat would be set up for another meeting with Clinton where he would be viewed

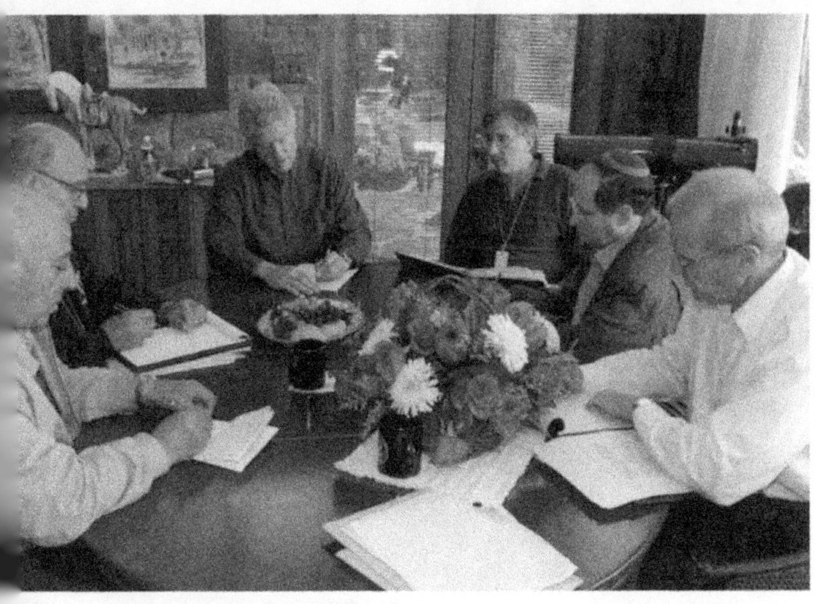

Clinton and negotiators talking inside at Camp David. From left: Abu Ala, Nabil Shaath, Clinton, Dennis Ross, Elyakim Rubinstein, Martin Indyk. (© Clinton Presidential Archives)

Clinton discussing the refugee issue with Rubinstein and Grinstein (facing camera) and (backs to camera) Nabil Shaath and Abu Mazen. (© Gidi Grinstein)

Territories, Palestinian Territories and areas in East Jerusalem which will be subject to Special Arrangements under Israeli sovereignty.]

4. The Expanded Area of Jerusalem ~~municipal area~~ will host the national capitals of both Israel and the Palestinian State.

Articles VII - Economic Relations
Article VIII - Water
Article IX – Legal Cooperation and Law Enforcement
Article X - Coordinating Mechanisms for Implementation
Article XI- Settlement of Differences and Disputes
Article XII- Final Clauses

For the Government of Israel

For the Palestine Liberation Organization

**Ross's slapdash changes to appease Barak on the most explosive summit topic—Jerusalem—which spelled the death of the Camp David drafting process.**

**Also at the request of the Israelis, Ross made an amendment to the sacrosanct negotiation bedrock: Resolution 242.**

REITERATING their commitment to United Nations Security Council Resolutions 242 and 338 and confirming their understanding that the FAPS is based upon and will lead to the implementation of Resolutions 242 and 338 between ~~them~~ → the basis for their implementation

VIEWING the FAPS as providing the basis for the resolution of the Israeli-Palestinian conflict and as an historic milestone in the creation of peace in the entire Middle East and between the entire Arab and Muslim worlds and Israel;

HEREBY AGREE AS FOLLOWS:

Article I: The Permanent Status Agreement and the End of the Israeli-Palestinian Conflict

1. The foregoing Preamble is an integral part of this Agreement

2. This Agreement constitutes the framework for resolving all the issues reserved for permanent status negotiations. It sets forth the principles, mechanisms and schedules for resolving each of these issues.

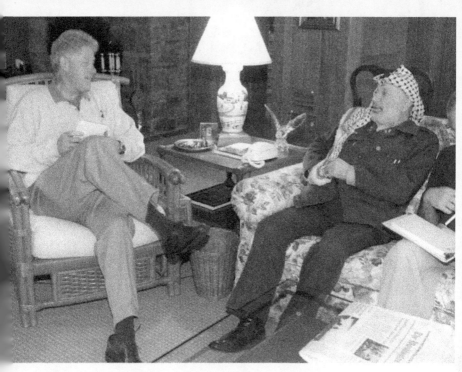

Clinton and Arafat talking inside. (© Clinton Presidential Archives)

Arafat, Clinton, and Saeb Erekat. (© Clinton Presidential Archives)

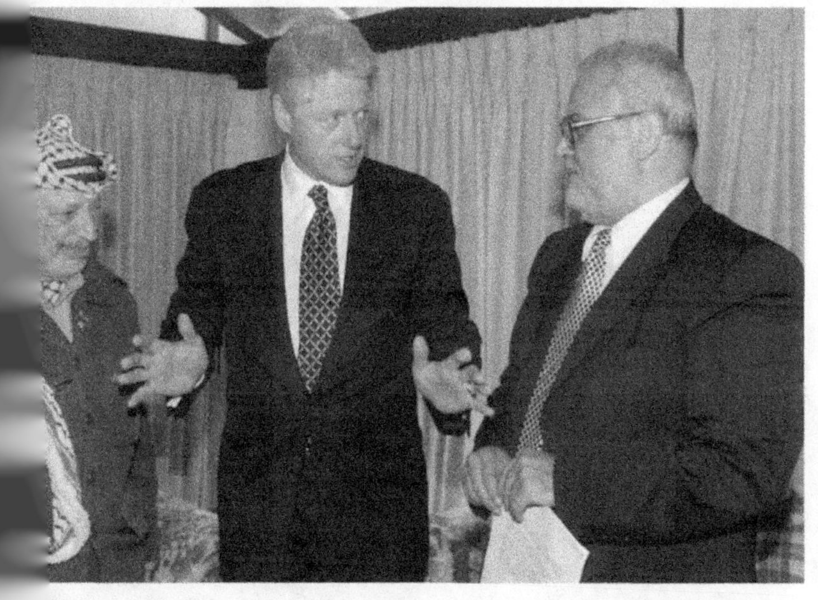

Barak, Albright, Berger, and Malley at Camp David. Albright often felt that Berger overstepped his bounds in the negotiations. This created internal divisions and heightened confusion at the summit. (© Clinton Presidential Archives)

Arafat looks at Clinton before the end of the Camp David summit. Clinton promised Arafat he wouldn't be blamed—and promptly went back on his word. (© Clinton Presidential Archives)

Ross, Albright, and Clinton have the last laugh just hours before announcing the collapse of the Camp David summit on July 25, 2000. Clinton's threat to let "all hell break loose" would be realized two months later. (© White House Photo/Author's Collection)

The author speaking with Israeli Defense Minister Shaul Mofaz, just one month after the Israeli Air Force bombed targets inside Syria, shattering a ceasefire in place since 1974. I told Mofaz of my conversations with Syrian officials, who still want full peace with Israel in exchange for Israel's full withdrawal from the Golan Heights. At right is Israel's Washington defense attaché, Major General Evry Sukenik. (© Author's Collection)

A roadside bomb killed three U.S. diplomatic security contractors in Gaza on October 16, 2003, a sad reminder of the increasing hazards of conducting U.S. diplomacy in the occupied territories. (© Diplomatic Security Service, U.S. State Department)

One of the many IDF towers standing watch over Palestinians in the Gaza Strip. (© Author's Collection)

American peace activist Rachel Corrie, just before and after being crushed by an IDF bulldozer. Even Americans expressing nonviolent opposition to the occupation are not immune to Israeli lethal force. (© International Solidarity Movement)

Young Palestinians forced to lie prone in front of a tank during the second intifada. (© WAFA)

A Palestinian suicide bombing at a pizzeria in Jerusalem on August 9, 2001, killed 15 and wounded about 130. (© Israeli Ministry of Foreign Affairs)

Two women hugging in front of demolished houses. (© WAFA)

as intransigent. The Israeli positions were progressing, and Dahlan didn't want the Americans to get the impression the Palestinians were uninterested.

But Ross, with the same disregard for Dahlan's entreaties as he had for Daoudi's at Shepherdstown, felt Barak's proposal was eminently fair and generous.[85] In the end it was for Arafat, not Dahlan, to reject, and it was as much a "test" of Arafat by both the Americans and Barak, to see if he could bring himself to make a deal on their terms.

• • •

**Clinton's departure for** Okinawa was approaching. Fearing a summit collapse, he was determined to leave no stone unturned. He summoned Arafat to Aspen, where they sat in the living room joined only by Helal, who was there to interpret. Clinton used every possible means to convince him to accept Israeli sovereignty over the Haram al-Sharif/Temple Mount, beginning with financial inducements. He promised:

> I will go to the G-8 meeting on Wednesday and I will ask them to provide the support your need for your state. What I ask you to do is to make a principled compromise on Jerusalem. It is not everything you want, but it's the price you have to pay.[86]

Arafat insisted he could not be bought, causing Clinton, increasingly desperate, to embody the persona of an interrogator. He alternated between persuasive rhetoric and strong body language; at one point he grasped Arafat's arms while pressing his forehead against Arafat's.[87] Such pressure tactics were precisely what Barak had wanted.

Joe Lockhart and a group of Clinton's advisers, including Ross, looked in on the meeting through a door in the adjoining room; they would later describe Arafat's reactions in the most unflattering manner. Lockhart offered his impression:

> I was like a kid off the street looking at these things. And I sat ten feet away from the last meetings with Clinton and Arafat, with Clinton pulling out everything, pleading with him, bullying him, using everything he could to try and push him to take the step toward this deal.
>
> I was completely convinced at that moment that Arafat wouldn't take any deal. I think he was at the point in his life where this sense of willingness to take huge risks was gone, and he looked at his legacy, and it was almost as if he became a smaller person. He sat there and in his mind, he was saying, "I'm not the Arab who is going to give up Jerusalem."
>
> I think it came down to Arafat and again, not being an expert, it struck me at that moment that we weren't going to make progress for another generation. . . . He was smaller than life that night. He looked like a feeble old man.[88]

It was hard for Arafat to say no to Clinton, whom he personally liked, but he stood firm in his refusal, reminding Clinton that the proposals looked no better coming from the president than they had when conveyed earlier from Ross to Dahlan. In the end, Arafat agreed to Clinton's request to mull it over and give some sense of finality as to whether or not it constituted a basis for continuing the summit.

• • •

**As the president** pondered whether to delay his trip to Okinawa any further, it became apparent that the summit was on life support. Worse, as the days and nights blurred into a constant stream of dialogue, his own delegation appeared ready to implode. The nerves of both State and White House/NSC were frayed over the possibility their summit might undermine the entire Oslo process and ruin all their hard work and effort, not to mention the legacy of peace they all wanted to be a part of.

But in their desperation to prevent disaster, they only helped create one, as the State and White House/NSC teams kept stepping on each other through uncoordinated and unprofessionally managed separate streams of dialogue. All of this was evident to both the Israeli and Palestinian teams.

The Palestinians were becoming less and less discreet with the president in voicing their belief that certain individuals, especially Ross, were damaging the talks. It was clear even to themselves that they were focusing more on how to defend themselves from American-Israeli proposals rather than taking the offensive or looking for openings. The Americans understood this and, at the risk that the Palestinians might completely shut down, the president had to make a stand. Unlike at Wye River in 1998, when Clinton and Ross ferried side by side between the parties, it became increasingly clear that, for the sake of keeping the summit together, the president would have to rely on his White House/NSC circle of advisers, whom he increasingly brought with him to important meetings. Echaveste, who was also at Wye River and other venues, offered a general opinion about Ross from her own non-foreign-policy vantage:

> Dennis spent how many years, you know? I think maybe part of the problem there too was maybe pending the solution. I think Dennis knew the issues as well as anyone [but] at a certain point he had forgotten that the people who were negotiating this deal were not . . . *the agreement was not his.* It was theirs to make. And there was at times a blurring of, "You should approach it this way or that." It was more of an intense desire to try and make a deal from Dennis than from either side.[89]

Both Clinton and Sandy Berger decided that, to the extent they could keep it discreet, the presence of Ross needed to be minimized.[90] There were significant risks in doing so, since it meant effectively changing horses in midstream. But with widespread fears over a repeat of the Shepherdstown/Geneva fiasco, they felt the cost was worth it.

In the hours after midnight on July 19, the Palestinians came back to Clinton with their reaction, prepared at the last minute by Erekat without the help of any of the NSU legal advisers. In the form of interrogatories, they sought clarification on the latest ideas, particularly with regard to the status of the Haram al-Sharif/Temple Mount. Berger convened the NSC team in the middle of the night to provide responses, under the guise of a "policy-planning meeting," without including Albright or Ross, perhaps hoping to avoid the oft-repeated Palestinian complaint that "Dennis Ross prepared these with the Israelis."

Berger technically included at least one State employee—Helal was almost always seconded to their team—but it did little to stem the outrage of Albright and Ross, who discovered their exclusion the following morning. More shouting matches followed, at least one of which was between Albright and Berger.

The air was superficially cleared, with the discord attributed to a "misunderstanding," but the damage had already been done. With the State and White House/NSC teams no longer working in tandem, observers increasingly saw Ross practicing jump shots on Camp David's basketball court or "checking in" on the talks at Emmitsburg. He was still obsessed with concluding a deal, though the ostracism would have hurt anyone in Ross's shoes. For Israelis and Palestinians, the shakeup meant they had to rechannel their ideas, which often required new explanations, adding to an already confused atmosphere. As for Albright, it had little effect on her practical role; both sides generally avoided her, since she lacked mastery of the topic. But the tensions between Albright and Berger remained "quite visible" to the Israelis. One of them politely described it:

> I can tell you that some very central envoys or officials in certain parts of the process were not as central as they were before Camp David II. I think that, for example, Robert Malley was much more persuasive with the president than Dennis Ross, Martin Indyk, or Madeleine Albright!
>
> Sandy Berger's influence on the president was most felt by the environment. Albright and Berger were fighting over the—not fighting, you know, between friends—for the attention of the president . . . . There wasn't a coherent logic that goes all the way from top to bottom.[91]

• • •

**The morning of** July 19 began a day of heightened drama and "borrowed time," as the president delayed his trip to see if the Palestinians would relinquish their claim to the Haram al-Sharif/Temple Mount. Following their discussions with the White House/NSC team in the wee hours of the previous night, the Palestinians sent a letter to the president saying unequivocally that the ideas being proffered on territory and Jerusalem contradicted the "fundamental principles of the peace process as established by the United States itself." Unconvinced, the White House/NSC team phoned Arafat at 3 A.M. for a "clear reply" over whether or not Clinton's ideas provided a basis to continue. Erekat delivered yet another letter, advising, "These ideas do not form a basis for negotiations," to which Bruce Riedel replied, "So it's over."[92]

This was not the way President Clinton wanted things to end, so the Americans decided to pull out the stops, reiterating that Israeli sovereignty over the Haram al-Sharif/Temple Mount could be sweetened with many billions in financial assistance. The Palestinians felt cheapened. But equally hurtful were Clinton's threats to Arafat that he would "wash his hands of the peace effort if the Palestinians wasted a historic opportunity."[93]

Most Palestinians viewed Clinton as moderately fair, though comments like these eroded their trust in his avowed commitment to a peace both sides could endure. There was disillusionment among Palestinians that he was hinging long-term American support for Middle East peace on Arafat's acceptance of an incomplete set of ideas, which everyone sensed were being forced by Clinton's political calendar. Similarly, Clinton's pleas that Barak's political troubles might bring down his government carried no more weight with Palestinians than they had before.

The Palestinian advisers urged Arafat to stay strong. From the reports conveyed to Gamal Abouali, a Palestinian legal adviser marooned at Emmitsburg, the Americans were resorting to a form of bullying, colonialist diplomacy that most third parties, including Britain, had long ago outgrown:

> Barak and Clinton seemed to think that by putting pressure on senior Palestinian leaders, and by attempting to isolate them from their advisers and public opinion, they could force the Palestinian side to accept a poorly thought out, one-sided and vague deal. . . . This approach was indicative of a somewhat colonial approach to diplomacy: bring in the natives, use immense amounts of psychological pressure, and hope they succumb. This approach was bound to fail.[94]

Arafat and Clinton met several times during the day; each time Arafat returned to his cabin showing expressions of anger, betrayal, and hurt over U.S. portrayal of him as the skunk in the room for not accepting Israeli sovereignty over the Haram al-Sharif/Temple Mount. Some of the Americans, especially Ross and Albright, accused him of sloganeering, while for Arafat, his refusals were based on absolute truth:

> The Palestinian leader who will give up Jerusalem has not yet been born. I will not betray my people or the trust they have

> placed in me. Don't look to me to legitimize the occupation! Of course, it can continue longer, but it can't last forever. No one can continue indefinitely to impose domination by military force—look at South Africa! . . . Our people will not accept less than their rights as stated by international resolutions and international legality.[95]

Further heated exchanges between Clinton and Arafat eventually degenerated into an absurd debate over religion, with Clinton pitting his Judeo-Christian perspective against Arafat's Islam. Danny Yatom recalled one exchange over the Haram al-Sharif/Temple Mount in which Clinton told Arafat, "In our Bible, the place is called the Temple Mount because the Jewish temples stood there."[96] Such grandstanding continued when Clinton "almost shouted" at Arafat, "It is impossible . . . to ignore the rights of Jews on the Temple Mount!"[97]

The goading proved almost unbearable for Arafat. After reaching an emotional low point, his responses became preposterous—at one point he insisted that "the Temple Mount was not in Jerusalem, it was in Nablus!" One offensive quip was all the Israelis and Americans needed as ammunition to later spear him both as a leader bent on denying important aspects of the Jewish faith and an unchanged revolutionary who wanted nothing less than the destruction of Israel. Everyone from the American side was bothered by the comment, including Gemal Helal:

> It was a huge Palestinian mistake to not recognize the holy status of the Temple Mount. They never recognized this. In fact, Arafat said the Temple Mount was in Nablus, then in Northern Yemen, and then Saudi Arabia. Arafat will never recognize their temple. Some Palestinian negotiators have in the past confided in me that, if they were to accept this, it would mean that their religion, Islam, is wrong. They could never do this. I've gotten pretty close to Arafat over the years, and one time I said to him, "I am a Christian, and if you tell

me that Christ never died on the Cross, I'm going to say 'fuck you.'" But Arafat failed to respect their belief. He viewed it as absurd, despite the fact that Jews or Christians might find the Koran's story of Mohammed riding a magical horse to heaven one night from Al Aqsa absurd.[98]

More fodder came from Arafat during an exchange on Jerusalem with Albright, dramatically reenacted in her memoir: "When I pushed the chairman to be more forthcoming, he gazed back fiercely and said, 'The next time you see me will be when you are walking behind my coffin.'"[99]

Such quotable commentary fit the agenda of those who sought to depict Arafat as either a coward or an unrepentant rejectionist unworthy of slain Egyptian leader Sadat or of Barak, who cloaked himself in the now-venerated mantle of the martyred Rabin. But for Ambassador Ned Walker, there was nothing untruthful about Arafat's fears:

> There was no way in hell that Arafat could ever have reached an agreement on Jerusalem. He doesn't represent the Islamic world. He had to have the support of other Arab countries or Islamic countries in order to do so. There would have to be a consensus behind it. Otherwise, no matter what he agreed to, if there were any compromises at all, he would be charged with having sold Islam out the window, and there would have been a *fatwa* on his head the next day. . . . It has nothing to do with personal weaknesses. It was an absolute fact—he would have been assassinated![100]

• • •

**The Americans generally** scoffed at Arafat when he invoked the considerations of the broader Islamic world. Only at the brink of the summit's collapse would the Americans decide it worthwhile to test Arafat's theory, hoping that Barak's insistence on asserting sovereignty over the Haram al-

Sharif/Temple Mount might suffice if it had the support of major Arab countries, several of which received substantial U.S. foreign and military aid.

Hoping someone could troubleshoot their efforts to win over support among figures like Mubarak, Crown Prince Abdullah of Saudi Arabia, or King Abdullah II of Jordan, for the first and only time Clinton summoned Ambassador Walker to spend a day at Camp David. Walker observed:

> The [world's Arab leaders] were all totally in the dark. The most they had was phone calls from Arafat, which are all intercepted and read. But there was no official U.S. communication to any of these guys. The Arab world was unprepared for this! . . . When the president, at the eleventh hour, called these various leaders and asked them to press Arafat to accept a compromise on Jerusalem, he got a resounding silence.[101]

Clinton first tried to work at the Egyptians discreetly, sending then-U.S. Ambassador to Egypt, Dan Kurtzer, to lobby President Mubarak in Cairo. There was one major catch: Kurtzer was not allowed to disclose what was being proposed. Not surprisingly, Mubarak refused Kurtzer's request to lean on Arafat. When that did not work, Clinton picked up the phone himself. Mubarak later related to Walker what was said:

> I was stunned! I get a call from the president of the United States, who tells me I've got to call Arafat and push him to take a compromise on Jerusalem. I asked him, "Well, what is the background? What are the terms?" And the President said, "I can't tell you because I pledged not to reveal the details of the negotiations in advance." [So I said,] thank you, Mr. President. There's nothing I can do for you.[102]

The same comical routine was repeated with the Saudis, as Secretary Albright worked the phones through Prince Bandar. She asked him to have Crown Prince Abdullah "call

Arafat and encourage him to accept what was offered." Bandar's deputy, Rihab Massoud, recounted the charade:

> Prince Bandar said, "But what is offered?" Albright responded, "Well, we cannot go into that with you." Bandar said, "Madam, how can I ask the Crown Prince to call Arafat to tell him, 'OK, we support you on this, you better take it,' when we don't know what's in it? Look, this is absurd! This is ridiculous!"
>
> Bandar suggested Albright speak with Foreign Minister Saud, who at the time was visiting in California. We go through the same shebang: "How can we ask somebody to accept a proposal when we don't know what's in that proposal?" Albright said, "Well . . . you have to trust us on this."
>
> "I'm sorry, I like you but we're not talking about the family jewels here that I can trust you with. We're talking about something far more important than that. And we have made it so clear that we have always maintained a policy—whatever the Palestinians agree to, we will agree and we will support. . . . We have been making this so clear, with one exception: Jerusalem."[103]

Instead of receiving Arab pressure, every phone call relayed to Arafat's cabin, according to Saeb Erekat, was a unanimous expression of support. The clumsy, ill-considered démarche had backfired on the Americans, some of whom later scorned the Arab leaders, including Mubarak, as obstructionists. From what Walker briefly observed, he left Camp David more concerned than when he had arrived:

> The guys who were running it . . . when they told me what they were talking about in terms of Jerusalem it just seemed like a joke to me! I mean, they seem to think that, first of all, it was this theory that Jerusalem was *only* the *third* most important site for Islam, therefore it's not as important as the Western

> Wall is to the Jews, their *first* most important site. How that thinking got started, I don't know. Certainly there was that sense that there was more room for Arafat to compromise on Jerusalem than there was for Barak to compromise on Jerusalem. That didn't make sense at the time. It still doesn't make sense. These are much more complex issues than that![104]

• • •

**As Clinton relayed** to Barak his inability to bring Arafat to an agreement on Jerusalem, Barak activated a number of public relations fallback plans that would allow him as graceful an exit from the summit as possible. Word was sent to the scores of Israeli journalists, many of whom were accompanying Barak on his plane, to have their bags packed and ready for a departure from Washington at 8 P.M. the night of the 19th. Barak prepared a letter for Clinton, thanking him for his efforts and warning that the Palestinians would have to "face the tragic results of this missed opportunity" while alleging a lack of "good faith" on their part.[105] Barak's intended audience, of course, was not President Clinton; the quotes were given to Barak's PR team in Emmitsburg, and thus quickly made their way across the world. In an Israeli radio interview Gadi Baltiansky, Barak's official spokesman, offered the following assessment:

> I certainly do not think that remaining in Camp David indicates any progress, let alone a breakthrough, nor re-establishment of mutual trust. Indeed, the talks revealed serious difficulties. From the Prime Minister's perspective, Arafat certainly did not rise to the occasion and displayed neither the flexibility necessary for achieving an agreement, nor the ability to make the kind of decisions that the summit required. The Prime Minister's staying is designed to try to exhaust every opportunity. Arafat clearly understands that the Prime Minister is not going to give up on any vital interest of Israel.[106]

One step behind Barak, the White House Communications Office issued a bland, two-sentence announcement of the failure: "The Summit has come to a conclusion without reaching an agreement. The President will return to the White House and will make a statement at the White House."

Many Israeli negotiators—save for hard-liners Meridor and Rubinstein—viewed Barak's warning of a summit collapse as a self-fulfilling prophecy. For several hours they cycled through his cabin, one by one, using his own summit logic against him. "If you walk away from the summit now," Barak was told, "you will not be credible when you tell the world you did everything you could." Barak could not ignore their arguments. He knew there were eleven others in his party who would likely speak out later, which posed a danger to his goal of keeping the Israeli public united. Any division within Israeli society over how he performed, Barak understood, would kill hopes for a post-summit political recovery and unravel his desire for Israel to be seen by the international community as having valiantly tried to end the occupation.

Most of the old-guard Palestinians had the opposite feeling. After the immense pressure that had come down on them, the Palestinians breathed a sigh of relief: they were proud Arafat had not capitulated to what they saw as an American-Israeli trap. But more importantly, they believed President Clinton would recognize the achievements that had been made and agree to their suggestion of reconvening negotiations in a few weeks. There were strong signals of how badly they wanted to depart. Aside from President Clinton, Abu Mazen was the only delegate allowed to leave Camp David, to attend the wedding of his son in Ramallah.

The Americans went to great lengths to get both sides to cool their heels. The State Department protocol office succeeded in delaying the Palestinians from loading their luggage into the waiting motorcade: "It would be rude to leave ahead of the President," they were told.

• • •

**Storm clouds, followed** by a deluge, reflected the mood of the Israeli and American team. Clinton phoned Arafat at 9:30 P.M. to see what could be worked out, but was interrupted by Arafat's bon voyage, which, since the summit's end appeared to be a foregone conclusion, he offered in a respectable way. Not amused, Clinton had several abrupt exchanges with the Palestinian leader. At one point Clinton walked the short distance to the porch at Arafat's cabin, where he made several personal appeals to Arafat in the presence of the Palestinian delegation. "Can't you change your mind?" he implored. There was a moment of silence, as Clinton took note of the rows of packed luggage stacked next to the diplomatic security motorcade, staged and ready to go. At the end of his limits, Clinton warned the Palestinians that, should they not take advantage of this last opportunity, "your cause will be frozen for another year or two."[107]

Barak's rejoinder came late, but not too late, in an eleventh-hour phone call to the president's cabin. Barak set a condition: he would stay as long as "Arafat agreed to negotiate on the basis of the ideas they had discussed the night before." For Clinton, this was just the adhesive he needed to keep the negotiations bound in his absence. Albright explained how the short-term fix worked:

> Clinton then went to Arafat and said he had persuaded Barak to stay. Because he thought it obvious, he did not specify that the discussion would have to be on the basis of the ideas presented the previous evening. Happy to talk when under the impression nothing else was required, Arafat agreed to remain.[108]

Whether it was misunderstanding or deliberate ambiguity on Clinton's part, the mood of the Palestinians changed.

Not all of them were eager to escape the Israeli-American pressure cooker, particularly the young-guard negotiators, who thrived in such an atmosphere. Asfur and Dahlan saw the summit's continuation as the best way to keep momentum going. Given that the Israelis had already begun their PR stealth campaign of blaming the Palestinians, they sensed that Barak would dead-end the peace process entirely—perhaps even provoke violence—should everything come to a close that night. Israeli counterparts Shahak, Ben Ami, Sher, and Grinstein, who happened to bump into Dahlan and Asfur inside the deserted Camp David cafeteria, were equally concerned. The two sides shared their assessments in what was described as an emotional scene. Their embraces signaled unspoken relief that both leaders had backed down, giving the summit a new lease on life.

At 12:45 A.M. on July 20, the breaking news around the world was enough to keep hope alive. It was vintage Clinton. With all the brevity of a man who was late to catch a plane, he briefly recounted his back and forth between Barak and Arafat, and while he could not go into details or offer any promises, the parties concluded that they wanted to stay and give peace a chance. He announced that Albright would hold the fort in his absence and wished the negotiators good luck until his return. His armada of limousines sped off into the night, leaving behind an electrified elementary school filled with journalists who did their part to boost the legions of hopeful well-wishers who prayed for a peaceful outcome.

• • •

**Alarm clocks were** set late on the morning of July 20, as both teams took use of the president's absence to catch a few extra hours of sleep after an exhausting nine days of negotiations. With Sandy Berger away in the company of the president, the next summit days were spent under the direction of Albright, who along with Ross wanted to revalidate their roles by shaping things before the president's return. John Podesta, who remained behind to administer the president's accumulating domestic business, observed:

> Once you have a presidential summit—once the president leaves—you're going to time out. If you know he's coming back, they're not going to negotiate this with the secretary of state. So you could unpack some stuff around the edges. . . . You could eat the days away and have a few discussions around the edges, but you're not going to do any real business until he's coming back, if you know he's coming back.[109]

Discouragingly, Barak blocked any discussions until Arafat agreed to the original understanding he had with Clinton on the basis for negotiations, prompting Albright and Ross to spend much of the day spinning their wheels in a fact-finding mission to "get to the bottom" of the screw-up.

To patch things up, Albright arranged for a dinner that night for both delegations. Once again Barak would not even so much as look at Arafat, much less exchange pleasantries with any of his negotiators. Several of Barak's negotiators were embarrassed; it was an uncomfortable scene for everyone. So sure was Barak that Arafat could not produce a deal that he remarked to Ben Ami, who was standing beside a wall clock, "If an agreement is reached with that character [Arafat], I will make that wall clock walk."[110]

Nothing, it appeared, could undo Barak's depression. He was angry to discover that Arafat was not going to negotiate on the basis he had proposed and fearful that his entire team—which had already received death threats from right-wing Israelis and other forms of political pressure on the Jerusalem issue—was now overexposed.[111] In Barak's view, Arafat had been exposed as a fraud when he brushed aside the prime minister's "winning card" on Jerusalem. For two straight days practically no one was permitted to see Barak, even his hosts. Only later did the American team discover what Barak had been up to when left to his own devices.

• • •

**Barak was tending** not only to Israeli domestic politics but to American politics as well. He had phoned presidential candidate George W. Bush, whose spokesman reported it as "brief . . . Barak let him know they had reached no breakthrough," while at the same time calling Al Gore, whose spokesman said, "Barak told the vice president that they were hard at work."[112] This in itself was not exceptionable. When things did not go his way following Clinton's departure, however, Barak's phone banking could no longer be explained away as harmless.

Barak called important allies in the American Jewish community, urging them to mobilize pressure against the Palestinians through the Clinton administration. According to Podesta, Clinton inured himself to these underhanded tactics, a favorite of many Israeli politicians. He recalled:

> There were a bunch of [Barak's] people who had—Sandy got the take on this more than I did—but some of his allies in the political community, mostly Jewish Americans, were calling in and this and that. I think [Clinton] basically didn't talk to anybody. [Clinton] just said, "Fuck this, I'm going to just try and see if I can get this thing done, let it go, and I'll just like worry about that later."[113]

When that was not enough, Barak worked on Hillary Clinton and on Al Gore's campaign staff. According to Leon Fuerth, who served as the vice president's national security adviser, Gore gave him explicit instructions to stay away from summit politics. Whether or not the same instructions were given to his political minions is unclear, but Gore's campaign advisers did make phone calls to Camp David. And Israel's report card on the Palestinians passed circuitously to Gore's campaign manager, Stan Greenberg, and Bob Shrum, his political adviser, through Tal Zilberstein, a partner of Greenberg's in Tel Aviv who retrieved Barak's updates by using the Israeli Defense Ministry's classified communications systems.[114] The discovery of Zilberstein's activities toward the end of the summit created quite a stir in Israel at the time, as he was a civilian without security clearance. An investigation followed, but as with the case of shady dealings during Barak's campaign for prime minister, they clearly served the bigger purpose of leveraging the president.

Indeed, there were seemingly no limits for Barak—not even with Hillary Clinton. In her memoirs she recounted how "Barak even called me asking for any ideas I might have to convince Arafat to negotiate in good faith."[115] She had received subtle endorsements from Barak in the past; he was quite aware of her precarious situation among the New York Jewish community. While she did not expand on what, if any, ideas she provided the Israeli prime minister, it is hard to imagine his call was purely about getting her negotiating advice.

Barak unleashed ruthless political spin even against members of his own team. Both Ben Ami and Shahak were suspicious when leaks to the Israeli media identified them as the ones responsible for pushing Barak further on Jerusalem. Barak would wait until they confronted him to downplay the reports and make his own denials. His desperation, apparent to many, left no illusions as to the lengths he would go should it come down to saving his own political hide.

• • •

**Albright's efforts to** reconvene the Israeli-Palestinian committee groups had little success. Barak, however, was enthusiastic about bilateral U.S.-Israeli discussions on one matter important to him: American military and economic inducements to broker an agreement with Palestinians. Bruce Riedel and

Martin Indyk took charge of these closely held discussions with Danny Yatom and Zvi Stauber, Barak's foreign policy adviser.[116]

According to Riedel, Barak requested a mutual defense agreement that included, among other things, a commitment by the United States to come to Israel's defense in the event of a future conflict. He also wanted bolder American assurances that, in the event Israel came under a nuclear attack, the United States would come to Israel's defense by counterstriking the aggressor with its own nuclear arsenal. All these alterations of the regional balance of powers, Riedel noted, were dependent on reaching an agreement.[117]

The American hosts experienced "sticker shock" when they heard Israel's request for direct U.S. financial aid: $35 billion. The ledger would have looked, according to Riedel, something like this: $15 billion to be set aside for "Israel's exclusive benefit"; $10 billion as hypothetical compensation for Palestinian refugees; and the final $10 billion to fund water desalination.[118] These staggering sums would have surely required Congressional approval, which, when leaked to Republican leaders Dennis Hastert, Dick Armey, and Tom DeLay, prompted their sending of a cautionary letter to Camp David: "We expect to be fully appraised [*sic*] of all aspects of the negotiations prior to entering into any commitments on behalf of the United States."[119] Certainly American taxpayers would raise questions about that much aid. Republican lawmakers also felt such expenditures were not being entertained in the interests of U.S. national security; according to one House Republican leadership aide, who spoke only on background, "Nobody wants to spend $40 billion on the president's legacy."

• • •

**Albright persisted with** her attempts to cheer Barak, even sending her bodyguards to comb local shops in search of a piano for him to play in his cabin. She hoped it would give him company, but after all the effort, he politely declined. For the other summit participants, Albright organized a movie night in the Camp David theater, allowing Israelis and Palestinians to lounge in the president's custom-made recliners as they watched action films.[120]

As the hours passed, the Palestinians became restless. After hearing that Albright was going to allow Barak an excursion outside of Camp David, Arafat pleaded for a similar field trip. He told the secretary, "Even in Gaza, we let the prisoners go free once a year!" Many of the Palestinians were eager to hit local shopping malls and stock up with gifts to take home to their families.

So on July 22, Albright arranged for a jaunt to her farm in Virginia, allowing some negotiators the opportunity to shop, while both she and Arafat retreated to her farm, the same place she had earlier taken Shaara during Shepherdstown. On a hot July afternoon the odd couple sat next to Albright's pool, watching her grandchildren do cannonballs.

On July 23, Barak was afforded the same opportunity to kill time, going by motorcade to the Civil War battlefield of Gettysburg, just forty-five minutes away. As he had earlier done for the prime minister during the Shepherdstown negotiations, when they took a break to visit Antietam and Harper's Ferry, Bruce Riedel guided Barak around the hills and ridge lines, the final resting site for 51,000 Americans who died, in part, because one side sought a territorial partition the other did not want. Barak told Albright on the way home his ideas about how the summit should continue: "He wanted the President to force Arafat to accept his ideas before negotiations resumed. He said we should tell the Palestinians that the United States would sever contacts with them if they did not yield."[121]

• • •

**Realizing that many** of their problems were stemming from the absence of an American drafting process, Ben Ami, Sher, and

Grinstein started their own initiative along with Erekat, Dahlan, and al-Omari. Even with Malley's helpful participation, the sides rejected each other's drafts. A similar initiative between Daniel Reisner, an IDF officer known for his drafting skills during Oslo, and al-Omari also led to failure. Neither side was authorized to make any moves, nor could the wide gaps be bridged, making all the more clear the weakness of not having assertive, constructive, third-party mediation.

Around the same time the Palestinians, through their cartographer Samih el-Abed, put forward their own map as a counterproposal to the Israeli one rejected earlier by Abu Ala. They sought to bridge the gaps between Barak's red lines, their own positions, and what had been conveyed to them according to their own notes. From their perspective, even if they accepted extended Israeli occupation of 12 percent of the West Bank as a "security zone" in the Jordan Valley, Barak's plans to hold on to the four largest settlement blocs of Ariel, Modi'in, Ma'ale Adumim, and Etzion would have functionally divided the Palestinian state into three noncontiguous sections, denying Palestinians the ability to exercise and enforce governmental and security functions, develop a coherent economic policy, or promote development opportunities.

To mitigate Barak's demands, al-Abed reconfigured the four blocs into what Gilead Sher described as "laces," so that rather than swallowing all the adjoining Palestinian villages amid the maze of settlements and bypass roads, the settlements' contiguity appeared in a way that represented small Israeli enclaves.[122] The Israelis rejected the map, which allowed annexation including 30-35 percent of the settlers in blocs on 2.5 percent of the West Bank, well below Barak's red line demand of keeping 80 percent of the settlers.[123] Sher would later return with a new Israeli proposal, offering to give them a state on 77.2 percent of the land, while 8.8 percent would be annexed and 13.3 percent along the West Bank border with Jordan would be under Palestinian sovereignty but

Israeli-occupied. Using the most charitable interpretation, the Palestinian state would have included roughly 91 percent of the West Bank/Gaza Strip, and this without factoring in the 5 percent that constituted areas of East Jerusalem, the territorial waters of the Dead Sea, and No Man's Land. Once again, the Palestinians rejected the Israeli percentages, designed by Barak as a means to keep most of the Jewish settlers happy.

The concerns of settlers were a worry for Barak throughout the summit. As they had been allowed to build their homes squarely in the midst of Palestinian desperation, the threat of violence heightened their paranoia. The largest settler group, the Yesha Council, furnished Barak the political cover he needed to stay rigid at Camp David, as it urged him to "return to Israel to prepare the army for violent confrontations with the Palestinians." Following Barak's premature declaration of the summit's end, their statement read, "The failure of Camp David has proved to everyone that Yasser Arafat is not a true partner for peace." Ariel Sharon added, "The concessions Mr. Barak has accepted are so great that we must organize early elections to form a national government that can reach a true peace while keeping Jerusalem."[124]

• • •

**The committee talks** had only slowly restarted—informally, at Barak's insistence—primarily on the issues of borders/security and refugees. The security discussions, held primarily through Dahlan and Yanai, were stuck due to Barak's hardline demands. Yanai read aloud a litany that sounded to Palestinians like the same old arguments they'd been hearing for years: that Israel needed to protect its narrow waist, which is the most populated area of the country; that even in peacetime it needed to protect itself, as there would always be states and groups that oppose peace; that even though it made peace with Jordan, it still needed the ability to protect itself from "an attack from the East" (presumably from Iraq); that as a matter of principle, Israel cannot rely on anyone else, even the United States, to defend the border with Jordan.

Further, Yanai specifically demanded that the IDF have two or three early-warning stations in the West Bank highlands; specific roads for the IDF's "emergency" use (the Israelis would, of course, decide what constituted an emergency); the right to deploy forces in an emergency along the border with Jordan; full security control over West Bank and Gaza Strip airspace; and joint Palestinian-Jordanian patrols to prevent the smuggling of weapons and possible infiltration by terrorist groups.

Dahlan gave an unbending defense of Palestinian requirements, reiterating that no agreement on security would be reached without full Palestinian sovereignty over the entire border with Jordan. Dahlan agreed to the principle of early-warning stations, which he would later regret, as well as joint patrols in specific areas and for a specific amount of time. For Palestinians, all the Israeli demands painted a picture of further occupation and dominance, and were not signs that Israel wanted peace.

With the gaps so wide, debates broke out over the formula they would follow even to begin the negotiations. The talks were given a boost with the arrival of CIA Director George Tenet, who was especially trusted by Dahlan. While Tenet's mediation was impressive, it came a bit too late. The central summit figure, President Clinton, was the only person to whom either side would reveal possible compromises. Real progress depended on his presence.

• • •

**At 6:25 P.M.** on July 23, the chopping blades of the President's helicopter, Marine One, heightened the drama among the negotiators, who had been eagerly awaiting his return. As both Clinton and daughter Chelsea disembarked into a waiting golf cart, he called out to those who had gathered, "Hi guys! I'm back. Let's get down to work." They knew Clinton could not stay with them at Camp David forever. This was clearly the home stretch.

After holding a strategy session, Clinton made clear his preference to break the teams out into marathon session on each of the core issues. The standoff on Jerusalem had not abated; worse, Barak had retracted his earlier willingness to concede Palestinian sovereignty over the Christian and Muslim quarters of the Old City. As all the issues came into focus, the status of the Haram al-Sharif/Temple Mount was identified as the most important, make-or-break point for both sides.

Perhaps believing he could warm up Barak on this issue through advancement on others, Clinton decided to pursue the issue of security first. Indyk, who noted earlier progress on security, was again thinking that because of Jerusalem, the only responsible exit was to settle for a partial deal. He recounted how the talks kept pointing right back to Jerusalem:

> We made some progress on security issues. I remember drafting a security protocol of what we agreed, but it got swamped in on the Jerusalem issue. I argued that we needed to do a partial deal—to defer Jerusalem and refugees. I drafted an agreement on this basis. . . . The reaction was, "Yes, good idea." But then we talked to the Palestinians and they said, "No, we can't do a partial deal." Barak was ready to do a partial deal, but I think it was too late. I know it was too late . . . .[125]

At 11:30 that evening, Clinton was indefatigable, bringing Albright, Ross, Berger, Tenet and Malley with him to start a three-way committee discussion on security that lasted throughout the night.[126] Abu Ala and Dahlan represented the Palestinian side; Ben Ami, Sher, and Yanai the Israelis. The Israelis were very clear with their long list of demands: three early-warning stations in the West Bank; three years to evacuate some of the settlements and outposts; five pre-positioned

IDF "supply bases" in the Jordan Valley for use in emergencies; three main roads all across the West Bank to provide immediate access to those bases; inspection oversight of the border crossings with Jordan and Egypt; control over Palestinian airspace, including civilian flyover rights; and exclusive use of the electromagnetic spectrum under the guise of "security needs," which for Palestinians was an important dynamic that would not just ensure Israel's control over radio frequencies but also guarantee Israel's economic hegemony over the booming cellular phone industry (in the months leading up to Camp David, the Israelis had leased the sphere to European companies for hundreds of millions).[127] Finally, the Israelis wanted the Palestinians to agree to have a "demilitarized" state, making external Palestinian security an eternal Israeli responsibility.

Even Clinton found some of the Israeli positions bothersome. He raised a set of thematic questions to clarify matters, such as who would decide when an "emergency situation" allowed IDF forces inside the Palestinian state, and how would a demilitarized state ensure its internal defense?[128] The Palestinians were irritated by the Israeli security demands, and the way in which discussions emphasized a "demilitarized" and "weak" Palestinian state. This evoked Oslo memories of Israel counting bullets and deciding internal Palestinian issues such as how many policeman could be employed. The Palestinians did not want to have an air force equipped with F-15 fighter jets, but they insisted on a dignified ability to police their own country.

This was especially important to Dahlan, who for years had been viewed with suspicion by many Palestinians as Israeli's security subcontractor. At the same time, he recognized that there were some Palestinians who opposed not only peace with Israel but also the Palestinian Authority itself. He acknowledged that in the initial years of independence, Palestinians might not be able to provide aspects of security most important to Israelis—along the border areas with Jordan. So with Arafat's approval, the Palestinians put forward a compromise: they told Clinton they were "prepared to provide security guarantees and to accept that U.S. or international troops be stationed in these areas."[129]

More significantly, though they insisted there could be no Israeli military presence in the West Bank, the Palestinians demonstrated a willingness to have joint Jordanian-American-Palestinian patrols along both Palestinian and Jordanian sides of the border area. The Palestinians thought that if the Israelis could not rely on Jordan, with whom they had peace, and the world's only superpower, their special friend and ally, the disagreement might not really be about security.

The Israelis utterly rejected not being allowed to patrol the borders of the future Palestinian state, going so far as to hint that the Jordanians wanted them to remain. Clinton was not about to take a position that did not err on the side of Israel's long list of security demands, but he nevertheless saw hope, because Arafat was willing to allow some form of multinational force.

On July 24, at 6 A.M., everyone turned in for a few hours of sleep. By 11 A.M. the president was awake and back to the negotiations, which next centered on refugees. The Palestinians again proposed that Israel accept the right of return in principle and then engage in discussions over how that right would be implemented. There were a number of logistical and financial burdens presented to the Palestinians, such as how Israel would feed, clothe, and employ the refugees they would absorb from the diaspora. Israel suggested allowing an unlimited number of refugees in Lebanon to leave their miserable camps and make a symbolic trip home, via the Fatima Gate along the Lebanon-Israel border—to their ultimate destination in the Palestinian state.

With knowledge that the right of return to Israel proper would be severely constrained because of Israel's "demographic concerns," the Palestinians looked for practical ways to shift emphasis to other aspects of Resolution 194, such as the creation of a compensation fund, from which remuneration could be given to refugees in lieu of physical return to Israel.[130] Most of the Israelis, but especially Eli Rubinstein, were unyielding on the question and refused to entertain this notion, which they believed would be an implicit Israeli acknowledgment of culpability for the refugee problem, thus making them legally vulnerable.

To throw the discussions off kilter, the Israelis raised counterclaims against the Palestinians, seeking compensation for the estimated 600,000 "Arab Jews" who were expelled from Arab states following the 1948 war. The Palestinians had sound defenses to these arguments, as both sides understood that the Palestinians were not responsible for those expulsions, nor had they materially benefited in any sense from what the Arab governments had done; quite the opposite, as the influx of Jewish immigrants in the new Israeli state after 1948 displaced the Palestinians even further from their homes.

The refugee issue was the last hand the Palestinians could play, and because of the order in which Clinton proceeded, absent an acceptable solution to Jerusalem, territories, and security, they were not in a position where it would have been wise to make far-reaching compromises.

There were other factors involved throughout the entire Camp David refugee talks that bothered Palestinians. Barak assigned the portfolio to Rubinstein, the most cautious and frustratingly hesitant Israeli negotiator, to work with Abu Mazen, himself a Palestinian refugee from the city of Safed, now inside Israel. Abu Mazen saw the appointment of Rubinstein as a clear signal that Barak did not plan to take the issue seriously. Meanwhile, the Americans and Israelis pursued the young-guard Palestinians to work around Abu Mazen's demand that first the right of return be recognized in principle. They took the matter up with Dahlan, Rashid, and Asfur, the latter of whom triggered Abu Mazen's deeply rooted animus. For the old-guard negotiators, such disrespect made them all the more rigid in their demands.

Talks next drifted into territory, which the President mediated separately with both sides, again resulting in neither side being pleased. According to Akram Hanieh, the Palestinians showed Clinton a map that detailed "how the annexations were designed to control the water resources and to fragment the territory into islands surrounded by settlement blocks."[131] This time the Palestinians revealed a willingness to accept Israeli annexation of 2 percent of West Bank land in order to accommodate settlers. For their part, the Israelis rejected such figures, including the Palestinian insistence on land swaps, at least in any meaningful sense. According to Helal:

> One of the ideas discussed was the idea of swapping territories. Israel could annex areas where there are settlement blocks, and in exchange the Palestinians get some territories from Israel proper. Contiguity was an issue. But the Palestinians were willing to go around it conditional on Israeli flexibility—the land had to be equal in size and quality. The Palestinians would say, "Don't give it to me in the Negev Desert." Portions of northern Gaza looked like a good spot. . . . The Palestinians showed flexibility that they would swap territories 1:1. However, the Israelis were not willing to go 1:1. They wanted a land grab of 1:6, 1:7, or 1:8.[132]

With still no breakthrough after several hours of back and forth, the president retired to his cabin to catch a few hours of sleep. Everyone was exhausted, and it became increasingly clear to Clinton's aides that the negotiations were almost out of gas. All arrows were pointing to Jerusalem, which Clinton indicated he would discuss personally with Arafat that evening. Again the issue pyramid was reversed, perhaps in the hope that with resolution of Jerusalem, the other issues might fall into place.

Surrounded by advisers Ross, Albright, Berger, Tenet, and Malley, the president received Arafat, Abu Ala, and Erekat at 9 that evening for one final, intensive sit-down on Jerusalem. From the moment the Palestinians walked into Aspen, the tension was palpable. Clinton began by divulging his latest sweetener: Arafat would receive a "sovereign presidential compound" inside the Muslim Quarter, for his exclusive use, placed aside the Haram al-Sharif/Temple Mount's thirty-acre complex.

For Arafat, such an offer demonstrated that Clinton was still missing the point: the dispute was not about giving him some form of "levitation chamber" near the Islamic holy shrine; rather, it was the unchanged reality that neither Palestinians nor the broader Islamic world would ever support a final-status agreement between Israelis and Palestinians that awarded Jewish sovereignty to an Islamic holy site. Arafat brushed off the compound idea, again evoking more images of Oslo and reformulated occupation: "So there will be a small island surrounded by Israeli soldiers who control the entrances. This is not what we are asking for. We are asking for full Palestinian sovereignty over Jerusalem occupied in 1967."[133]

A range of threats was leveled against Arafat for not giving in. Among them, that America would wash its hands of the peace process; the Palestinians would bear the entire responsibility; the United States would freeze bilateral relations; and Congress would freeze any foreign aid. Malley, who was present during the exchange, later quoted Clinton's tongue lashing:

> If the Israelis can make compromises and you can't, I should go home. You have been here fourteen days and said no to everything. These things have consequences; failure will mean the end of the peace process . . . . Let's let hell break loose and live with the consequences.[134]

According to the Palestinians, Arafat, wedded to his own heroics, gave a *sotto voce* reply:

> A revolution has taken place in these talks—the two sides now know exactly the other's positions. We did not waste time here. If anyone imagines that I might sign away Jerusalem, he is mistaken. I am not only the leader of the Palestinian people; I am also the vice president of the Islamic Conference. I also defend the rights of Christians. I will not sell Jerusalem. And I will not allow for a delay in discussions on Jerusalem, not even for one minute.
>
> You say the Israelis moved forward, but they are the occupiers. They are not being generous—they are not giving from their pockets but from our land. I am only asking that UN Resolution 242 be implemented. I am speaking only about 22 percent of Palestine, Mr. President.[135]

Clinton persisted that his ideas on Jerusalem were reasonable and something he could live with, bringing Arafat's most quoteworthy reply: "Do you want to come to my funeral? I would rather die than agree to Israeli sovereignty over the Haram al-Sharif."[136]

Erekat broke into the silence that followed, pleading with Clinton to see the progress made, adding that for the sake of peace, the summit should not be brought to an end amid threats and recrimination. As the meeting came to a close, Clinton shook Arafat's hand, telling him, "You're an honest, honorable man. You've shown firmness in defending your positions. For that, I respect you, as I respect your demands."[137]

• • •

**From 10 that** evening until after midnight on July 25, Clinton summoned Ben Ami and Erekat for the final Camp David session, to again lay down his final ideas on dividing East Jerusalem and to prepare for the day after the summit's end, which had not been given much thought. As the issues started to heat up, the negotiations once again descended into a debate over religious claims to the Haram al-Sharif/Temple Mount. As Clinton looked on, Ben Ami and Erekat debated one another as to whether or not Solomon's Temple once stood on the Temple Mount where the Haram al-Sharif exists today.[138]

Clinton broke the two apart, giving Erekat one last set of ideas to take back to Arafat for his approval. Like so many of the other propositions at Camp David, the president's ideas represented a confused logic of "either . . . or," and were qualified as hypothetical—he did not know if Barak would accept them.

Erekat took notes as Clinton described one option: the Palestinians could choose functional autonomy (but not sovereignty) over the inner East Jerusalem neighborhoods with full sovereignty over the Christian and Muslim quarters of the Old City and Israeli annexation of the Jewish and Armenian quarters. As a second option, Clinton said they could have full sovereignty in the inner East Jerusalem neighborhoods with functional autonomy in the Christian and Muslim quarters of the Old City, the practical arrangements of which could be worked out later. The offer on the Haram al-Sharif stood the same for both: the UN Security Council and Morocco would grant Palestinians "sovereign custody" over the Haram, including both the al-Aqsa and Dome of the Rock mosques, while Israel would retain "residual sovereignty" to preserve their claim to the land beneath, where Jews believe the ruins of the Temple Mount lie. The offer for Arafat to have a presidential compound, which could be placed next to the al-Aqsa Mosque, could likewise be thrown in. So confusing were the ideas put forward that Nabil Shaath would later say, "You would need a GPS navigational system in your shoes to negotiate Barak's Jerusalem."[139]

Clinton asked both Ben Ami and Erekat if they were ready to accept these proposals as a basis to continue the summit. Given that he had earlier retracted from ceding sovereignty over the Christian and Muslim quarters, it was quite possible that Barak would have rejected Clinton's ideas. But both Ben Ami and Clinton perhaps felt that, if the summit was going to collapse, better to have it come to an end with Arafat's "no." According to Ben Ami, "I told [Clinton] that for a change, I was not going to comment until the Palestinians replied."[140] Erekat, who knew what the answer would be—not only for himself, but for Arafat as well—dutifully excused himself and with his notes walked back to Arafat's cabin, where the entire Palestinian delegation was waiting.

• • •

**At various points** in between, Malley, Helal and Tenet circulated in and out of Birch, all taking a stab at lobbying Arafat to accept Clinton's ideas on Jerusalem. There was an understood inadequacy to the offer on Jerusalem, which Helal later acknowledged: "What the Palestinians were offered, no Arab leader could accept."[141] But as servants on the president's team, it was their duty to make a spirited try.

All their efforts were for naught. Arafat reiterated that follow-on negotiations should begin, as the gaps were beginning to narrow. But such an answer could not satisfy the political needs of either Barak or Clinton, who after almost a year of pursuing negotiations exclusively with Syria were now trying to rush the Palestinians to an agreement on their terms, according to their own political timetables.

At 3:15 A.M. on July 25, Erekat and Dahlan carried their negative response to Aspen, where Clinton stood waiting. Erekat read from the letter, thanking the Americans for their dedicated efforts and emphasizing the desire to seek additional negotiations. Exhausted, Clinton said, "I was expecting a response like this."[142] Letting out a sigh of desperation in the direction of Berger and Albright, Clinton uttered the words of a man worn down by three high-profile summits with nothing to show for it. "I don't like to fail," he said.

"Particularly at this."[143] It is uncertain whether or not Clinton's intended audience was Dahlan and Erekat. To be sure, both Albright and Berger, as mentioned earlier, had significant clashes throughout the summit that, in addition to the other internal administrative problems, repeatedly undercut Clinton's ability to bridge the gaps. It also left both Israelis and Palestinians with the feeling that more could have been accomplished if only those in charge had spent less time bickering and more time hosting a methodical, structured, and professional summit.

Dahlan and Erekat walked back to Birch. Once inside, they found their colleagues gathered around Arafat, all commiserating. Abu Mazen, Abu Ala, Abed Rabbo, Shaath, and Hanieh each took their turns consoling Arafat, teary-eyed from all the personal attacks and threats by the American president over the past two weeks. "You made the right decision," they told him. The young, American-educated NSU attorneys, some of whom were allowed up for the final summit day, likewise rejoiced in what they described as "immense relief" that Arafat and the PLO had avoided a cave-in similar to what they had done with Oslo. So sure were they that Arafat would wilt in the glare of Clinton's intimidation that many of them had prepared letters of resignation, which they prayed they would not have to deliver.

While the Americans had helped move both sides closer, the piecemeal ideas collected during the various committee meetings bore no resemblance to a coherent "offer," as far as the Palestinians were concerned. From their review of the notes on all the collective positions described at Camp David, the makings of an enduring peace for generations of Palestinians to come was nowhere to be found. Instead, they had heard all the trappings of yet more occupation—the land, the sky, the water, and finally, the holy sites and Jerusalem. Moreover, there had yet to be Israel's historic acknowledgment of its role in creating the refugee problem, even amid the alternative remedies the Palestinians were coming closer to accepting. Instead, the focus was aligned with Barak's diktat: how to keep hope alive for Jewish settlers seeking permanent homes within the remaining 22 percent of historic Palestine while conceding a nominal statehood in exchange for an end to conflict.

Noticeably absent from the congregation were Rashid and Dahlan, both of whom were in a separate room weighing the events privately. While Dahlan strongly rejected many of the American-Israeli ideas that had been presented, he was overcome with the same feeling that all sides had missed an opportunity for peace. Bitter feelings would be directed toward the two of them afterward, particularly toward Rashid, who all along promoted the idea that "every square inch of Palestine is as sacred as the other" under the concept of a land swap. Even though the Israelis only reluctantly accepted the latter—in the most charitable interpretation, at a rate of 1:9—Rashid, in the view of some of his peers, was succumbing to the blandishments of the Americans and, as a result, had talked a more compliant game than the others to keep the negotiations centered on him.

• • •

**The Americans and** Israelis knew the Palestinians' single greatest fear was that they would be blamed if the summit failed. Several Palestinians described the fear of blame as a sixth sense that never left them; they knew that Clinton was not the only one concerned with his foreign policy legacy, and that several of the American negotiators, including Ross, Berger, and Albright, were noticeably concerned with how history would judge their role in the confusing summit. In the view of the Palestinians—and indeed some Israelis—the attempt by the world's greatest superpower to resolve one of the most complex disputes in the world in a fortnight had been disastrous.

The Palestinians were well aware of Barak's domestic fears,

both from the right wing and the center/left groups he had so arrogantly alienated in the previous weeks. They were given a preview of the blame game on July 19, when Barak prematurely announced the summit's collapse, designating Arafat the guilty party. But the Palestinians underestimated Barak's determination to stick to his twofold PR strategy of maintaining internal unity and sustaining international legitimacy.

All throughout the summit, Barak had been reading polling data and marketing plans prepared by Stan Greenberg, who was in Jerusalem keeping tabs on how Israelis would react to the relinquishing of occupation over Arab East Jerusalem. Whether or not Greenberg shared these polls with his other VIP clients, including Clinton and Al Gore, is still unknown, though some, including Ross, clearly indicated that he did prior to the summit. According to reports of Greenberg's mid-summit findings, the most important conclusion made from their research was that, no matter what, Barak must not emerge from the summit looking like "a sucker to Arafat," meaning "an Israeli leader who concedes Israeli security and the walls of Jerusalem."[144]

As the Americans prepared a draft communiqué announcing the close of the summit, there was one friend on the American team Barak knew he could rely on to further his PR objectives: That person, Barak knew, was Dennis Ross, the envoy who had invested eight years in managing the Oslo process. Ross was by all accounts furious at both the Palestinians in general and Arafat in particular. It did not help matters that Ross had been excluded from certain meetings with Palestinians, and that most of his time had been spent having private discussions with Barak.

At that precise moment, Barak saw in Ross a willing conduit to get across the Israeli PR position on the podium of the president of the United States. With scores of caveats, Dan Meridor, whom Barak charged with crafting what would later be described as the "blame speech," bluntly revealed how both he and Ross spent the final predawn hours of the summit:

> It was something that Clinton had to do—it was . . . he was in power to levy. He was demanded by us to do it. We said to. Again, I was in part of these meetings, in some of them. I went to Dennis before the end of the meeting. I sat with Dennis for two hours and we sort of drafted what he would say. Barak really stretched his neck all the way, and is losing all of his life—politically—because he went that far . . . . [I] and Dennis stayed the whole night. It was like . . . two hours or whatever and it was before the collapse of the talks. And we drafted, more or less, what would be the final statement. We demanded this and they said that. I came with a brief and things and I sat before with Barak and we decided what we would ask of the American group. Barak went all the way and Arafat did not. And I think it was . . . it was fair![145]

• • •

**In a last**-minute panic before the parties went their separate ways, Albright discovered that aside from the opening day of the summit, the Americans would not be able to honestly tell journalists that as mediators they had really brought Arafat and Barak together. After barely getting any sleep, Clinton called Arafat and Barak together, where he would show them a trilateral statement, prepared the night before by Aaron Miller. Determined, in his words, to "put a happy face on things," and also to offset the visible anger at the Palestinians by some Clinton aides, especially Berger, Miller drafted what was called the "marshmallow text."[146]

Among the boilerplate items for agreement that Clinton read aloud were commitments to put an end to decades of conflict and achieve a just and lasting peace; continue efforts to conclude an agreement on all permanent-status issues; base those commitments on Resolutions 242 and 338 and to create an environment free from pressure, intimidation, and threats of violence; avoid unilateral actions that prejudge the outcome of negotiations; resolve differences by good-faith negotiations; and lastly, an agreement from both sides that the United States will remain a vital partner in the search for peace and that both parties will continue to consult closely with Clinton and Albright in the period ahead.

As the Palestinians went to pack their bags, the Israeli and American teams were still busied with preparations for how Barak and Clinton would spin the summit. Everyone was asked to refrain from making any statements ahead of the president, who was holding a noontime press conference back at the White House. Barak, for his part, would delay just one half-hour, holding his own in a motel in Frederick, Maryland. The Palestinians were in an altogether different mode, still overwhelmed by the summit's failure. Hours afterward, the Palestinians would discover the president's breach of his solemn commitment, which some Israelis, Palestinians, and even Americans believe was the proximate cause for the second intifada. As Clinton had threatened, all hell was about to break loose.

# • EPILOGUE •

# *The Politics of Blame*

AT THE WHITE House on July 25, Clinton delivered his concluding remarks on the Camp David summit. His comments were the result of pressure from the Israelis, his own genuine anger and frustration, and the combustible mood of the American team—the feeling that, as John Podesta put it, "Arafat actually had been exposed as the guy who couldn't make the deal."[1] Aaron Miller points out that the American side also felt "resignation, disappointment, and incredulity that we convened a summit."[2] The latter sentiment could not be outwardly acknowledged at the time, of course; it would surely have caused an uproar.

Choosing the path of least resistance presented what must have been a crisis of conscience for President Clinton. But after trying to resolve a longstanding conflict in fifteen days, when the previous fourteen months were squandered chasing after a new Israeli prime minister's missteps and confused priorities, Clinton made a conscious decision to break his pledge to the Palestinians—the weaker party whom it had never hurt to criticize in the past—and blame their leader,

Yasser Arafat, for the failure. Despite Clinton's admirable hard work and yearning to reach an agreement, his decision to cast blame had unintended, pernicious consequences both for the future of the Middle East and U.S. national security.

It began with Clinton's hallmark play on words, which subtly moved from perfunctory "appreciation" of both sides to an excessive exaltation of Barak. He lauded Arafat for little more than showing up:

> Prime Minister Barak showed particularly courage and vision, and an understanding of the historical importance of this moment. Chairman Arafat made it clear that he, too, remains committed to the path of peace.

Carnivorous reporters seized on the contrasting depictions, prompting the president to answer with partial truths and dissembled "clarifications":

> . . . There were some very, as I said—it has been reported the prime minister took some very bold decisions, but we were in the end unable to bridge the gaps. . . . Let me be more explicit. I will say again: we made progress on all of the core issues. . . . The Palestinian teams worked hard on a lot of these areas. But I think it is fair to say that at this moment in time, maybe because they had been preparing for it longer, maybe because they had thought it through more, that the prime minister moved forward more from his initial position than Chairman Arafat, on—particularly surrounding the questions of Jerusalem.

> . . . My remarks should stand for themselves, not so much as a criticism of Chairman Arafat, because this is really hard and never been done before, but in praise of Barak. He came there knowing that he was going to have to take bold steps, and he

did it. And I think you should look at it more as a positive toward him than as a condemnation of the Palestinian side.

Before Clinton's address ended, Barak took the podium at a motel in Frederick, Maryland, where he extended Clinton's tone of recrimination:

> The government of Israel, and I as prime minister, acted in the course of the Camp David summit out of moral and personal commitment, and supreme national obligation to do everything possible to bring about an end to the conflict—but not at any price—while at the same time, strengthening the State of Israel, and Jerusalem as its capital. . . . We touched the most sensitive nerves, but regretfully—with no result.
>
> We were not prepared to relinquish three things: the security of Israel, those things that are holy to Israel, and the unity of our people. If we will be faced with the alternative between compromising one of these and a confrontation, the choice is clear to every Israeli.

For Barak, the political lesson of the failed Geneva summit was that he could best abate domestic infighting by heightening his rhetoric against the Arabs. In fact, his descriptions of the Palestinians at Camp David, in particular Arafat, were near-verbatim repetitions of what had been said about Asad:

> . . . if we find ourselves in a confrontation, we will be able to look straight into the eyes of our children and to say that we have done everything to prevent it. In the face of dangers and risks before us, we must put aside all our differences and unite, as we have known to do so many times in the past. . . . We can look in the mirror and say: In the past year, we have exhausted every possibility to bring an end to the 100-year-

> old conflict between us and the Palestinians, but regrettably the conditions were not ripe.
>
> . . . Arafat was afraid to make the historic decisions necessary at this time in order to bring about an end to the conflict. Arafat's positions on Jerusalem are those which prevented the achievement of an agreement. . . . We must not lose hope. The vision of peace is not dead, but it suffered a heavy blow because of the Palestinians' stubbornness.

Once again, Barak depicted himself as the lonely dancer at the Arab-Israeli prom, with no partner to perform the tango of peace:

> . . . We'll leave no stone unturned on the way to check whether it's possible to make a peace with out neighbors without violating our national interest. But I emphasize that it takes two to tango. We cannot impose it on them. We are ready, and if a partner will be there, there will be peace.

In a Ministry of Foreign Affairs statement released that day, the Israeli criticisms sought legitimacy in President Clinton's "praise of Barak," which enabled the blame to be extended not only to Arafat but to the broader Arab world:

> Point 4: . . . President Clinton, in his statement following the summit, praised the flexibility shown by Prime Minister Barak and the Israeli delegation during the talks. . . .
>
> Point 6: During the course of the summit, the Palestinian leadership showed that it had not yet internalized the need to demonstrate flexibility and compromise on a number of key issues. In particular, the positions presented by Arafat with regard to Jerusalem prevented the achievement of an agreement. The leadership of the Arab world did not provide Arafat with sufficient backing for a more flexible stance.

Before their departure, the Israeli delegation churned out enough spin to satiate the press for weeks, months—even years—ahead. Dan Meridor told reporters, "Once again the Arabs blew it. . . . We know, unfortunately, after the last two weeks that we have no partner."[3] Elyakim Rubinstein stayed behind in Washington, summarizing for an eager pro-Israel crowd at the Washington Institute for Near East Policy, including many five-star journalists, how it was that the Palestinians refused to abandon their red lines: "It became clear that the Palestinians were not willing to deviate from their historical position. . . . An opportunity was missed."[4]

One year later, Israeli journalist Aluf Benn described what happened aboard Israeli Air Force One on the flight home to Tel Aviv:

> . . .Barak decided that all the members of the delegation should give their account of the summit. . . . The result was that the trip home turned into a flying press conference that went on for hours, in the air and at the stopover in Rome. Everyone gave interviews at great length and rehashed the official version, which held that Barak was a distinguished, visionary leader, while Arafat was a recalcitrant rejectionist who was leading his nation to a historical calamity.[5]

On July 26 Barak stepped off his plane at Tel Aviv Airport to an awaiting military honor guard and obligatory show of supporters. Israelis everywhere watched as he addressed the disappointed crowd, emotionally eulogizing why peace could not be reached with Palestinians:

> Fifteen days ago, I set out from Jerusalem, the heart of the Jewish people, on a mission of peace in Camp David. In the name of millions of citizens raising their eyes in hope and in prayer, I embarked to try and complete the task begun by the late Menachem Begin, and for which the late Yitzhak Rabin gave his life.

> I embarked to try and strengthen Jerusalem, our capital, to enlarge and buttress it for generations to come with a firm Jewish majority.
>
> I embarked to try and ensure that a majority of the settlers in Judea and Samaria would for the first time live under Israeli sovereignty.
>
> Today I can return from Camp David and look into the millions of eyes and say with regret: We have not yet succeeded. We did not succeed because we did not find a partner prepared to make decisions on all issues.
>
> Today the entire world knows that Israel desires peace. Today the entire world knows that we conducted negotiations willingly and honestly.
>
> . . . To our neighbors, the Palestinians, I say today: "We do not seek conflict. But if any of you should dare to put us to the test, we will stand together, strong and determined, convinced in the justness of our cause in the face of any challenge, and we shall triumph."

• • •

**Killing time in** cushy hotel suites at the Ritz Carlton hotel in Pentagon City, Virginia, the Palestinians waited as Arafat's jet readied for takeoff at nearby Andrews Air Force Base. In a blunder of gargantuan proportions—the worst act of negligence during his delegation's entire two-week time in America—Arafat decided to turn the other cheek, without so much as making a departing statement.

The Palestinian PR personnel assumed they could never successfully challenge the Clinton-Barak narrative. They simply surrendered to the notion that the American press will always side with Israel. But they also firmly believed the situation at home was too explosive to mire themselves in a fight they felt they were destined to lose. There was one hastily held news conference, in which Saeb Erekat optimistically projected, "After the conclusion of the Camp David summit, the prospects for achieving a comprehensive peace between Palestinians and Israelis on all issues is much more viable than [at] any time."[6] When asked why Clinton and Barak were blaming the Palestinians, Hassan Abdel-Rahman, the PLO's Washington representative, simply denied that it was happening: "I don't think President Clinton blames President Arafat." The counterarguments Abdel-Rahman did offer amounted to incoherent, uninventive fingerpointing, a reflection of his limited capacity. In the wake of a professionally engineered campaign against the Palestinians, this was much too little and far too late.

After a quiet Washington departure, Arafat stopped on his way home to Palestine to pay homage to Egyptian President Mubarak at the Ras al-Teen palace in Alexandria, overlooking the Mediterranean. There Arafat told reporters his desire to keep talks going: "As President Clinton said yesterday, it is possible to go back one more time next month to Washington or to any other place he himself chooses."[7]

Later that day, at Gaza International Airport, Arafat emerged from his plane to a triumphant reception such as he had not received since he returned from exile in Tunis in 1994. Thousands of Palestinians greeted him, waving flags and carrying large banners. As he stepped off the plane, ululating women rejoiced that the Palestinian leader had not surrendered their rights. Zealous fans quickly swarmed Arafat, hoisting him above their heads, a sharp contrast to the somberness and disappointment projected by Barak and Clinton. With microphone in hand, Arafat pumped the crowd: "Jerusalem does not belong only to the Palestinian nation, but to the entire Arab nation, all the Muslims and Christians of the world."[8] For those who disagreed, Arafat offered his rhetorical beverage of choice—"Let them drink from the sea at Gaza."

For the first time in a while, the Americans and Israelis actually succeeded in making Arafat quite popular among all the Palestinian camps. Even those intellectuals and activists who had frequently criticized Arafat over Oslo, like Hanan Ashrawi and Marwan Barghouti, lent unusually strong support. Ashrawi, who accompanied the Palestinian delegation to Washington but did not negotiate, said, "Arafat has survived because he knows what his people want, and he has led them." She added that the American-Israeli territorial percentages meant "a truncated Palestinian state, fragmented internally and surrounded externally, and that would have produced more conflict."[9] Fatah rival Barghouti said, "There is still a chance for negotiations. The summit failed, but that does not mean that it's the end of the negotiations. It is the end of this round, but not of the peace process."[10]

This mindset, of course, was precisely what Barak did not want the Palestinians to have. According to Yossi Beilin, who had been excluded from Camp David, Barak's intent was to "freeze the situation that had been created at the end of the Camp David summit" because he felt that "the support he was getting from the peace camp in Israel made him think that reopening the negotiations would expose him to new Palestinian ideas which he would be unable to accept."[11]

September 13 was around the corner, and the Palestinians believed that through more dedicated negotiations, the areas of disagreement from Camp David might be lessened even more. Nabil Shaath expressed it best: "This is the first offer any Israeli has ever made on Jerusalem. We're determined to keep engaged. This is not the last step. This is the first serious one."[12]

• • •

**Needless to say,** Arafat's victory dance did not go over well in either Tel Aviv or Washington, where the blame intensified.

On July 26, Sandy Berger told American viewers on CNN, "The Palestinians, with respect particularly to the issue of Jerusalem, were not as prepared to compromise, and to give—let go of the—some of their traditional positions, in order for the larger good of creating a Palestinian state."[13] At the same time, during a less flashy interview on PBS, Albright differed: "I don't think it's really useful to place blame."[14] But she acknowledged later, in her memoirs, how "with Israeli and American negotiators now free to provide background to the press, the imbalance in the President's words gained added weight," which she herself later contributed to.[15]

With its customary knee-jerk support for Israel, Congress rapidly set down the "Middle East Peace Process Support Act" on July 26, which, among other things, took note of the "repeated Palestinian threat to declare an independent state unilaterally after September 13." The Support Act, co-sponsored by Hillary Clinton's opponent in the New York Senate race, Representative Rick Lazio, promised Israelis a "prohibition of United States assistance" to the Palestinians as well as other gifts, including use of the Israeli-proxy UN Security Council veto, should the international community rally behind the Palestinians.

Not to be outdone, Hillary Clinton told New York reporters, "Any unilateral declaration of Palestinian statehood would be entirely unacceptable and should be met with a cutoff of United States assistance."[16]

Politically, once the decision by her husband had been made to levy blame, no one in the administration could unring the bell. The relatively short leash Clinton afforded Barak was stretched to its limits in ways that could have been predicted, but were ignored in the heat of anger. Rhetoric from all angles against Palestinians steepened. Barak began to fall prey to his own spin, looking like a sucker for having made Arafat such a "generous offer." The debonair and politically astute Egyptian ambassador to the United States, Nabil Fahmy, pointed out the consequences:

> The result was that you lost the Israeli public opinion. You participated in discrediting the Palestinian negotiator completely by putting all the blame on him.
>
> [Arafat] became a demon for the supporters of the Israeli left, a demon for the Israeli right, and he became a hero for the Palestinian right. So, it's an actual fact, you pushed the two parties apart. Also, you ended up discrediting Barak: as much as you wanted to put the blame on Arafat, you explained it in such a black-and-white manner—that "Barak offered so much and Arafat said nothing"—that Barak came out looking like an idiot who had offered everything from his plate and gotten nothing in exchange.
>
> The traditional Anglo-Saxon logic of this is that someone has to be blamed—if you're going to end up with something that fails, you have to blame somebody. You're not going to blame Barak, because you want him to be re-elected. So you blame Arafat.[17]

The IDF establishment, under the helm of Shaul Mofaz, was particularly rattled. In a Knesset briefing on July 25, Mofaz told lawmakers of reports that Palestinians were smuggling in antitank missiles in preparation for war.[18] Word was leaked to the media the following day that Mofaz had given the OK to Jewish settlers to take "all necessary measures," including the use of live ammunition, to repel any attacks.[19] One Jewish settler in the West Bank, who told reporters he recently moved there from California, confirmed, "As soon as the Indians come over the hill, we will have war on our hands."[20]

The threat of violence no longer centered on Jewish settlements, however, as criticism of the Palestinians for their refusal to accept Jewish sovereignty over the Haram al-Sharif/Temple Mount heightened tensions within the Old City itself. On July 26, reports quoted in the Israeli paper *Ma'ariv* warned of military intelligence assessments that confrontation could erupt in Arab East Jerusalem. In a radio interview that day, Israeli police chief Yair Yitzhaki assured listeners that "we are taking care of the Temple Mount with very large police forces and with a lot of technology and a lot of manpower. . . . We know the best [Palestinians] can hope for is children fighting against Israeli tanks on CNN."[21]

Indeed, much press attention was paid to the preparations being made among the Palestinian people to brace themselves for conflict. For decades in Palestine, children and teenagers had attended summer camps to learn basic military tactics, including how to handle automatic rifles. Israelis have similar, far more organized programs, as preparations for mandatory military service at the age of 18 begin early. And in the United States such training, commonly called JROTC and designed to prepare youth to defend the country, is viewed as patriotic. But for the jaundiced eyes of some Western commentators—who ignored the effect that IDF exercises in the occupied territories leading up to Camp David had on the mindset of Palestinians—the images of Palestinian children graduating from these camps were taken as evidence that Palestinians were training their youth not in self-defense but to bring about the destruction of the Jewish state.

The worsening attitudes on all sides—including the United States—was a great concern to CIA officials on the ground. CIA officer Melissa Mahle remembered that, in light of the combustible security situation before and during the summit, there was a degree of surprise among her peers at the winds of blame, especially as they originated from the White House:

> The U.S. mission had been advised that there would be no blame game because the mission was very concerned about what the impact of that would be on the Palestinian street—and on the Israeli street as well, for that matter. We were very concerned about the security environment. It was a very

> tense time, a bit of a pressure cooker. And we were concerned about the safety of American citizens in the area.[22]

Mixed reactions came from Hamas spiritual leader Sheik Ahmed Yassin, who through one Reuters journalist offered Israelis something positive: a truce in exchange for a complete withdrawal from the West Bank, Gaza, and East Jerusalem (which would require the dismantling of all settlements), as well as the right of return, though he did not specify modality or implementation of the latter.[23] On the other hand, as blame intensified, Yassin described the failure of Camp David as "another indication that the only choice we have is resistance. Only by force are we able to retain our rights."[24]

Amid the charges that Barak had weakened Israel's security, Clinton came to the rescue in an Israeli television interview on July 27, promising that, because of Barak's delivery on the Lebanon withdrawal and stellar Camp David performance, the United States would bolster its strategic military relationship with Israel, adding hefty financial assistance to further "modernize the IDF." The most controversial gift Clinton pledged to Israeli TV-watchers was his announcement that he might move the U.S. Embassy in Tel Aviv to West Jerusalem after all, a surprise for many, even in the United States, but especially in the watchful Arab and Muslim world. In a way that indirectly signaled negotiations were over, Clinton plaintively reasoned:

> I have not done so because I didn't want to do anything to undermine our ability to help to broker a secure and fair and lasting peace for Israelis and for Palestinians. But in light of what has happened, I've taken that decision under review and I'll make a decision sometime between now and the end of the year.

Again his contrast was clear: "The Palestinians did make some moves at these talks that have never been made before.

And while I made it clear in my statement, I thought that the prime minister was more creative and more courageous . . . it is true that while the Palestinians, themselves, didn't make some moves on Jerusalem, that Israel did more. But nothing that I think undermined the vital interests of the people of Israel." In response to a question as to why his powers of persuasion didn't bring a deal, Clinton said, "It wasn't really a matter of charm. Believe me, if I could have prevailed by charming, cajoling, arguing, or just deprivation of sleep, we would have a deal."

The most important aspect of Clinton's interview was not his Jerusalem Embassy pledge but rather his identification of the crucial element needed to reach an agreement that, ironically, his own castigation of the Palestinians would prevent from happening:

> I don't know if anybody else will ever put the time in on this that I have, or have the kind of personal, almost religious conviction I have about it. But, keep in mind, this is an evolutionary process. If we don't finish—and I believe we can, and I still believe we will—but if we don't finish this year, the negotiating teams for the two sides, and the attitudes of the people will be in a different place than they were because of all that has happened . . . and especially because of what happened at Camp David, as long as there is a constructive attitude taken about it.

• • •

**Days later, while** vacationing with the New York elite in the Hamptons, Hillary bolstered her husband's stance in a radio interview: "It's clear that Prime Minister Barak came committed to reaching a deal that would guarantee peace and security for Israel and the entire region. And I'm sorry that Chairman Arafat didn't show the same commitment." With a one-upmanship her opponent could not beat, the First Lady reassured New York listeners of the desire she had to see the world's most influential person—her bed partner—move the American embassy to Jerusalem "before the end of the year."[25]

In major American newspapers, journalists best known for their contempt for Palestinians introduced fictitious Camp David details to further the Israeli propaganda effort. On July 27 William Safire of the *New York Times* editorialized:

> Three pictures on the front page of the Times told the Camp David story: Ehud Barak stunned and dismayed, Bill Clinton shattered—and Yasir Arafat grinning broadly. Why? Because Arafat gave up nothing. . . . We offered Arafat virtually all of the West Bank, including the vital Jordan Valley, requiring the uprooting of 40,000 Jewish settlers. [Barak] offered what amounts to right of return of thousands of Palestinians to Israel, backed up by a reported huge commitment by Clinton to pay Palestinians around the world to not return. And most unthinkable only a year ago, [Barak] offered to share sovereignty with a new Palestinian state in portions of Jerusalem. . . . You have to sympathize with Barak, a good man learning diplomacy the hardest way. Through Clinton, he offered Asad all the Golan Heights, only to be rebuffed. He offered Arafat virtually all the West Bank, and was scorned again. Land for peace? The land Arab leaders want is the land of Israel. . . . In time, an Israeli unburdened with Barak's concessions will find a Palestinian interlocutor who wants peace too.

Lally Weymouth, daughter of the late *Washington Post* media mogul Katharine Graham, had this to say on July 28 in an op-ed in their family publication titled "Waiting for Arafat":

> At Camp David, according to reliable reports, Israeli Prime Minister Ehud Barak actually expressed willingness to give Arafat—as part of an overall agreement—94.5 percent of the West Bank, as well as a foothold in Jerusalem.

After 14 days, an intransigent Arafat turned down a deal. U.S. officials say it fell apart over Jerusalem. . . . Arafat has always played a double game, wearing a uniform while talking of peace. . . . When Binyamin Netanyahu was prime minister, the Americans blamed him for slowing the peace process and praised the Palestinian Authority. But with Barak willing to go for a generous settlement, Arafat was put on the spot, and he revealed his true colors.

Apologists for Arafat will try to argue that he has opposition and can act only with Saudi Arabia and Egypt firmly on board. It may be nice for the PLO chairman to receive backing from his Arab brothers, but the fact is that he controls the West Bank with an iron hand. . . .

Lining up support for what was to come, Weymouth said:

Barak shared with congressional leaders his concern that if Arafat declares an independent state, there will be violence. Arafat, one hopes, will get the message and act before such violence flares up. If he does not, the fault lies squarely with him.[26]

On July 27, *New York Times* editorialist Thomas Friedman offered his own conclusions. He appeared to be stunned to learn that sovereignty of the Old City and the Haram al-Sharif/Temple Mount had been debated; all along he had promoted the outlying village of Abu Dis as the appropriate capital of the Palestinian state. The question Friedman posed to America was embodied in his patronizing characterization of the Palestinians and Arafat:

And so it really comes down to this: Who is Yasir Arafat? Is he Nelson Mandela or is he Willie Nelson? That is, is he a man ready for a historic compromise, or would he just prefer to sing the old songs? . . .

> Why didn't Mr. Arafat seize on that with a serious counteroffer? One view in the U.S. camp is that the Palestinians still don't know who they want to be when they grow up. They still prefer to whine and play the victim. Another view says, hold on, Mr. Arafat knows he has to engage, but he needed to show his people he could say no before he says yes.
>
> My own view is a mix. I believe Mr. Arafat presides over a decentralized, disenfranchised and dysfunctional national movement that, against all odds, has managed to survive Arab regimes that wanted to control it and Israeli governments that wanted to destroy it. He survived all these years by bobbing, weaving, straddling and never making an irrevocable decision. But now he is at the moment of truth. He must do something he has never done before: clearly define not just what the Palestinians want, but what they also believe the Jews are entitled to, and then split the difference and take responsibility.

Barak had convinced Clinton that they would have to blame the Palestinians to save the Israeli left; instead, it dealt the left a severe blow. On July 28, Amos Oz, a celebrated Israeli writer and peacenik, announced his defection in a *New York Times* op-ed:

> I pause to reflect. I remember how in the old days a single phone booth would have sufficed to contain the entire national assembly of Israeli peace activists. We could literally count ourselves on the tips of our fingers, a tiny minority among minorities. Today everything is different. More than half the nation is with us.
>
> And yet the Palestinians said no. They insist on their "right of return," when we all very well know that around here "right of return" is an Arab euphemism for the liquidation of Israel.

> The Palestinians have a right to their own free and independent Palestine. But if they also want to have Israel, they should know that they will find me ready to defend my country: an old peace activist ready to fight for the survival of Israel. I believe this to be the last opportunity: the Palestinians must choose if they want a new Saladin, or to really work for peace.

On July 31, the collective Israeli burnout with Barak and the Labor Party's inability to deliver peace on both the Syrian and Palestinian fronts became clear in the country's presidential election results. Shimon Peres threw his hat in the ring for the ceremonial post—one of the few he had not held in his long and distinguished career—but was defeated by Likud candidate Moshe Katsav. He was riding the coattails of Sharon, who hailed the growing consensus that "Barak is leading us in a very dangerous way."[27]

In the Knesset, Barak barely survived multiple votes of no-confidence. Finally, on August 2, following the formal resignation of Foreign Minister David Levy, who alleged that Barak had stretched too far on Jerusalem at Camp David, the Knesset voted by a 61-51 majority to hold new elections. Since the Knesset headed into recess that same day, the matter would be shelved until October 29—a week before the U.S. elections—unless a quorum of legislators convened a special session in the interim. This only heightened American empathy for Barak, who had been standing on eggshells for some time. In the event any agreement with the Palestinians was reached, it would first have to pass a Knesset referendum vote with a supermajority, which meant approval from Likud and those Knesset members who had ditched Labor when they voted for Katsav.[28]

Although just one week had passed since Camp David, time and the political energy necessary to conclude an agreement—especially in the crucial arena of public affairs—had been wasted in what can only be described as industrial-strength stupidity. Officially sanctioned American and Israeli blame was nailing the coffin shut on peace while setting the stage for a cataclysmic turn that would endanger the safety and security of the entire region. As both a direct participant in the talks and a historian of the conflict, Aaron Miller now reflects in hindsight on the consequences of ending Camp David in blame. "On July 25," says Miller, "any serous effort to reach an agreement came to an end."[29]

• • •

**For the education** of those still wedded to the thesis that Camp David failed because the Palestinians turned down a generous offer, conscientious American and Israeli participants have come forward with the truth—and some embarrassing details—that should put an end to this myth. In fact, there is evidence that even Bill Clinton doesn't believe the hype. A prominent Israeli who had the opportunity to dine with Clinton privately in 2003 told me the former president said to him, "If Yitzhak Rabin were alive, I would have gotten an agreement out of Camp David." The implication is clear: it couldn't have been all Arafat's fault.

In July 2002, when I first began the research that led to this book, I visited Aaron Miller in his Foggy Bottom offiice, where he cautioned me to be watchful of what I was told. "Part of the problem in analyzing Camp David II," he said, "is that the personal agenda and heat of the moment have colored it. The current players can't do it." Though Miller had plenty of criticism for what he described as Palestinian "passivity" at the summit, he made the following crucial point:

> There was not a formalized, written proposal that covered the four core issues. There was no deal on the table. None of the issues were explained enough in detail to make an agreement, though the Israelis made an interesting argument on Jerusalem.[30]

Miller's statement supported the arguments Robert Malley had made publicly the summer before in his seminal article for *The New York Review of Books.* (The same afternoon I talked to Miller, I visited the adjoining cubicle of Gemal Helal, and was riveted by his similar version of events. He warned me that it was impossible to understand why Camp David failed without a careful study of the doomed Syrian track.)

After a period of despondency in the Bush administration, Miller opted for retirement in January 2003. A true believer in peace, he took up a position with the nonprofit group Seeds of Peace, promoting reconciliation among Arab and Israeli teens. In a speech at Tel Aviv University in May 2004, the text of which he gave me, Miller made a significant public statement corroborating Malley's arguments, connecting the Geneva failure with that of Camp David:

> We couldn't see it at the time, but Geneva was a dress rehearsal for what was to come at Camp David. . . . So you put down an offer that your interlocutor cannot accept, you hope that the Americans can sell it to him but if they can't you then go ahead and blame and expose the other side. This was what happened at Geneva and this was what we were in store for at Camp David. . . . As a consequence of the decisions taken by all the parties, admittedly with varying degrees of responsibility, a perfect storm was brewing, a perfect storm of misjudgment, of misconception and mistake, and little did we know at the time that circumstances were about to be set into motion that would have this perfect storm wash away virtually everything we had tried to achieve for the preceding decade.

It was not the first time I had heard such criticism from an American participant. Of the ideas discussed at Camp David, Ambassador Ned Walker had earlier told me, "There is no way in hell the Palestinian people would have accepted this thing. It's hard enough to imagine the Israelis accepting it." [31]

Hearing a nearly identical assessment from one of Barak's

most senior negotiators, however, took me by surprise. When I asked General Amnon Lipkin-Shahak in January 2003 if it is accurate to say the Palestinians turned down a deal at Camp David, he shook his head no. Without any prompting, he continued:

> It was not a real dialogue. Look, in the first day when we went to Camp David, there was no dialogue. Then we started to talk. The Palestinians had no suggestions whatsoever. The Israelis put maps that were known to Palestinians months earlier, so in the beginning the Palestinians saw nothing. It was not that it wasn't prepared; it was premature for this kind of summit! It's like bringing, now, Saddam Hussein and George Bush to a sealed room and tell them, "You have forty-eight hours to reach an agreement." I don't think it's going to work!

Contrast Shahak's response to that of a senior State Department official who insists on anonymity:

> Was there an actual peace document? No. But there was certainly enough paper! Were they American ideas—were they Israeli ideas? You know, how do you present Israeli ideas because they wanted them presented as American ideas? You know, there is a lot of other stuff here. The only person I think really has the best story on this is Dennis.

This certainly sounds like confirmation of the American-Israeli collusion alleged by the Palestinians and others, and repeatedly denied by both the Israelis and Americans. I pressed my interlocutor on this question—whether, as Rob Malley alleged, there had been inappropriate collusion at Camp David. I was told, "Probably. But, you know, I mean part of it is that the Israelis are our allies!" This is hardly a ringing endorsement of the claim that Washington served as a constructive, honest broker in the negotiations.

At a September 2003 conference in Washington celebrating the twenty-fifth anniversary of the Egyptian-Israeli Camp David Accords, I asked Jimmy Carter about his involvement with the Clinton administration. He explained:

> When Clinton was first elected, I came up to Washington and met with Warren Christopher and Madeleine Albright and offered anything that I could do to help with the Middle East peace process. And they told me in very nice and friendly terms that they could handle the situation, since so many of them had been involved in my own administration. So they never did call.

I asked Carter what would he have told Clinton if his advice had been sought.

> I think Clinton did the best he could after he had been in office seven years. My advice would have been [to] make a major effort the first six months, or first year, which he did then finally at Camp David, instead of waiting seven years! . . . I don't say that in a critical way, because he had a lot of other things. I think he made a genuine effort, and I think he did the best he could.

Former Vice President Walter Mondale likewise told me he was not contacted. His assessment was similar to Carter's:

> I think the problem in the second Camp David process was that it got started so late. Everybody knew that Clinton's term was about to end, and there was not enough comprehensive groundwork that we had. . . . That took years, and, although the pattern was established there, it wasn't ripe.

Former Ambassador Samuel Lewis, who served in Tel Aviv from 1977 to 1985 and briefly in the Clinton administration at the State Department's Policy Planning Division, offered a more detailed opinion:

> President Clinton believed very deeply in his persuasive powers to get people together. He could usually convince almost anybody of anything. But I don't believe there was anything comparable to the preparation in great detail ahead of time, and much of this I also blame on Barak, who didn't come clean, apparently, with Clinton, as to what he was prepared to do—nor with any of his own staff.
>
> Barak's style did no facilitate having really good preparation for that meeting, so Clinton went in there not knowing what Barak was going to propose. I don't think there was anything analogous to what Sadat did with Carter. Sitting down, he went over with Carter all of his potential fallback positions. That didn't happen—I'm quite certain—with Clinton and Barak. And I blame Barak as much. But I don't think Clinton pressed him as much as he would have liked. Clearly, the staff work was much more helter-skelter. It was prepared under duress in a way, because Barak was pushing for a meeting. A lot of people involved felt that it was premature, and Arafat said he was not ready.
>
> Clinton, actually, is a tremendously absorbing reader. He can take a briefing paper, take a few pages, inhale it, and have it part of himself. But he's not—he doesn't demand the kind of highly complex staff work that Carter did.

Lewis's point that the Clinton administration wasn't adequately prepared and simply didn't know Barak's bottom lines was repeated to me by several officials involved in or close to the talks. They had similar regrets about not resisting Barak's pressure to convene the summit prematurely, and the unfortunate tendency to follow his lead at Camp David. Malley was the first to confirm this, followed later by several others, including Ambassador Walker, Toni Verstandig, and—for the first time publicly (before making it a footnote in her book)—Secretary Albright. Walker offered to me how:

> the problem was that nobody knew what Barak had in mind. They went to Camp David cold. They didn't have any idea where Barak was coming from or what he was willing to do. Maybe the president did, maybe Barak and the president had spoken, but the guys at the bottom lines, at the Aaron Miller and Schwartz level and so on, didn't have a good sense of what was possible.[32]

Albright maintains that Barak put forward an "unbelievable plan" and that "Arafat literally sat on his hands" and "did not contribute anything, nor did his people," but she was willing to be self-critical:

> The problem was that Barak did not want to give us his bottom line before he came, and he did not also want even to discuss it. So we don't have time or the possibility—to use Dennis's always-favorite word—to "condition" the Arab leaders. So instead of getting help from all the Arab leaders when we started making phone calls about it, they weren't willing to help us because they didn't know the full context of what it was about . . .[33]

Verstandig saw this as part of the larger Camp David disaster:

> Look, you never go into a negotiation without knowing an endgame! We went in to the most high-stakes of negotiations not only not knowing an endgame; we didn't know what Israel's positions were—their final bottom line positions on Jerusalem. We saw them unfolding in front of us.[34]

Malley had a similar explanation:

> I think we followed Barak's lead and his advice on tactics, on strategy, on substance, on process, far too much. I think there are several explanations. First is, simply, our mistake. We shouldn't have. We should have stood up to him more and said "this won't work." Second, is because [Barak] did have a

> constant stream of ideas and proposals that went beyond the point where many of his predecessors to the conflict didn't—we were taken by that. Third is that the Palestinians weren't offering a counterstrategy that we could look at as "maybe we should go this way." It was very much one strategy. We should have had our own. We did have our own preferred one, but if the parties were not prepared to go that way and one party was offering another way out and we saw that Barak was taking risks that came—we went along with that. I think it was a mistake, by following too blindly. But Barak did what he thought he had to do. He was pressuring us to take a certain route. We should have resisted . . .[35]

After leaving office, Malley went on to play a commendable behind-the-scenes role in drafting the Geneva Accord, a 2003 document that removed Oslo's killer ambiguities and has been accepted by many Israelis, Palestinians, and prominent world leaders as the best possible solution to the conflict—even winning Clinton's endorsement.

• • •

**The week after** Camp David ended marked the beginning of a battle by Clinton and Barak against Arafat over the important issue of international support. Arafat hoped the world would stand behind his efforts to declare statehood—recall that he had earlier deferred this move in response to Clinton's May 1999 request. At Sharm in September 1999 he was again promised a new date for statehood by the seventh anniversary of Oslo, in September 2000—but after trips to European, Asian, and Arab capitals, the receptions were mixed, and in some instances, cool. Everywhere Arafat was greeted with the long arm of American influence, or, in some instances, the Israelis had already gotten there first. No one, it seemed, was willing to run afoul of the president of the United

States. This further embittered Arafat against Barak and, more importantly, Clinton. At least in this arena, Arafat's globetrotting was not a success.

The White House lobbied not only Europe but the Arab world as well, dispatching Ambassador Walker on a whirlwind trip:

> I went to thirteen governments in fifteen days. I can't remember how many governments. I went to every Arab government that we have relations with, and I talked to the principal leader in each case—the head of state in every case. I reported on what went on at Camp David II, what were the problems; my principal role was to try and see if there was a way to break through on the Jerusalem issue.

Walker's travels brought unexpected flexibility from the Arab world:

> Nobody was excluding the possibility of an agreement, even Saudi Crown Prince Abdullah. . . . He said, "Look, what you have to keep in mind is that any settlement you come up with can't be a lawyer's settlement—it has to be understandable to the people." And I said, "Well, what if we had an agreement where your Muslim constituents could travel all the way to the al-Aqsa Mosque, pray, and go home and never see an Israeli or go through a barrier? And he said, "That would be something we could work with." What I'm getting at is there was not a hardened position.[36]

The American press, however, was either unaware of or disregarded this flexibility, instead hurling accusations at Arab leaders who would not pressure Arafat on the Jerusalem discussions at Camp David—the substance of which was probably unknown to these reporters. On August 1 in the *New York Times*, Thomas Friedman took aim at Mubarak in one of his favorite rhetorical ploys, the make-believe letter; he called this one "Memo from President Clinton to President Mubarak":

> Dear Hosni: I'm writing you this letter by hand on White House stationery because it is a personal note from a friend. Hosni, I have to tell you how disappointed I and all my foreign policy aides were with your behavior during the Camp David summit. I am going to be frank with you, you're skating on thin ice here. The number of people on my foreign policy team, or in Congress, who have a good word to say about you or Egypt today could be counted on one hand—maybe on no hands. More and more people are asking me: What exactly are we getting out of our relationship with Egypt—not to mention $30 billion in aid to Egypt since 1978?

• • •

**Away from the** limelight, two important channels were quietly racing against the clock to bring about a final agreement. One involved very lengthy and extensive talks principally between Saeb Erekat and Gilead Sher; another involved Egyptian mediation between Israelis and Palestinians. Both were a testament to the desire among many in the region to save the hopes for peace. For all their work, however, the unprofessional attitudes within the Clinton administration—still riding the wave of blame—led to perhaps the greatest American missed opportunity in Arab-Israeli intervention.

On July 31, Sher and Erekat began the first of some forty covert meetings throughout August and September to reverse the harmful course that had been set since the summit's end. Mohammed Dahlan, Mohammed Rashid, and Omar Dajani frequently joined the group, as did Israel Hasson, Shlomo Ben Ami, and Gidi Grinstein from the Israeli side. The core work, however, was done by Sher and Erekat, who spent time combing the neighborhoods of Jerusalem on foot. With the help of aerial maps, they made a determined effort to understand how the parameters of peace would look from the ground. They developed an especially close friendship as a result of their undercover meetings in Jerusalem, Tel Aviv, Ramallah, Jericho, New York, and Washington.

Unfortunately, the aims of their leaders were elsewhere, still playing the blame game and fighting over international support at a time when the upper echelons of the Clinton administration were beginning to turn passive. It was as if the White House felt the Camp David controversy should be sidelined during the vacation month of August, especially sacrosanct to Washington politicians. And the key American players were already looking ahead to the fall elections.

Clinton immersed himself in fundraising for his wife; attending dinners with the American Jewish community, many of whom were elated over Al Gore's selection of Senator Joe Lieberman to be his running mate (a true landmark for the American Jewish community); and being on hand in Los Angeles for the several days of cheerleading at the Democratic National Convention, which he had always wanted to enter without any Arab-Israeli controversy sticking to his heels.

Clinton made just one attempt to reach out to the Arab world, granting a newspaper interview with the Egyptian paper *Al Hayat* on August 10. However, his previous interview on Israeli TV, particularly his statement about wanting to move the Israeli embassy to Jerusalem, cast a shadow over his protestations of sympathy for Palestinian suffering.

The day before the *Al Hayat* interview, Arafat told Clinton of the back channels he had authorized to continue negotiating for peace. Arafat wrote a letter to the president asking him to convene a follow-up summit, where the leaders could integrate what had been discussed at Camp David with the advances of the Sher-Erekat channel. The timing of Arafat's request, just days before the Democratic convention, presented the White House with a new difficulty. Inevitably it fell on the shoulders of Dennis Ross, who took ownership of the decision-making, and angrily waved away Arafat's request. Later, Ross said:

> What were we supposed to do? Arafat, at Camp David, indicated no readiness to do anything. If we were to chase after him at that point then you would tell him that that kind of negotiating behavior was fine. You know what they were saying, right? Arafat goes back to a hero's welcome for being defiant—the tradition of the Palestinian movement once again reinforced: "Don't agree to anything; prove how you rejected everything!" And then right after that, what do you think he did? He came back and said, "OK." He sent a letter to me saying, "Let's hold another summit." [Erupts in laughter.] Like, "Well fuck you! [More laughter.] You know? We just shot our wad! You go out as a hero for being defiant—on what conceivable basis should we convene a summit without having some confidence that you'll actually behave differently?[37]

The effects of Ross's burnout and hardening attitude—in many respects far worse than that of Barak or Arafat—still haunts many Israeli, American, and Palestinian negotiators. Ned Walker was repulsed:

> That was stupid. Absolutely stupid on the part of anybody that made that kind of statement. But you've got to remember that everybody's emotions were running high by that time. Arafat, to defend him, he had no way he could accept what they were offering on Jerusalem. And you cannot sell al-Aqsa [Mosque] the way they were trying to sell it to the Islamic world.

Regarding Ross's dismissal, Walker laments:

> . . . it was a missed opportunity. It got personal and the reasons had nothing to do with it. First of all, it got personal in a sense that Clinton felt that his future had been robbed

> from him—the great chance. Second, Dennis had to, you know, feel really—this was something he had worked on for fifteen years collapsing in front of his face. I mean, you don't get engaged . . . all of these people are human and have human emotions. It would take an extraordinary person to say, "Well, OK, let's go to the next one."

Ross was not too bothered to leave the talks behind as he headed off to Israel for his annual family vacation, first spending two days at the Gaza beach home of Mohammed Dahlan, which one diplomat described as Dahlan's gesture to "suck up" to the central American envoy and shift his destructive mood. From there Ross continued on to Eilat, where he spent the bulk of his time. The Israeli and Palestinian negotiators would find his presence in the region all but useless. One Israeli negotiator raged about an exchange he had when a dispute between Erekat and Sher required the immediate clarification by the Camp David hosts. He recalled:

> I personally tried to reframe the caption of Camp David with our counterparts Saeb Erekat and Mohammed Dahlan—to try and reassemble the pieces of Camp David . . . into one coherent agreement. We did that in almost daily session in Jerusalem, Tel Aviv, and elsewhere, mainly during August, and then part of September. But when we asked the Americans to anchor the agreements that were achieved at Camp David—for example, [with regard to] the security [discussions] during a night meeting with the president, where [we] went point by point on an American presidential agenda on the early-warning stations and the emergency deployment and we kind of concluded it to our satisfaction—it was a closed issue.

When they contacted Ross on vacation, however, they learned he was not feeling up to task. An Israeli who spoke with Ross revealed what the envoy's real problem was: there were no Camp David records to go from:

> Then during the negotiations after Camp David II, the Palestinians reopened all of the [security issues]. So we called the Americans. . . . We asked them, "Hey, isn't this the set of agreements that we reached on security at Camp David?" And they just said "Aaah . . . more or less." They weren't firm and positive about it—even the records of Camp David! You know what Dennis told me? "We don't have records of Camp David"! [Shouting angrily.] Hey! Come on! Do I have to hold the records, or what? Did I summon the meeting at Camp David? Or did Barak invite Arafat and Clinton to spend some time with him at Camp David? Come on! There were no anchors! There was no infrastructure for the continued negotiations! So we [had to] start everything afresh.

Arafat was dejected when his calls for another summit were brushed aside. Observers recall sensing that dangerous thoughts began entering his head: perhaps, were he to hold out for a while, a victory by candidate George W. Bush—whose campaign alignment with former Secretary of State James Baker brought back positive memories of George H.W. Bush's toughness on Jewish settlements—would bring an administration more to his liking. Many friends of the Palestinians—including some in the State Department—were worried about the buzzings of a better Middle East peace process under George W. Bush. Diplomatic cables were sent from Tel Aviv and Jerusalem showing the daily Palestinian headlines and editorials that alluded to how the Palestinians might finally get a "fair shake" if only the Americans elected a Republican. This was made all the more attractive when some considered—perhaps with a degree of anti-Semitism—the influence Joe Lieberman would have as vice president under Gore, who almost always gave Israel his unwavering backing and was a favorite of the American Israel Public Affairs Committee.

Palestinians should have exorcised any such fantasies following the mid-August visit by the Bush campaign's top foreign policy adviser, Condoleezza Rice, who through her actions and words raised doubts about how an incoming President Bush would handle the complexities of the Arab-Israeli peace process—or not. It was clear to several at the U.S. consulate that Rice, an expert on Russia, knew little about the conflict. In such instances, the default rule for any U.S. politician is a pro-Israel tilt. But many were surprised by the outright refusal of Rice to even meet or shake hands with any of the Palestinians during her several-day visit. It is less than clear what advice Rice received from Ross, whom she had come to know and trust from their days together at the Reagan National Security Council. But on August 14, her statements to Israelis were just what Ross would have ordered from any of his menu of policy suggestions from the Washington Institute for Near East Policy: "Governor Bush understands," Rice said, "and I certainly understand, that Israel is our friend whatever happens in the peace process." In an Israeli TV interview later that evening, Rice laid out how a Bush presidency would defend "the only democracy in a very tough neighborhood":

> I think you would see with [Bush] a very strong emphasis on an upgraded, indeed a stronger security relationship with Israel, for instance, in the area of ballistic missile defense, where we may be able to do some things together to counter the emerging threat of countries like Iraq and Iran who are trying to acquire weapons of mass destruction.[38]

Days later, while being courted in the town of Yokne'am, one of the earliest Jewish settlements now within Israel near Haifa, Barak told Rice, "We are at a very sensitive stage . . . I hope that logic will win out and that the Palestinian side will show the flexibility and openness needed to reach an agreement shortly." Should they not, Barak told Rice and reporters, "we will at least enjoy a great deal of support in the world and know how to stand united against anything that the future may bring."[39]

Aware of the chronic Palestinian inability to gauge domestic American politics, one diplomat went so far as to contact Arafat privately for an off-the-record discussion in which he told the Palestinian leader that he would be making a grave mistake to think an improvement would come with Bush's election.

Not all hope was lost, however, as top Egyptian officials stepped up their pace through direct dialogue, particularly on the topic of Jerusalem and all the legal avenues opened up at Camp David for the very first time. Extensive consultations were held. The possible solutions ranged from designating the entire plaza area "sovereignty to God" status to designating Palestinian sovereignty over the Haram al-Sharif and Israeli sovereignty over the Wailing Wall, with the UN Security Council designating the earth in between a corpus separatum, an echo of the original plan suggested by the UN General Assembly in 1947 for the entire city.

Nabil Shaath quickly took these ideas to his team of NSU lawyers in Ramallah, who had been working around the clock on legal papers since the collapse of the summit, the PLO leadership finally seeing their worth. The leadership, including the late Faisal al-Husseini, the PLO minister for Jerusalem, was intrigued. Husseini directly discussed the compromise with Yossi Beilin, who over the years had become a friend.

• • •

**By the end** of August, after extensive consultations with both sides, the Egyptians had put together a document to resolve all the core issues of the Israeli-Palestinian conflict. The timing seemed right to deliver it to Clinton personally, as the president was traveling to Africa. So Mubarak arranged for an impromptu meeting on August 29 in the

VIP lounge of Cairo International Airport as the president's plane refueled.

According to Hesham Youssef, who at the time was a senior adviser to Foreign Minister Amr Moussa, the Egyptian document addressed all the outstanding issues—refugees, borders, security, and, most importantly, Jerusalem—which essentially stole the Americans' thunder, putting forward a realistic solution that both sides could live with, which the Americans had not done during and after Camp David. As the Egyptians claim to this day, almost all the items included in their paper that day were later embodied in the "Clinton parameters" of December 23, 2000. With the Millennium UN General Assembly Summit in New York scheduled to begin on September 6, the idea was to take advantage of the opportunity, when virtually every head of state in the world, including Arafat and Barak, would be in Manhattan.[40]

Unfortunately, yet another opportunity was missed to avert the brewing disaster. Dennis Ross made sure the entire world understood there would be no trilateral meeting at the UN. Before announcing his return to Israel, where he was still vacationing, Ross shot down the Egyptian idea with more delaying tactics:

> . . . The plan right now is to have separate bilaterals between the president and Chairman Arafat, and the president and Prime Minister Barak. And he'll also be seeing other regional leaders. But the focus is really on what can be done with the two of them separately. . . . I think our focus right now is let's work the substance and focus more on the substance, and we'll focus on the procedure at a point when we're satisfied that we have the substance to a point where it makes sense to make a procedural move. The president has always said that—since Camp David—that he would be prepared to get together with the leaders when he saw a readiness to make decisions.

The details of the Egyptian plan were shared with both sides. It called for Palestinian sovereignty over 94 percent of the West Bank plus 1 percent of Israel proper, in all likelihood on the edges of Gaza, bringing the total to 95 percent. This was little more than the parties had discussed on their own—Ben Ami recalled that his side was talking about 93 percent in exchange for a 2 percent land swap in addition to Israel's important concession of dropping the demand for further long-term occupation of the Jordan Valley.

Back in Israel, Ross, Miller and members of the American peace team began playing catch-up to the work of Sher and Erekat, taking field trips of their own through the Old City. They canvassed block by block, even looking at individual homes that would be affected, particularly in the Armenian Quarter. But their efforts were going too slow for the reality facing both sides; the Israelis, feeling Barak could not stretch any further without a "push" in the form of an American proposal, individually pleaded with the Americans to set down their plan. Ben Ami recalled:

> Throughout this period, we were really waiting for the Americans to work out a package that would be presented to both sides. In this period I personally pressured the Americans to work the collective memory that was created at Camp David into a document: to collate all the presidential summations that were recorded there, and out of them build a comprehensive proposal.[41]

Sensing the American aversion to a summit, the Israelis, like the Egyptians, argued with Ross to use the upcoming UN meeting to offer a proposal. One Israeli, who at the time acted outwardly against it to appease Barak, described with the utmost frustration:

> Why a summit? We didn't need a summit! It was the General

> Assembly of the UN in September. . . . It could have been the perfect venue![42]

When asked why the United States decided to delay presentation of a plan, Gilead Sher snapped:

> Ask them! Because they were ready, and the packaging was ready toward the first week of September. . . . We had numerous meetings between Camp David II and the beginning of the UN General Assembly in September. The package deal was ready. We discussed it with them, the details. . . . I don't know why they were reluctant to put them on the table.[43]

• • •

**On the eve** of the General Assembly, more pressure was brewing to reach an agreement on Jerusalem. The six-member Gulf Cooperation Council, comprising Saudi Arabia, Qatar, Bahrain, Oman, Kuwait, and the United Arab Emirates, met in Riyadh with what appeared to be a unified front behind the Egyptians. Crown Prince Abdullah had this to say:

> Israel makes a grave mistake if it thought that the peace process can move forward while it ignored the legitimate rights of the Palestinian people to return and to establish an independent state on its own land. . . . Israel would be making an even greater mistake if it imagined that the Arab and Islamic world would remain silent towards the unilateral steps it is taking in Jerusalem.[44]

Yossi Beilin, strongly promoting a three-way UN meeting, wrote this of Barak's reaction:

> Barak thought it would be a mistake to make a move at that point. At a conference in Tel Aviv on September 1, he promised that if an agreement was signed at the meeting with

> Clinton and Arafat in New York, he would "build a Jerusalem stronger and greater than ever, with a Jewish majority, a Jerusalem that will gain recognition by the whole world as the capital of Israel. And if that happens, no struggle will be more exhilarating to wage, on the streets and at the junctions."[45]

On his flight to New York, Barak told journalists, "I've put Arafat up against a wall, the way he was in Beirut in 1982," a good way to sum up his agenda toward the Palestinians during the three-day UN event.[46] Barak arrived in New York not to sound out agreements with Clinton or Arafat; rather, he was intent on courting the international community to line up with him against Arafat. Just as at Camp David, Barak purposefully avoided the Palestinian leader. At one point the two happened to enter the same elevator, whereupon Arafat turned to Barak's wife, asking sarcastically, "Who is this guy next to you?"[47] Eyes straight ahead, Barak ignored Arafat with a stony silence that seemed to doom all hopes of a post-summit negotiation.

Behind closed doors, Barak and his delegation worked the Americans over for increased military assistance, which they justified by the strong rise in popularity of Ariel Sharon, who was promising better security. The Clinton administration had already proposed $250 million in addition to their normal allotment that year. But the Israelis kept insisting on a full $1 billion supplemental. In addition, they asked Clinton to upgrade the U.S.-Israeli relationship from "major non-NATO ally" to "strategic, major non-NATO ally." Objections anew over the block of the Phalcon radar sale to China were raised by Deputy Defense Minister Ephraim Sneh; he said it "gave the United States a veto over Israel's national interests."[48]

With all the criticisms of the Palestinians for not putting forward a "counteroffer" at Camp David, meaning something other than a restatement of their entitlements under international law, Arafat brought with him to New York an idea to resolve Jerusalem by according sovereignty over the

Haram al-Sharif/Temple Mount to the Organization of the Islamic Conference, chaired by the King of Morocco, whose monarchy had well-established relations with Tel Aviv; the idea was to guarantee access to the holy sites to all religions.[49] For both the American and Israeli teams, it was unacceptable to involve an organization that included some countries designated by the United States as sponsors of terrorism, like Syria, Iran, Iraq, and Libya. So instead of exploring the proposal to spread this burden among the Islamic world—with full knowledge that the United States and international allies would never waver in their defense of Israel—the idea was dismissed out of hand.

Nothing on Jerusalem had been committed to paper by the Americans since Ross's handwritten shenanigans on the third day of the summit. The Americans were still unwilling to put down a plan of their own and would resign themselves, in the case of Albright, to goading Arafat into more religious debates over the holy sites, resulting in his predictable fits of anger. These were curious arguments for Albright, who was not an especially religious person and who professed to learn that she was herself of Jewish origin only belatedly, upon taking her post as secretary of state. Such exchanges with Arafat at the Waldorf Astoria never made it into her memoirs; only Arafat's reaction: "I met again with the Palestinian chairman and probed to see whether he had moderated his position. Arafat rose from his seat, shaking his fists, and stormed out of the room."[50]

After a meeting with President Clinton that also made little progress, Arafat quickly tried to patch things up with the secretary in his customary way: by covering her with kisses. This always made witnesses blush and afterward elicited lengthy complaints from her to her advisers. Nothing could repair her negative impressions of Arafat:

> His behavior in September in New York would make one think that there wouldn't have been any particular advantage

> to it. . . . Clinton and I, in many respects, it would have been nice to do more—always—but . . . I mean . . . he just didn't respond.

She then gets to the real reason why no further summit was called:

> By then I think Barak was in more difficulty domestically in terms of what he had already proposed [at Camp David].[51]

For Palestinians, there were little advances in their bilateral talks with UN member states, whose support Arafat had counted on in fulfilling a September 13 declaration of statehood. He prepared to return to the region, hoping that by leaving behind his central negotiators, the deadlock between the leaders might break. In an outgoing CNN interview that his aides imprudently arranged amid Arafat's feelings of betrayal, hurt, and paranoia, the Palestinian leader made a mockery of himself before the entire world, validating many of the U.S. and Israeli rumors that he was coming unhinged. He alternated between a rude, belligerent attitude toward his host, Christiane Amanpour—whose sharp tone merely reflected the popular spin that everyone in the West had been fed by Clinton and Barak—and an inexplicable, craven refusal to admit that Clinton had blamed him for the failure of Camp David.

• • •

**Everyone breathed a** sigh of relief as September 13 passed without a unilateral declaration of Palestinian statehood. Despite Ross's oft-repeated claims that Arafat never made a decision until "one second to midnight," there was still nothing for Arafat to decide, as an American proposal had still not been presented since the failed Camp David summit. American Jewish leaders like Abe Foxman, national director of the

Anti-Defamation League, took a more direct interest, visiting with Arafat to assess the situation for himself and his organization. Foxman sounded optimistic at the conclusion of his meeting, noting that the two discussed "things that are doable." But he also pointed out the predicament of Arafat, who at that point, he said, had not "decided on what to sign, when to sign."[52]

After the UN General Assembly, short meetings were held, with little success. So the parties headed back to the region, where talks continued on September 17 at the King David Hotel. Erekat, Dahlan, and Dajani, along with counterparts Sher, Hasson, and Grinstein, tried once again to thrash out the elements of an agreement from all their cumulative exchanges. In the absence of an American interlocutor with reliable records, they first had to fight over whose notes from Camp David were more accurate. Sher thwarted Palestinian attempts to bring along Rob Malley or the newly designated consul general, Ron Schlicher, both of whom the Palestinians trusted. Sher plainly admitted to Palestinians his fear that they might harden their positions. Sher instead preferred to report to a mediator friendlier to his team, Ambassador Indyk, who they believed would be returning to the region in just a couple of days.

Unbeknownst to them all, Indyk was back in Washington deeply embroiled in an investigation that had been launched into his mishandling of classified information, both at the embassy in Tel Aviv, where his lax security practices were described by colleagues as the most abhorrent they had ever witnessed, and on domestic and international trips, where he drafted classified memos on his personal computer, in violation of federal law, State Department rules, and common sense. Albright had grown tired of Indyk, whom she had never gotten along with personally, and pressure from the Senate Intelligence Committee afforded her an easy pretext to strip him of his security clearance, which made him a visitor at the embassy where he presided. He even required a Marine escort to get to his office, the utmost in humiliation.

To be on the safe side, the State Department Office of Professional Responsibility, where I later worked, assessed that, given the total picture of Indyk, as well as the nature of the secret information he mishandled, a referral to the FBI was warranted—a move that raised the specter of possible criminal prosecution—and raised questions in the press over Indyk's possible involvement in espionage. After a string of embarrassing security lapses within the department, the decision to suspend Indyk's access to sensitive national security information at such a critical time was not without controversy. Though the FBI never brought criminal charges against Indyk, accusations by the pro-Israel Anti-Defamation League of anti-Semitism compared Indyk's plight to the Dreyfus Affair in France. Indyk's troubles, and the ADL's defense of him, were reminders of the risk Clinton had taken when he granted expedited citizenship and high-level appointment to Indyk, whose résumé arguably indicated no greater ties to the United States than to Israel and its interests. And given Indyk's background as an intelligence officer in Australia in the 1970s, his carelessness regarding security matters aroused the utmost suspicion.

One benefit of not having American involvement in the exchanges between Israel and the Palestinians was that it led to more candor—there was no need to posture for the Americans. To negotiators like Sher, extensive American involvement by Ross and others, in addition to evoking Palestinian charges of bias, had also weakened the Israelis. As he describes it:

> I feel like we Israelis have sacrificed a lot of our positions because of that biased tag that was put on Dennis Ross and on others—on Madeleine Albright—all the same. Arafat used to say to Clinton, "These guys are working for the Israelis, not for you!" . . . Believe me, we did a lot to try and

> convince the Palestinians that whichever proposals came from the American side was just as unacceptable to us as they were to them! But, unfortunately, they did not believe us.[53]

Thus, without American involvement, the Israelis opened their positions on security, but not before Sher offered a chilling prediction of the need to work fast. His verbatim remarks at the time were:

> My opinion is that we have one week to ten days to work peacefully. I suggest we move on with drafting and try to put on paper at least two of the agreed sections—the four chapters. This should take no more than two to three days. Then we can proceed with I's and P's in sub-articles. This is complementary to the American effort—to the political effort.

Palestinians listened for four hours to the Israeli ideas on the first area, security. The parties broke to meet the following day, on September 18 at the same hotel, where they heard a reaction from Dahlan, who felt the Israelis had only slightly altered since Camp David. His words were nevertheless a striking demonstration of how, even at this late hour, both sides were still disputing the most basic definitional issues:

> What surprised me in your presentation was the way you conceptualized what you want. It's based on the redeployment of the Israeli forces—redrafting Israeli control over the Palestinians. You are seeking to continue your mandate over the Palestinians. I didn't detect that you want to move from the interim mentality to the permanent-status mentality. Under your approach, you're offering a few dark corridors, which, if entered, will pull us deeper and deeper into darkness. I looked through your agreement with Egypt, which did not involve all of this. The threat to Israel from Egypt at the time was from all the Arab countries. The PLO and Israel are now working together. Our strategic thinking is that we move

> from the hostility stage to the stage of friendship. . . . Our interests are tied, whether we like it or not. We have confronted a certain segment of the Palestinians society, and we were victorious. . . . Both sides are commited to fight terror. We're serious about it; we've been doing it now, when we're weak.

Dahlan railed against the steady emphasis of the Americans and Israelis over creating a "weak" Palestinian state, objecting again to the choice of definitions:

> I understand that you don't want a militarized state that can attack Israel or assist others in attacking Israel. But we cannot accept the phrase "demilitarized state." I suggest a state with "limited arms" or "defensive arms." Without using the phrase, we can reach an acceptable agreement.

There were more heated exchanges, but unlike talks where Americans had been present, this did not destroy the feelings of civility and confidence in the other side as a partner for peace. The negotiators drafted a rigorous schedule for the next several days in Jerusalem and Jericho. As the meeting came to a close, Sher had this to say of the rumors that an American draft was nearing its presentation:

> I'm willing to try to put on paper something significantly different from our current written text that goes along the lines of certain things that were said today and certain tacit understandings said today—and show it to you tomorrow. Because the alternative is that we will get screwed up by the American text. And there's no assurance to the contrary. We've seen the U.S. documents before. You've rejected them. We've rejected them—quite bluntly. No one knows what the sensitivities and problems are better than us. If we don't identify the divergences in every issue of the main, core issues, we cannot move forward, because we can't frame the trade-offs that the leaders will have to make at the end of the process.

• • •

**As each day** ticked beyond September 13, and with an agreement appearing nowhere in sight—quite the opposite, as on the evening of September 19 Barak announced he was suspending all talks, only to reverse himself under severe international pressure[54]—it became clear that something had to give. Tensions on both the Israeli and Palestinian street were building, and CIA officials were sending ominous reports back to Director Tenet in Langley. Melissa Mahle described the scene:

> It was a very eerie period there—that's the best way to describe it. The tension—and I'll speak specifically about the West Bank because that's where I was spending the vast majority of my time—you could feel the tension in the air. It was as though all Palestinians were waiting for the other shoe to drop. Everybody knew something was going to happen. They didn't know what it was that was going to happen, but they were certainly concerned . . . prior to Camp David, certainly, there was a sense of desperation that began to pervade, and then after Camp David failed, this sense of desperation then became an angry desperation.

Mahle related the effects of the American-Israeli blame campaign:

> There was always a belief within the Palestinian leadership and on the street and certainly within the security apparatus that only the U.S. would be able to deliver an agreement. . . . When the blame was laid on the doorstep of Arafat it was one of those moments that the Palestinians said, "We've been abandoned—totally!"[55]

In late September, the Egyptian pressure to table a working proposal intensified, much to the chagrin of the Israelis, who feared their ideas sided too heavily with the Palestinians. In a meeting with Shlomo Ben Ami, Amr Moussa proposed having the Temple Mount/Haram al-Sharif entrusted to the UN Security Council, which Ben Ami rejected. In an Israeli radio interview after meeting the following day with French President Jacques Chirac, who was also strongly pushing the parties, Ben Ami told listeners, "I informed [Moussa] of my reservations about one primary component—Israel's place on Temple Mount. We will naturally reject any ideas where the Israeli link to the site is adulterated."[56]

As the U.S. delay in presenting a plan dragged on, at least one Israeli newspaper began examining the reasons. On September 22, the right-wing *Jerusalem Post* carried a story citing a "source close to the negotiations" that alleged Clinton was "wavering on a plan to grant custodianship of the Temple Mount to the Palestinians" out of fear it could harm the campaigns of his wife and Al Gore. "What if most American Jews don't like it?" said the source, who added, "It doesn't take that many votes to bring down Hillary Clinton."[57] Word of the possible linkage between her campaign and the Jerusalem question caught the attention of Ariel Sharon, who in a breakfast meeting in New York on September 24 with members of the Conference of Presidents of Major American Jewish Organizations lamented, "Imagine that the future of the Jewish people is now dependent on the fact of the election of a member of the Senate of the U.S."[58]

This provocation of Sharon's led to more pandering by Rick Lazio, who sought to distance himself from all the Clinton talk of a "divided Jerusalem":

> I have a 100 percent record of support for the state of Israel. I've been a tireless advocate for Israeli security. I'm not the person who called for a "Palestinian state." As a matter of fact, I've opposed that. I'm the one who's called for a commitment to an undivided Jerusalem under the control and the sovereignty of the state of Israel.[59]

• • •

**The Clinton administration's** diplomacy may have been stagnant, but at least some Jewish Americans tried to make a constructive contribution. Perhaps believing that part of the problem lay in the terrible personal relations between Arafat and Barak, the late Daniel Abraham, the Slim-Fast magnate, used his considerable wealth to promote a peace mission. According to Yossi Beilin, Abraham cajoled Barak into extending a dinner invitation to Arafat.[60] (Charles Enderlin told me that Abraham's role in this dinner was negligible, if at all, and that the main organizers were Sher, Grinstein, Erekat, and Ghaith al-Omari.) Save for their accidental face-off in the UN elevator in September, they had not actually met since Camp David.

The dinner took place on the evening of September 25 at Barak's home in the affluent suburb of Kochav Yair, right next to the Green Line dividing Israel from the West Bank. Arafat had always complained about Barak's mistreatment of him, so observers were heartened to see the two of them walking arm and arm through Barak's garden.[61] Ben Ami, who described Barak as "not a very pleasant person. . . . He is closed and introverted and there is no emotional contact," would later tell his wife, "Barak wants an agreement so badly that he is ready to change his personality."[62] Phoning in from Washington, Clinton heard from Barak a single phrase that must have utterly surprised him: "I am going to be the partner of this man in a way better than Rabin."[63] Barak later downplayed his phone message:

> We were at a major, last minute effort and I saw that it makes sense to be as positive as possible both in content and in statements. But I was less optimistic at the time. . . . I didn't see Arafat at any moment really focused on taking action to do something about it. But I thought that in spite of my own doubts, it makes a point to try. . . . [It will] enable it so that

> when we reach the end of this road, we will know. If we will have to say that we ultimately decided that Arafat is not a partner, we should be able to convince our own people, we should be able to convince honest people in the world.[64]

Before departing, Arafat made a point of mentioning reports in the press that Sharon was planning a trip to the Haram al-Sharif/Temple Mount in the coming days. Arafat pointed out how provocative such a trip would be. Though he knew of Barak's propensity to dismiss such concerns, he pleaded anyway. "This visit [would] make a big story not only with us, with all the Muslims all over the world," Arafat later said of the exchange. "He didn't listen to me."[65]

Arafat was not about to be the one to stop negotiating. He dispatched his team to meet with Barak's in Washington that night, where talks resumed at the Pentagon City Ritz Carlton on September 26. Ross, who claims the American "ideas" had been ready for presentation, had this to say of criticism that the United States had lagged too much in the months after Camp David:

> I think you have to understand that in September we did move. We were ready to go ahead and present ideas in September. We had one last request from the Palestinians to have "one more round." It was made as a joint request, but as Gilead Sher said to me, this was a favor to Saeb because "Saeb wanted one more round for us to find out before we presented the ideas," which would be what each side could live with.[66]

But Erekat was not the only one hesitant to see what Ross was putting together. Both sides were uncertain about being presented with an American document as a fait accompli. When I asked one senior White House observer why the parameters were delayed, the official told me on background:

You see, this pisses me off. Because of fucking Israel! The Israelis didn't want them to be put forward because Barak didn't want them tabled because he was worried about his election. . . . My recollection, in December, was that there were certain proposals that Barak didn't want put forward because he didn't think he could sell them back home. Also, realize that the U.S. is pro-Israeli. Clinton was the first president who first reached out to Palestinians—like no other—but at the end of the day, Clinton was a pro-Israeli president. When push came to shove, Clinton wasn't going to—if Barak said don't put this in front of him, he wouldn't do it. What can I say—they're our closest ally!

Aaron Miller had this to say:

There's no mystery here and there is no need for secrecy; I can categorically tell you that the parameters were not nearly ready by September; that while we were in the process of developing them we were in no way, shape or form prepared to present them. Most of October and even part of November was consumed by travel to Sharm and to Paris in an effort to defuse the intifada that had begun on September 28. The fact [that] we were making revisions on the parameters up until the very day they were presented on December 23 demonstrates that we were not ready, certainly not as early as September. We didn't even begin to re-engage in the wake of Camp David until August, and that flowed into conversations with Israelis and Palestinians in Washington in the first part of September. . . . That, combined with a lack of clear strategy and dithering over what the parameters should be, produced the delay.[67]

As far as the Palestinians were concerned, the Camp David experience proved that American ideas were vetted so thoroughly with the Israelis that they lost any value, so maybe it was better to continue intensive bilateral talks directly with the Israelis. If the Americans were stationed nearby, maybe they could break an impasse and help bridge an agreement substantially made by the parties themselves—as Israelis and Palestinians had done in Oslo, as the Egyptians and Israelis had largely done on their own before Jimmy Carter called them to a summit, and as Israelis and Jordanians had done. Alternatively, the Americans could incorporate any progress into their own proposal.

Instead of focusing on negotiations, however, the Ritz Carlton talks became centered on crisis management, as it became clear that Barak was going to allow Sharon's visit. Sharon cleverly publicized how he wanted it viewed. "We are not visiting Judaism's holiest site with a message of provocation, but with a message of peace," he said, adding, "The Temple Mount is the most sacred place, it is the basis of the existence of the Jewish people, and I am not afraid of riots by the Palestinians."[68]

That day, the Egyptian ambassador to the United States, Nabil Fahmy, joined Dahlan and Erekat in their suite. Afterward Fahmy briefed Mubarak in Cairo on what Ross's words of wisdom about Sharon's visit had been, which, Fahmy recalls, were "Don't overplay it," "Don't react," and "Barak can't stop the guy."[69]

Ross's reaction had been no better than Barak's with Arafat days earlier. Ross absolves himself of any responsibility for not acting more forcefully to stop the Sharon visit. This was in many ways because Ross, especially after Camp David, was loath to extend himself on behalf of the Palestinians. In addition, he figured that the Palestinian reaction to the visit would be a test for Arafat: any adverse reaction would be further proof that Arafat—who Ross believed reigned supreme over his constituents in the autonomous sectors of the territories—had no interest in a peaceful resolution of the conflict. Afterward Ross proclaimed that Arafat "cultivated" the atmosphere that exploded with Sharon's visit:

> I knew we were headed toward an explosion. For eight months we had been hearing from intel—Israeli intelligence—how bad the mood was on the Israeli street, on the Palestinian street, and sooner or later it was going to spill over. And, you know, Arafat cultivated this! This is classic Arafat, because he saw the value of it. He saw it as a pressure on the Israelis and, of course, he ignored that it might become a pressure on him.

Of the talks in Washington on the eve of Sharon's visit Ross had this to say:

> Arafat knew from his negotiators that this was very promising, and he did nothing to stop the violence. And we told him, because we had information that the violence was going to take place the next day—we told him we wouldn't present the ideas if there was violence. . . . I think from Arafat's standpoint he thought the violence would create pressure on us and on the Israelis. I mean, look, you got to look historically at how many times at big moments Arafat calculated correctly. His track record is not very good![70]

• • •

**Despite all the** warnings, on the sunny morning of Thursday, September 28, Ariel Sharon and his followers went ahead with their promenade on the Haram al-Sharif. Encircling Sharon were more than 1,000 border police and Shin Bet agents. While Sharon and his swarm did not enter al-Aqsa or the Dome of the Rock mosques, the thirty-minute walk around the Islamic holy site was for many Palestinians akin to seeing a known arsonist holding a gas can and matches—with police aiding and abetting. Sharon is, after all, especially infamous for his role in the gruesome Phalangist massacre of Palestinians at the Beirut refugee camps of Sabra and

Shatila in 1982. Yet, despite all the publicity his actual visit received, the reaction that day was surprisingly tame; with the exception of a few who chucked stones as the procession departed, there was no violence.

The following day was an entirely different matter. Many Palestinians saw Sharon's visit as an American-backed demonstration of Jewish ownership over the Jerusalem holy sites—pitting Judaism versus Islam—which could not go unanswered. Indeed, Sharon later said his purpose that day had been to "actualize Israel's sovereignty over" the Temple Mount.[71]

For many Palestinians on their way to the Haram al-Sharif that Friday, this was no ordinary gathering. Many youth activists and members of Fatah's tanzim arrived with more than prayer in mind. As they filed out of the mosques, they confronted Israeli police outside. What happened next has been well documented. A fact-finding commission established the next month at Sharm el-Sheik tasked with finding ways to "end the violence, prevent its recurrence, and to find a path back to the peace process," was led by former U.S. Senator George Mitchell. In a letter to Mitchell, Clinton urged the commission to "steer clear of any step that will intensify mutual blame or finger pointing." The commission described the first day of the second intifada:

> A large number of unarmed Palestinian demonstrators and a large Israeli police contingent confronted one another. According to the U.S. Department of State, "Palestinians held large demonstrations and threw stones at police in the vicinity of the Western Wall. Police used rubber-coated metal bullets and live ammunition to disperse the demonstrators, killing 4 people and injuring about 200. According to the Government of Israel, 14 Israeli policemen were injured."[72]

Outraged over the lethal Israeli response to unarmed demonstrators, the Fatah Higher Leadership Committee convened that evening in Ramallah, bringing together the leaders of grassroots activists to prepare for further demonstrations. As always, inter-Palestinian politics came into play. Although the secretary general and committee chair was Husayn al-Sheikh, whom Arafat had appointed earlier that year after demoting Marwan Barghouti from the same position, there was little any the committee members could do to stop Barghouti's calls for coordinated protests at checkpoints and settlement outposts throughout the territories the following day, including in Jerusalem.

In a curious way, Arafat's political situation was a mirror of Barak's: he had almost no political reserves to draw on, and since Sharon's visit had touched on the explosive question of Jerusalem's holy sites, he would have looked like a quisling had he ordered his constituents not to react, especially in light of the deadly response that Friday by Israeli police. Barak hadn't done anything to stop a provocation that he knew would unleash pent-up feelings of rage—why should Arafat be the one to turn the other cheek? The more troubling question for Arafat, however—who at the time feared losing control to Barghouti, as he briefly had during the Nakba riots in May—was whether or not Barghouti and his followers would have listened had Arafat tried to stop them.

The second intifada exploded that Friday and Saturday, the last two days of September, when, according to B'Tselem, an Israeli human rights group, the IDF killed fifteen Palestinians, including four children, while the Israeli security forces suffered one casualty.[73] The death of 12-year-old Mohammed al-Dura, shot by the IDF at the Netzarim checkpoint in Gaza as he cowered under his father's arms behind a barrel, would be captured live by a French TV crew and broadcast around the world. This killing aroused the fury of Palestinians, indeed of Arabs and Muslims everywhere, and helped turn what might have been brief clashes into a full-scale intifada. (In Egypt, Mohammed Tantawi, the most respected cleric and sheik of al-Azhar Mosque, issued calls for

Palestinians to "engage Israel in armed confrontation."[74] Al-Qaeda would also use the killing for recruitment purposes; in a seldom-studied videotape made in the summer of 2001, just months before the devastating September 11 attacks, Osama bin Laden condemned Israeli brutality against Palestinians, showing the al-Dura killing repeatedly. Al-Qaeda expert Peter Bergen believes this killing both increased sympathy for al-Qaeda and "definitely moved up" planning for terrorist operations.[75]) Arafat initially hoped to ride the wave of outrage in Europe and the Arab and Muslim world against the IDF's harsh response. Barak understood this, and also how critical it was to build support for the IDF's iron fist not just within Israel but in the international arena as well. For these reasons, Barak's government and its supporters in the United States unleashed one of the greatest PR frauds in history, still dominating the American and Israeli media to this day.

This PR spin is compounded from the blame that began at Camp David. The line is that Arafat's true face was exposed when he rejected Barak's "generous offer" that would have brought peace; that Arafat abandoned negotiations after Camp David because all along his real intent has been to destroy the Jewish state; and that his rejectionism and the outbreak of violence in September 2000 demonstrate that Israel has no partner for peace.

A March 2001 report issued by a United Nations Commission on Human Rights fact-finding team buttressed the claims of many observers that Isreals' heavy-handed response to demonstrations fueled the intifada. It found the government in blatant violation of not only the Fourth Geneva Convention but the laws of armed conflict, specifically the "principle of proportionality," which the IDF ignored from the very beginning.[76] Bar Ilan University Professor Menachem Klein, who at the time was an external adviser to Shlomo Ben Ami (Ben Ami, who was Barak's minister of internal security with responsibility over Israeli police, had declined on legal grounds to prohibit Sharon's visit), reflected on the effects of the IDF's escalation, which Barak sanctioned:

> At some time between mid-May to late September, Barak approved the operational and tactical plans of the IDF to halt the intifada. These included the massive use of snipers by IDF, which brought about heavy Palestinian dead and wounded in the first days of the intifada. In my opinion, these casualties had the effect of turning a single violent clash on the Haram al-Sharif after Sharon's visit into a national intifada.[77]

A remarkable investigative report in 2002 by Israeli journalist Ben Caspit revealed just how brutal the IDF's actions had been:

> About 3 weeks after the outbreak of the intifada, the head of the Intelligence Unit of the IDF, while visiting the Central Command, asked one of the officers how many bullets the IDF had shot since the beginning of the violence. When it turned out that no one knew, and after a short investigation, everyone in the room turned pale when they heard the numbers: the IDF, in the first few days of the intifada, shot 700,000 bullets of different kinds in the West Bank and about 300,000 more in the Gaza Strip—about 1 million bullets in total.[78]

After two more years and many more casualties, Major General Amos Malka, who was the head of the IDF's Military Intelligence (MI) branch until 2001, along with Mati Steinberg, an Arab affairs adviser to the Shin Bet, went public with their strikingly similar description of events to Israeli journalist Akiva Eldar. As Eldar puts it:

> Both of them share the argument that the top Israeli security echelon contributed to fanning the flames. Malka relates that about a month after the intifada began, he was on his way to the Gilo neighborhood in Jerusalem, [and] he asked Yossi

> Kuperwasser, at the time the intelligence officer of the Central Command (and today head of the research division), how many 5.56 bullets the command had fired that month. "Kuperwasser got back to me with a number of 850,000 bullets. My figure was 1.3 million bullets in the West Bank and Gaza. This is a strategic figure that says that our soldiers are shooting and shooting and shooting. I asked, 'Is this what you intended in your preparations?' And he replied in the negative. I said, 'Then the significance is that we are determining the height of the flames.' I brought the issue up at Central Command discussions, but [IDF Chief of Staff Shaul] Mofaz went with the militant bit from the very first day and all along the way."[79]

Just as hawks in the U.S. Defense Department were to do in gathering intelligence to justify the Iraq war, Barak "cherry-picked" the intelligence that suited his political agenda. In this case it was served up by Kuperwasser, a rightist, and his Shin Bet director, Avi Dichter, who had replaced Ami Ayalon months before the intifada. Kuperwasser and Dichter trumped the dissenting opinions of subordinates.

General Malka has alleged that then-Brigadier General Amos Gilad, who at the time served as his subordinate in the MI research division, bears personal responsibility for providing patently false oral briefings to cabinet and Knesset members once the intifada started. It was Gilad, Malka insists, who spoon-fed Barak's line that Arafat was not a partner for peace, that he had chosen a strategy of violence after Camp David, and that he insisted on the right of return to destroy Israel demographically. Malka identified Gilad as a "very significant factor who influenced many people." Malka couldn't have been blunter: "I say, with full responsibility, that during my entire period as head of Military Intelligence, there was not a single research department document that expressed the assessment that Gilad claims to have presented to the prime minister [Barak]."[80] Colonel Ephraim Lavie, who handled the Palestinian portfolio under Gilad's command, likewise backed Malka, attesting, "I can unequivocally say that in the written official assessments of the research department there was no conception so prevalent nowadays." With social pressure in Israel still strongly committed to this dogma, Lavie admitted he had not come forward until 2004 so as to "protect the reputation and credibility of military intelligence." In the wake of these revelations, Knesset Member Shimon Peres demanded an investigation into Gilad for his briefings, describing them as "stupid, exaggerated theories," which, he lamented, have "contributed to . . . the decision to carry out a unilateral disengagement instead of trying to reach an agreement with the Palestinians."[81]

The myth that Arafat cultivated the intifada and is psychologically unable to make peace with Israel took deep root in America too, of course. But the U.S. intelligence apparatus has its own refutation to match Malka's revelations: a thirty-five-year veteran clandestine CIA officer and adviser to Director George Tenet told me, first, that Arafat did not plan the second intifada; second, that the status quo theory that "he couldn't get what he wanted negotiating so he chose the path of violence" is a lie. Third, Jibril Rajoub, head of the Preventive Security Organization for the West Bank, had predicted that violence would erupt, and was the one who told Arafat to urge Barak to block Sharon's visit (an important point, as Ben Ami would testify under oath before an internal commission of inquiry investigating Israeli shooting of Palestinian citizens in October 2000, the Or Commission, that Rajoub had OK'd the visit). Finally, Arafat even phoned the White House on the eve of Sharon's visit to beg Clinton to weigh in on Barak. Amid the internal finger-pointing in Washington that would later arise, the CIA officer told me that he took the unusual step of confirming this for himself: Arafat's message was not taken by Clinton; rather, it was handled by Dennis Ross.

Another CIA officer involved in the events corroborated these four points and added firsthand knowledge on two additional points. First, at least one West Bank mukhabarat commander protested Sharon's planned visit directly with the Shin Bet, obviously to no avail. Second, though these reports were sent to Washington at the time for consumption by the State Department, NSC, and White House, it was not uncommon for lead Middle East envoy Ross to dismiss CIA conclusions in favor of the assessments he liked from Israeli intelligence.

These revelations, though late in arriving, are important, as they demonstrate how even at this late stage in the Oslo process, the Palestinians were willing to make a good-faith attempt to fulfill their responsibility to prevent violence, which they were certain the Sharon visit would bring. But more importantly, the revelations also reflect the way in which the intelligence services of another country can influence Washington policy.

• • •

**Even in the** first days of the clashes, Egyptian diplomats sensed disaster. At a breakfast meeting in New York, Foreign Minister Moussa pleaded with Albright to act quickly and set down the package the Egyptians had delivered in late August. But the Americans still felt little sense of urgency as, according to Moussa's spokesman, Albright vaguely promised, "There will be intensive consultations during the months of October and November," and that the United States "will not stop until an agreement is reached."[82] To this day, Egyptian diplomats believe the Americans were deliberately negligent.

As the situation deteriorated Albright arranged round-the-clock talks in Paris with Barak, Arafat and various deputies. Arafat demanded an international inquiry into the violence and Barak resisted. Arafat was furious at the death toll, not only in the territories but in Israel too, where in the first week or so of the uprising thirteen Palestinian citizens of Israel who were demonstrating in solidarity with their comrades were shot dead.

At one point in the talks, after shouting about Barak, "This man does not respect me!" the Palestinian leader burst out the door and headed toward his limousine. Albright practiced a little coercive diplomacy, ordering, "Do not let him leave. . . . Shut the gates!" There were more theatrics, quite depressing in retrospect; at a late hour, Barak came storming outside with a secure cell phone in hand, telling President Clinton words to the effect of, "You don't understand what I'm dealing with. Even your FBI once told me these people are incapable of telling the truth—they have no cognitive dissonance. Arafat is a liar and he is only playing games." (Such crude racism would appear in print less than two years later, when, in the *New York Review of Books,* Barak was quoted by Israeli historian Benny Morris as saying that Palestinians "are products of a culture in which to tell a lie . . . creates no dissonance. . . . They don't suffer from the problem of telling lies that exists in Judeo-Christian culture. Truth is seen as irrelevant."[83])

On October 7, the UN Security Council condemned, by a vote of 14-0 with the United States abstaining, Israel's aggression and the high toll of Palestinian casualties. The American ambassador Richard Holbrooke's lecture on the necessity to refrain from "finger-pointing and recrimination" was too late in arriving.

A second horrific incident occurred on the afternoon of October 12. As hundreds of Palestinians marched through downtown Ramallah to bury their latest intifada casualty, two IDF reservists who had gotten lost, Yossef Avrahami, 38, and Vadim Norvich, 33, drove up alongside the procession. As a mob attacked them, Palestinian policeman came to their defense, moving the two swiftly to a nearby police station.[84] The police were quickly overwhelmed, however, and the soldiers were brutally beaten and stabbed to death. As with al-Dura, their fate was captured by a television crew outside. A jubilant Palestinian was seen tossing a lifeless body from a second-story window, displaying his blood-stained hands to the cheering crowd below. Just as the al-Dura killing fueled Palestinian rage and a thirst for revenge, so the Ramallah lynchings would do the same for the Israeli public, already primed by Barak's PR machine to believe that the Palestinians were solely to blame for the violence. Journalist Ben Caspit later identified the "bloody hands" incident as Barak's own "breaking point":

> Barak, according to eyewitnesses, went crazy with rage and immediately asked to prepare F-16 airplanes to attack many Palestinian targets at once. He would not answer to calls from then U.S. Ambassador Indyk and spoke, in closed forums, of an "Armageddon War." His aides and close political associates tried different tactics to calm him down and in the end the F-16s were replaced by fighter helicopters. Gaza received its heaviest shelling ever. Israel abandoned its self-restraint, and the entire conflict went up a notch—probably more than one—overnight.[85]

Despite an emergency high-level summit in Sharm el-Sheik on October 16, attended by Arafat, Barak, Clinton, Mubarak, King Abdullah, Kofi Annan, and other senior EU leaders, the resulting calls for a cease-fire, investigation by an independent commission, and recommitment to negotiations went mostly ignored. By the end of October, the number of Palestinian killed by Israeli security forces rose to an even 100, including twenty-nine children; Israeli civilians, presumably Jewish settlers, killed two Palestinians in the occupied territories. On the Israeli side, four security personnel and six civilians were killed inside the occupied territories.[86]

• • •

**In Washington, the** election season was in high gear, so the Clinton administration wanted to avoid any controversial moves on the Arab-Israeli issue. Congress made clear its stance, passing a resolution in mid-October that expressed its "solidarity with the State and people of Israel," alleging: "Whereas the Government of Israel made clear to the world its commitment to peace at Camp David, where it expressed its readiness to take wide-ranging and painful steps in order to bring an end to the conflict, but these proposals were rejected by Chairman Arafat."[87]

American media support was, of course, firmly behind the Israelis. Thomas Friedman's October 13 *New York Times* op-ed, titled "Arafat's War," told American readers how the Palestinians were to blame:

> Mr. Clinton pointedly, deliberately—and rightly—stated that Israeli Prime Minister Ehud Barak had offered unprecedented compromises at the summit—more than 90 percent of the West Bank for a Palestinian state, a partial resolution of the Palestinian refugee problem and Palestinian sovereignty over the Muslim and Christian quarters of the Old City of Jerusalem—and that Yasir Arafat had not responded in kind, or at all. . . .
>
> Mr. Arafat had a dilemma: make some compromises, build on Mr. Barak's opening bid and try to get it closer to 100 percent—and regain the moral high ground that way—or provoke the Israelis into brutalizing Palestinians again, and regain the moral high ground that way. Mr. Arafat chose the latter. . . .[88]

*USA Today* journalist Jack Kelley—who at one point was nominated for a 2001 Pulitzer Prize for his "eyewitness" intifada coverage, only later to be terminated after an internal investigation found that he engaged in "sweeping and substantial" journalistic fraud,[89] including the use of fictional Israeli intelligence sources—wrote an extensive piece on October 23 that accused Palestinians of "professionally organized attacks using kids as a cover."[90] Sourcing "other Israeli intelligence officials," Kelley went on to convey the preposterous claim that "satellite photos reveal that heavy artillery is being moved around the Palestinian-controlled territories in the West Bank and Gaza." The artillery, of course, never materialized.

Many in the Middle East had hoped the Israeli-Palestinian negotiations would start up again once the U.S. presidential election was over. But the razor-thin margin and the long-drawn-out dispute over the Florida balloting threw Washington into turmoil, further delaying progress on the Israel-Palestine front, even as casualties on both sides mounted. For the first time ever, Barak deployed F-16 fighter jets against Palestinian Authority buildings, including key security structures like prisons and police stations, which would damage the PA's ability to keep order and fight terror.[91]

In symbolic response to Barak's activation of the Israeli Air Force, Ambassadors from Egypt and Jordan—the only countries at peace with Israel—were recalled from their Tel Aviv posts, further estranging Israel from the only front-channel ties it had with the Arab world. Further frictions emerged between Barak and the Clinton administration over the Sharm el-Sheik Fact Finding Commission, led by former Senator George Mitchell, because of Barak's protests that they not arrive amid the violence, which he feared would result in a report blaming Israel (this gambit would be attempted again, with more success, a year and a half later, when Israel would successfully prevent a UN investigation of the IDF's April 2002 invasion of Jenin).

Separate dialogues with Arafat through Shimon Peres/Gilead Sher and Yossi Ginosar/Amnon Lipkin-Shahak likewise failed, the latter resigning his role in protest after witnessing how "specific detailed agreements he reached with his Palestinian counterparts [Dahlan] were later ignored by [Israeli] military personnel on the ground." [92]

• • •

**A new factor** was introduced on December 9, when Barak resigned as prime minister. He feared that he would be defeated by Netanyahu in general elections scheduled for May, and that he had better chances going to special elections earlier, on February 6, against Sharon. And if he could propose a peace referendum, it would only increase his prospects.

Clinton also realized time was running out; now that the American elections were over, the coast was clear to restart intensive negotiations (Hillary had won her Senate race handily and, in a controversial December 12 ruling, the Supreme Court handed the presidential election to George W. Bush). The parties were invited to Washington's Bolling Air Force Base in late December in an attempt to pick up from where talks had left off in the days before the intifada. The most significant development, aside from having American reengagement, was a concession proposed by Shlomo Ben Ami, which he admits was made "without consulting anyone." According to Ben Ami, it was for Palestinians to have "sovereignty over the Temple Mount" so long as they "would undertake not to conduct excavations there because the place was sacred to the Jews." But Ben Ami insisted that the Palestinians make a statement proclaiming that "the site is sacred to the Jews."[93] But the Palestinians balked, fearing that such recognition could backfire if the Israelis withdrew the offer—a strong possibility, considering that Barak hadn't authorized it and that other members of the Israeli delegation were angry with Ben Ami for making the offer without Barak's authorization; at least one negotiator, Israel Hasson, threatened to resign.[94]

The bickering paused when the parties were summoned to the White House on the bitterly cold morning of December 23, a momentous occasion they had all been expecting. The White House was at the peak of its Christmastime splendor, as it would be the last holiday Clinton would spend there as president. The anxious delegations listened intently as Clinton began his historic remarks. Even though he was leaving office, Clinton was still skittish about offering a written proposal. Apparently not having learned his lesson from Camp David's sloppy procedures, he once again decided to convey his ideas orally, reading at dictation speed. The president began with some qualifiers:

> We know you're working hard. But at the rate you're going, you won't make it. What I'm going to give you is not a U.S. proposal, but rather our idea of what will be needed on core issues to reach an agreement. If either side refuses to accept these parameters, they're off the table. We can talk about refinements, but these ideas are not to be negotiated. I would like answers from your leaders in four days.[95]

Next Clinton read his ideas, later referred to as the "Clinton parameters": On territory, the Palestinian state would control 94-96 percent of the West Bank, with a 1-3 percent swap from Israel proper (as at Camp David, the working assumption by all parties remained that all of Gaza would be returned to the Palestinians). On security, Israel would be allowed several warning stations in the Jordan Valley, and the withdrawal would be carried out over a thirty-six-month period, with an international force monitoring implementation. On Jerusalem, "Arab areas are Palestinian and Jewish ones are Israeli. This would apply to the Old City as well." Regarding the Haram al-Sharif/Temple Mount, Clinton offered two alternatives: either Palestinian sovereignty over the Haram and Israeli sovereignty over the Western Wall "and the sacred space to Judaism [Holy of Holies] of which it is a part"; or "Palestinian shared sovereignty over the Haram and Israeli sovereignty over the Western Wall and shared functional sovereignty over the issue of excavation under the Haram . . . " Regarding refugees and the right of return, "the guiding principle should be that the Palestinian state will be the focal point for Palestinians who choose to return to the area without ruling out that Israel will accept some of these refugees." Clinton closed his remarks by saying, "These are my ideas. If they are not accepted, they are not just off the table; they also go with me, when I leave office."[96]

• • •

**Both Israelis and** Palestinians were perplexed with the many ambiguities in Clinton's presentation, which, because Clinton insisted they "could not be negotiated," only "refined," meant they would have to clarify differing interpretations on their own.

On Jerusalem alone, there was the introduction of a new term, "Holy of Holies," which, according to Dr. Moshe Amirav of Haifa University, whom Barak had appointed after Camp David to advise him on Jerusalem, was a demand made by Barak that no other Zionist leader—including David Ben Gurion, Moshe Dayan, and Menachem Begin—had ever insisted on. According to Amirav, "Holy of Holies" refers to an area of "four square meters which the High Priest would enter on Yom Kippur." But according to Amirav, Barak applied this term to "the entire plaza, including the mosques."[97] Another potential deal killer for Palestinians was the proposal to have "shared functional sovereignty" over the issue of excavation under the Haram al-Sharif mosques, which only required "that mutual consent would be requested" (my emphasis) prior to any digging.

Both sides wanted clarifications. Eventually both would accept the parameters, but both would express reservations. Barak convened his negotiators on the evening of December 24. Yossi Beilin wrote of the decision that emerged:

> No one suggested that we should not adopt the outlined plan. It was decided that Israeli reservations would be prepared, and

> that the proposal should be presented for the endorsement of the full government without delay. On December 28, at a meeting of the government, the plan was endorsed in principle together with permission to send reservations that had not been presented to the government for endorsement.[98]

Many in Barak's government, opposing both the known and unknown of Clinton's parameters, raised strong objections before the vote took place. Dan Meridor said, "I am totally opposed to dividing Jerusalem for Zionist reasons and because of matters of policy." Meridor went on to threaten, "If there is an agreement that gives away parts of the Old City, I will vote against it. And if it is put to the public in the election as a referendum, I would oppose it by supporting Sharon."[99] Attorney General Rubinstein, in a "personal letter" to Barak on December 25 that was leaked to the press, offered his unsolicited opinion on the legality of Barak's continuing negotiations that could bind a future Israeli government. According to an editorial in the *Jerusalem Post*, Rubinstein questioned "the wisdom of negotiating an agreement when the 'midwife' is a U.S. president about to leave office," while at the same time he raised doubts over whether or not the Palestinians would even abide by an agreement.[100]

There were fears among the Israeli team that an agreement would not pass a referendum or be accepted as legitimate. But Barak figured that, as in the past, he could get Clinton to agree to his terms—and that because of this, he might be able to get his colleagues' agreement. He was the first to respond to the president with a qualified "yes." Ben Ami described the reservations and qualifiers:

> Clinton, in his proposal, did not make reference to the "sacred basin"—the whole area outside the Old City wall that includes the City of David and the Tombs of the Prophets on the road to the Mount of Olives. We demanded that area, in

> which there are hardly any Arabs, but the Palestinians refused. During the night, there was a very firm phone call between Barak and Clinton on this subject, because we were afraid he would decide against us. As a result of that call, the subject remained open. Clinton did not refer to it. . . . We sent the Americans a document of several pages containing our reservations. But as far as I can recall, they were pretty minor and dealt mainly with security arrangements and deployment areas and control over passages. There was also clarification concerning our sovereignty over the Temple Mount. There was no doubt our reply was positive. . . [101]

On the Palestinian side, Arafat showed detailed interest while listing his own reservations in a letter faxed to Clinton on December 28. It is worth reprinting the letter in full, in order to puncture yet another myth of Palestinian rejectionism, this one regarding the Clinton parameters; namely, that the Israelis accepted them while the Palestinians rejected them. (Ross diligently spread this fairy tale, as did the president himself. Saeb Erekat told me what Clinton had told him when the former president was visiting the region in the spring of 2001 and had dinner with Erekat, who asked Clinton why he falsely told the world that Arafat had rejected his parameters. "I was with [Arafat] when he told you 'I accept your parameters with the following reservations and qualifications!'" Erekat exclaimed to Clinton, who sheepishly replied, "I was told if I didn't say this there would not be a peace camp in Israel—that Barak would be over." So much for Bill Clinton's integrity and courage.)

Here's what Arafat wrote in his letter to the president:

> Mr. President, please allow me address you with all the sincerity emanating from the close friendship that ties us, and the historical importance of what you are trying to do. I want to assure you of my will to continue to work with you to reach

a peace agreement. I need your help in clarifying and explaining the basis of your initiative.

I need clear answers to many questions relating to calculation of land ratios that will be annexed and swapped, and the actual location of these territories, as well as the basis for defining the Wailing Wall, its borders and extensions, and the effect of that on the concept of full Palestinian sovereignty over al-Haram al-Sharif.

We understand that the idea of leasing additional territory is an option we have the right to reject, and is not a parameter of your bridging proposals. We also presume that the emergency Israeli locations are also subject to negotiations and to our approval. I hope that you have the same understanding.

I have many questions relating to the return of refugees to their homes and villages. I have a negative experience with the return of displaced Palestinians to the West Bank and Gaza during the Interim Period. Because the modalities remained tied to an Israeli veto, not one refugee was allowed to return through the mechanism of the interim agreement, which required a quadripartite committee of Egypt, Jordan, Israel, and Palestine to decide on their return. Equally, I don't see a clear approach dealing with compensation of the refugees for their land, property and funds taken by Israel under the aegis of the Israeli custodian of absentee property.

I feel, Mr. President, that the period for Israeli withdrawal specified in your initiative is too long. It will allow the enemies of peace to exploit the time to undo the agreement. I wonder if the "Period" is one of the fixed parameters of your proposal; a "basis" that cannot be changed.

Mr. President, I have many questions. I need maps, details, and clarifications that can help me take the necessary decisions with my leadership and people.

I would like you to appreciate that I do not want to procrastinate or waste time.

We need a real opportunity to invest once more your determination and creativity to reach a fair and lasting peace with you efforts and during your presidency.

I remain, Mr. President, ready to pay you a visit at the White House, in the shortest possible time if you find this visit appropriate, to discuss with you the bridging proposals and to exchange views on ways to develop them further.

Please accept my highest regards and best wishes,

Yasser Arafat[102]

As with any other contract or important binding document affecting the fate of nations, it would have been unconscionable for either the Palestinians or the Israelis to make any commitment to Clinton's guidelines without having the clearest understanding of all the terms presented. In this regard, Arafat's request was not only not obstructionist but the minimal fulfillment of his critical responsibilities as Palestinian leader.

There were two possibilities Arafat had to consider. First was Barak's upcoming re-election. Though that became less and less likely as the violence wore on and the Israeli public hardened, the Palestinians had good reason to believe a new Barak government might allow for the beginning of negotiations over Clinton's ideas, despite Clinton's threats that they would leave office with him. The Saudi ambassador to the United States, Prince Bandar bin Sultan, has revealed in a March 2003 *New Yorker* interview how the incoming Secretary of State-designate, Colin Powell, sent Arafat assurances through Bandar that the incoming Bush administration would enforce any deal made by Clinton.[103]

For Arafat, that consideration had to be balanced off another possibility—a Sharon victory in February—which looked more probable as each day passed. As the Palestinians saw it, if Sharon was elected after the Palestinians had unequivocally deposited their acceptance of Clinton's parameters, Sharon would use these Palestinian concessions—retreating from UN Resolutions 242, 338, and 194—as a new baseline, which he would try to whittle down further.

In a meeting at the White House on January 2, Arafat formally gave Clinton his qualified "yes," though the reservations and explanations he requested still stood. The next day in a press conference, White House spokesman Jake Siewert confirmed this, adding, "Both sides have now accepted the president's ideas with some reservations." Gilead Sher arrived in Washington days later to seek clarification for his side. But both returned empty-handed, as the influence, attention, and capabilities of the Clinton administration had come to its nadir.

As polls began to show overwhelming support for Sharon's election, there seemed little utility in keeping up the talks. Negotiations did in fact take place at the Egyptian resort of Taba in late January, where the gaps lessened. But the Bush administration forbade any U.S. participation, restricting the deputy consul general in Jerusalem to holding debriefing meetings, and only with Israelis. It was simply too late for serious negotiating. Gilead Sher says, "I was against Taba. So was Amnon Shahak. So were others. This was no time for negotiations. There was no political time. There was nothing we could do better than we did before."[104] As Barak himself put it, in his interview with PBS's *Frontline* a year and a half later:

> There was no way to make an agreement. It was the height of the election campaign. . . . I saw it as a last kind of opportunity to see whether Arafat's mind is changed somehow. So it was clear to me that there was no sense in trying to negotiate; I did not even allow our people to establish a delegation that sits together with a Palestinian delegation.
>
> But I saw that there is no other better use for this time—before I [stand for re-election] and before President Clinton leaves office forever—than to give Arafat a last chance to signal a change in his mind. And at the same time, if this is not the case, [it was a chance] to let other leaders of the Israeli left—namely people like Yossi Sarid or Yossi Beilin—who were not personally involved in the frontline of these negotiations, to get a first-hand impression of . . . the Palestinians.[105]

Amnon Lipkin-Shahak used somewhat less diplomatic language in a discussion with me: "Taba was bullshit. Taba was an elections exercise—don't trust nothing! Taba was not aimed to reach an agreement. Taba was aimed to convince the Israeli Arabs to vote."[106]

If Taba could not be called a committed diplomatic negotiation by the parties then in power, the participants did at least pursue fruitful avenues of discussion that will stand as a model for serious future negotiations. The Geneva Accord, a kind of virtual peace agreement hammered out by Yossi Beilin, Robert Malley, Yasser Abed Rabbo, Ghaith al-Omari, and others, was in fact developed from what had been discussed at Taba; Geneva stands as the closest that Israeli and Palestinian diplomats have come to a reasonable two-state solution.

• • •

**Though the Clinton** team understandably had bitter feelings toward the incoming Bush administration regarding the disputed election, the new team was nonetheless entitled to an objective depiction of what had taken place, especially on matters that so deeply affect U.S. national security interests. But by this point the American-Israeli spin was out of control, and it would have been extremely difficult for Clinton to acknowledge his mistakes and frustrations publicly.

In a 2004 fundraising speech, Vice President Dick Cheney offered his account of the outgoing advice Clinton's team gave to President Bush:

> I'm always struck by the memory that I'll always carry of January 20, 2001, when President Bush and I were sworn in. We went to—as is traditional that day, you go to church service, and then you go over to the White House and have coffee with the outgoing administration. . . .
>
> And Bill Clinton talked repeatedly all day long about his disappointment in Yasser Arafat, and how Arafat had, in effect, torpedoed the peace process. Arafat was in the White House and the West Wing more often than any other foreign leader during the eight years of the Clinton administration. Bill Clinton did everything he could to try to put together a settlement and came fairly close. In the final analysis, Arafat refused to say yes.[107]

A similar exhange also took place between Clinton and incoming Secretary of State Colin Powell at 4 o'clock on January 20, in which Clinton urged Powell not to invest any energy in dealing with Arafat. Dennis Ross, who was leaving government to return to the pro-Israel Washington Institute for Near East Policy (while moonlighting as a Fox News Middle East analyst), would later give Powell a more extensive briefing. Ross adopted an especially cynical stance; according to Gilead Sher, Ross's advice for Powell was, "Don't believe a word Arafat says—he's a con man."[108] Although on most policy matters the incoming administration refused to follow the Clinton team's advice, in this area they readily accepted it.

Because of what was accepted as Camp David orthodoxy, better stated as the untruths of Camp David, the ideological advice provided by Bush's advisers filled the new president's intellectual vacuum, laying the groundwork for a destructive American Middle East policy that gives blanket endorsement to Sharon's unilateralism and refusal to negotiate. Not only has this exacerbated a disastrous course of events that has left the region a shambles; it has undermined the global reputation of all Americans, undermined the country's ability to fight terror, and made it much more difficult to forge coalitions on other essential fronts.[109]

With candor and genuine regret, Aaron Miller recalled how he joined Ross during the Powell briefing. Powell, impressionable on the topic and one of the most fair-minded members of the new administration, heard four hours of Ross's tainted version of what had happened in the previous year and a half, including at the Camp David summit. Miller offered me the following mea culpa: "Like any brief," said Miller, "You don't want to give centrality to how you fucked up. Dennis could have never brought himself to do it, and neither could I".[110]

# *Notes*

## CHAPTER ONE

[1] William B. Quandt, "Clinton and the Arab-Israeli Conflict: The Limits of Incrementalism," *Journal of Palestine Studies* 30, no. 2 (Winter 2001), 27.

[2] Ned Walker, interview by author, February 19, 2003.

[3] State Department political appointee, interview by author.

[4] Shimon Peres, speech at the Washington Institute for Near East Policy, February 22, 2004.

[5] Joe Lockhart, interview by author, April 18, 2003.

[6] Benny Morris, *Righteous Victims* (New York: Knopf, 1999), 650.

[7] "U.S. 'Hired Guns' Leave Their Mark on Israeli Politics," Cable News Network (CNN), May 1999. News on-line. Available from http://www.cnn.com/SPECIALS/1999/israeli.elections/stories/israel.us.sidebar/. Accessed October 29, 2003.

[8] Assaf Bergerfreund, "Barak Campaign Uses Money Intended for Immigrants," *Ha'aretz,* September 10, 2003.

[9] *Ibid.*

[10] "Clintonism in Israel," *Wall Street Journal,* February 10, 2000.

[11] Madeleine Albright, interview by author, July 7, 2003. Albright stated, "The advantage of doing Syria was that Rabin had really bitten the bullet on it and had done so much . . . we kept trying to persuade Netanyahu that he could wrap himself in Rabin on that."

[12] Deborah Sontag, "Issue of Troops in Lebanon Energizes Israeli Election," *New York Times,* March 6, 1999.

[13] Charles Enderlin, *Shattered Dreams: The Failure of the Peace Process in the Middle East, 1995-2002* (New York: Other Press, 2003), 69–70.

[14] Zoe Danon Gedal, "Arafat, Israeli Elections, May 4, and U.S. Policy," *Peacewatch Anthology,* 1999 (Washington DC: Washington Institute for Near East Reporting, 2000), 7.

[15] William B. Quandt, *Peace Process* (Washington, DC: Brookings Institution Press, 2001), 357.

[16] William B. Quandt, Appendix X, "Extract from 'Letter from Bill Clinton to Yasser Arafat.'" Available from http://brookings.edu/press/appendix/appen_x.htm. Accessed October 29, 2003.

[17] "Arafat Welcomes Clinton Offer on Peace 'Within One Year,'" CNN, April 26, 1999. Available from http://www.cnn.com/WORLD/meast/9904/26/israel.PA.lestinians/index.html. Accessed October 29, 2003.

[18] Ehud Barak, Agence France-Presse, April 27, 1999. The Balfour Declaration was the 1917 British promise to create a Jewish national home in Palestine.

[19] Dennis Ross, interview by author, November 12, 2002.

[20] David Maraniss, *First in His Class: A Biography of Bill Clinton* (New York: Simon & Schuster, 1995), 455.

[21] Maria Echaveste, interview by author, November 12, 2002.

[22] *Ibid.*

[23] He obtained 56 percent of the vote, with a twelve-point lead over the incumbent Netanyahu.

[24] John F. Harris, "Going for Broke, Coming Up Short," *Washington Post,* July 26, 2000.

## CHAPTER TWO

[1] "Barak's Victory Speech," BBC, May 18,1999. Available from http://news.bbc.co.uk/1/hi/world/monitoring/346507.stm. Accessed October 29, 2003.

[2] In the final analysis, Barak won the election with a strong Jewish majority.

[3] "Barak's Victory Speech," BBC, May 18, 1999. Available from http://news.bbc.co.uk/1/hi/world/monitoring/346507.stm. Accessed October 29, 2003.

[4] Salim al-Hoss, Reuters, May 18, 1999.

[5] Saeb Erekat, Agence France-Presse, May 18, 1999.

[6] Amnon Lipkin-Shahak, interview by author, January 21, 2003.

[7] State Department political appointee, interview by author.

[8] Melissa Boyle Mahle, interview by author, January 25, 2004.

[9] Senior intelligence official, interview by author.

[10] Patrick Cockburn, "The Mystery of Mr. Barak," *Independent,* July 7, 1999.

[11] James Bennet, "Aides Disavow Mrs. Clinton on Mideast," *New York Times,* May 8, 1998.

[12] James Dao, "New York's Palestinian State," *New York Times,* February 28, 1999.

[13] Avi Shlaim, *The Iron Wall* (New York: Norton, 2001), xvii.

[14] Gilead Sher, interview by author, August 19, 2003.

[15] "Barak Takes Helm: Launches Israel on Course for Peace," CNN, July 6, 1999. Available http://www.cnn.com/WORLD/meast/9907/06/israel.barak.03/. Accessed October 29, 2003.

[16] Tribune News Services, "Barak Will Allow Continued Work on Settlements, Right-Winger Says," *Chicago Tribune,* June 1, 1999.

[17] Toni Verstandig, interview by author, December 19, 2002.

[18] See, for example, the essays collected in Said's *Peace and Its Discontents* (New York: Vintage, 1996) and *The End of the Peace Process: Oslo and After* (New York: Pantheon, 2000).

[19] David Sharrock, "Arafat Declares a Day of Anger Over Settlers," *Guardian,* June 3, 1999.

[20] Edward Said, foreword to Noam Chomsky, *Fateful Triangle: The United States, Israel, and the Palestinians* (Cambridge: South End Press, 1999), viii.

[21] Omar Dajani, "Surviving Opportunities," unpublished text for the U.S. Institute of Peace, September 15, 2003.

[22] Ami Ayalon, speech at the Carnegie Endowment for International Peace, December 12, 2003.

[23] Melissa Boyle Mahle, interview by author, January 25, 2004.

[24] Haydar Abdel Shafi, interview by author, May 22, 2003.

[25] Joel Greenberg, "Jewish Settlers Waste No Time in Housing Start," *New York Times,* May 19, 1999.

[26] Toni Verstandig, interview by author, December 19, 2000.

[27] Nabil Shaath, interview by author, November 27, 2002.

[28] Eytan Bentsur, *Making Peace: A First-Hand Account of the Arab-Israeli Peace Process* (London: Praeger, 2001), 166.

[29] The text of the Oslo Agreement Declaration of Principles is available at http://www.palestinecenter.org/frameeduc.html.

[30] Melissa Boyle Mahle, interview by author, January 25, 2004.

[31] "Barak's Victory and the Peace Process," *Palestine Center for Policy and Survey Research,* no. 41 (1999). Available from http://www.pcpsr.org/survey/cprspolls/99/poll41a.html. Accessed October 29, 2003.

## CHAPTER THREE

[1] Sidney Blumenthal, *The Clinton Wars* (New York: Farrar, Straus & Giroux, 2003), 777.

[2] Martin Indyk, speech, delivered at the Center for Policy Analysis on Palestine on June 3, 1999, tape available at the Palestine Center Library, Washington, DC.

[3] Kathleen Christison, *Perceptions of Palestine: Their Influence on U.S. Middle East Policy* (Los Angeles: University of California Press, 1999), 249.

[4] Martin Indyk, interview by author, October 9, 2002.

[5] Martin Indyk, "Are Comprehensive Negotiations Feasible?" *Peacewatch/Policywatch Anthology*, 1991 (Washington, DC: Washington Institute for Near East Reporting, 1991), 3.

[6] Gemal Helal, interview by author, September 6, 2002.

[7] Al Kamen, "Choice for Israel Took Unconventional Route," *Washington Post,* February 2, 1995.

[8] Laura Blumenfeld, "Three Peace Suits," *Washington Post,* February 24, 1997.

[9] Martin Indyk, interview by author, October 9, 2002.

[10] Blumenfeld, *op. cit.*

[11] Martin Indyk, "Near East Report," *Interview,* April 20, 1998.

[12] Gemal Helal, interview by author, October 8, 2002.

[13] Partaking in host-country internal politics is prohibited by State Department regulations and under international law could be construed as an interference inconsistent with diplomatic rights and privileges.

[14] Ned Walker, interview by author, February 19, 2003.

[15] Judy Dempsey, "Barak's Bridge Over Troubled Lands," *Financial Times,* June 19, 1999.

[16] Helena Cobban, *The Israeli-Syrian Peace Talks: 1991-1996 and Beyond* (Washington, DC: U.S. Institute of Peace Press, 1999), 64.

[17] Martin Indyk, delivered at the Center for Policy Analysis on Palestine, June 3, 1999, tape available at the Palestine Center Library, Washington, DC.

[18] Dennis Ross, *Acting with Caution: Middle East Policy Planning for the Second Reagan Administration,* Policy Paper 1 (Washington, DC: Washington Institute for Near East Policy, 1985).

[19] Ross was also aided by a strong recommendation from outgoing Secretary of State James Baker, who pleaded with incoming Secretary of State Warren Christopher that Ross remain in government for the sake of having continuity in Middle East policy.

[20] Cobban, *op. cit.,* 5.

[21] Charles Enderlin, *Shattered Dreams,* 114-116.

[22] Aluf Benn et al., "Talks on Wye to Resume in 10 Days," *Ha'aretz,* July 12, 1999.

[23] Ann Compton, Antonio Mora, *ABC Good Morning America* (Transcript #99071502-J01), July 15, 1999.

[24] Enderlin, *Shattered Dreams,* 114-116.

[25] Nitzan Horowitz, "America Will Walk With You," *Ha'aretz,* July 16, 1999.

[26] "Barak Sought Direct Contact With Clinton," *White House Bulletin,* July 19, 1999.

[27] Danna Harman, Elli Wohlgelernter, "Barak Predicts Peace Deals Within 15 Months," *Jerusalem Post,* July 18, 1999.

[28] "Barak Sought Direct Contact With Clinton," *White House Bulletin,* July 19, 1999.

[29] Quandt, *Peace Process,* 359.

[30] Horowitz, "America Will Walk With You," *Ha'aretz,* July 16, 1999.

[31] Senior intelligence official, interview by author.

[32] Harman, Wohlgelernter, "Barak Predicts Peace Deals Within 15 Months," *Jerusalem Post,* July 18, 1999.

[33] Enderlin, *Shattered Dreams,* 114.

[34] Tony Walker and Andrew Gowers, *Arafat: The Biography* (London: Virgin Books, 2003), 406.

[35] "Barak Sought Direct Contact With Clinton," *White House Bulletin,* July 19, 1999.

[36] State Department political appointee, interview by author.

[37] Barbara Slavin, "U.S.-Israel Panel to Review Security Needs," *USA Today,* July 22, 1999.

[38] Harman, Wohlgelernter, "Barak Predicts Peace Deals Within 15 Months," *Jerusalem Post,* July 18, 1999.

[39] *Ibid.*

[40] Bill Clinton, "Press Conference by the President," *White House Office of the Press Secretary,* July 21, 1999.

[41] Quandt, *Peace Process,* 359.

[42] Toni Verstandig, interview by author, December 19, 2002.

[43] Gemal Helal, interview by author, September 6, 2002.

[44] Senior State Department official, interview by author.

[45] Madeleine Albright, interview by author, July 7, 2003.

[46] Ann Compton, Antonio Mora, *ABC Good Morning America* (Transcript #99071502-J01) July 15, 1999.

## CHAPTER FOUR

[1] Deborah Sontag, "In Honoring Hassan, Israelis Bare Intrigue in Cause of Peace," *New York Times,* July 26, 1999.

[2] Danna Harman, et al., "Morocco's King Hassan Dies," *Jerusalem Post,* July 25, 1999.

[3] Danna Harman, "Clinton Puzzled by Barak's Absence," *Jerusalem Post,* July 26, 1999.

[4] John Podesta, interview by author, February 12, 2003.

[5] Deborah Sontag, "Israeli's Peace Initiative Pauses After Death of Morocco's King," *New York Times,* July 24, 1999.

[6] *Ibid.*

[7] Robert Kilborn et al., "News in Brief," *Christian Science Monitor,* July 26, 1999.

[8] Syrian official, interview by author.

[9] Danna Harman et al., "Morocco's King Hassan Dies," *Jerusalem Post,* July 25, 1999.

[10] Sandy Berger, "Barak, Arafat Report to Clinton on Their July 27 Meeting," *White House Report,* July 28, 1999.

[11] Luc de Barochez, Agence France-Press, July 27, 1999.

[12] "Latest Israeli Peace Efforts Draw Praise from Egypt," *Chicago Tribune,* July 30, 1999.

[13] Charles M. Sennott, "Barak-Arafat Meeting Marked by Disagreement," *Boston Globe,* July 28, 1999.

[14] Ilene Prusher, "Barak Meets Arafat to Rekindle Peace," *Guardian,* July 28, 1999.

[15] *Ibid.*

[16] "Latest Israeli Peace Efforts Draw Praise from Egypt," *Chicago Tribune,* July 30, 1999.

[17] Sandy Berger, "Barak, Arafat Report to Clinton on Their July 27 Meeting," *White House Report,* July 28, 1999.

[18] Enderlin, *Shattered Dreams,* 117.

[19] Ilene Prusher, "Barak Meets Arafat to Rekindle Peace," *Guardian,* July 28, 1999.

[20] Barbara Slavin, "Israeli Leader Is New, But Style Is Familiar," *USA Today,* September 3, 1999.

[21] Danna Harman, "Egypt Does Not Reject Wye Changes," *Jerusalem Post,* July 30, 1999.

[22] Ilene Prusher, "Barak Meets Arafat to Rekindle Peace," *Guardian,* July 28, 1999.

[23] Gilead Sher, *Just Beyond Reach* (Tel Aviv: Yediot Ahronot, 2001), 43.

[24] "Latest Israeli Peace Efforts Draw Praise from Egypt," *Chicago Tribune,* July 30, 1999.

[25] Luc de Barochez, Agence France-Press, July 27, 1999.

[26] "Latest Israeli Peace Efforts Draw Praise from Egypt," *Chicago Tribune,* July 30, 1999.

[27] Jamie Rubin, "Albright Postpones Middle East Visit at Barak's Request," *State Department Report,* August 9, 1999.

[28] Martin Sieff, United Press International, August 24, 1999.

[29] "Arafat Asks U.S. to Help Peace Talks," Associated Press, August 23, 1999.

[30] Jane Perlez, "Mideast Standoff Remains Unresolved as Albright Visits," *New York Times,* September 3, 1999.

[31] Martin Sieff, United Press International, August 24, 1999.

[32] Jane Perlez, "Israel and PLO, With Help of U.S., Reach an Accord," *New York Times,* September 4, 1999.

[33] The specific language states, "Recognizing the necessity to create a positive environment for the negotiations, neither side shall initiate or take any step that will change the status of the West Bank and the Gaza Strip in accordance with the Interim Agreement." Available from http://www.yale.edu/lawweb/avalon/mideast/mid024.htm. Accessed October 29, 2003.

[34] Barry Schweid, "Albright Forced to Mediate W. Bank Pact," *Chicago Sun-Times,* September 2, 1999.

[35] Jane Perlez, "Israel and PLO, With Help of U.S., Reach an Accord," *New York Times,* September 4, 1999.

[36] *Ibid.*

[37] State Department political appointee, interview by author.

[38] Accounts taken from *Ma'ariv,* September 8, 1999, and *IsraelWire,* September 9, 1999.

[39] U.S. Department of State, Office of the Press Secretary (Jerusalem), September 3, 1999.

[40] Jane Perlez, "Israel and PLO, With Help of U.S., Reach an Accord," *New York Times,* September 4, 1999.

[41] Lee Michael Katz, "Mideast Breakthrough Largely Illusion," United Press International, September 4, 1999.

[42] *Ibid.*

[43] Madeleine Albright, "American Letter of Assurance," PLO Negotiation Affairs Department. Available from http://www.nad-plo.org/speeches/us1.html. Accessed October 29, 2003.

[44] Taria Halonen, "European Letter of Assurance," PLO Negotiation Affairs Department. Available from http://www.nad-plo.org/speeches/eu1.html. Accessed October 29, 2003.

[45] Jane Perlez, "Israel and PLO, With Help of U.S., Reach an Accord," *New York Times,* September 4, 1999.

[46] Enderlin, *Shattered Dreams,* 120.

[47] "The Sharm el-Sheikh Memorandum on Implementation Timeline of Outstanding Commitments of Agreements Signed and the Resumption of Permanent Status Negotiations; September 4, 1999," The Avalon Project at Yale Law School. Available from http://www.yale.edu/lawweb/avalon/mideast/mid024.htm. Accessed October 29, 2003.

[48] U.S. Department of State, Office of the Press Secretary (Damascus), September 4, 1999.

## CHAPTER FIVE

[1] U.S. Department of State, Office of the Press Secretary (Jerusalem), October 27, 1999.

[2] Israel crossed the line on October 5, 2003, when its fighter planes bombed a Syrian village that Prime Minister Ariel Sharon alleged was a "terrorist training camp."

[3] Tanya Reinhart, *Israel/Palestine: How to End the War of 1948* (New York: Seven Stories Press, 2002), 73.

[4] "Sovereignty and Territorial Issues at the Heart of Final Status Talks," Foundation for Middle East Peace, *Report on Israeli Settlement in the Occupied Territories*, vol. 10, no. 1 (January-February 2000). Available from http://www.fmep.org/reports/2000/v10n1.html. Accessed October 29, 2003.

[5] The concept of a territorial "swap" was not embodied in the Israeli-Egyptian 1978 Camp David Accords, and was only discussed later with the Israeli-Jordanian peace agreement. Jordan agreed to lease a few hundred acres of land to Israel—while keeping full sovereignty—in exchange for water. The idea of a land exchange was broached again on the Palestinian-Israeli track at Camp David 2000 but rejected because the Israeli offer was not equitable; i.e., it didn't involve a swap of land in equal size and value. Asad at least had the virtue of consistency, by always insisting on the specific land Syria was entitled to under 242. He would never accept even the discussion of a swap.

[6] Bouthaina Shabban, "The Future of Syrian-American Relations" (delivered at the Brookings Institution on June 18, 2003), transcript available at Brookings Institution, Washington, DC.

[7] "Mubarak, al-Assad Hold News Conference in Cairo," Arab Republic of Egypt Radio (Cairo), December 23, 1995; translated in FBIS-NES-95-247.

[8] "Israel Agreed to Leave All the Golan Heights," *Guardian*, November 24, 1999.

[9] Cobban, *The Israeli-Syrian Peace Talks: 1991-1996 and Beyond*, 62.

[10] *Ibid.*

[11] "Albright, al-Shara Press Conference in Syria," U.S. Department of State, Office of the Spokesman (Damascus, Syria), September 4, 1999.

[12] Senior diplomat involved in Synai Isreali negotiations, interviewed by author.

[13] Daniel Sobelman, "Albright Told Asad Barak Recognizes 1967 Lines, Lebanese Paper Claims," *Ha'aretz*, September 10, 1999.

[14] Danna Harman, "Chirac Has No Syrian Message for Barak," *Jerusalem Post*, September 23, 1999.

[15] Senior diplomat involved in the Syrian-Israeli negotiations, interview by author.

[16] *Ibid.*

[17] Enderlin, *Shattered Dreams*, 126.

[18] Senior diplomat involved in the Syrian-Israeli negotiations, interview by author.

[19] Enderlin, *Shattered Dreams,* 126.

[20] Gilead Sher, interview by author, August 19, 2003.

[21] Gemal Helal, interview by author, September 6, 2002.

[22] U.S. Department of State, Office of the Press Secretary (Washington, DC), December 12, 1999.

[23]Chemi Shaley, "Arafat Refused and All the Rest Is Gossip," *Forward,* July 27, 2003. Available from http://www.forwarDCom/issues/2003/03.07.25/arts3.html. Accessed October 29, 2003.

[24] State Department political appointee, interview by author.

[25] Joe Lockhart, interview by author, April 18, 2003.

[26] Jane Perlez, "Israel and Syria to Reopen Talks, Clinton Reports," *New York Times,* December 8, 1999.

[27] David Makovsky and Janine Zacharia, "Clinton Awaits Asad's Answers," *Jerusalem Post,* November 18, 1999.

[28] Jane Perlez, "Israel and Syria to Reopen Talks, Clinton Reports," *New York Times,* December 8, 1999.

[29] Martin Indyk, interview by author, October 9, 2002.

[30] Enderlin, *Shattered Dreams,* 125.

[31] William A. Orme Jr., "While Barak's Allies Rejoice, His Political Foes Find Fault," *New York Times,* December 10, 1999.

[32] Deborah Sontag, "Fresh Air for the Middle East," *New York Times,* December 15, 1999.

[33] *Ibid.*

[34] Reinhart, *Israel/Palestine,* 78.

[35] Bradley Burston, "Right-Wing Extremists Threaten Barak Over Golan Issue," *Toronto Star,* December 16, 1999.

[36] Natan Sharansky, interview by author, September 17, 2003.

[37] Gary C. Gambill, "Barak Faces Obstacle in Road to Peace with Asad," *Middle East Intelligence Bulletin,* vol. I, no. 12, December 1999.

[38] Deborah Sontag, "Fresh Air for the Middle East," *New York Times,* December 15, 1999.

[39] Bradley Burston, "Right-Wing Extremists Threaten Barak Over Golan Issue," *Toronto Star,* December 16, 1999.

[40] *Ibid.*

[41] Deborah Sontag, "Fresh Air for the Middle East," *New York Times,* December 15, 1999.

[42] Uri Sagi, interview by author, August 26, 2003.

[43] Enderlin, *Shattered Dreams,* 128. Account confirmed by Martin Indyk, interview by author, August 27, 2003.

[44] Uri Sagi, interview by author, August 26, 2003.

[45] Enderlin, *Shattered Dreams,* 128. Account confirmed by Martin Indyk,

interview by author, August 27, 2003. Indyk told me that he plans to further expound on this meeting in his upcoming memoirs. His account is vigorously disputed by both Uri Sagi and Riad Daoudi, who believe that Barak's trepidation came weeks later, before the Shepherdstown summit. Amnon Lipkin-Shahak also believes that Barak's "cold feet" came on the eve of Shepherdstown.

[46] Hussein Agha and Robert Malley, "Camp David and After: An Exchange," *New York Review of Books,* June 13, 2002.

[47] Uri Sagi, interview by author, August 27, 2003; Riad Daoudi, interview by author, November 8, 2003; John Lancaster, "Syria and Israel Are Set to Meet Again in January," *Washington Post,* December 17, 1999.

[48] Uri Sagi, interview by author, August 27, 2003.

[49] *Ibid.*

[50] Amnon Lipkin-Shahak, interview by author, January 21, 2003.

[51] Madeleine Albright, interview by author, July 7, 2003.

[52] Deborah Sontag, "Fresh Air for the Middle East," *New York Times,* December 15, 1999. According to *My Life* by Bill Clinton (New York: Alfred Knopf, 2004, p. 885), Asad also agreed to allow a secret delegation of forensic experts to travel to Syria, in order to try and locate the remains of three missing Israelis from the Lebanon war. Although their bodies were not located, this also indicated Assad's genuine desire to make peace.

[53] Martin Indyk, interview by author, October 9, 2002.

[54] Uri Dan, "In this Grand Puppet Show, Bill Clinton Is Pulling All the Strings," *Jerusalem Post,* December 30, 1999.

[55] Deborah Sontag, "Religious Faction Says It Will Quit Barak's Cabinet," *New York Times,* December 28, 1999.

[56] Ilene Prusher, "PR Plan to Win Israeli Approval," *Christian Science Monitor,* January 10, 2000.

[57] David Zev Harris, "Sharon: White House Thinks It Can Buy Israelis," *Jerusalem Post,* January 5, 2000.

[58] *Ibid.*

[59] *Ibid.*

[60] Ariel Sharon, "Why Should Israel Reward Syria?" *New York Times,* December 28, 1999.

[61] "Israel-Syria Talks to Be Held in West Virginia," CNN, December 1999. Available from http://edition.cnn.com/1999/WORLD/meast/12/21/mideast.talks/. Accessed October 29, 2003.

## CHAPTER SIX

[1] Charles Enderlin, interview by author, August 31, 2003.

[2] Madeleine Albright, interview by author, July 7, 2003.

[3] Enderlin, *Shattered Dreams,* 128.

[4] Uri Sagi, interview by author, August 26, 2003.
[5] *Ibid.*
[6] Enderlin, *Shattered Dreams,* 132.
[7] Imad Moustapha, interview by author, September 1, 2003.
[8]Jamie Rubin, "On-the-Record Press Briefing, Middle East Peace Process," U.S. Embassy to Israel. Available from http://www.usembassy-srael.org.il/publish/peace/archives/2000/january/me0104b.html. Accessed October 29, 2003.
[9] *Yediot Ahronot,* January 3, 2000.
[10] Enderlin, *Shattered Dreams,* 133.
[11] Bouthaina Shabban, interview by author, June 18, 2003.
[12] Walid Moallem, interview by author, June 2, 2003.
[13] Martin Indyk, interview by author, October 9, 2002.
[14] Walid Moallem, interview by author, June 2, 2003.
[15] Rihab Massoud, interview by author, August 27, 2003.
[16] Madeleine Albright, *Madam Secretary* (New York: Miramax Books, 2003), 476.
[17] Hussein Agha and Robert Malley, "Camp David and After: An Exchange," *New York Review of Books,* June 13, 2002.
[18] Dennis Ross, interview by author, November 12, 2002.
[19] A non-paper is a diplomatic tool for crafting hypothetical positions for each party to negotiations, and thus facilitating talks, while avoiding attribution and enhancing deniability.
[20] Martin Indyk, interview by author, October 9, 2002.
[21] Bouthaina Shabban, "The Future of Syrian-American Relations" (delivered at the Brookings Institution on June 18, 2003), transcript available at Brookings Institution, Washington, DC.
[22] Nina Noring, "The Withdrawal Clause in UN Security Council Resolution 242 of 1967: Its Legislative History and the Attitudes of the United States and Israel since 1967" (Washington: Office of the Historian, U.S. Department of State, 1978), 2.
[23] Donald Neff's paper provided by William Quandt in interview by author, August 28, 2002.
[24] Madeleine Albright, interview by author, July 7, 2003.
[25] Lally Weymouth, "We Want Our Land Back," *Newsweek,* October 11, 1999, 55.
[26] Albright, *Madam Secretary,* 478.
[27] Danna Harman and Janine Zacharia, "Barak Denies *al-Hayat* Report," *Jerusalem Post,* January 10, 2000.
[28] *Ibid.*
[29] "Israel-Syria Peace Talks to Resume Saturday Night," CNN, January 7, 2000. Available from http://www.cnn.com/2000/WORLD/meast/01/07/israel.syria.03/. Accessed October 29, 2003.
[30] Riad Daoudi, interview by author, November 8, 2003.

[31] Clinton, *My Life,* 886.
[32] Senior State Department official, interview by author.
[33] Clinton, *My Life,* 886.
[34] Joel Greenberg, "Leak of Negotiating Document Puts Focus on Golan Settlers," *New York Times,* January 14, 2000.
[35] Martin Indyk, interview by author, October 9, 2002.
[36] Joel Greenberg, "Leak of Negotiating Document Puts Focus on Golan Settlers," *New York Times,* January 14, 2000.
[37] Janine Zacharia and Danna Harman, "Syria Puts Talks on Hold," *Jerusalem Post,* January 18, 2000.
[38] *Ibid.*

## CHAPTER SEVEN

[1] Dennis Ross, interview by author, November 12, 2002.
[2] Walid Moallem, interview by author, June 2, 2003.
[3] Riad Daoudi, interview by author, November 8, 2003.
[4] State Department political appointee, interview by author.
[5] "Israeli Military Intelligence Warns: U.S. Technology Can't Replace Security Value of Golan Heights," Zionist Organization of America, March 23, 2000. Available at http://www.zoa.org/pressrel/20000323b.htm. Accessed October 29, 2003.
[6] "U.S. Generals' Letter to Capital Hill," Jewish Institute for National Security Affairs, March 22, 2000. Available at http://www.gamla.org.il/english/article/2000/march/golan.htm. Accessed October 29, 2003.
[7] Aluf Benn et al., "Barak: Past PMs Set Syria Talks on '67 Lines," *Ha'aretz,* February 28, 2000.
[8] According to Sagi, "I personally don't think he wanted Albright to steal the show. He saw it as a political show and he thought it was a better way to do business face to face with Clinton. Also, it is impossible to go secretly to Damascus, in Albright's case." Uri Sagi, interview by author, August 26, 2003.
[9] Bouthaina Shabban, interview by author, June 18, 2003.
[10] *Ibid.*
[11] Senior diplomat involved in the Syrian-Israeli negotiations, interview by author.
[12] Rihab Massoud, interview by author, August 27, 2003.
[13] Senior intelligence official, interview by author.
[14] Rihab Massoud, interview by author, August 27, 2003.
[15] Elsa Walsh, "Profiles: The Prince," *The New Yorker,* March 24, 2003.
[16] Rihab Massoud, interview by author, August 27, 2003.
[17] *Ibid.*

[18] Rihab Massoud, interview by author, August 27, 2003.
[19] Senior White House official, interview by author.
[20] State Department political appointee, interview by author.
[21] Joe Lockhart, interview by author, April 18, 2003.
[22] *Ibid.*
[23] State Department political appointee, interview by author.
[24] Martin Indyk, interview by author, October 9, 2002.
[25] Senior diplomat involved in the Syrian-Israeli negotiations, interview by author.
[26] Madeleine Albright, *Madam Secretary* (New York: Miramax Books, 2003), 480.
[27] Madeleine Albright, interview by author, July 7, 2003.
[28] Albright, *Madam Secretary,* 480.
[29] Enderlin, *Shattered Dreams,* 141.
[30] *Ibid.*
[31] *Ibid.*
[32] *Ibid.*
[33] Bouthaina Shabban, interview by author, June 18, 2003.
[34] State Department political appointee, interview by author.
[35] Walid Moallem, interview by author, June 2, 2003.
[36] Enderlin, *Shattered Dreams,* 142.
[37] Bouthaina Shabban, interview by author, June 18, 2003.
[38] Albright, *Madam Secretary,* 480.
[39] Bill Clinton, March 28, 2000, news conference. Government Printing Office, "Weekly Compilation of Presidential Documents," Information Access Company, April 3, 2000.
[40] *Ibid.*
[41] Charles Babington and Howard Schneider, "White House Hopes Pressure Will Help Soften Asad's Stance on Peace With Israel," *Washington Post,* March 28, 2000.
[42] Douglas Davis, "Barak: Syria to Blame for Summit's failure," *Jerusalem Post,* March 31, 2000.
[43] Uri Dan, "Syria Rips Biased Bill Over Israel," *New York Post,* March 31, 2001.
[44] "Clinton Puts Pressure on Syria," BBC, March 30, 2000. Available at http://news.bbc.co.uk/1/hi/world/middle_east/695402.stm. Accessed October 29, 2003.
[45] *Ibid.*
[46] Uri Dan, "Barak Feeling the Heat in Asad Talks," *New York Post,* April 9, 2000.
[47] Douglas Davis, "Bashar Asad in Line to Succeed His Father," *Jerusalem Post,* April 3, 2000.
[48] Elsa Walsh, "Profiles: The Prince," *The New Yorker,* March 24, 2003.
[49] *Ibid.*

[50] Amos Perlmutter, "Clinton and Asad: Exercise in Futility," *Washington Times,* April 5, 2000.
[51] Amos Perlmutter, "The Importance of Being Asad," *Foreign Affairs,* July/August 2000.
[52] Uri Dromi, "Master of Missed Opportunities," *Boston Globe,* April 1, 2000.
[53] After being named president by the Supreme Court, George W. Bush would appoint Zoellick to become his U.S. trade representative.
[54] "A Conversation with Leon Fuerth and Robert Zoellick," Peacewatch/Policywatch Anthology, 2000 (Washington, DC: Washington Institute for Near East Reporting, 2001), 291.
[55] *Ibid.*
[56] Niyazi Gunay, "Presidential Candidates on Middle East," Policywatch 490, WINEP, October 3, 2000. Available at http://www.washingtoninstitute.org/watch/Policywatch/policywatch2000/490.htm. Accessed October 29, 2003.
[57] *Ibid.*
[58] Barry Schweid, "Peace Process Likely Set Back," Associated Press, June 11, 2000.

## CHAPTER EIGHT

[1] Hussein Agha and Robert Malley, "Camp David: The Tragedy of Errors," *New York Review of Books,* August 9, 2001.
[2] "Shattered Dreams of Peace Interviews Ehud Barak," *Frontline,* PBS, 2002. Available at http://www.pbs.org/wgbh/pages/frontline/shows/oslo/interviews/barak.html. Accessed October 29, 2003.
[3] State Department political appointee, interview by author.
[4] Dennis Ross, interview by author, November 12, 2002.
[5] Martin Indyk, interview by author, October 9, 2002.
[6] John Podesta, interview by author, February 12, 2003.
[7] Albright, interview by author, July 7, 2003.
[8] Madeleine Albright, *Madam Secretary,* 289.
[9] It is worth noting President Asad's scrupulous enforcement of the 1974 Syrian-Israeli cease-fire agreements: there have been no instances of cross-border attacks against Israel from Syria.
[10] Madeleine Albright, interview by author, July 7, 2003.
[11] *Ibid.*
[12] Omar Dajani, "Surviving Opportunities," U.S. Institute of Peace, September 15, 2003.
[13] William Quandt, interview by author, August 28, 2002.
[14] Dennis Ross, interview by author, November 12, 2002.
[15] Martin Indyk, interview by author, October 9, 2002.

[16] State Department political appointee, interview by author.
[17] According to Ned Walker, "The only one that has any *real* background in the Arab world is Gemal Helal. I mean, Dennis has never spent any real time in the Arab world. Aaron Miller never has. I mean, they have spent a lot of negotiating time, but they never had any real personal experience." According to Maria Echaveste, "He [Helal] was an integral part of those discussions. He was not just an interpreter! He brought insight that others didn't have by virtue of who he is and his knowledge. . . . The President would turn to him and say, 'What do you think, Gemal?'"
[18] Gemal Helal, interviews by author, July 11-December 17, 2002.
[19] Toni Verstandig, interview by author, December 19, 2002.
[20] Bruce Riedel, interview by author, November 4, 2002.
[21] Ned Walker, interview by author, February 19, 2003.
[22] Ned Walker, interview by author, July 16, 2003.
[23] Amnon Lipkin-Shahak, interview by author, January 21, 2003.
[24] Uri Sagi, interview by author, August 26, 2003.
[25] *Ibid.*
[26] Walid Moallem, interview by author, June 2, 2003.
[27] Riad Daoudi, interview by author, November 8, 2003.
[28] Ned Walker, interview by author, February 19, 2003.
[29] Walid Moallem, interview by author, June 2, 2003.
[30] Uri Sagi, interview by author, August 26, 2003.
[31] Walid Moallem, interview by author, June 2, 2003.

## CHAPTER NINE

[1] Aaron Miller, interview by author, March 12, 2004.
[2] See Hanan Ashrawi, *This Side of Peace: A Personal Account* (New York: Simon & Schuster, 1995), and Allegra Pacheco, "Flouting Convention: The Oslo Agreements," in Carey, ed., *The New Intifada: Resisting Israel's Apartheid* (New York: Verso, 2001), 181-206.
[3] Ashrawi, *This Side of Peace*, 260.
[4] Baruch Kimmerling and Joel S. Migdal, *The Palestinian People: A History* (Cambridge, MA: Harvard University Press, 2003), 356-60.
[5] Melissa Mahle, interview by author, January 1, 2004.
[6] Mohammed Dahlan, interview by author, May 22, 2003.
[7] http://www.unhchr.ch/html/menu3/b/93.htm.
[8] Elyakim Rubinstein, interview by author, March 1, 2004.
[9] *Ibid.*
[10] Kelly Wallace, "Sharon: 'Occupation' Terrible for Israel, Palestinians," CNN, May 26, 2003.
[11] Lee Hockstader, "Settlement Expansion Threatens to Derail Peace Process," *Washington Post*, December 6, 1999. Hockstader cited figures

provided by Peace Now.

[12] Palestinian Academic Society for the Study of International Affairs, (PASSIA). See http://www.passia.org/palestine_facts/pdf/pdf2003/sections2/6-Land.pdf. Gilead Sher disputes these statistics. In an interview with me he coyly remarked, "I don't think there was any *initiated* settlement expansion. There were expansions on private land as well as governmental acquisitions that were confirmed or approved prior to his election that he respected and then let the work be done according to tenders already awarded and in process. But he did not *initiate* any new expansion of settlements or issue new governmental tenders."

[13] PASSIA, http://www.passia.org/index_pfacts.htm.

[14] Linda Gradstein, "Reaction of Israelis Settlers," NPR, September 19, 1999.

[15] It is a common but false assumption that most Israeli settlers are ideologues who believe the territories should become a permanent part of "Eretz Yisrael." In fact, a majority have no particular attachment to the territories, and live there only because the Israeli government gives huge subsidies, including tax breaks and other benefits, to encourage the growth of settlements. But the organized settler lobby speaks for the Greater Israel ideologues, not the non-ideological, "suburban" settlers.

[16] PASSIA, http://www.passia.org/index_pfacts.htm. See also the Applied Research Institute-Jerusalem, http://www.arij.org/paleye/monthley/99-9/.

[17] PASSIA, http://www.passia.org/index_pfacts.htm.

[18] Palestine Center for Human Rights, http://www.pchrgaza.org/Intifada/Settlements_stat.htm.

[19] Amira Hass, "PA Calls for Halt on Settlement Activity, Authority Accused of Kowtowing," *Ha'aretz*, September 29, 1999.

[20] Fourth Geneva Convention, Article 49, paragraph 6.

[21] Toni Verstandig, interview by author, December 19, 2002.

[22] Nabil Shaath, interview by author, November 27, 2002.

[23] Mohammed Dahlan, interview by author, May 22, 2003.

[24] State Department political appointee, interview by author.

[25] Martin Indyk, interview by author, October 9, 2002.

[26] Nabil Shaath, interview by author, November 27, 2002.

[27] Mohammed Dahlan, interview by author, May 22, 2003.

[28] Melissa Boyle Mahle, interview by author, January 25, 2004.

[29] Ned Walker, interview by author, February 19, 2003.

[30] Madeleine Albright, interview by author.

[31] "Islamic Jihad Rejects Israeli-Palestinian Final-Status Talks," BBC News, quoted from *Al-Sharq al-Awsat*, London, September 14, 1999.

[32] "Terror Remark by Opposition Leader Stirs Israel," *Chicago Tribune*, March 8, 1998.

[33] Toni Verstandig, interview by author, December 19, 2002.
[34] Melissa Mahle, interview by author, January 25, 2004.
[35] Amira Hass, "PA Cracks Down on Hamas, Arrests Top 3 Members," *Ha'aretz,* August 9, 1999.
[36] Avi Machlis, "Pipe Bomb Heralds Mideast Peace Talks," *Financial Times,* November 8, 1999.
[37] Danna Harman and Lamia Lahoud, "Yassin Distances Himself from Netanya Bombings," *Jerusalem Post,* November 8, 1999.
[38] Lamia Lahoud, "PA Finds Huge Hamas Explosives Cache in Hebron," *Jerusalem Post,* December 12, 1999.
[39] Mike O'Connor, "Bomb Injures 22 Israelis; Peacemakers Meet," *Washington Post,* January 17, 2000.
[40] Gemal Helal, interview by author, July 17, 2002
[41] "Expulsion of Palestinian Residents from the South Mt. Hebron Area," October-November 1999, B'Tselem—The Israeli Information Center for Human Rights in the Occupied Territories, February 2000, 8.
[42] Aluf Benn, "News: At the Summit, Bold Political Gambles," *Ha'aretz,* November 3, 1999.
[43] Danna Harman, "Barak Upset Over Arafat's Words at Rabin Memorial," *Jerusalem Post,* November 3, 1999.
[44] Aluf Benn, "News: At the Summit, Bold Political Gambles," *Ha'aretz,* November 3, 1999.
[45] Aluf Benn, "Wear Them Down, Wear Them Out," *Ha'aretz,* November, 16, 1999.
[46] Lee Hockstader, "Israeli Troops Dismantle Shrine to Extremist Who Killed Muslims," *Washington Post,* December 30, 1999.
[47] Sakher Abu el Oun, "Ross Ends Middle East Peace Mission Empty-Handed," Agence France-Presse, February 28, 2000.

## CHAPTER TEN

[1] Danna Harman, Lamia Lahoud, and Margot Dudkevitch, "Ross Arrives Amid Row Over Withdrawal," *Jerusalem Post,* November 16, 1999.
[2] Dennis Ross, State Department Official Remarks (Jerusalem), November 16, 1999.
[3] Enderlin, *Shattered Dream,* 138.
[4] Gilead Sher, interview by author, August 19, 2003.
[5] Edwin Chen, "Arafat, Barak Pledge Anew to Make Peace," *Los Angeles Times,* November 3, 1999.
[6] Nomi Bar-Yaacov, "Israel, Palestinians Lock Horns Over UN Land-for-Peace Resolution," Agence France-Presse, November 9, 1999.
[7] Ned Walker, interview by author, February 19, 2003.
[8] Charles Enderlin, interview by author, August 31, 2003.
[9] Omar Dajani, "Surviving Opportunities," unpublished paper, September 15, 2003.

[10] Nabil Shaath, interview by author, November 27, 2002.
[11] Martin Indyk, interview by author, October 9, 2002.
[12] Nina Gilbert, "Likud Establishes Headquarters to Fight for Jerusalem," *Jerusalem Post,* January 31, 2000.
[13] David Zey Harris, "Barak Questioned on Election Funding," *Ha'aretz,* January 20, 2000.
[14] Deborah Sontag, "Barak Delays 3rd West Bank Transfer, Angering Palestinians," *New York Times,* January 17, 2000.
[15] Danna Harman and Lamia Lahoud, "Barak Tells Arafat: Don't Expect Abu Dis in Next Pullout," *Jerusalem Post,* January 18, 2000.
[16] BBC Summary of World Broadcasts, citing Israel Channel One, "PNA Officials Say Barak's Refusal to Hand Abu Dis Over 'Odd,'" January 28, 2000.
[17] Lamia Lahoud, "Arafat Laments Delays in Peace Talks," *Jerusalem Post,* February 1, 2000.
[18] Danna Harman, Lamia Lahoud, and Janine Zacharia, "Arafat Bolts Summit," *Jerusalem Post,* February 4, 2000.
[19] Deborah Sontag, "Frustrated Arafat and Barak End Session," *New York Times,* February 4, 2000.
[20] Gideon Samet, "Declare Victory and Pull Out," *Ha'aretz,* February 9, 2000.
[21] "Israel on Alert After Hamas Bomb Plot Foiled," Agence France-Presse, March 3, 2000.
[22] "Israelis, Palestinians, Trade Threats," AP Wire, March 3, 2000.
[23] "Palestinian Police Release 18 Hamas Members," BBC, from Voice of Israel radio, March 12, 2000.
[24] Enderlin, *Shattered Dreams,* 137.
[25] *Ibid.*
[26] Danna Harman, Lamia Lahoud, "PM Offers Arafat Land Compromise," *Jerusalem Post,* February 28, 2000.
[27] Aluf Benn, "Israel and Palestinians to Resume Talks in Washington," *Ha'aretz,* March 9, 2000.
[28] Danna Harman, Margo Dudkevitch, "Pullback Approved by Inner Cabinet," *Jerusalem Post,* March 16, 2000.
[29] Ilene R. Prusher, "Widening the Jerusalem Envelope," *Christian Science Monitor,* March 21, 2000.
[30] *Ibid.*
[31] Tanya Willmer, "Israel to Hand Over West Bank Land to Palestinians," Agence France-Presse, March 19, 2000.
[32] "Israel Frees Palestinian Prisoners for Muslim Holiday," Agence France-Presse, March 20, 2000.

## CHAPTER ELEVEN

[1] State Department political appointee, interview by author.

[2] Senior White House official, interview by author.

[3] This was apparent not only to State Department officers but to Palestinian negotiators as well. Mohammed Dahlan commented, "Dennis Ross was the man who was in charge. With all respect to Secretary Albright, she didn't release any wonders about the file unless she had the agreement of Dennis Ross. She didn't say anything about [the] situation unless she had the agreement of Ross. Even in some press conference when she was talking, she was also looking at Dennis, just to have his agreement: 'Am I doing it right or wrong?'" Interview by author, May 25, 2003.

[4] State Department political appointee, interview by author.

[5] State Department political appointee, interview by author.

[6] Ned Walker, interview by author, February 20, 2004.

[7] To be sure, almost all information related to U.S. negotiations in the Arab-Israeli peace process are over-classified by the government. Even so, the storage or processing of these discussions on unauthorized computers is a violation of federal criminal law. The September 2000 State Department and FBI investigation into Martin Indyk's processing of highly classified material on his personal laptop is discussed in the final chapter of this book.

[8] Ari Shavit, "End of a Journey," *Ha'aretz,* July 15, 2002.

[9] Office of the Press Secretary, White House, April 11, 2000.

[10] "Pope Backs Right to Palestinian Homeland," Agence France-Presse, March 22, 2000.

[11] "Speech of the Holy Father John Paul II," Available at http://www.vatican.va/holy_father/john_paul_ii/travels/documents/hf_jpii_spe_20000322_deheisheh-refugees_en.htm. Accessed October 28, 2003.

[12] Saeb Erekat, interview by author, April 7, 2004.

[13] Roy Gutman, "Barak Turns to U.S. for Input," *Newsday,* April 12, 2000.

[14] Gideon Levy, "Settlers' Friends in High Places," *Ha'aretz,* April 9, 2000.

[15] Foundation for Middle East Peace, *Report on Israeli Settlement in the Occupied Territories,* Vol. X, No. 4, available at www.fmep.org.

[16] Ghassan Khatib, "End the Cease-Fire," April 12, 2000. Available at http://www.fmep.org/reports/v10n3.html.

[17] "The Peace Process, Bir Zeit, etc.," Palestine Center for Policy and Survey Research, no. 48 (2000). Available from http://pcpsr.org/survey/cprspolls/2000/poll48a.html. Accessed October 29, 2003.

[18] Melissa Mahle, interview by author, January 28, 2004.

[19] Dahlan learned Hebrew from his jailers, a skill that would later give him an edge as a negotiator.

[20] "Barak Rejects Shin Bet Recommendation on Releasing Palestinians," *Yediot Ahronot,* April 29, 2000.

[21] Margot Dudkevitch and Lamia Lahoud, "Four Palestinians Wounded in Prisoner Day Rioting," *Jerusalem Post,* April 18, 2000.

[22] Danna Harman and Janine Zacharia, "Clinton: There's Hope for Rapid Movement on the Israeli-PA Track," *Jerusalem Post,* April 12, 2000.

[23] Enderlin, *Shattered Dreams,* 145-46.

[24] *Ibid.*

[25] Omar Dajani, interview by author, April 3, 2004.

[26] Martin Indyk, interview by author, October 9, 2002.

[27] Enderlin, *Shattered Dreams,* 147.

[28] Hussein Agha el al., *Track-II Diplomacy: Lessons from the Middle East* (Cambridge, Mass: MIT Press, 2003), 2.

[29] Amnon Lipkin-Shahak, interview by author, January 21, 2003.

[30] Gilead Sher, interview by author, August 19, 2003.

[31] Par Nuder, e-mail exchange with author, September 22, 2003.

[32] *Ibid.*

[33] Agha el al., *Track-II Diplomacy,* 78.

[34] *Ibid.*

[35] Omar Dajani, interview by author, April 10, 2004.

[36] Enderlin, *Shattered Dreams,* 148, and Shavit, "End of a Journey," *Ha'aretz,* July 15, 2002.

[37] Shavit, "End of a Journey," *Ha'aretz,* July 15, 2002.

[38] *Ibid.*

[39] Naseer Aruri, *The Dishonest Broker* (Cambridge, Mass: South End Press, 2003), 151.

[40] Ari Shavit, "End of a Journey," *Ha'aretz,* July 15, 2002.

[41] *Ibid.*

[42] Saud Abu Ramadan, "Chief Palestinian Negotiator Resigns," United Press International, May 15, 2000.

[43] From Gilead Sher, "Negotiating in Times of Crisis," paper and lecture delivered at the Wharton School, University of Pennsylvania, August 19, 2003.

[44] Dennis Ross, interview by author, November 12, 2002.

[45] Gilead Sher, interview by author, April 11, 2004.

[46] Aaron Miller, interview by author, March 12, 2004.

[47] Aaron Miller, interview by author, July 11, 2002.

[48] Rob Malley, interview by author, July 30, 2002.

[49] Gemal Helal, interview by author, July 17, 2002.

[50] Gilead Sher, interview by author, April 11, 2004.

[51] Par Nuder, e-mail exchange with author, September 22, 2003.

## CHAPTER TWELVE

[1] Aaron Miller, interview by author, March 12, 2004.

[2] Daniel Sobelman, *New Rules of the Game: Israel and Hizbollah After the Withdrawal From Lebanon* (Tel Aviv: Jaffee Center for Strategic Studies, 2004), 29.

[3] Melissa Mahle, interview by author, January 25, 2000.

[4] Hugh Dellios, "Israelis Fear Latest Outbreaks Show Arafat No Longer Controls Masses," *Chicago Tribune,* May 17, 2000.

[5] Deborah Sontag, "Palestinian Forces Exchange Gunfire With Israeli Troops," *New York Times,* May 16, 2000.

[6] Enderlin, *Shattered Dreams,* 149.

[7] Deborah Sontag, "Palestinian Forces Exchange Gunfire With Israeli Troops," *New York Times,* May 16, 2000.

[8] "Israeli-Palestinian Gunfights Erupt in "Day of Rage" Protests," Agence France-Presse, May 19, 2000.

[9] Sobelman, *New Rules of the Game,* 30.

[10] Sobelman, *New Rules of the Game,* 38.

[11] Larry Kaplo, "Israel Speeds Lebanon Pullout," *Atlanta Journal and Constitution,* May 24, 2000.

[12] Ben Lynfield, "Hezbollah's Victory May Be New Blueprint for Intifada," *The Scotsman,* May 26, 2000.

[13] Lisa Beyer, "Courage Under Fire: Ehud Barak Makes Good on His Promise to Withdraw," *Time,* June 5, 2000.

[14] Senior intelligence official, interview by author.

[15] Toni Verstandig, interview by author, December 19, 2002.

[16] Ari Shavit, "End of a Journey," *Ha'aretz,* July 15, 2002.

[17] Lee Hockstader, "Barak Insists Israel Will Not Discuss Status of Jerusalem," *Washington Post,* June 5, 2000.

[18] *Ibid.*

[19] Uzi Dayan, speech at the Washington Institute for Near East Policy, December 15, 2003.

[20] Uzi Dayan, interview by author, December 15, 2003.

[21] Hussein Agha and Robert Malley, "Camp David: The Tragedy of Errors," *New York Review of Books,* August 9, 2001.

[22] Enderlin, *Shattered Dreams,* 163.

[23] Enderlin, *Shattered Dreams,* 162.

[24] "Arafat, Clinton Confer, While Israeli-Palestinian Talks Stumble," CNN, June 15, 2000. Available from http://www.cnn.com/2000/WORLD/meast/06/15/clinton.arafat.01/. Accessed October 29, 2003.

[25] Enderlin, *Shattered Dreams,* 163-64.

[26] Malley, interview by author, July 30, 2002.

[27] State Department political appointee, interview by author.

[28] *Ibid.*
[29] *Ibid.*
[30] Michael Janson, "Arafat to Reassess Declaration of Statehood," *Irish Times,* August 18, 2000.
[31] Gilead Sher, interview by author, August 19, 2003.
[32] Enderlin, *Shattered Dreams,* 167.
[33] Ari Shavit, "End of a Journey," *Ha'aretz,* July 15, 2002.
[34] Natan Sharansky, interview by author, September 17, 2003.
[35] "Threats to Quit Still Hang Over Barak Coalition," Agence France-Presse, June 28, 2000.
[36] State Department Office of the Spokesman (Jerusalem), "Remarks of Secretary Albright," June 28, 2000.
[37] Nabil Shaath, interview by author, November 27, 2002.
[38] Saeb Erekat, interview by author, May 24, 2003.
[39] Madeleine Albright, interview by author, July 7, 2003.
[40] Nabil Abu Rudeineh, interview by author, May 25, 2003.
[41] Dennis Ross, interview by author, November 12, 2002.
[42] Thomas Friedman, "The Real Deal," *New York Times,* May 2, 2000.
[43] Thomas Friedman, "Mideast Reality Check," *New York Times,* May 23, 2000.
[44] Jim Hoagland, "Middle East Peace Will Not Be Part of Clinton's Legacy," *Chicago Tribune,* June 9, 2000.
[45] Yossi Alpher, "Barak Was Willing, and So Were U.S. Jews." Available at http://www.bitterlemons.org/previous/bl150702ed26.html. Accessed October 28, 2003.
[46] *Ibid.*
[47] John F. Harris, "Bush Advisor's Remarks Criticized," *Washington Post,* July 13, 2000.
[48] Thomas Friedman, "Just Do It," *New York Times,* July 4, 2000.
[49] Richard A. Clarke, *Against All Enemies: Inside America's War on Terror* (New York: Simon & Schuster, 2004), 224.
[50] Sidney Zion, "Jewish Votes Trouble for Hil," *New York Daily News,* June 6, 2000.
[51] Janine Zacharia, "Bush Tones Down Pledge to Move Embassy," *Jerusalem Post,* May 23, 2000.
[52] Lisa L. Colangelo and William Goldschlag, "Israel Parade's No Walk in Park for Hil," *New York Daily News,* June 5, 2000.
[53] Sidney Zion, "Jewish Votes Trouble for Hil," *New York Daily News,* June 6, 2000.
[54] Dennis Ross, interview by author, November 12, 2002.
[55] John Podesta, interview by author, February 12, 2003.
[56] Martin Indyk, interview by author, October 9, 2002.
[57] Aaron Miller, interview by author, March 12, 2004.
[58] Saeb Erekat, interview by author, May 24, 2003.

[59] Martin Indyk, interview by author, September 5, 2002.
[60] Martin Indyk, interview by author, October 9, 2002.
[61] William B. Quandt, *Camp David: Peacemaking and Politics* (Washington, DC: Brookings Institution, 1986), 196.
[62] Conor Cruise O'Brien, *The Siege: The Saga of Israel and Zionism* (New York: Simon & Schuster, 1986), 461.
[63] Quandt, *Camp David,* 196.
[64] *Ibid.*

## CHAPTER THIRTEEN

[1] Like Barak, Arafat had problems with his de jure foreign minister, Farouk Qaddoumi (Abu Lutf), who had opposed the Oslo process from the outset, even refusing since 1993 to return with the PLO leadership from Tunis.
[2] Israeli negotiator at Camp David, interview by author, May 13, 2004.
[3] Aluf Benn, "The Selling of the Summit," *Ha'aretz,* July 27, 2001.
[4] *Ibid.*
[5] Gilead Sher, *Just Beyond Reach* (Tel Aviv: Yediot Ahronot, 2001), from an English translation of chapter 9 supplied by Sher to the author.
[6] Martin Indyk, interview by author, October 9, 2002.
[7] Sher, *Just Beyond Reach,* chapter 9.
[8] Amnon Lipkin-Shahak, interview by author, January 21, 2003.
[9] Joe Lockhart, interview by author, April 18, 2003.
[10] Dennis Ross, interview by author, November 12, 2002.
[11] Sher, *Just Beyond Reach,* chapter 9.
[12] Enderlin, 182.
[13] *Ibid.*
[14] William Quandt, interview by author, August 28, 2002.
[15] Hussein Agha and Robert Malley, "Camp David: The Tragedy of Errors," *New York Review of Books,* August 9, 2001.
[16] John Podesta, interview by author, February 12, 2003.
[17] Nabil Shaath, interview by author, November 27, 2002.
[18] Israeli negotiator at Camp David, interview by author, May 13, 2004.
[19] Aaron Miller, interview by author, March 12, 2004.
[20] Sher, *Just Beyond Reach,* chapter 9.
[21] Madeleine Albright, *Madam Secretary,* 485 and 478.
[22] Albright, interview by author, July 7, 2003.
[23] Enderlin, *Shattered Dreams,* 194.
[24] Saeb Erekat, interview by author, May 3, 2004.
[25] Saeb Erekat, interview by author, May 3, 2004.
[26] Albright, *Madam Secretary,* 478.
[27] Akram Hanieh, "The Camp David Papers," *Journal of Palestine Studies,* Winter 2001 (Vol. XXX, No. 2), 75-97.

[28] Gilead Sher, interview by author, August 19, 2003.
[29] Maria Echaveste, interview by author, November 12, 2002.
[30] Madeleine Albright, interview by author, July 7, 2003.
[31] Israeli negotiator at Camp David, interview by author, May 13, 2004.
[32] Saeb Erekat, interview by author, May 3, 2004.
[33] Sher, *Just Beyond Reach*, chapter 9.
[34] *Ibid.*
[35] Dan Meridor, interview by author, May 25, 2003.
[36] *Ibid.*
[37] Ari Shavit, "End of a Journey," *Ha'aretz*, July 15, 2002.
[38] Gemal Helal, interview by author, September 26, 2002.
[39] Enderlin, *Shattered Dreams*, 202.
[40] Sher, *Just Beyond Reach*, chapter 9.
[41] Ari Shavit, "End of a Journey," *Ha'aretz*, July 15, 2002.
[42] Martin Indyk, interview by author, October 9, 2002.
[43] Yossi Beilin, *Touching Peace: From the Oslo Accord to a Final Agreement* (London: Weidenfeld & Nicolson, 1999), 121.
[44] Enderlin, *Shattered Dreams*, 194.
[45] Enderlin, *Shattered Dreams*, 203.
[46] Hanieh, "The Camp David Papers."
[47] Saeb Erekat, interview by author, May 3, 2004.
[48] Dennis Ross, interview by author, November 12, 2002.
[49] Senior State Department official, interview by author.
[50] John Podesta, interview by author, February 12, 2003.
[51] Mohammed Dahlan, interview by author, May 22, 2003.
[52] Ari Shavit, "End of a Journey," *Ha'aretz*, July 15, 2002.
[53] Dan Meridor, interview by author, May 25, 2003.
[54] Dan Meridor, interview by author, May 25, 2003.
[55] Rob Malley, interview by author, July 30, 2002.
[56] Charles Enderlin, interview by author, May 1, 2004. Enderlin recounts that several Palestinian negotiators told him this in strictest confidence. He would not reveal who they were.
[57] Gemal Helal, interview by author, September 26, 2002.
[58] Sher, *Just Beyond Reach*, chapter 9.
[59] Albright, *Madam Secretary*, 488.
[60] Ari Shavit, "End of a Journey," *Ha'aretz*, July 15, 2002.
[61] Sher, *Just Beyond Reach*, chapter 9.
[62] Applied Research Institute—Jerusalem, "The Withdrawal Percentages: What Do They Really Mean?" January 2001. Available at http://www.poica.org. Accessed October 28, 2003.
[63] Sher, *Just Beyond Reach*, chapter 9.
[64] Akram Hanieh, "The Camp David Papers."
[65] Heidi J. Gleit, "Masses Turn Out Against Summit," *Jerusalem Post*, July 17, 2000.

[66] Michael Kramer, "Hillary Denies, Clinton Fumes at Charges She Made Racist Comment," *New York Daily News,* July 17, 2000.

[67] Michael Kramer and Corky Siemaszko, " 'God It's Hard,' Clinton Says of CD Peace Process," *New York Daily News,* July 17, 2000.

[68] Dan Meridor, interview by author, May 25, 2003.

[69] Israeli negotiator at Camp David, interview by author.

[70] Hussein Agha and Robert Malley, "Camp David: The Tragedy of Errors," August 9, 2001.

[71] Albright, *Madame Secretary*, 489.

[72] William Quandt, interview by author, August 28, 2002.

[73] Martin Indyk, interview by author, October 9, 2002.

[74] Dennis Ross, interview by author, November 12, 2002.

[75] Maria Echaveste, interview by author, November 12, 2002.

[76] Toni Verstandig, interview by author, December 19, 2002.

[77] *Ibid.*

[78] Albright, *Madam Secretary*, 489.

[79] Ari Shavit, "End of a Journey," *Ha'aretz,* July 15, 2002.

[80] Robert Malley, speech at the Palestine Center, March 7, 2001. Available at www.palestinecenter.org.

[81] Amnon Lipkin-Shahak, interview by author, January 21, 2003.

[82] Hanieh, "The Camp David Papers."

[83] Enderlin, *Shattered Dreams,* 228.

[84] Ari Shavit, "End of a Journey," *Ha'aretz,* July 15, 2002.

[85] Recall that Daoudi had cautioned Ross against promoting the 1923 International Boundary for the Golan instead of the June 4, 1967, line.

[86] Jane Perlez and Elaine Sciolino (quoting Sandy Berger's recollection), "Against Backdrop of History, High Drama and Hard Talks at Camp David," *New York Times,* July 28, 2000.

[87] *Ibid.*

[88] Joe Lockhart, interview by author, April 18, 2003.

[89] Maria Echaveste, interview by author, November 12, 2002.

[90] One State official told me this had nothing to do with Ross's ideology or opinions on the issues: "There was already enough pro-Israeli bias among us all to go around," he said. The official said Berger and Ross got along fine, and that the shift had more to do with this being a White House show, and that it would thus be inappropriate to have Ross there.

[91] Israeli negotiator at Camp David, interview by author.

[92] Hanieh, "The Camp David Papers."

[93] *Ibid.*

[94] Gamal Abouali, interview by author, May 8, 2004.

[95] Hanieh, "The Camp David Papers."

[96] Uri Dan, "Rewriting History Is Hard to Do," *Jerusalem Post,* August 17, 2001.

[97] *Ibid.*
[98] Gemal Helal, interview by author, July 17, 2002.
[99] Albright, *Madam Secretary*, 488.
[100] Ned Walker, interview by author, February 19, 2003.
[101] *Ibid.*
[102] *Ibid.*
[103] Rihab Massoud, interview by author, August 27, 2003.
[104] Ned Walker, interview by author, February 19, 2003.
[105] Janine Zacharia, Danna Harman, and Lamia Lahoud, "Barak: PA Not Negotiating in Good Faith," *Jerusalem Post*, July 20, 2000.
[106] http://www.israelemb.org/summit-camp_david/2000071900.html.
[107] Hanieh, "The Camp David Papers."
[108] Albright, *Madam Secretary*, 490.
[109] John Podesta, interview by author, February 12, 2003.
[110] Ari Shavit, "End of a Journey," *Ha'aretz*, July 15, 2002.
[111] Israeli official at Camp David, interview by author.
[112] "Barak Phones Bush, Gore to Give Updates," *Florida Times-Union*, July 17, 2000.
[113] John Podesta, interview by author, February 12, 2002.
[114] Aluf Benn, "The Selling of the Summit," *Ha'aretz*, July 27, 2001.
[115] Hillary Clinton, *Living History* (New York: Simon & Schuster, 2003), 518.
[116] Bruce Riedel, "Camp David—The US-Israeli Bargain." Available at http://www.bitterlemons.org/previous/b1150702ed26extra.html.
[117] *Ibid.*
[118] *Ibid.* If Israel gave up some of the strategically placed West Bank settlements, it would no longer be able to take water from the many aquifers located below.
[119] Dave Boyer, "Clinton Warned on Cost of Mideast Deal," *Washington Times*, July 18, 2000.
[120] Albright, *Madam Secretary*, 491.
[121] Albright, *Madam Secretary*, 492.
[122] Sher, *Just Beyond Reach*, p. 202 of Hebrew edition (translation supplied by Charles Enderlin).
[123] Enderlin, *Shattered Dreams*, 242.
[124] "Barak Is Conceding too Much," *The Australian*, July 21, 2000.
[125] Martin Indyk, interview by author, October 9, 2002.
[126] Enderlin, *Shattered Dreams*, 244.
[127] The Israelis argued that they needed to control the electromagnetic sphere for military purposes; they also argued that the Palestinians did not have the technical capability to manage it.
[128] Enderlin, *Shattered Dreams*, 246, 247.
[129] Hanieh, "The Camp David Papers."
[130] According to General Assembly Resolution 194 (December 1948),

"compensation should be paid for the property of those choosing not to return and for loss of or damage to property which, under principles of international law or in equity, should be made good by the Governments or authorities responsible."

[131] Hanieh, "The Camp David Papers."

[132] Gemal Helal, interview by author, July 17, 2002.

[133] Hanieh, "The Camp David Papers."

[134] Hussein Agha and Robert Malley, "Camp David: The Tragedy of Errors," *New York Review of Books,* August 9, 2001.

[135] Akram Hanieh, "The Camp David Papers."

[136] Enderlin, *Shattered Dreams,* 253.

[137] Enderlin, *Shattered Dreams,* 255.

[138] Lee Hockstader, "Unique Opportunity Lost at Camp David," *Washington Post,* July 30, 2000.

[139] Tony Walker and Andrew Gowers, "Fear and Loathing at the Camp David Talks," *Australian Financial Review,* July 28, 2003.

[140] Ari Shavit, "End of a Journey," *Ha'aretz,* July 15, 2002.

[141] Gemal Helal, interview by author, July 17, 2002.

[142] Hanieh, "The Camp David Papers."

[143] Albright, *Madam Secretary,* 493.

[144] Akiva Eldar, "The Goal: To Avoid Looking Like a Sucker," *Ha'aretz,* July 27, 2000.

[145] Dan Meridor, interview by author, May 25, 2003.

[146] Aaron Miller, interview by author, March 12, 2004.

## EPILOGUE

[1] John Podesta, interview by author, February 12, 2003.

[2] Aaron Miller, interview by author, March 12, 2004.

[3] "Israelis, Palestinians Differed on Much, But Shared Camaraderie at Camp David," Canadian News Wire, July 28, 2000.

[4] "Camp David Collapse: A Behind the Scenes Assessment by a Participant," summarizing Elyakim Rubinstein. Washington Institute for Near East Policy, Number 272, July 26, 2000. *Peacewatch/Policywatch Anthology 2000.* 106-7.

[5] Aluf Benn, "The Selling of the Summit," *Ha' aretz,* July 21, 2001.

[6] "Camp David Talks Not a Full Failure, Palestinian Negotiator Says," CNN, July 25, 2000. News online. Available at *http://www.cnn.com/2000/WORLD/meast/07/25/mideast.summit.04/.*

[7] "Arafat Comes Home a Hero," *Ha'aretz,* July 27, 2000.

[8] Richard Boudreaux, "Summit Aftermath: Arafat Returns Home to Hero's Welcome," *Los Angeles Times,* July 27, 2000.

[9] Months later, Palestinians would publish a map based on the ideas kicked around at Camp David, graphically corroborating Ashrawi's

claims. The Israelis still have not publicly released a map to refute the Palestinian assertion.

[10] Ben Lynfield, "In Mideast, Vows to Keep Dealing," *Christian Science Monitor*, July 27, 2000.

[11] Yossi Beilin, *The Path to Geneva* (New York: RDV Books, 2004), 179.

[12] Richard Boudreaux, "Summit Aftermath: Arafat Returns Home to Hero's Welcome," *Los Angeles Times*, July 27, 2000.

[13] Bill Hemmer, "Berger: Israel More Willing to Be Creative and Flexible at Camp David Summit," *CNN Morning News*, July 26, 2000.

[14] "Interview with Secretary of State Madeleine Albright," *The News Hour With Jim Lehrer*, July 25, 2000.

[15] Madeleine Albright, *Madam Secretary* (New York: Miramax Books, 2003), 493.

[16] William Goldschlag, "Hillary Says Zap Arafat's Aid if Palestinians Declare State," *New York Daily News*, July 26, 2000.

[17] Nabil Fahmy, interview by author, February 26, 2004.

[18] Nina Gilbert, "Mofaz Warns of Conflict Following Summit Failure," *Jerusalem Post*, July 26, 2000.

[19] "Settlers Get Okay to Use Live Ammunition," *Ha'aretz*, July 26, 2000.

[20] Charles M. Sennott, "Barak, Arafat Return to New Dynamics," *Boston Globe*, July 27, 2000.

[21] Dan Ephron, "Violence Feared in Wake of Failed Talks; Israel Tightens Security as Focus Shifts to Deadline," *Washington Times*, July 26, 2000.

[22] Melissa Mahle, interview by author, January 25, 2004.

[23] Lamia Lahoud, "PA Official: Yassin's Offer Encouraging," *Jerusalem Post*, July 25, 2000.

[24] Avi Machlis, "Hamas Capitalizes on Failure of Talks," *Financial Times*, July 27, 2000.

[25] Verena Dobnik, "Hillary Clinton Blames Arafat for Breakdown of Peace Talks," Associated Press, July 29, 2000.

[26] Lally Weymouth, "Waiting for Arafat," *Washington Post*, July 28, 2000.

[27] "Barak Wins One/Loses One," *Newsday*, August 1, 2000.

[28] Beilin, *The Path to Geneva*, 175.

[29] Aaron Miller, interview by author, March 12, 2004.

[30] Aaron Miller, interview by author, July 17, 2002.

[31] Ned Walker, interview by author, February 19, 2003.

[32] Ned Walker, interview by author, February 19, 2003.

[33] Madeleine Albright, interview by author, July 7, 2003.

[34] Toni Verstandig, interview by author, December 19, 2002.

[35] Robert Malley, interview by author, July 30, 2002.

[36] Ned Walker, interview by author, February 19, 2003.

[37] Dennis Ross, interview by author, November 12, 2002.

[38] Joshua Brilliant, "Bush Advisor: We'll stand by Israel," UPI, August 14, 2000.

[39] Herb Keinon, "Ben Ami: Second Summit Should Be Held Only if Success Ensured," *Jerusalem Post,* August 16, 2000.
[40] Heshaum Youssef, interview by author, May 19, 2003.
[41] Ari Shavit, "End of a Journey," *Ha'aretz,* July 15, 2002.
[42] Senior Israeli negotiator, interview by author.
[43] Gilead Sher, interview by author, August 19, 2003.
[44] Herb Keinon, "Barak and Arafat to Meet With Clinton This Week," *Jerusalem Post,* September 3, 2000.
[45] Beilin, *The Path to Geneva,* 181.
[46] Charles Enderlin, *Shattered Dreams: The Failure of the Peace Process in the Middle East, 1995-2002* (New York: Other Press, 2003), 276.
[47] Jane Perlez, "With Hopes Fading Fast, Clinton Meets with Barak," *New York Times,* September 10, 2000.
[48] *Ibid.*
[49] Enderlin, *Shattered Dreams,* 277
[50] Albright, *Madam Secretary,* 494.
[51] Madeleine Albright, interview by author, July 7, 2003.
[52] Herb Keinon, David Franklin, Lamia Lahoud, "Source: Hillary's Campaign Delays US Jerusalem Plan," *Jerusalem Post,* September 22, 2000.
[53] Gilead Sher, interview by author, August 19, 2003.
[54] Beilin, *The Path to Geneva,* 183.
[55] Melissa Mahle, interview by author, January 25, 2004.
[56] "Israel: Acting Foreign Minister Says Talks Pause Announcement 'Technical Move,'" *BBC Worldwide Monitoring,* quoting Voice of Israel radio, September 20, 2000.
[57] Herb Keinon, David Franklin, Lamia Lahoud, "Source: Hillary's Campaign Delays US Jerusalem Plan," *Jerusalem Post,* September 22, 2000.
[58] Marilyn Henry, "Sharon Objects to Linking Jerusalem Future to Hillary's Campaign," *Jerusalem Post,* September 24, 2000.
[59] Elizabeth Moore and Stephanie Saul, "Seeking Jewish Support/Senate Candidates Meet With Influential Leaders," *Newsday,* September 27, 2000.
[60] Beilin, *The Path to Geneva,* 185.
[61] Enderlin, *Shattered Dreams,* 284.
[62] Ari Shavit, "End of a Journey," *Ha'aretz,* July 15, 2002.
[63] Quote from PBS video transcript of *Frontline*'s "Shattered Dreams of Peace: The Road From Oslo," June 27, 2002.
[64] "Interviews: Ehud Barak," PBS Transcript, Available at *http://www.pbs.org/wgbh/pages/frontline/shows/oslo/interviews/barak.html.* Accessed October 29, 2003.
[65] *Frontline,* "Shattered Dreams of Peace."
[66] Dennis Ross, interview by author, November 12, 2002.

[67] Aaron Miller, e-mail to author, April 13, 2004.

[68] Beilin, *The Path to Geneva,* 189.

[69] Nabil Fahmy, interview by author, February 26, 2004.

[70] Dennis Ross, interview by author, November 12, 2002.

[71] Beilin, *The Path to Geneva,* 189.

[72] Report of The Sharm el-Sheikh Fact Finding Committee, April 30, 2001.

[73] Monthly casualty charts available from B'Tselem, the Israeli Information Center for Human Rights in the Occupied Territories, *www.btselem.org.*

[74] Beilin, *The Path to Geneva* , 195.

[75] Peter Bergen, interview by author, June 1, 2004.

[76] *Question of the Violation of Human Rights in the Occupied Arab Territories, Including Palestine,* UN Commission on Human Rights, Economic and Social Council. Report submitted March 16, 2001.

[77] Menachem Klein, "The Origins of Intifada II and Rescuing Peace for Israelis and Palestinians." Lecture at the Foundation for Middle East Peace, October 2, 2002. Available at *http://www.fmep.org/analysis/klein_origins_of_intifada_II.html.* Accessed October 29, 2003.

[78] Ben Caspit, "Two Years Into the Intifada," from *Ma'ariv* weekend magazine,September 6-13, 2002. Hebrew translation provided by the Economic Cooperation Foundation, available at *http://www.jfjfp.org/maariv_caspit.htm.* Accessed October 29, 2003.

[79] Akiva Eldar, "Popular Misconceptions," *Ha'aretz,* June 11, 2004.

[80] Akiva Eldar, "Popular Misconceptions," *Ha'aretz,* June 11, 2004.

[81] Akiva Eldar, "Opposition Demands Probe of Gilad's 'Erroneous' Evaluations," *Ha'aretz,* June 11, 2004.

[82] Hishem Youssef, interview by author, May 19, 2003.

[83] Benny Morris and Ehud Barak, "Camp David and After—Continued," *New York Review of Books,* June 27, 2002.

[84] Keith B. Richburg, "A Bloody Act Born of Rage," *Washington Post,* October 13, 2000.

[85] Ben Caspit, "Two Years Into the Intifada," *Ma'ariv* weekend magazine, September 6-13, 2002.

[86] Statistics from B'Tselem, *www.btselem.org.*

[87] "Concurrent Resolution Concerning the Violence in the Middle East," 106th Congress, second session. Introduced in the House as H. Con. Res. 426, passed with Senate concurrence on October 12, 2000.

[88] Thomas Friedman, "Arafat's War," *New York Times,* October 13, 2000.

[89] Blake Morrison, "Ex-USA Today Reporter Faked Major Stories," *USA Today,* March 19, 2004.

[90] Jack Kelley, "West Bank Street Clashes Now Organized Warfare; Palestinian Sniper Network," *USA Today,* October 23, 2000.

[91] Enderlin, *Shattered Dreams,* 327.
[92] Ben Caspit, "Two Years Into the Intifada," *Ma'ariv* weekend magazine, September 6-13, 2002.
[93] Ari Shavit, "End of a Journey," *Ha'aretz,* July 15, 2002.
[94] Enderlin, *Shattered Dreams,* 333.
[95] Albright, *Madam Secretary,* 496.
[96] Enderlin, *Shattered Dreams,* 334-38.
[97] Aryeh Dayan, "Barak Began Referring to the 'Holy of Holies'," *Ha'aretz,* December 9, 2002.
[98] Beilin, *The Path to Geneva* , 223.
[99] Gil Hoffman, "Dan Meridor Threatens to Support Sharon for PM," *Jerusalem Post,* December 28, 2000.
[100] "Stretching the Law," *Jerusalem Post,* January 4, 2001.
[101] Ari Shavit, "End of a Journey," *Ha'aretz,* July 15, 2002. The "several pages" of Israeli reservations have yet to be made public in full.
[102] "Unofficial Translation of Letter by President Yasser Arafat to President Bill Clinton," December 28, 2000. Copy obtained by author from official source.
[103] Elsa Walsh, "Profiles: The Prince," *The New Yorker,* March 24, 2003.
[104] Gilead Sher, interview by author, August 19, 2003.
[105] "Shattered Dreams of Peace," PBS *Frontline,* June 27, 2002.
[106] Amnon Lipkin-Shahak, interview by author, January 21, 2003.
[107] "Remarks by the Vice President to the Los Angeles World Affairs Council," Beverly Hills, California. The White House, Office of the Vice President, January 14, 2004.
[108] Gilead Sher, *Just Beyond Reach,* draft translation provided by Sher to author.
[109] With regard to Iraq, for example, many in the international community and on the Arab street have found the Bush administration's avowed desire to build a democratic Iraq disingenuous, especially as the United States continues to finance and defend the apartheid treatment of Palestinians by the Sharon government.
[110] Aaron Miller, interview by author, March 12, 2004.

# *Acknowledgments*

**MY DECISION TO** write on this topic was partly the result of personal interest and partly a graduation requirement for my master's thesis at Georgetown University. Two visiting Israeli professors, Aaron Klieman and the late Ehud Sprinzak, ensured that I became one of those students who, rather than running scared, delved deeper into the topic. Once I began my research, Dr. Francis X. Winters of the School of Foreign Service influenced my use of the interview method, just as he had done in his book examining the unintended consequences of President Kennedy's decision to allow the assassination of the president of South Vietnam in 1963. Dr. William Quandt of the University of Virginia, Dr. Naseer Aruri of the University of Massachusetts, and Dr. Samih Farsoun of American University were all kind enough to review portions of my research and encourage me to form a narrative of the accounts as I wrote. My thesis mentor, Dr. Yvonne Haddad of the Georgetown history department, provided constant guidance, commiseration and unwavering patience while I peeled the layers of the onion.

From my first interviews with Aaron Miller and Gemal Helal, I made sure never to leave a meeting without a recommendation of whom I should speak with next. While everyone was generous in providing contacts, there are two people in particular I must recognize: Ambassador Dennis Ross, who despite my critical questions was nonetheless willing to share with me his contacts; and his assistant, Marguerite Dale, who ensured that letters of introduction and appointments were arranged both in the United States and Israel. Both offered crucial support when I was stuck amid a wave of violence and IDF operations on the Gaza side of the Erez crossing. From Washington, they contacted Israeli Defense Minister Shaul Mofaz, who made sure that I eventually passed through the closure. Special thanks to you, Minister Mofaz: Though one phone call from Washington allowed me to circumvent the full experience of what Palestinians go through every day, I was allowed at least a momentary glimpse into the well of frustration, anger, and humiliation caused by an occupation that makes no sense even to the soldiers I encountered, who expressed their own embarrassment, and in one instance, bought me a lunch to apologize.

Aside from weighing the different accounts collected during the course of my research and interviews, one of the greatest challenges in writing this book has been to track down the participants—scattered throughout the United States, the Middle East, and Europe—and convince them to talk on matters that in some cases are still very painful. Whether it was because I was an unassuming grad student or simply because the burden of withholding information proved too much—or simply because no one else had bothered to interview them—they were willing to talk to me. Many recognized the immeasurable harm that has resulted from the Clinton-Barak diplomacy of blame—so much so that they risked incriminating themselves or friends for the sake of setting the record straight. If John F. Kennedy's Profiles in Courage were still taking candidates, they would have my nomination. They know who they are, and they have earned my respect and utmost admiration.

In Gaza, my appreciation goes to Ghaleb Darabya, Majdi Khaldi, Mohamed Adwan, Mohannad Aklouk, Ammar Hijazi, Nour Odeh, Yahya, Nasser Elawa, Basil Jebril, Rania

Kharma, Haydar Abdel Shafi, and the families in Gaza who, despite the misery of occupation and their understandable unhappiness with my government, nevertheless washed my clothes, fed me, and extended me a hospitality that still makes my eyes water. In the West Bank, my admiration to NSU friends Diana Buttu, Andrew Kuhn, Michael Tarazi, Yaser Dajani, and Stephanie Khoury. Ron Schlicher and Omar Dajani were motivators from beginning to end. Thanks also to my excellent host while I conducted my Israel and West Bank interviews, Mark Dennis. In Syria, my thanks go to Bashar el-Azmeh and family; also, Miriam and Manar Taleb from the Foreign Ministry.

In Israel, my thanks and friendship to journalist Charles Enderlin, whose seminal work, *Shattered Dreams*, was based, in large part, on contemporaneous recordings and interviews of those directly involved. Charles was gracious enough to allow me to freely quote from his book; he also reviewed my own interviews, pointing out areas both of overlap and further extension of the record. Gilead Sher and Gidi Grinstein, both of whom I deeply respect, were kind enough to offer points of clarity and answer questions. Many more are answered in Sher's own book, Just Beyond Reach, which fully deserves translation from Hebrew into English.

Thanks to cartographer Jan de Jong for allowing me to reprint his maps, kept current by his work in the field, often at the risk of his life. The assistance of Emma Lennartsson, of the Swedish prime minister's office, and Sherry Cooper from the Saudi Embassy in Washington allowed me to collect two very unique perspectives. Semper Fidelis to Special Agents Fernando Matus, Frank Arnot, Tony Diebler, John Kelly, and Chris Bakken, with whom I shared memorable experiences on travels during the period covered in my book. I am indebted to many others, including the Naji family, Kim Bondy, Don Mackenzie, Lance Root, and Capt. Bert Steele, USMC.

Ghadah Alrawi and Carl Bromley of Nation Books were key supporters of my research from the very outset. Once the writing process began, Ruth Baldwin, demonstrating the patience of Job, gave me all the time needed to pursue my research, even beyond the many missed due deadlines. I could not have been any luckier than to be introduced to Roane Carey, author and senior editor of *The Nation* magazine; without his devotion, understanding of the topic, and surgical editing skills, this book would have remained an incomplete set of chapters on a dusty Georgetown library shelf. It is worth mentioning that, while all the people mentioned above played crucial roles in helping me prepare this book, I am responsible for the ideas, arguments, and criticisms expressed, and for any mistakes, which will inevitably surface with the passage of time, publication of memoirs, and declassification of materials.

My gratitude and lifelong affection goes to my mother, brother, and sister. Above all else was the support and encouragement of an amazingly talented and beautiful woman who changed my life and stood beside me throughout most of this undertaking, through the countless hours and many lonely nights I spent slouched over a laptop while your patience, love, and commitment endured. If only, my love, if only…

# Index


## A

Abbas, Mahmoud. *see* Abu Mazen
Abed Rabbo, Yasser, 166, 167, 192, 197, 199, 201, 202, 209, 253
  fistfight, at Camp David II, 279
Abdullah, Crown Prince of Saudi Arabia, 307–308
Abdullah II (king of Jordan), 49, 55, 176, 307
Abu Ala, 150, 177–178, 202, 203–204, 205, 207, 208, 209, 211, 224, 274–276, 278
Abu Dis, 174–175, 176–177, 190, 215, 237
Abu Mazen (Mahmoud Abbas), 150, 170, 201, 203, 203–204, 204–205, 205, 206, 209–210, 253, 276, 278, 279
Adam Smith Institute, 171
Agence France-Presse, 162–163
Albright, Madeleine, ix, 4, 34, 44, 52, 217
  on Barak, 45
  at Camp David II, 257, 271, 275, 293, 306
    in charge, 312, 313, 315
    hosts field trip, 316–317
  in Geneva, 100, 102–103, 114, 116–117
  handling of negotiations questioned, 183–184
  in the Middle East, 230–234
  personality, 98
  position in Clinton administraton, 97–98, 106, 108, 184, 224, 259, 302–303
  pro-Israel stance, 151, 152
  Sharm Agreement, 54-56, 64-65
  on Shepherdstown failure, 127
  at Syrian negotiations, 79, 81–82, 85, 85–86, 87
  on Syrian negotiations, 113, 114–115, 115–116
  and Wye River Agreement, 52–53, 54
Allon Plan, 189
Allon, Yigal, 189, 201
Alpher, Yossi, 238–239
American Israel Public Affairs Committee (AIPAC), 32, 35, 109, 227–228
American University, 106
Anata (Anathoth), 181, 193–194
Andrews Air Force Base, 224
annexation, 207, 238, 328
  of Jerusalem, 227–228
anti-Americanism, 140
al-Aqsa Mosque, 174, 282
Arafat, Yasser, 6, 7, 8
  addresses United Nations, 147
  asks for U. S. intervention, 52
  at Camp David II, 316–317,

326–327
blamed for failure, 304, 331–332
meets with Clinton, 299–300, 303–306
plans departure, 310–311
and co-optation of terrorists, 156–159
credibility, 222
at Hassan funeral, 49
meets with Barak, 49–50, 173–175
meets with Clinton, 175–176, 225–226, 228–229
at Camp David II, 299–300, 303–306
and Oslo agreement, 150
and the PLO, 135–136, 137, 138
popularity, 27, 29–30, 192–193, 195, 215
Shin Bet attempts bolster, 196–197
and Ross, 184, 186, 226–227
seeks support, 176
on settlement expansion, 161
shakes Rabin's hand, 136
signs Oslo Accord in secret, 63
signs Sharm Agreement, 55
threatens Palestinian independence, 11–12
visits White House, 19
wins Nobel Peace Prize, 4
Asad, Bashar-al, 224
Asad, Hafez al-, 40, 48–49, 63, 68, 73, 83, 167
dies, 223–224
failing health, 98, 100, 102
in Geneva, 87–88, 94–96, 124–125, 127
blamed for failure, 106–109, 111–112
reacts to offer, 96–97, 100–102, 102, 102–103, 105
and Ross, 184
Asfur, Hassan, 205, 206, 208, 224, 253, 278, 312
fistfight, at Camp David II, 279
Ashrawi, Hanan, 135, 136–137, 159, 204
Ayalon, Ami, x, 28, 33, 66–67, 178

## B

Balfour Declaration, 12
Baltiansky, Gadi, 78, 86, 309
Bandar bin Sultan, 95, 95–96, 102, 106, 124, 125–126, 308
Barak, Ehud, 5, 8
1999 election campaign, 9–10, 12–13
acceptance speech, 14–16
angers Clinton, 110–111
at Camp David II, 282–283, 316–317
behavior at, 282–283, 289–290, 313–314, 316–317
enlists Jewish community, 313–315
leaks information, 314–315
makes offer, 294–296
plans departure, 307–309
public relations, 307–309, 331–333
career, 10, 202, 253
chokes on peanuts, 288–289
Clinton supports, 9–10, 12–13, 18–19
after failed Syrian negotiations, 103–104
coalition government, 21–24, 179, 181, 189–190, 222–223
under criminal investigation, 175
at Hassan funeral, 49
implementation of Sharm. *see* Sharm agreement
leaks propaganda, 93–94

and Lebanon, 61–62
meets with Arafat, 40–41, 49–50, 173–175
and Oslo Accords, 28–29
on Palestinian terrorism, 155–156
personal characteristics, 17–18, 44
and public opinion, 176–178, 260–261
public relations, 74–75
and Ross, 184
and settlement expansion, 152, 160–163, 163, 172
signs Sharm agreement, 55
and Syria first, 37, 40–41
Syrian negotiations, 87–88, 89, 104–105, 111–112, 130
and Golan Heights, 71–72, 77, 79–80, 127
importance, for legacy, 76
offers 1923 International Boundary, 100–102
withholds information, 78
threatened with assassination, 70–71
and Wye River Agreement, 51–52, 53
Barak, Nava, 38
Barghouti, Marwan, 214–215
Baz, Osama el-, 53
Begin, Menachem, 117, 244, 245
Beilin, Yossi, 23–24, 276
Beit Ula village, 145–146
Ben Ami, Shlomo, 179, 188–189, 199, 202, 206, 207, 229, 230–231, 253
at Camp David II, 265, 283–284, 295, 311–312
Ben Ami, Shlomo, 24, 104, 178, 211
Ben-Zeev, Yoram, 238–239
Benvenisti, Meron, 181
Berger, Sandy, 4–5, 34, 68, 96, 184, 187, 225, 227–228
at Camp David II, 257–258, 271–272, 283, 293, 301–302, 329–330
and Malley, 113
position in Clinton administraton, 97–98, 106, 229
at Syrian negotiations, 79, 85–86, 99–100
Bethlehem, 181
Blair House, 73, 74, 85
Bolling Air Force Base, 192, 197
*Boston Globe*, 107–108
Britain, and Resolution 242, 84
Bronfman, Charles, 9
Bush, George H. W., 32, 38
Bush, George W., 108, 109, 238–239, 313–314

## C

Camp David compound, 251
Camp David I, 244–245, 262, 263–264, 290
Camp David II, 110–111, 126–127, 265–266, 294
accommodations, 252–253
American draft
amended, 267–269
Barak rejects, 265–266, 269
Palestinians reject, 270
produced, 262–264
taken off the table, 272
American team, 257–258
inefficient organization of, 291–293
infighting, 290–294, 300–301, 301–302, 302, 329–330
Jews on, 276–277
unpreparedness of, 263–265
Arafat at. *see* Arafat, Yasser, at Camp David II
and Barak. *see* Barak, Ehud, at

Camp David II
borders discussed, 319–320, 324–325
Clinton at
and Barak, 289–290
favors Israel, 260–262, 265–266
meets with Arafat, 299–300, 303–305
offends Palestinians, 274–276
returns, 320–324
close of, 333–334
cultural issues, 276–277
drafting abandoned for oral presentations, 270, 294
attempts to remedy, 317–318
field trip, 316–317
fistfight, 279
Islamic world not consulted, 306–308
Israeli participants, 253
legal team, 254–255
Israeli public relations, 255–256
Israel's request for U. S. aid, 315–316
Jerusalem proposal, 273–274, 287–289, 295–296, 325–327, 328–330
Arafat rejects, 297–300, 303, 329–330
and larger Islamic world, 306–308
land swaps, 287–288, 297
leak prevention, 251–252
Israeli plans to circumvent, 255–256
leaks, 316
negotiations, 272–274, 283–285
opens, 258
Palestinians, 253–254
lack of media outlets, 256
lauded by Ross, 277–279
legal support denied access, 254
mistrust of Americans, 259–260
offended, 274–276
offer map, 318–319
perception of Israeli-US alliance, 276–277
respond to proposal, 301–302
plans for, 233–234, 238–244
destined to fail, 248–249
refugees discussed, 279–282, 319–320, 323–324
religious debate, 304–306, 327–328
and Resolution 242, 262, 263
security discussed, 319–320, 321–323
simulation exercise, 283–284
terms of reference, lack of. *see* Camp David II, and Resolution 242
*Camp David* (Quandt), 244, 246, 262, 290
CAPS (Comprehensive Agreement for Permanent Settlement), 56
Carter, Jimmy, xi, 19, 20, 84, 244, 245, 263–264
wins Nobel Peace Prize, 117
Carville, James, 9, 75
Centrist Party, 253
Chabad, 7
China buys radar technology, 184–185, 189
Christian Zionists, 148–149
Christopher, Warren, 64, 137
CIA (Central Intelligence Agency), 17, 29, 33, 195, 219–220
and the PLO, 138–139, 142, 154, 178
Clarke, Richard, 240
classified information mishandled, 186–187
Clinton administration

and Barak campaign, 9-10
and Geneva negotiations, failure analyzed, 117–118
handling of negotiations questioned, 183–184
at Harpsund, 210–212
infighting, 97–98, 101–102, 106, 116, 257
at Camp David II, 290–294, 301–302, 329–330
Jewish Americans in, 276–277
and Palestinian terrorism, 139–141
pro-Israel stance, 148–149
and public opinion, 285–286
and settlement expansion, 152
and Syrian negotiations, 121–123
Clinton, Bill
agrees to Camp David summit, 223–224
anger at Barak, 110–111
at Camp David II. *see* Camp David II, Clinton at
credibility, 94, 95, 96
lost, with Syrians, 106
displeased with staff, 183–184
favors Israel, at Camp David II, 260–262, 274–275
guarantees Sharm implementation, 180, 215, 222
at Hassan funeral, 49
impeached, 3
and Israeli-Syrian negotiations, 68, 91
legacy, 76, 235–236, 331
meets with Arafat, 175–176, 225–226
at Camp David II, 299–300, 303–305
meets with Barak, 41–42
as negotiator, 259–260, 299, 303–304, 310–311, 312, 330
and Netanyahu, 8–9, 41
opens Camp David II, 258
on Palestinian independence, 11–12
prepares for Camp David II, 244–245
spins Geneva failure, 103–104, 105
supports Barak, 9–10, 12–13, 18–19, 175, 217
after failed Syrian negotiations, 103–104
supports Palestine, 19–20
supports Peres, 6–7, 7–8
and Syrian negotiations, 72, 80, 85–86, 87, 100-101, 110-111
post-failure, 93
promises Asad 1967 line, 94–96
Clinton, Chelsea, 321
Clinton, Hillary Rodham, 19–20, 41, 240–241, 314, 315
accused of anti-Semitism, 241, 286
CNN, 87, 225
Cohen, William, 44, 185
Columbia University, 26

## D

Dahlan, Mohammed, x, 50, 117, 138, 141–142, 149, 151, 196, 205, 224, 232–233, 254, 278–279, 298
at Camp David II, 277–278, 283–284, 311–312, 331
Dajani, Omar, x, 26–27, 116–117, 171, 199, xii
Dan Hotel, Tel Aviv, 14
Daoudi, Riad, xi, 65–66, 78, 87, 92, 126
Dayan, Moshe, 222, 277
Dayan, Uzi, 221–222
Dheisheh refugee camp, 192
Dome of the Rock, 174

**E**

Eban, Abba, 84, 107, 108
Echaveste, Maria, ix, 13, 258, 271, 291, 292, 293, 301
Edna village, 145–146
Egypt, 63, 81, 84, 117, 183, 233
Egypt/Israeli peace process, 244–247
Enderlin, Charles, 198
Erekat, Saeb, x, 15–16, 51, 150, 176, 181, 192, 197, 201, 202, 224, 225, 232–233, 233, 243, 253
 at Camp David II, 278, 283–284
Eran, Oded, 167, 192, 197, 198, 200–201, 204
European Union, 55, 171, 176
evictions. *see* settlements, and evictions
Executive Order 12947, 141

**F**

FAPS (Framework Agreement for Permanent Settlement), 56, 157, 174
 negotiations, 166–182, 224–225
  and Resolution 242, 168–169
  stalled, 197
Fatah Party, 195, 196–197
 credibility, 213–214
 Hawks, 205
 and terrorism, 215–216
final-status issues, 50, 51, 174–175, 198–199
 refusal to address, 172–173
First Additional Protocol, Fourth Geneva Convention, 142–143
First Zionist Congress, 30
Foreign Affairs, 107
Four Mothers, 218
Fourth Geneva Convention, 135, 136, 142–143, 144
Friedman, Thomas, 236–237, 239
Fuerth, Leon, 108–109, 314
fundraising, political, 7, 9–10

**G**

Gaza, 237
 safe passage, to West Bank, 180
 seaport, 165
Gaza Preventive Security, 50
Gaza Strip, 30, 168, 173, 199, 207
 map, xvi
 security, 138
 settlement expansion, 146
 violence in, 216
Gesher Party, 231
Gilad, Amos, 10, 217
Ginosar, Yossi, 180, 253
Giuliani, Rudolph, 20
Golan Heights, 4, 49
 Israeli occupation, 18, 23, 70
  Barak offers withdrawal, 69–71
  Rabin offers withdrawal, 63–64
 map, xiii
 subsidies for, 62–63
Golani Brigade, 77
Goldberg, Arthur, 84
Goldstein, Baruch, 161–162
Gore, Al, 20, 108, 228, 240, 241, 314
Green Line, 201
Greenberg, Stanley, 9, 9–10, 12–13, 315
Grinstein, Gidi, x, 229, 253, 265, 288–289, 293–294, 311–312
Gutnick, Joseph, 7

**H**

*Ha'aretz*, 93–94, 193
Hamas, 6, 10, 28, 29, 133–134, 153, 154, 178
 anti-Arafat rhetoric, 157–158
 and the PLO, 156–157, 158, 159

political prisoners, 196–197
public support for, 195
role in community, 154–155
and terrorism, 155, 156–157, 157–159, 215–216
al-Hamma, 91–92, 120
handshake, Rabin-Arafat, 136
Hanieh, Akram, 254, 270
Har Homa, 8, 139–140, 141
Harakat al-Muqawama al-Islamiya (Islamic Resistance Movement). *see* Hamas
Haram al-Sharif/Temple Mount, 174, 220, 250, 273, 282, 285, 295, 297–298
religious significance, 304–306, 327–328
*hasbara*, 93–94
Hassan (king of Morocco), 47–50
Havat Maon, 160, 163
Hebron, 8, 49, 161–162, 181, 199
Hebron Protocol, 1997, 28
Helal, Gemal, ix, 67, 79, 99, 197, 257
at Camp David II, 257, 274, 282–283, 305
on co-optation, 159
on Geneva negotiations, 119–121
at Harpsund, 210–211
Herbst, John, 257
Herzog, Yitzhak, 175
Hezbollah, 35, 64, 96, 214
conflict with IDF, 218–219
in Lebanon, 61–62, 190
Hoagland, Jim, 237–238
Holocaust, 250–251
Holy Sepulcher, 250
Hussein (king of Jordan), 48

I

Indyk, Jill, 38
Indyk, Martin, ix, 5, 31, 34–35, 37–38, 52–53, 71, 183, 228
appointed to National Security Council, 36, 37
backs Syria first, 44, 63, 66, 67
at Camp David II, 257, 291, 315–316
at Eilat, 200
on Geneva negotiations, 99, 118
handling of negotiations questioned, 183–184
prepares Camp David II briefing, 244
pro-Israel stance, 150
and settlement expansion, 116, 148–149, 151–152
and Syrian negotiations, 79, 82, 90, 120
Intercontinental Hotel, Geneva, 96
Iran, 35, 75, 154
Iraq, 35, 75
Israel
1996 election, 5–7
1999 election, 9–10, 13, 17–19
coalition government, 23–25, 189–190, 231–232, 245, 260–261
creation of state, 212
expansionists in, 30–32
intelligence, 28–29, 36–37
military actions, 7, 8
military capabilities, 62, 76
Ministry of Foreign Affairs, 201–202
negotiates with Syria. *see* Syrian negotiations
plans withdrawal from Lebanon, 65
political left, 23, 104
political right, 215–216, 215–216. *see also* Likud Party; National Religious Party (NRP); Shas (Orthodox Sephardic Party)
preparedness, for negotiations, 170–171
public opinion

and Camp David II, 285–286, 331–332
on stalled Palestinian talks, 177–178
on withdrawal from Lebanon, 190
relations with Morocco, 47–48
religious school system, 74
response to Palestinian independence, 11
sells U. S. radar technology, 184–185, 189
settlements. *see* settlements
support for Syrian peace, 75–76
Syria, relations with, 10
violence in, 6, 213
Israel Defense Forces (IDF), 145–146, 153, 160, 187–188, 193–194
casualties, 217–218
clashes with Palestinians, 197, 215–216, 215–218
communications system, 314–315
Intelligence Research Division, 217
Operation Field of Thorns, 178–179
plans to defend settlements, 221–222
Israeli Democracy Institute, 107
Israeli-Jordinian peace agreement, 1994, 10
Israeli proposed final status, 2000 (map), xvii
Israeli proposed final status, 2001 (map), xviii
Izz al-Din al-Qassam Brigade, 155

**J**

Jabal Abu Ghneim, 8, 139
Jaffee Center for Strategic Studies, Tel Aviv University, 75
Jerusalem, 174, 220–221, 261
discussed at Camp David II, 273–274, 287–289, 295–296, 297, 325–327, 328–329
proposal, 297–300
religious significance, 250
Jerusalem Embassy Act of 1995, 227–228
*Jerusalem Post*, 105–106
Jewish Americans, 9, 75, 93, 237, 238–239, 241, 313–314
in Clinton administration, 276–277
Jewish Institute for National Security Affairs, 93
John Paul II, Pope, 191–192
Jordan, 63, 189, 233
Jordan Valley, 199, 207, 284
*Journal of Strategic Studies*, 106

**K**

Khalidi, Ahmed, 204
Khatib, Ghassan, 194–195
Kimmerling, Baruch, 137
Knesset, 18, 22, 70, 75, 181
Kol Shalom, 237
Kosovo, 4–5
Kurtzer, Daniel C., 148, 307

**L**

Labor Party, 18, 37, 74, 189
Lake Tiberias (Sea of Galilee), 81, 83, 85, 91, 100–101
land swaps, 201, 220, 287–288, 297
Larsen, Terje Roed, 43
Lazio, Rick, 240, 241
Lebanon, 7, 15–16, 90, 96
Israel plans withdrawl, 61–62, 65, 75, 190
Israel withdraws, 214, 218–220
fear of attack after, 217
Israeli occupation, 187–188

Levy, David, 23, 48, 52, 77, 78, 87, 231–232, 245
Levy, Gideon, 193
Levy, Yitzhak, 23, 70, 181, 191
Lewinsky, Monica, 3, 20
Lieberman, Joe, 228
Likud Party, 7, 18, 19, 23, 69, 74, 75, 174, 191–192
  criticism of Barak, 176, 179
Lindh, Anna, 203–204
Lipkin-Shahak, Amnon, x, 16, 78, 126–127, 179, 202, 203, 253, 259, 272, 311–312
Lockhart, Joe, ix, 8, 251–252, 258, 259–260, 299, 299–300

**M**

Ma'ale Adumim settlement, 30, 145, 194
Madrid summit, 29, 204
Mahle, Melissa Boyle, x, 17, 29, 33, 139–140, 151–152
  on terrorism, 156–157
*Making Peace Among Arabs and israelis: Lessons from Fifty years of negotiating Experience* (USIP), 248–249
Malley, Robert, ix, 66, 79, 98, 99–100, 110–111, 112–113, 192, 197, 210–211, 227
  at Camp David II, 262-263, 265, 268, 281–282, 291, 295
Mandatory Palestine, 82–83
Maon Farm, 160, 163
Massoud, Rihab, xi, 95–96, 307–308
Meir, Golda, 245
Meretz, 21, 190
Meridor, Dan, 253, 279–281, 280–281, 287
Migdal, Joel, 137
Miller, Aaron, ix, 52–53, 66, 148, 187, 192, 197, 213, 224, 237, 243
  at Camp David II, 257, 265
  at Harpsund, 210–211
  and Syria first, 67
Milosevic, Slobodan, 4
Moallem, Walid, xi, 78, 92, 102, 126, 127–128
  on Syrian negotiations, 127–129, 130
Mofaz, Shaul, 158, 178, 217
Mohlo, Yitzhak, 167
Mondale, Walter, xi, 245–246
Moratinos, Miguel, 176
Morocco, 47, 298
Moskowitz, Irving, 30, 140
Mossad, 253
Mount Hebron settlement, 160
Mount of Olives/Ras al-Amud settlement, 140
Mubarak, Hosni, 51–52, 55, 107, 176, 183, 107, 242, 307
Muhammad VI (king of Morocco), 298
*mukhabarat*, 138
Muqata, 232–233

**N**

Nablus meeting, 230–231
Nakba Day (al-Nakba), 212
  1998, 216
  demonstrations, 214–218, 223
Nasrallah, Hassan, 214, 218
National Religious Party (NRP), 21, 22, 23, 70, 181, 191, 231, 245
National Security Council (NSC), 5, 34, 36, 183
  at Syrian negotiations, 79
Negotiation Support Unit, 171–172, 254
negotiations, back channel, 203–206
  conflict with official, 204, 209
  Israeli/Palestinian, 201–203

and Oslo process, 147–148
Syrian. *see* Syrian negotiations, back-channel
Netanyahu, Benjamin, 4, 5–6
character, 8
international support for, 7
as Prime Minister, 7, 8–9, 24–26, 26, 30
legacy of distrust, 51
response to Palestinian independence, 11
and settlement expansion, 152
*New York Daily News*, 241, 286
*New York Post*, 105
*New York Times*, 48, 75, 216, 236
*New Yorker*, 115–116
1967 line, 66, 226, 246–247, 263, 274. *see also* Resolution 242
1923 International Boundary, 66, 82–83, 86, 91, 92, 100, 120
Nuder, Pär, xi, 204–205, 205, 212,

O

Olmert, Ehud, 174
Omar, Ibrahim, 66, 78
Omari, Ghaith al-, x, 254
Operation Field of Thorns, 178–179
Organization of the Islamic Council, Jerusalem Committee, 298
Orthodox Jews, 7, 18
Orthodox Sephardic Party (Shas), 70, 74, 104, 190
Oslo Accords. *see also* Sharm agreement
Oslo Accords, 1993, 4, 10–11, 16, 23
bias towards Israel, 137–138, 142, 143–144
failings of, 29–30, 32, 133, 136–137
and settlement expansion, 150–151
failure to implement, 25–28, 29, 32–33, 140–141, 151
and Barak, 43–44, 142–143
Palestinian, 216–217
and PLO, 142–143, 159
and terrorism, 158
origins of, 203
back-channel, 147-148
Palestinian Islamic Jihad statement, 153–154
and the PLO, 134–140
and settlement expansion, 161–162
Oslo II (1995), 56

P

Palestine
anger in, 213–214
anti-Americanism, 140
and FAPS negotiations, 166–182
independence, 11–12, 19
military actions, 8
military capabilities, 178–179
under Netenyahu, 24–26
and Oslo Accords, 10–11
Pope John Paul II visits, 191–192
public opinion, 177–178
relations with Israel
under Barak, 14–17
discussed at Hassan funeral, 49
rights denied, 250–251
settlements. *see* Settlements
and Syria first, 67
Palestinian Authority, 6, 12, 26, 56, 133–134
and co-optation of terrorists, 156–159
equation of terrorism with settlements, 140–143
formed, 138

funding for, 171–172
preparedness, for negotiations, 170, 171–172
structure of, 171
Palestinian Islamic Jihad (PIJ), 133–134, 153–154, 196–197
and the PLO, 159
Palestinian negotiations, 116–117, 210–211
Andrews Air Force Base, 224–225
Eilat, 197–201, 202
Harpsund, Sweden, 206–212, 220–221
leaked to media, 209–210, 220–221
information mishandled, 187-188
Palestinian Prisoner Day, 197
Palestinian protesters, 197
Palestinian refugees. *see* refugees, Palestinian
Palestinian Research Center, 195
Palestinians, as Israeli citizens, 15
Peace Now, 145
Peres, Shimon, 6–7, 14, 179
1996 election, 7
in Barak government, 23
and king Hassan, 47–48
and Syria, 64
wins Nobel Peace Prize, 4
Perle, Richard, 109, 238–239
Perlmutter, Amos, 106, 107
Persson, Goran, 204
Phalcon radar technology, sale to China, 184–185
PLO (Palestinian Liberation Organization), 26, 26–27, 30. *see also* Fatah party
and co-optation of terrorists, 158–159
credibility, 213–214
forms Palestinian Authority, 138
and Hamas, 156–157, 158, 159
internal rivalry, 205–206
and Preventive Security Organization (PSO). *see* Preventive Security Organizaton (PSO)
recognition of, 134–138
and failure to implement, 142–143
and loss of popularity, 139–140
status of, 170–171
structure of, 138–139
and Yasser Arafat, 137, 138
Podesta, John, ix, 258, 263, 278
at Camp David II, 241–242, 291, 312–313, 314
on Syrian negotiations, 113
Pollard, Jonathan, 8, 36
Preventive Security Organizaton (PSO), 138
benefits Israeli economy, 153
co-optation policy, 158–159
methods, 138–139
prisoners, political, 52–53, 55–56, 56, 213
indoctrination, 195–196
release of, 52–53, 164, 165, 178, 180, 181–182, 192, 196–197, 225
rioting, 197
protesters, Palestinian, 197

**Q**

al-Qaeda, 240
Qana refugee camp, 7
Quandt, William, xii, 117
*Camp David*, 244, 246, 262, 290
Qurei, Ahmed. *see* Abu Ala

**R**

Rabin deposit, 64–66, 73, 81–82, 87, 93, 96, 105–106, 127, 167

Rabin, Leah, 14, 162
Rabin, Yitzhak, 14–15
  assassinated, 4
  offers withdrawal from Golan Heights, 64
  recognizes PLO, 137
  shakes Arafat's hand, 136
  signs Oslo Accord, 63–64
  wins Nobel Peace Prize, 4
Ramadan, 80, 85–86
Ramon, Haim, 104
Rashid, Mohammed, 224, 277–278, 331
Rasmussen, Nick, 186
Reagan administration, 38
Red Crescent Society, Palestine, 29–30
refugee camps, 192
refugees, Palestinian. *see also* right of return
  camps, 192
  discussed at Camp David II, 279–282, 319–320, 323–324
  discussed at Harpsund, 207–209
  discussed at White House, 226
Republican Party, 38
Resolution 181, 208
Resolution 194, 226
Resolution 242, 226. *see also* 1967 line
  and Camp David I, 274
  at Camp David II, 262, 262–263, 268–269
  and Egyptian/Israeli negotiations, 245–246
  and FAPS negotiations, 168–169
  and Palestine, 135, 137, 159, 198, 204, 207, 211, 233, 238, 246–247
  and Syria, 86, 91–92, 119–120
Resolution 338, 159, 211, 268–269
Resolution 425, 188, 233
Riedel, Bruce, ix, 79, 86, 96, 106, 121–122
  at Camp David II, 258, 315–316
right of return, 208, 211, 237
  discussed at Camp David II, 261, 281–282, 323–324
Ross, Dennis, ix, 5, 27, 31–32, 35, 52–53, 61, 65, 149, 183, 197, 237
  Arab dislike for, 93, 184, 186, 226–227, 228
  backs Syria first, 63
  at Camp David II, 254, 265, 267–269, 271–272, 277–278, 291, 291–292, 298, 300–301, 312, 313
  Camp David II role, 257
  at Eilat, 199–200
  and Geneva negotiations, 101–102, 105, 118–119, 127–129
  handling of negotiations questioned, 183–184, 186–187
  at Harpsund, 209–210, 212
  in the Middle East, 233
  and Palestine, 137
  position in Clinton administraton, 97, 98, 123–124, 183–186
  pro-Israel stance, 38–39, 115, 116, 148–149, 185–186, 188–189, 234–235
    and Jerusalem Embassy Act, 227–228
    and settlement expansion, 151
    and Sharm implementation, 165, 172
  and Syria first, 68
  and Syrian negotiations, 67, 68, 79
  at Syrian negotiations, 82
  on Syrian negotiations, 113–114
  and Syrian negotiations
    comments on failure, 90–91
    in Geneva, 99
    post-failure, 91–93
Rubinstein, Elyakim, 143–144,

166–167, 175, 253, 255, 323–324
Rudeineh, Nabil Abu, x, 254
Rudman, Mara, 185
Russian Jews, 22, 70, 272–273

## S

Sadat, Anwar, 244, 245, 246
Sagi, Uri, x, 65–66, 71, 77, 78, 126
  on failure of negotiations, 127
  at Syrian negotiations, 80
  on Syrian negotiations, 127, 128–129
Saudi Arabia, 95
Sayeret Matkal, 253
Schliker, Ron, 257
Schwartz, Jonathan, ix, 79, 197, 228
  at Camp David II, 268
  at Harpsund, 210–211
Sea of Galilee (Lake Tiberias), 81, 83, 85, 91, 100–101
Seagram's Distillers, 9
Seale, Patrick, 40
Second FRD, 164, 174, 175, 176
Serbia, 4–5
Serra, Sulieman, 79
settlements, 93, 139–141
  annexation, 207, 238
  discussed at White House, 226
  and evictions, 144–145, 162–163
  expansion of, 144–150, 172, 192–193
    Clinton administration supports, 148–151, 150–152
    and evictions, 156, 160, 193–195
    and Oslo process, 150–151
    retaliation. *see* Hamas
  IDF plans defense of, 221–222
Shaara, Farouk al-, 56, 64–65, 68, 69, 216
  on Geneva failure, 105–106
  at Syrian negotiations, 85
  and Syrian negotiations, 87–88
  at Syrian talks, 71–72, 78, 80–81
Shaath, Nabil, x, 32, 54, 148–149, 172, 172–173, 232, 253, 263
Shabban, Bouthaina, x, 79, 94, 99, 101, 126
Shafi, Haydar Abdel, xii, 26, 29–30
Sharansky, Natan, x, 23, 70, 104, 191, 231, 286–287
Sharm Agreement, 64–65, 142, 153–154, 158. *see also* Oslo Accords
  implementation, 164–166, 171–189
    Barak reneges, 224–225
    negotiations suspended, 177–178
    prisoners released, 178, 181, 181–182
    three-village upgrade, 174–175, 176–177, 190–191, 215
    United States guarantees, 180
  and release of prisoners, 164
  signed, 54-56
  and settlement expansion, 160
Sharm-el-Sheikh, xiv, 6
Sharon, Ariel, 18, 69, 75, 80, 144, 174, 191, 216, 246, 286–287
Shas (Orthodox Sephardic Party), 70, 74, 104, 190, 245
Shepherdstown negotiations, 79, 128, 175
  failure, analysis of, 126–127
Sher, Gilead, x, 21, 50–51, 166, 167, 191, 203, 206, 209, 229, 230–231, 253
  at Camp David II, 270, 272, 283–284, 293–294
  and Syria first, 66–67
Sherman, Wendy, 79, 257
Shin Bet, 28–29, 33, 178, 195
  attempts bolster of Arafat, 196–197

Shrum, Robert, 9, 314
Siegman, Henry, 107
Six-Day War, 83, 120, 189, 207–208
Sneh, Ephraim, 71, 222
South Lebanon Army (SLA), 218–219
State Department, 4, 5, 17, 30, 33, 34, 35, 219–220
  Bureau of Intelligence and Research, 98–99
  Near East Affairs, 186
  and Syria first, 67–68
Stauber, Zvi, 78, 315
Sweden, as facilitator, 203–207
Syria
  breaks from Palestinian cause, 63–64
  military capabilities, 62
  negotiates with Israel. *see* Syrian negotiations
  post-Sharm negotiations, 64–65
  relations with Israel, 10, 48–49, 62–63. *see also* Syria first
  support for Palestinian Islamic Jihad (PIJ), 154
Syria first, 35–38, 187
  rationale, 35–36
Syrian negotiations, 61-130
  Andrews Air Force Base, 71-74
  Arab opposition to, 86–87
  And Asad, Hafez al-. see Asad, Hafez al-, in Geneva
  back-channel, 95–96, 102, 106, 115, 124–125, 125–126
  Barak offers withdrawal from Golan Heights, 73
    withdraws offer, 86–87
  borders committee, 79–81, 86–87
  Clinton administration on, 112–114
  Clinton at, 72, 81–82, 85–86, 87
  failed, public reaction, 87–89
  Geneva, 94-103
  Israeli opposition to, 69–71, 74-75, 82, 87–88, 90, 104
  and normalization, 81
  and Rabin deposit. *see* Rabin deposit
  sequelae of, 126–127
  Shaara addresses press, 71–72
  Shepherdstown, 77-89
  take focus from Palestine, 179, 187
  United States involvement, 65–66, 72
  and water resources, 82–83, 85, 91–92, 99, 100–101, 105–106, 114–115, 120

## T

*tanzim. see also* Fatah party
Tel Aviv University, 75
Temple Mount/Haram al-Sharif, 174, 220, 250, 273, 282, 285, 295, 297–298
  religious significance, 304–306, 327–328
Tenet, George, 8, 258, 320
terrorism, 155–156
  and co-optation of terrorists, 158–159
  Hamas, 155, 156–157, 157–158
  Israeli, 161–162
  Palestinian Authority, 139–141
  and Palestinian Islamic Jihad (PIJ), 153
  settlement expansion as, 140–143
Third Further Redeployment, 173, 180, 223, 224–225, 226
Third Further Redeployment Committee, 56
three-village upgrade, 174–175, 176–177, 216
  Barak reneges, 216, 222–223, 224

torture, 140, 196
Track-II diplomacy, 201–202, 201–203
Tunis, 134, 135
tunnel intefada, 213

U

U. S. Institute of Peace (USIP), 248–249
United Nations
  Charter, 63
  position on settlements, 147
  Relief and Works Agency For Palestinian Refugees, 208
  Security Council, 8
    and Palestine, 141–142
    Resolution 181, 208
    Resolution 194, 208
    Resolution 242. *see* Resolution 242
    Resolution 425, 188
University of Virginia, 117

V

Verstandig, Toni, ix, 25–26, 31, 148, 219–220, 294
  at Camp David II, 257, 293, 296
  on Syrian negotiations, 121–122

W

Walker, Ned, ix, 37, 152, 169–170, 186–187, 257
  at Camp David II, 306
  on Syrian negotiations, 122–126, 128
Waqf, 8
Washington Institute for Near East Policy (WINEP), 32, 35, 35–36, 108
*Washington Post*, 238
*Washington Times*, 106–107, 107
West Bank, 30, 49, 116–117, 168, 173, 189, 198–199, 201, 207, 237
  safe passage, to Gaza, 180
  security, 138
  settlements, 160, 161–162
Western Wall, 8
Woolsey, James, 93
Wye River Agreement, 8–9, 28, 29, 142, 225
  implementation, 56
    avoidance of, by Israel, 40–41, 41–42, 49, 50–51, 51–52, 176–177
  and release of prisoners, 52–53, 55–56, 56
  renegotiated, 51–54

Y

Yanai, Shlomo, 253, 319–320
Yassin, Ahmed, 155, 197
Yatom, Danny, 48, 253, 304–305, 316
Yisrael Ba'Aliyah Party, 22, 23, 70, 104, 181, 191, 231, 245

Z

Zadok, Merav Parsi, 44
Zilberstein, Tal, 13, 315
Zionist Organization of America, 93, 286
Zionists, 30, 37
  in United States, 93, 148, 286

CPSIA information can be obtained
at www.ICGtesting.com
Printed in the USA
BVHW031757190620
581667BV00001B/2